Typewriter Killer:
H. Beam Piper

by
JOHN F. CARR

Pequod Press

Typewriter Killer: H. Beam Piper

John F. Carr

All Rights Reserved
Copyright © 2015 by John F. Carr

This book may not be reproduced or transmitted in whole or in part, in any form or by any means electronic or mechanical, including photocopying, scanning, recording, or any information storage or retrieval system, without prior permission in writing from the author or publisher.

First Edition 2015

Printed in the United States of America
Second Printing, 2016
V 10 9 8 7 6 5 4 3 2

ISBN: 978-0-937912-68-3

Piper Books & Related Works

Terran Federation Books

Federation
Empire
The Uller Uprising
Four-Day Planet
The Cosmic Computer
Space Viking
Little Fuzzy
Fuzzy Sapiens
Fuzzies and Other People
Fuzzy Ergo Sum
Caveat Fuzzy
The Last Space Viking
Space Viking's Throne
The Merlin Gambit

Paratime Books

Paratime
Time Crime
The Complete Paratime
Lord Kalvan of Otherwhen
Great Kings' War
Kalvan Kingmaker
The Hos-Blethan Affair
Siege of Tarr-Hostigos
The Fireseed Wars
Gunpowder God

H. Beam Piper Books

H. Beam Piper: A Biography
Typewriter Killer: H. Beam Piper

ACKNOWLEDGEMENTS

Much of this book could not have been fully realized without the scholarship and help of John Anderson who has carried on a lively correspondence with the author for over 30 years; David Johnson who has kept H. Beam Piper's torch burning at his Zarthani.net web site and provided the updated Piper bibliography; Tom Rogers who has provided invaluable and rare documents and Dennis Frank, keeper of the records and my first reader. And, H. Beam Piper, without whose writings and historical scholarship, we would all be the poorer.

Plus, I'd like to thank Don Coleman for his generosity in sharing "The Early Letters" and Mike Knerr for providing me with his unpublished manuscript, "PIPER." R.I.P.

I'd also like to thank the following copyeditors, Victoria Alexander, Dwight Decker, Dennis Frank, Mike Richardson, Larry Hopkins, Wolfgang Diehr and David E. Williams for their copyediting efforts and help in making this a better book.

TABLE OF CONTENTS

Preface 13

Part I   **The Young Writer**
1. The Beginning 19
2. The Young Author 25
3. Brothers of the Quill 31
4. The Tiadaghton 38
5. Three Wishes 45
6. Moment of Greatness 54
7. The Unholy Trinity 64

Part II   **Published at Last**
8. Time and Time Again 73
9. He Walked Around Horses 80
10. Rebel Raider 86
11. Day of the Moron 93
12. Murder in the Gunroom 98
13. New Friends 102
14. The Uller Uprising 110
15. The Collaborators 115
16. On Writing 120

Part III   **Big Changes**
17. The Lovebirds 131
18. The Case of the Missing Gun 140
19. Harriett Piper RIP 149
20. The Dark Side 158
21. Knife Edge 168

Part IV   **From New York to Williamsport**
22. The Big Move 175
23. Graveyard of Dreams 188
24. Back in the USA 201
25. Ministry of Disturbance 208

Part V	**The Science Fiction Novels**	
	26. Little Fuzzy	219
	27. When in the Course	230
	28. Four-Day Planet	237
	29. Junkyard Planet	242
	30. Naudsonce	250
	31. Little Fuzzy Sold At Last!	255
	32. Space Viking	260
	33. Fuzzy Sapiens	269
	34. Fuzzies and Other People	277
	35. The Kalvan Saga	285
	36. Afterwards	313
Bibliography		321
Appendix	Appendix I: Paratime	331
	Appendix II: Piper Story Log	355
	Appendix III: The Future History	365
	Appendix IV: The Terro-Human Future History Chronology	373
	Appendix V: The Terro-Human Future History	401
	Appendix VI: The "Lost" Fuzzy Novel	409
	Appendix VII: The Continuing Worlds of H. Beam Piper	431
	Appendix VIII: H. Beam Piper Bibliography	451

As long as a book would write itself, I was a faithful and interested amanuensis and my industry did not flag; but the minute the book tried to sift to my head the labor of contriving its situations, inventing its adventures, and conducting its conversations I put it away and dropped it out of my mind. The reason was very simple...my tank had run dry; the story...could not be wrought out of nothing.

Mark Twain

Preface

"For all his knowledge, Beam was no dry intellectual. He was a storyteller; a man who could keep you up all night with his books and his tales. He had respect for the intellect and for intellectuals, but he was never one of the breed. He was a cavalier."

Jerry Pournelle
Federation
Preface

Henry Beam Piper was born March 23rd, 1904, the only issue of Harriett L. (Mauer) Piper and Herbert Orr Piper. Both of his parents were middle-aged. As Piper researcher David Hines pointed out, "The Piper-Maurer union was, for the time, an unusually late marriage for both; Harriett was three days shy of 40 when she gave birth to their first and only child." At the beginning of the twentieth century, childbirth was perilous for all women, but especially risky for a first time mother approaching 40 years of age. Not only was childbirth dangerous, but there was a good chance of birth defects or of giving birth to a child with Down's Syndrome.

As an only child born late in Harriett Piper's life, he was feted and spoiled by his mother. Anne McGuire, the wife of John J. McGuire, told her daughter, Terry, "Beam's Mother treated him like a prince. He could do no wrong in that household. She made all his meals and did all the housekeeping." Piper lived with his mother in her small apartment until her death in 1955, where she cooked his meals and generally took care of him.

H. Beam Piper was one of the most enigmatic writers in the field of science fiction. He appeared suddenly and from out of nowhere in 1946 at the top of his form and went on to write a number of memorable short stories in the premier science fiction magazine of the time, *Astounding Science Fiction*, under legendary editor John W. Campbell. Piper quickly became friends with many of the top writers of the day: Lester Del Rey, Fletcher Pratt, Robert Heinlein and Sprague de Camp.

Piper wrote in the vein of Robert Lewis Stevenson, Arthur Conan Doyle and Mark Twain. Wonderful adventure stories that appealed both to the "men" in boys, and to the "boys" in men. First and foremost, he was a storyteller. Piper had the knack of engaging the reader in far-off worlds in time and space. His protagonists were heroic; his antagonists villains of the blackest stripe. Piper's stories will live as long as there are dreams of derring-do, rip-roaring adventure and fights-to-the-death between good and evil.

During his life, Piper made sure the spotlight was on his creations, not himself. Even those who counted Piper among their friends knew little about the man and his life as a railroad guard for the Pennsylvania Railroad in Altoona, Pennsylvania. Piper was very protective over his personal privacy and had a Victorian view of publicity and self-promotion. Mike Knerr put Piper into perspective with the comment in "PIPER," his unpublished biography: "Part of the reason for the mystery of Piper lies in his origins. His life was common, his formal education almost non-existent and his knowledge of writing gleaned primarily through a voracious appetite for reading that could never be sated. When he died he was reading, ironically, *Captain Blood Returns*. I took it back to the library for him. Early in his life he knew his way around a library and grew up reading the various pulp magazines of the time."

What was H. Beam Piper like? He was a lean man of medium height, with a pencil thin mustache—in the style of Errol Flynn and David Niven—and dark hair. He was rarely seen without a pipe and cane. A thin patrician nose bridged two flint-hard eyes which would occasionally twinkle as though he were aware of some crucial insight into the foibles of mankind. Those who met him describe him as a courtly gentleman of the old school. Most described his manner as Victorian, which is ironic since Piper viewed himself, at least during his twenties, as a Bohemian. Having worked for three decades as a yard bull for the Pennsy Railroad, he was not one to suffer fools gladly.

Not married until late in life, he did have an eye for the ladies. As Jack McGuire, Jr. (the son of John J. McGuire, Piper's only literary collaborator) told me: "From then on Beam became a constant presence in our house. My mother stated she was very naïve then, and would sometimes invite Beam for dinner, and he would say, 'No, Anne, tonight I'm going out to beat the bushes.' My mother later understood that to mean he was going out to meet a woman."

Jack reiterated, "Beam was always a lady's man. Sometimes Beam would take me and Terry along with him to the local taverns—we called him 'Uncle' Beam while he trolled for women."

Paul Dillinger, an old school friend, shared the following memory of H. Beam Piper in a letter: "My most vivid remembrance of him was his recalling attendance at a movie, which from its description sounded like *THEM*. Anyway, he said about the time the giant insects appeared he stalked out in disgust. Another man who exited at the same time struck up a conversation with him, including the question of whether Piper had ever read any science fiction. 'Hell,' Piper said, 'I WRITE the stuff!'"

Piper enjoyed the role-playing and mystery involved in 'hiding' his real self. Mike Knerr noted: "Beam wanted to be what he believed a man should be, a living example of what he put on paper and, when he failed in his quest, he could not allow it to be seen.... His life, and the various myths that swirled around him, is as difficult to bring into focus as the character of the man himself. Swathed in secrecy and a verbal smoke screen of self-produced fiction, he lived out his final years in a lonely, frustrated existence that few people, if any, understood. Except when it suited his purposes, he refused to discuss his past and his origins and, when he did, he frequently lied. He generally summed up everything with a favorite expression: 'Man is born, he suffers, he dies; so far, I've done two thirds of this.'"

PART ONE

The Young Writer

CHAPTER ONE

The Beginning

H. Beam Piper was born on March 23rd, 1904; he was the only son of middle-aged parents. His mother, Harriett Piper, was almost forty when he was born. He was doted over and given full run of the Piper household. Don Coleman describes his parents thusly, "They had always been a part of his existence and remained clearly 'near the window'...always addressing them as 'mother' and 'father' rather than mom and pop had produced...a personal reverence. 'Mother' was always there, so the saying goes, being able to relate so much knowledge of the War Between the States—she having been born shortly before its ending." Harriett Piper's tales led to his fascination with the Civil War, and his expertise of the war's chronological history. His interest in this period of history was certainly influenced by his identification with his namesake, Henry Beam Piper, also known as H. Beam Piper, who was a Captain in the Union Army and a decorated war hero. His grandfather's name is still inscribed on a Civil War memorial plaque in downtown Altoona.

Very little is known about H. Beam Piper's father, Herbert Orr Piper. He was born March 7th, 1870 in Greensburg, Pennsylvania. At the time of his death, December 26th, 1936, Herbert Piper was working for Penn Central Power and Light as an office clerk. His residence was 1936 Fairview Street, Altoona and he was a member of the First Presbyterian Church.

The wedding announcement in the *Altoona Mirror* noted the groom was "an employee of the Juniata shops (Pennsylvania Railroad)." Piper's father was probably instrumental in getting him a job with the Pennsy. According to Wikipedia: "The Pennsylvania Railroad was the largest railroad by traffic and revenue in the U.S. for the first half of the Twentieth century. Over the years, it acquired, merged with or owned part of at least 800 other rail lines and companies. At the end of 1925, it operated 10,515 miles of rail line; in the 1920s, it carried nearly three times the traffic as other railroads of comparable length, such as the Union Pacific or Atchison, Topeka & Santa Fe railroads. Its only formidable rival was the New York Central (NYC), which carried around three-quarters of PRR's ton-miles.

"At one time, the Pennsylvania Railroad was the largest publicly traded corporation in the world, with a budget larger than that of the U.S. government and a workforce of about 250,000 people. The corporation still holds the record for the longest continuous dividend history: it paid out annual dividends to shareholders for more than 100 years in a row."

Herbert Piper worked at a number of jobs, teamster, meter man and lastly office clerk At Pennsylvania Central Light & Power. According to his Certificate of Death, Herbert Piper died of a heart attack ("Myocardial disease") at age 66 on December 26th, 1936. He was buried two days later in the Maurer family plot.

Mike Knerr noted in his unpublished book, "PIPER," that "Beam seldom talked about his father, except in relation to the older Piper's firearms, but he once showed me a picture of him. It was taken in 1922, at an area hunting camp, showing him holding his new .32 Winchester Special at a kind of port arms. The photo displays a small-boned, thin-faced man with the stern look of the 'frontier' in his eyes and a walrus mustache dripping from his upper lip.

"His father taught young Beam about firearms early in life and the love of them stayed with him. In later years he mentioned that he half believed that he had cut his first tooth on the barrel of his dad's old 32/20 Colt revolver. Herbert gave him a smoothbore caplock and taught him how to hunt. Armed with his 'fowling piece,' together with shot and a flask of powder, Beam tramped the woods of Blair County and brought his kills back to the family larder....

"Beam was fourteen when the United States entered the war in France and he may have been younger when he hunted blackbirds with his old muzzle-loading shotgun. His statement [about hunting blackbirds—jfc] could have hinted at the poverty of his parents, or it could have simply been a notation on a lack of game. On the other hand, it could well have been a doting mother preparing what her young son brought home from the woods."

While Piper was too young for the armed services in World War I, he was too old to join up for World War II. In a phone conversation, John McGuire Jr. told me, "Most of Beam's friends had seen service in World War II, and it was obvious that having missed two World Wars Piper felt he'd missed out on a rite of passage." He had this to say to Mike Knerr about his "service" in World War II: "Beam joined the local 'home guard' unit after Pearl Harbor and served for the duration. 'We did a damned good job, too,' he said laughing, 'There wasn't a single German soldier in all of Blair County!'"

Harriett L. Maurer was born March 26th, 1864, at Juniata Gap and was six years older than her husband. Both parents were members of the First Presbyterian Church in Altoona. David Hines noted, "According to her obituary, she was survived by 'a number of nieces and nephews,' but I do not know whether she came by them through siblings of her own or through her marriage to Herbert."

H. Beam Piper and both of his parents are interred at Fairview Cemetery in Altoona and all three graves are within the Maurer family plot. H. Beam Piper's grave is between his mother's and Brother Maurer, an Episcopalian minister, who died after H. Beam Piper. As a lifelong atheist and possessor of a very dry sense of humor, I'm sure Piper would be amused about their close placement.

To Piper, mundane reality—no matter how odd and fascinating—was no match for his fertile and dramatic imagination. One of the best examples of Piper's inventiveness at work were the tall tales he told about his marriage to Elizabeth Hirst. The basic "cover story" was reported by John H. Costello in *Renaissance*, a science fiction fanzine: "Nearing sixty, he embarked on a disastrous marriage. An expensive European honeymoon, and subsequent divorce proceedings, wiped out his life's savings and left him, in the words of Lester Del Rey, 'with hardly enough money to put bread on the table.'" Jerry Pournelle reported, "Beam told me that his wife married him for an expensive French vacation!"

Mike Knerr was incensed when I reported this in *Federation* and went out of his way, through the offices of Ace Books, to enlighten me: "Just more Piper bullshit!," he told me over the phone. "Beam loved Betty until his dying day." Knerr wrote in his unpublished biography, "PIPER": "Many are of the opinion that Beam married a French woman, and, according to him, 'she only married me for an expensive Paris vacation.' He told this to several people, including me, and he lied, as usual. Betty simply spoke French, as well as read it to some extent, and she definitely did *not* marry Beam on any such notion. Hirst is scarcely a French name and anyone whose home is in Carmel (a rather well-to-do area) doesn't need a thousand dollar a year writer to use for a vacation."

While Piper could stretch the truth about himself: he had zero tolerance for lies and less than honorable behavior from his friends and acquaintances—and, as will be shown, he was intolerant of their misbehavior to an extreme degree. The protagonists of his stories and novels were straightforward and said what they meant, and meant what they said.

In another attempt to shade the truth, Piper was reported as saying that his father was a minister, which was what John H. Costello reported in the fanzine, *An Infinity of Worlds*. This was given verisimilitude (since Piper was the kind of author who put a lot of himself and his life in his stories) by the fact that the father of Calvin Morrison, the protagonist in "Gunpowder God" and *Lord Kalvan of Otherwhen*, was a minister. I reported that information in my introduction to *Federation*, a collection of Piper's early future history stories, and Paul Schuchart, a lifelong friend of Piper's, wrote me this correction: "Beam's father was NOT a Presbyterian minister, but worked for the electric company. My father was a Methodist minister at Llyswen, a suburb of Altoona, and we lived about a half block from where Beam and his mother and father lived." Mike Knerr added, "Beam's tall tales about himself crop up all the time, even the one that states his father was a minister. Unfortunately, this is more *Piper-fostered* fiction...."

Little is known about Piper's childhood and school years. In "PIPER," Knerr had this to say: "He came from a relatively poor family and was raised in a small town whose population probably never had a writer in their midst. He worked at a menial job, struggling for everything he owned and everything he knew. College was totally out of the question and his help was needed at home." To cover up his inability to continue school, Piper often said he hadn't entered college because he wanted to spare himself "the ridiculous misery of four years in the uncomfortable confines of a raccoon coat." He went to work for the Pennsy Railroad at age eighteen, after getting kicked out of high school, and stayed with the PRR until he resigned in 1956.

Beam's friend Paul Schuchart noted in his February 18th, 1981, letter, "I agree with you when you said Beam never had a formal education, but he probably read more books than most professors. I graduated from Washington and Lee in Lexington. My recollection was that Beam was thrown out of Altoona High School because he shot the bottoms out of several test tubes in the chemical lab."

Piper scholar David Hines, who conducted extensive research in Altoona, found little to add: "Very little information from Beam Piper's youth survives; the earliest photograph of him I know of is circa 1953. I hoped to find a picture of him in the high school yearbook, but to no avail. Piper left high school (as you know, he was reportedly thrown out) before graduating, and in those days only the Seniors' photos were included in the yearbook. He must have made an impression, though: on page 57 of the 1921 Annual for Altoona High School, the feature 'Who's Who in the Sophomore Class' contains this line: 'We feel sure Beam Piper will be president of our class when we are seniors.' This is the sole record of H. Beam Piper's scholastic career. Altoona High School officials could find no record of an H. B. Piper ever attending high school there."

The September 1953 issue of *The Pennsy*, a monthly newsletter published by the Pennsylvania Railroad Company, includes an article on page 7 about H. Beam Piper titled "Typewriter 'Killer:" "Mr. Piper, night watchman at Altoona Works, is a part-time author with a record of 25 published short stories [mostly 'lost' non-fiction pieces for local newspapers—jfc], a murder mystery which the New York Times called 'an unusually fascinating first novel,' and a historical article to which Walt Disney bought the movie rights.

"The story, 'Time and Time Again,' was a fantasy about a man who gets killed in World War III in 1975 and revives to find himself at the age of 13 in 1945, with full knowledge of everything that was to happen until his 'death' in 1975. The story was published in *Astounding Science Fiction*, republished in a U.S. anthology, then translated for a German anthology and finally presented as a radio show over NBC.

"Things picked up for Mr. Piper thereafter, with stories in such magazines as *Future, Amazing Stories, Weird Tales* and *Space Science Fiction*, and an article about Colonel John S. Mosby, the Confederate guerrilla leader, which appeared in *True*."

*   *   *

Piper wrote his letters with a view to "posterity," and was not above "editing" them to ensure that it was the "ideal past" that survived; fortunately, Ferd Coleman, his best friend, thought they were all important. Unfortunately, all but two of Piper's unpublished works were "torn up and burned," either in gleeful pyromania with J.J. McGuire, or in his fireplace in melancholy solitude. Before his marriage to Elizabeth Hirst, he burned all his pre-1955 diaries in one big bonfire.

Some writers are born with the golden touch, they write easily and quickly, selling almost everything they produce. Science fiction author Robert Silverberg is a good example of this type of gifted writer; he sold stories to the science fiction pulps as a teenager in New York and for a long time was so prolific he was writing science fiction stories that were appearing in some magazines in the same issue under several pseudonyms. But for H. Beam Piper, the path to his writing career was long and torturous.

CHAPTER TWO

The Young Author

During his middle-aged years, H. Beam Piper was well loved by the science fiction and mystery community, but not well known outside them. Piper loved to drink and talk late into the night about politics, history and writing at science fiction conventions and writers' gatherings. He was a gifted storyteller and raconteur, and a damn good mimic. His sharp eye for detail often captured the foibles, quirks and idiosyncrasies of his fellow humans, which he related with great gusto and style. However, he told his writer friends and fans very little about his "other life," working as a night watchman at the Juniata Yards, or about his camping and hiking expeditions. He told them nothing about his childhood or young adulthood and *most importantly*—his personal life.

I had a lot of information about the last decade of Piper's life, thanks to Mike Knerr who had sent me his unpublished Piper biography, "PIPER," but after twenty years of research—other than Paul Schubert's letter regarding the test tube shooting in the chemistry class at Altoona High School—I had uncovered nothing about H. Beam Piper's life before his first story appearance in *Astounding Science Fiction*. Neither Fred Ramsey (a local SF fan and the founding owner of Webster's Book Store in State College) nor David Hines (a dedicated Piper scholar who sought out Piper's surviving former friends in Altoona and Williamsport) had been able to uncover anyone who knew Piper during the time he lived in Altoona despite numerous visits.

Nor did it help that in the intervening years since his death, all of Piper's former residences had been demolished and turned into parking lots. I despaired of ever learning anything about his youth and early writings until I received a letter from Don Coleman, the son of Piper's best friend, in 1991. Don Coleman wrote to tell me about a manuscript, entitled "The Early Years," he'd assembled which contained the collected correspondence between H. Beam Piper and Ferdinand (aka Ferd) W. Coleman starting in the early 1920s. Don had run across my name in the first Piper short story collection *Federation* which I had edited and assembled for Ace Books.

Having read Robert A. Heinlein's posthumous *Grumbles From the Grave*, Don thought he might be able to sell Piper's and his father's collected correspondence to a publisher and thought I might be of help in this quest. I quickly wrote him back and asked him to send me a copy so that I could determine its value. When the full manuscript arrived, I felt like Bouchard Pierre-François, the discoverer of the Rosetta Stone. For the first time, I had an actual window into Piper's past, a collection of more than a hundred letters between H. Beam Piper and his best friend, Ferd Coleman, starting with a Piper letter dated August 26th, 1926 (when Beam was 22 years old).

In his 1991 cover letter, Don wrote: "Beam Piper was my friend for over thirty years and when reading recollections of him by anyone other than my own family; it really set me to reminiscing of Beam's early years—the times he struggled and dangled about—before becoming a noted science fiction author. Literally, hundreds of letters passed between him and his closest compadre during these 'struggling' years—my father. I consider many of these scribblings to be classic and [they] should not be hidden away among the obscurities of the den bookshelves, forever.

"The meeting of Piper and Coleman came about during a gathering of the Pennsylvania Alpine Club at the mountain home of Colonel Henry W. Shoemaker, the prominent [Pennsylvanian] folklorist and historian, and a staunch supporter of this extraordinary group. Shoemaker's retreat, affectionately named 'Restless Oaks,' is nestled in the mountainous environs of McElhattan, (located some 20 miles up the river from Williamsport) where he authored numerous folk tales of early Pennsylvania, and was actively involved with issues of conservation of wildlife and forest lands within the Commonwealth. The Colonel loved the woods and wilds, and thrived upon the historical values of the surrounding beauty—just as the likes of the young and industrious Coleman, and the young and ambitious Beam Piper. Although the Colonel was a mutual friend of both, this particular occasion brought the two together for the first time, and needless to say, they became thoroughly absorbed in discourse."

Colonel Shoemaker was a local character of some political and social note in Central Pennsylvania. Piper's first published work in 1927 was a catalogue of Colonel Shoemaker's gun collection published as "compiled by H. Beam Piper, *A Catalogue of Henry Wharton Shoemaker Weapons at Restless Oaks in McElhattan Pennsylvania*, publisher *Times Tribune Co.,* Altoona, Pennsylvania." In addition, his first mystery novel, *Murder in the Gunroom*, was dedicated to Colonel Shoemaker.

Don Coleman writes, "Beam seems to have regarded Shoemaker as a mentor of sorts. A wealthy man, self-made, also without formal education, I think Beam saw a hopeful precedent for himself in Shoemaker's success and aspired for something similar. They met and worked together because of their interest in history, writing and weapons. He made much money from his paper and was a LARGE presence in the community."

"Restless Oaks is gone now. But it was in McElhattan, near the West branch of the Susquehanna, east of Lock Haven. This location on the northern boundary of Kalvan's future Hostigos must have been paradise to the industrial city dwelling Piper.

"Woods full of game. Second growth forest, maybe seventy-five years in from the first harvest. The house was located near a small stream at the northern end of a narrow gap that led into Sugar Valley. A site that to someone lost in the love of medieval warfare would have seen as a wonderful place for a castle."

At the time they met at Restless Oaks, both H. Beam Piper and Ferd Coleman saw themselves as Bohemians (the pre-World War II equivalent of beatniks), and often mocked conventional views of religion, bourgeoisie morality and politics. One of Piper's 1927 letter closers was "Yours for

Free Love and Atheism, Beam." This is not the Victorian image that Piper presented to the world of science fiction in the 1950s and '60s.

The same was true with Piper's dress, the formal attire (even when dining alone or writing he wore a tie), wearing capes and slouch hats at night in Altoona; he believed in an unconventional lifestyle and got joy out of offending those who considered themselves the pillars of conventional morality and society. It's not surprising that he fit in well with both the mystery and science fiction crowds.

* * *

As Don Coleman recounts, "Ferd W. Coleman was born in 1904. He attended a Catholic school and of course, back then, eleven years enveloped the complete curriculum. He loved to write, and poetry seemed to be his wont, but he knew one couldn't live on poetry alone. He never attended college. He would challenge the world with his own self-learned wisdom.

"Ferd was a very smart man; an intellectual. His vocabulary was extraordinary. I also considered Beam an intellectual, but visibly eccentric. Dad was an avid reader; he wore prescription glasses at eight (or younger) and had a profound interest in poetry.

"He established the *Shopper's Guide* in 1922 at age 18. He wanted to do something entirely different from the ordinary. He wanted a paper solely dedicated to advertising—not a newspaper. He felt this was giving the patron a more personal communication between the tradesman and the housewife. He concluded the paper would pay for itself, and that not a select few, but everyone, would receive it.

"His initial publications measured half a newspaper page (sliced down the middle)—both sides, originally giving him a net revenue of some eight to ten bucks! He started in a small area called Newberry, which actually is within the west side of Williamsport. I don't know who printed the paper originally, but when it eventually became more than just a single sheet, blossoming to a full page and finally into six and eight-page editions, Dad hired out to the Sunbury *Daily Item* (thirty miles downriver) to print the publication. After sometime with the *Item*, he began running syndicated columnists such as Walter Winchell, *et. al.*"

Don Coleman paints a vivid picture about the beginnings of the Piper/Coleman friendship: "We have here two outdoorsmen—one a publisher of a budding shopping newsletter; the other a night watchman and part-time writer, employed by the Pennsylvania Railroad system—what seemingly appears a most unlikely incompatible pair. Coleman, having not yet approached the mature age of 21 years of life, but completely sound, had somewhat deviated from those who were unable to keep up with his cunning demeanor—until now! After lengthy conversations, Coleman was confronted with the fact that he'd met a man who was as ingenious as himself. Could this be true?

"He quickly learned that Beam Piper was spontaneous in response to solving and resolving the queries and qualms of the day—and each found that *neither* could tolerate idle conversation. And neither would admit to egoism. So on this day in December, 1925, a matchless friendship was born.

"Both men loved the mountains where rambling forests and gentle streams were real, and where wild game flourished with grandeur.... Despite Coleman's animosity towards the use of lethal weapons, both he and Piper were avid collectors of antique weapons. Beam was primarily an accumulator of antique weapons and accessories, while Ferd expanded more into other items of value such as spinning wheels, apple wood rockers and other articles of antique furniture. Both were historians who, whenever time permitted, were continually exploring the life and traditions of the early Dutch settlers to the West Branch Valley.

"...Aside from the great outdoors, each possessed another and greater common amour...that of writing. Coleman was editor and publisher of the Williamsport *Shopper's Guide,* which he established in 1922—a device that took its rank among the initial shopping newspapers in the nation.

"Piper spent his nights as a watchman amid the Pennsylvania Railroad shops and yards in Altoona, a community that was quite prominent in railroad repair, and a bustling hub of the [rail] systems. The nature of his job required cognizance of the system's security about the vast railroad yards, and his riding the line as a railroad *dick* brought him within or about the confines of Williamsport numerous times...And he was continually writing both day and night. Whenever his ideas surfaced—even while performing his railroad responsibilities—they were immediately put to paper. Murder investigation and history were his primary literary goals at this time. And sleep was secondary, of course."

CHAPTER THREE

Brothers of the Quill

Piper began writing in his teens. The *Pennsy* article "Typewriter Killer" has this to say about the young Piper. "Mr. Piper's success hasn't come without sweat. When he began working for the PRR in 1922 as a laborer, at the age of 18, he already was an author of two years standing. He was using all his pocket money for postage, regularly sending out stories to the magazines and just as regularly getting them back. It wasn't until 1946, when he had been writing for 26 years, that he made his first sale."

Later in the *Double-Bill Symposium* [a science-fiction fanzine], Piper clarifies this: "In my teens, which would be in the early 1920s, I decided that what I really wanted to do was write; I wasn't sure what, but I was going to write something. About the same time, I became aware of science fiction, such as it was then, mostly H.G. Wells, and fantasy, Bram Stoker, H. Rider Haggard, and then I began reading the newer science (more or less) fiction—Burroughs, Merritt, Ralph Milne Farley, Ray Cummings, *et al.* This was the Neolithic, or Hugo Gernsback, period of science fiction, and by this time I was a real 200-proof fan.

"This first enthusiasm waned slightly after a while. I got interested in history and historical fiction, and for some time read little else in the way of fiction, and every historical novel I read started me reading up on the history of the period involved. I wanted to know just who this guy Richelieu was and why D'Aartagnan & Co. had such a down on him. Then the Prohibition period was in full swing, and I became interested in Chicago gangsters for a while. All the time, I was scribbling stories, few of which ever got finished, thank God!"

The "Typewriter Killer" article further states: "Mr. Piper, a tall, slim man with sharply chiseled features, and a sinister black mustache, could pass for a villain in his own mystery novel. He spends the somber midnight hours patrolling through the Altoona shops, watching out for trespassers and possible fires." While financial circumstances dictated that he work as a night watchman for the Pennsylvania Railroad to support himself and his writing habit, Beam used those "circumstances" to *his* best advantage, working the graveyard shift and working on story ideas as he made his rounds of the car shops or, when he had the opportunity, penning rough drafts at work.

It doesn't take much imagination to see Piper—with a slouch cap, cape and black overcoat—wandering the deserted car shops, where they kept the boxcars, locomotives and railroad flatcars, late at night in a light drizzle like some wraith, talking out the story complications of his latest yarn. Woe to the bum or wrongdoer who ran into Mr. Piper, for—if needed—he could dispense Billy Club justice with nether sentimentality nor rancor—just the firm application of *force majeure*.

I suspect there were several benefits to this job that kept him steadily employed as a night watchman for over thirty years. First, he worked late at night and didn't have a boss watching over his shoulder. It was a lot like working for himself. From Piper's diary entries it's obvious that he had a lot of freedom as to the hours and days worked which allowed him to take long visits to New York to attend writers' meetings and meet with editors and other members of the writing clan. Finally, he got free railroad passes which he used frequently to travel from Altoona to Williamsport (to meet with Ferd and other hunting friends) and to New York.

All writers put something of themselves in their work; Piper probably more than most. Many of his stories are set in rural settings not unlike that of the Appalachian Mountains where he spent most of his life. In *Little Fuzzy*, the protagonist, Jack Holloway, a grizzled, self-sufficient old prospector on the frontier world of Zarathustra, describes Piper justice, in answer to the question: "'Haven't had any trouble lately, have you?'

Holloway replies: 'Not since the last time.' The last time had been a couple of woods tramps, some out-of-work veldbeest herders from the south, who had heard about the little bag he carried around his neck."

H. Beam Piper's lack of sentimentality and penchant for writing *real* characters probably did not help him make story sales at a time when outlaws and gangsters were glorified in movies and fiction. As, in most things, he was out of step with the times; this never changed. It only took him another twenty years of unsuccessful writing before he found a field where 'being out in left field' was a compliment, not a put-down.

While he had little faith in the afterlife, it's quite obvious Piper was quite interested in living his life fully and wanted to make his mark as a serious author. Probably the major cement of the Ferd Coleman/H. Beam Piper friendship was their love of words, literature, word play and writing. Don Coleman gives us a good view of how his father regarded Piper's writing: "Ferd W. Coleman, as a writer himself, surely was capable of tossing barbs of criticism at H. Beam Piper, as well as Joseph Conrad or Ernest Hemingway or any other author of the day, if need be—but in the early going he acknowledged Piper as potentially a good contributor. The force with which Piper put his thoughts to paper (letter writing)—his philosophies and beliefs and the simple advising of his own doing—were extremely welcomed by Coleman."

"...I am sincere, Beam, when I write I enjoyed your letter so much. I think it should not be difficult for you to know why, since nuts or pioneer souls, as you will, like yourself and me, are difficult to discover, with the alternative that such associates as I tolerate are quite commonplace, and, as to letters I receive few, and those of no consequence…. Further, Beam, your letter was well written and convinces me without more ado on that score that you *can* write. Your only drawback, as I fathom you, is that which I told you last Christmas at 'Restless Oaks'—you haven't *lived.* ...However the extent of your background, Beam, I wish you would forward me some of the dope you have written. I know I should be keenly interested in it…."

Piper fired back: "As for myself, I have been doing little or nothing except writing, and that at another unspeakably cheap pot-boiler. I had a little trouble in developing that story I told you about—the one in which a soldier of fortune has the love affair with the married woman and gets bumped off in a duel—and I laid it by until the Muse would get into working order again."

This desultory way of working was typical of Piper until the day he died. He would get an idea, try to work it into a story, then write draft after draft trying to make the story work. He would work and work at a story, often abandoning it at the eleventh hour, because of some suspected flaw. Then he would literally pine over it, as he waited for divine inspiration—or desperation—to help him finish the story. Unfortunately, none of Piper's unpublished works from this era survived his death so it is impossible to do an objective analysis. His diaries and his letters clearly demonstrate that Piper was rarely satisfied with his stories, even those that were published, and rewrote them over and over.

Don Coleman writes: "…as for Piper, only after drafting his thoughts in longhand, scratching out and adding and re-penning an idea, would he eventually turn to tapping the keys of his anchored 'Underwood' with the final veneer—and never without at least one carbon copy… Invariably a Piper miscarriage would wind up making a return trip to 400 Wordsworth Avenue, it being slammed down aside the typewriter unopened, as meticulously as immediate frustration would allow. And after experiencing the existing disappointments, he would never let the presence of a publisher's rejection impede the continuity of thought he carried.… He would return to the draft he was penning until the segment…was complete. Then, after feeling content with what he had written, he would grasp and scrutinize the package of denial."

Piper wrote to Ferd: "I've been up to the ears for the last week with one thing or another, chiefly re-writing that story, so you haven't heard from me sooner. I think that I have the thing fixed about as I want it and Monday I start finishing it up; smoothing out the rough spots, making the sentences a little better and typing it off.… I toned down the religious argument quite a good bit, as I thought that some of the 'intellectual' readers of the magazine might object. Disgusting, but I think that it had to be done. Likewise, I reduced the conversation between the man and girl to the proper level of imbecility.

"Well, enough of this. It's always tiresome to talk shop, particularly when it comes to recounting the devices by which stories are rendered comprehensible to the 'booboise,' so I will shift to more amusing topics...."

Even in his twenties, Piper knew what he was aiming for. He took his career seriously, realizing that he would have to put in a long apprenticeship, and that he wouldn't start out at the top. He needed to develop his technique and in that era literary fiction was largely done by those with a Yale or Harvard degree. One needed a certain pedigree or the 'right friends' to become published in *The New Yorker* or *American Mercury*. Piper had foregone a formal education and so served his apprenticeship in the pulp magazines, rude and colorful magazines that were pitched to readers of westerns, romances, crime stories, mysteries and tales of other worlds.

"I did another potboiler, fifteen thousand words of eyewash about the Rum Row whisky-trade. In it I succeeded in killing off almost the entire cast of characters and introduced several pitched battles in the manner of Herrin, Ill. If those buggers want a 'clean story of swift-moving action,' they shall have it, so help me, Allah! I hope it sells. If it does, I'll be able to take a few months and write something decent—that novel I was telling you about, for instance.

"I was very careful to stipulate that it be published under an assumed name. I don't want that sort of thing thrown in my teeth when I'm writing good stuff. I regard a piece of poor work in the same light as a bastard offspring—it is wise not to acknowledge it publicly. When, twenty years hence, I am known as an author, I don't want to have people say, 'Oh, hell, he wrote for *Black Mask* and *Brief Stories!*' Their money is just as good as the *American Mercury's*, but damnit, their reputation isn't."

This statement provides further evidence Piper was taking himself seriously as a writer even as far back as 1926. Of course, he had no way of knowing that his first story would not be published for another twenty years! By the 1940s, he was no longer worried about being published in the pulps, or about his future *literary* reputation. Thus, he used his real name on his first published story, "Time and Time Again" for *Astounding Stories.*

Ferd Coleman, another frustrated would-be author, was very supportive of his best friend's career. "I sincerely hope you cash in on the manuscript, Beam. You not only deserve to because of your persistence but frankly I believe there is excellent material and tolerable technique behind your work. I forgot whether you told me you subscribed to the *Author and Journalist* when I asked you at McElhattan. If you do not, let me know and I shall send you a batch."

As with just about everything concerning hunting, antique firearms, the outdoors, politics, Piper had strong views regarding writing manuals and magazines that catered to would-be-writers, like himself. "You ask if I have subscribed to the *Author and Journalist.* I have not. Saving your presence and asking your pardon, I solemnly hold that trade journals, while excellent for carpenters, undertakers, real-estate dealers, cheesemongers, etc., are not for artists, particularly for authors.

"The same thing, by the way, applies also to the numerous Author's Leagues and Writer's Associations.... As for the ten thousand Schools of Story-Writing, words cannot help me express my opinions.

"However, I retain a partially open mind. If you have any copies of the magazine, I accept your offer. Mail them on, informing me whether or not you want them returned, and I will give them the once-over, as a true agnostic should, to see if there is any wheat in what I think is a Gargantuan chaff-heap. This is, however, only a personal opinion, subject, like Bannerman's prices on ammunition, to change....

"Also, I would be glad to glance over any of the stories you have written, the stories, I mean, that you were telling me about, if any of them are finished.

"With sincere hopes that you are well and out of jail, I am, as ever, Your fellow ballock [testicle] of the devil—Beam."

Piper's condescending air towards self-help journals doesn't stop him from accepting them—even if he described them as "bunk." As with most unpublished authors, he was still searching for the 'key'—either within himself, or the New York publishing establishment—that would open the magical doors of publication. It's a formidable structure and Piper had already spent several years beating his head against it in frustration.

Piper also worried story ideas like a mastiff chewing a big bone. In March of 1927 he wrote Coleman about another idea for the soldier of fortune story. "You know, I've decided that I'll not write that thing about the soldier of fortune and the married lady as a short story, but as a novel. After I got to thinking it over, I saw that there was too damn much to it to be disposed of in any few thousand words. Those two characters, the man in particular, simply can't be hammered down into a short story at all, and the characters, or at least the one main character, will make a good story out of it if handled right. Of that I am firmly convinced."

CHAPTER FOUR

Tiadaghton

By 1927, his frustration at not getting published building, Piper was working hard to figure out what was wrong with his technique or style, a question that often frustrates many beginning writers. Sometimes it is a good thing people can't see into the future, since Piper had nineteen more years of these kinds of questions to go over before his first story sale.

He wrote to Ferd: "By the way, that story that I was working on at Brookside has gone forth and returned three times. (*Argosy-Allstory, Black Mask,* and the Street and Smith gang) Now, you read it. What in hell's amiss with it? Or have I been sending it to the wrong place? I am not unmindful of my promise to buy a keg of moonshine and go off somewhere with you if it sells. I hope it does. Cold sober, we have had a hell of a good time. Gloriously tanked, we could hold revel as the gods and heroes do in Valhalla.

"By the way, do you know anything about this course in fiction writing that Columbia University runs? Anything good, that is? I see rather plainly that there is something wrong with my stuff—these damn blood-and-thunder potboilers, I mean—but the thing is to find out what it is. And how to remedy it. I don't mean the correspondence course, but the course conducted at the University. Let me know your opinion on this."

In another undated letter, Piper attempts to analyze why he's not selling his work. "I received the book, along with a letter from the Colonel, just as I was starting on a hunting trip, and this is the first opportunity that I have had to answer either. I found it interesting simply to no end and for one thing, it showed me just what was wrong with that fool murder mystery story I wrote about a year ago. As I see it, there wasn't a damned thing right about it.

"I am convinced that that rum-running story, 'Drink and the Devil,' is a total loss. Maybe I can sell it after Al Smith gets elected (President), but with all this prohibition sentiment it won't go. I think I'll rewrite it, changing the characters from Twentieth Century bootleggers to Seventeenth Century buccaneers. The W.C.T.U won't object to murdering Spaniards and stealing pieces of eight as they do to selling whisky. Yours, for Rum, Royalism and Rebellion, Beam.

"P.S. I was glad to get the book, as I think I told you, and, having read and re-read it, I will bring it with me when I come down. I found a good bit that was profitable in it."

Piper first mentions his projected trilogy ["Tiadaghton"] based on local Pennsylvania history in a January 23rd, 1928 letter to Ferd Coleman: "I received the *Otzinatchson* (a history of the West Branch Valley of the Susquehanna: its first settlement, accounts of the privations endured by the early pioneers, Indian wars, predatory incursions, abductions and massacres, together with an account of the Fair Play System.) on the same afternoon that I mailed you my letter regarding the meeting, and I am delighted with it. I'd say, off hand, that it is worth all I am going to pay for it ($15), both as a history of the valley in which I spent some of the happiest days of my life and as a source of information and material for my projected series of three novels dealing with the Fair Play Man. As to the latter, I think it will serve as the foundation, to which I will build up my other research into old records, oral traditions and such like. I find, however, that the author is most damned infernally disorderly and digressive, but I will arrange some kind of an index by which I can put it in proper chronological order, and also prepare a bibliography, which it sadly wants. Then, with such notes as I may see fit to append, I will have a first class tool for the work I have in mind."

According to Don Coleman, "Piper's mention of 'Fair Play Men' centers around the early boundary given the western borders of Lycoming

County. There was a question as to whether Lycoming Creek, which flows just west of Williamsport to be the bonafide [sic] boundary, or the Tiadaghton (Pine Creek), which lay further west. If anyone trod west of Lycoming Creek, they would risk being hunted down by the Indians. Many settlers, feeling a strong sense of deception by the Indians in the treaty of 1768, believed the Tiadaghton to be the true western boundary and thus would move on across the line. In order that protection be given these wandering pioneers—within all this-of-a-sudden no man's land, the Fair Play system was implemented. Beam would tie this in with his proposed 'trilogy!'"

On January 28th, 1928, Ferd replies: "Anent your manuscripts, please go damned slow. Take your own counsel of two months back, derived from Sabatini, read, read, read, the lives, the histories, the very guts of locality, over many a night's midnight oil or gas, in home, not in auto and street, before attempting to write a line of historical romance. My novels of Nippenose [Nippenose Township became part of Lycoming County when Lycoming County was also formed from Northumberland County in 1795—jfc], crude as they are, must have been pioneer works because there is so little of the particular valley, and less of that distinct people; I, in fact, had to adopt with them the welcome which all Berks County Dutch accord strangers, I had practically to sleep with them in order to learn them. The condition, by good fortune, is different with you, not that you may not want to sleep with whomever you may find—but you have splendid research facilities. Let me tell you, boy, you said on your previous visit to me that you didn't want so much the possession of *Otzinatchson*, as you did the information it contained…"

Piper wrote back: "I fear you are laboring under a trifling misconception regarding the manuscript that I said I'd send you. I don't mean the manuscript of "Tiadaghton," the first of my trilogy on the Fair Play Men, I mean the manuscript of that short story which I outlined to you while drunk, and which I am calling 'Moment of Greatness.' Great Thor, I don't even have any ideas as to what the story of "Tiadaghton" will be. I'll have to wait until I've finished my research, first, as there will be absolutely no liberties taken with history and it will be necessary to discover what actually happened on the West Branch in the ten years' time about which I write before I can say what *fictitiously* happened.

"As to how I will gather that material, I mean to put in almost, or possibly more than, a month on the West Branch, both in the library and doing field work among the Oldest Inhabitants, Local Historians, and Hill-Billies [stet], not to forget the various historical societies, D.A.R. chapters, etc. I look to the last-named organization in its various ramifications, together with the Lycoming and Clinton County Historical Societies for some valuable data, as a historical novel accurately portraying a period in their own locality's history would be all cream for them, particularly with a note of acknowledgement in the book. But don't spring this on your own society until the arrangements are completed for my trip next summer...."

According to Don Coleman, "the Otzinatchson referred to in the letters relates to the Delaware Indian derivation given the West Branch (and immediate valley areas) of the Susquehanna River which, of course, is most prominent with the Clinton and Lycoming county regions of the Commonwealth.... At this time in their lives, the *Otzinatchson* book was the most informative source of Eighteenth Century regional history, to which Piper especially, intended to research and portray...in his yet-to-be-started novel.

"The letters also bring up reference to Tiadaghton, another name given by the Delawares. There may also be questions as to how the name came about, but Pine Creek, (a tributary running north of the Susquehanna just west of Jersey Shore) is represented as the Tiadaghton, and apparently its banks were happy hunting grounds for these two correspondents...."

Piper had difficulty giving birth to new ideas; in part because of his own overly critical view of his work. Plus, good ideas did not come easy to him, or ideas that *he viewed* as worthy of writing. He had very high standards, regardless of what kind of story or what market he was aiming for. So, his story production was slow, even when he was writing full time in the 1950s and no longer working as a night guard in the Altoona Yards.

In this April 18th, 1928 letter, written after he had finished the rewrite of "Moment of Greatness," he talks about his next story. "This done,

I am going to grind out another yarn, the action of which takes place at Mr. Sauel Wallis' 'Muncy Farms,' shortly before the Revolution. As it is to be a story of about the same length as the other, I think that what I can get out of the *Otzinatchson* and out of some of Col. Shoemaker's stuff will be quite enough for local color. There will be a number of actual characters—Wallis and his lady, Michael McAvoy, the gardener, and perhaps 'Hawkeye' Grove and Martha Gribblestone, as well as three or four purely fictitious ones. The story is quite too long to outline here, however, or, rather, too complicated, and I will spare you until I see you again."

Piper was as much interested in writing historical fact as he was fiction, especially in the early years of his career since it combined his two great passions. Unfortunately, other than the Mosby piece, "Rebel Raider," that was published in *True* magazine, there are no surviving examples of his historical non-fiction, most of which was published in local low-circulation newspapers, such as Coleman's *Shopper*.

In an October 12th, letter, he queries Ferd about one of his short pieces, "By the way, I wonder if you'd publish a little sketch that I have written of the activities of the Quakers during and prior to the Revolution? I am not expecting any remuneration, but simply wrote the thing as an antidote to a lot of nonsensical whoop-la that is being made over that sect at present, and to correct certain erroneous impressions now prevailing. For Ames & all Prohibitionists (to the left is a sketch of a tomahawk)."

Ferd replies on the 16th, "You may submit your Quaker ms. If not too lengthy and provocative I shall be pleased to publish it on a week when ads are low."

Even at this early date, Piper worked off and on at the Pennsy Yards, as demonstrated in this October 21st, letter. "However, I think I can keep myself at the typewriter and as I don't need to work overtime now, I can come home less tired than before and do more efficient work." It appears, other than the fact that Altoona was a one-industry town (Pennsy R.R.), that he worked his night guard job around his real job—writing. Unfortunately, later in life, when the Pennsy went into bankruptcy, he had no alternative way of making a living, but—in 1928—those days are far off and Piper is still full of piss and vinegar—or gunpowder.

In his letter of October 21st, he added, "Have a few good ideas for articles or short stories that I'll try to do something about in a pot-boiling sort of way. I'll tell you about them, maybe, when I see you again.

"As for the Quaker sketch, I'm not troubling to send it, for it is rather violent for you and besides, I doubt you could get it published before the election, and it would be valueless after. It's purely propaganda to combat the Hooverites yelling about Sir 'Erbert being a Quaker. I'm sending it to the Johnstown *Democrat*, edited by Warren Worth Bailley, and I expect that it will do good work, especially as many of his readers are Irish and will sympathize with ye 'dirty Irish' whom ye Quakers so despised.

"By the way, for the love of Christ, Ferd, don't vote for Hoover! VOTE AS YOU DRINK! For Rum, Romanticism and Rebellion! Beam"

Commenting about one of Piper's projected novels, Ferd wrote: "… While you have learned many lessons and gleaned many observations in this brief experience with the fleeting lady [a young woman who worked in an antique shop that Piper had a crush on], don't think that equips you for a novel. You are in something of a heat just now, and I would advise at least a half year's wait, and then consider the matter. You have lost a good deal of time on worthless manuscripts, you know."

Piper did not take criticism well, not even from his best friend. His reply of January 18th scorches the paper it's written on: "Even more am I amused by the little schnit [sic] of literary criticism with which you close. In the first place, the story might be possible if I only saw the girl for ten minutes on a railroad coach and never after that. In the second place, I told you the main particulars of the story twice already. You were drunk on both occasions. Once you yelled that it was a 'mashterpeesh!' and the other time you thought it was the bunk. If I knew on which occasion you were drunker, and, by consequence, more competent to judge such things, I'd know which verdict to accept. I laughed like hell when you advised me to wait A HALF A YEAR!!! Ye Gods, where are your thunderbolts! If I get it started inside of ten, I'll be doing well."

Things are getting so hot that Piper ends his letter with a white flag! "After so many insults as I have hurled in your teeth in the above screed I feel it time to close, as ever, with the same friendly feeling as before."

In an October 13th, 1929, letter, Piper wrote about a new novelette that he's just finished. "I will be down, Allah willing, about that time. Maybe sooner, if I hear favorably from a novelette of about 30,000 words that I've just sent off. It's gang-war stuff, with murders, and men put on the spot and taken for a ride, and police raids, and "pineapples" [grenades—jfc], and Thompson guns, and bootlegging, and white-slavers, and crooked officials, and a special police officer hero who wades up to his ears in gangster gore and cleans up the town and marries the girl. The girl, by the way, runs a sort of an antique shop. As Louie Bardo says, 'Get it?'

"'Racket-Town' has, to date, a record of three rejections, from *Argosy*, *Blue Book* and *Adventure*, and I am sending it out again today. Have masses said and candles burned to insure its acceptance."

In a May 25th, 1930, letter, he wrote: "'Racket-Town' now has the magnificent record of five rejections. At present it is out for the sixth time, and should I receive a check for it prior to Friday, I promise you that Williamsport will be painted a deep crimson and the City Fathers will be out at the pocket for a considerable repair-bill as a result of the celebration."

On July 7th, "I arrived home in good condition.... On my arrival I found 'Racket-Town' home again, for the seventh (7th) time. This time it was from Street & Smith, and, instead of the usual printed slip I got a personal letter with it. They complain (*mirable dictu*) of insufficient action. Well, I'll let them have one that won't have that drawback. The entire plot will be as follows: —Bang! Bang! Bang! Some of these days I'll arrive, if I keep on like this."

CHAPTER FIVE

Three Wishes

Piper did most of his writing in the "gunroom," as he called it, in the Altoona apartment on Wordsworth Avenue he shared with his mother. The *Pennsy* article, "Typewriter 'Killer,'" provides a vivid description of Piper's gunroom. "On the cluttered desk in H. Beam Piper's study are a miniature cannon that can go off with a big bang, a cigarette lighter made of a hand grenade and a pistol serving as a paperweight. Hanging on the walls and resting on bookcases are about 80 antique pistols and revolvers and about 50 stilettos, poniards, rapiers, broadswords and other lethal weapons. But the only way he ever kills anybody is with his typewriter....

"Today, his collection ranges from a four-hundred-and-fifty year-old French sword and a four-hundred year-old Spanish poniard with a gold-inlaid blade to a small brass cannon once mounted on a pioneer's block-house during the Indian fighting days and a 9-millimeter pistol of the type used by German SS troops during World War II."

By the 1950s, H. Beam Piper was not one to verbalize his innermost feelings either in person, in his diary or in his letters. Fortunately, he does reveal a lot of his inner self in letters written to his close friend Ferd Coleman during the 1920s. In response to a 1930 chain letter from Colonel Shoemaker, which is supposed to pay off magically in three wishes, he tells Ferd what his wishes would be. "My first choice from the gods' bargain-counter would be, of course, a good break up the river from Williamsport and below Lock Haven [this is in reference to a lady he was interested in—jfc], and my second, a million dollars. My third would be the ability to make some impression on the flinty hearts of a lot of these 'lousey'[sic] publishers. I leave that third because I think that I have that ability to do it in time, but I wish to Jesus I could hurry the process up a little."

This is a rare look into Piper's view of his fledgling 'writing career'—which is still going nowhere after ten years of hard work—and his mounting frustration. Very few individuals will continue to persevere at their art in the face of constant rejection. It's only his own belief in himself, and that of a few 'trusted' friends like Ferd, that keep this dream of becoming a published author alive. Unbeknownst to him, fifteen more long years of editorial rejections wait before him until he makes his first sale.

On November 7th, 1930, Ferd Coleman wrote: "I enclose two good-looking tear sheets from the Historical Edition of the *Shopper's Guide*, issued yesterday. These tear sheets are intended to be a copy of your contribution, and a copy of Shoemaker's story. Under separate cover I am sending you two full additional copies. If there are additional copies of certain clippings of articles you wish, advise. I have followed out your instructions otherwise in sending copies to three certain persons."

Piper wrote back the next day: "Received the copies and tear-sheets of the Historical Edition. I thought it was a damn fine get-up generally. I noted that the other copies had been sent out. Well done!

"Altoona is having a double dose of Hoover Prosperity, just now. All the railroad shops will be closed the 23rd to the 5th next month, and the 'lousey' hole I work in shut down yesterday. In a way, it's a nice thing for me, as I'm busy as the devil on my writing. I'll tell you about that when I get down, too. My idea is to put out a couple of book-length stories in the next six months…the sort that are designed for popular consumption, made up in equal parts of true love, deep dyed villainy and gore, with pure minded heroes, heroines remaining *virgo intactis* until they lawfully become otherwise at the very last and happy endings, with all the villains killed off. Then, I'm going to take what money I get out of this wretched stuff, take an apartment either in Harrisburg or Williamsport, so as to be near a good library, and get to work on 'Tiadaghton.'

"By the way, I've decided to change the name from 'Tiadaghton' to something else, as I'm afraid a title so difficult of pronunciation would be hard to sell, not to publishers, but by publishers to the public. What do you think? And can you make any suggestions as to the new title? You see, the Hoi Polloi would have a hard time twisting their tongues around Tiadaghton, would be apt to forget it after they heard it and would be afraid to discuss if for fear of mispronouncing it and being thereby ridiculed, and that doesn't sell books. In passing, it will probably cost me $1,800 to live while I'm writing the damned thing, and after it's finished it'll be a good break if I get a grand out of it. Stick to journalism, Fernando! The Muse is a hell of a paymistress."

The last statement is truly prophetic, considering Piper's finances during the last decade of his life. Still, knowing full well that he would have trouble making a living as a writer, Piper persevered. It certainly shows his dedication to his art since his first published story would not appear for another sixteen years.

* * *

H. Beam Piper was an atheist who sometimes teetered on the fence of agnosticism. A fence that Ferd, a former Catholic, would encourage him to walk. This letter on February 22nd, 1928, shows Ferd Coleman's own creed, or lack of: "I regret that I cannot pray for you (Beam) in the form of Litanies to the Blessed Virgin, or candle-burning to St. Anthony. You are certainly aware that I no longer have faith. You remember I admire these practices only as beautiful ritual, and despite further learning on my part in future years, because it is a part of the Human Comedy, indulged in by the populace of centuries, I know I shall always esthetically flutter in witness of Catholic ritual, both the mob as well as the stolid priest scenes.

"Each man's ability to accede to the values of this life lies within his own consciousness and I can only suggest that the desire of your mind for a summer on our cherished West Branch be constantly thought of, and ere the time does come a means will have been found."

While the two friends acted and felt as brothers, they also argued like brothers, as can be noted in this series of dispatches following Piper's appendicitis operation in March of 1928: It opens with Ferd's March 30th, 1928 apology: "I've been rather an ass, Beam, for I wished to write you all the past week, but didn't—in spite of your evident condition, in spite of our friendship, etc., etc. I am sending you under separate cover a small volume, the diary of an unknown Englishman, visiting in the Muncy Valley in 1838....

"Oh, how I shall emit preachments when first I see you. How I shall besmirch you with verbosity that 'as I have said,' 'as I have said,' and 'as I have said,' tardy camping habits are not good for the system, canned foods are vitriol to the system, insufficient exercise is of ill advantage, etc. Perhaps you shall prefer the hospital confines to my eventual shrewing, for, while learning of your true condition from your letter...was a distinct shock, I was not overly surprised, for I, ah I, I am a proper liver, am I."

Piper fires back a reply on April 2nd: "Listen, ass! When we meet again—and I hope it won't be soon—I don't want to hear any hygienic lectures. Remember, you are a passivist [sic], sworn to turn the other cheek, and if you even start to say 'I told you so'—Furthermore, the simple fare of the field is not at all to blame for my condition, nor, God wot, is lack of exercise. I get entirely too much of that. Nor is canned food, for sixty percent of what you eat at that so excellent hash-house is likely to be canned, and canned food has the advantage of having been prepared under much more scientific and sanitary conditions than prevail in the majority of home kitchens, my own included. As to your own dietary preferences, it has always been my opinion that shredded wheat is fit only for horses and milk for an even less dignified order of domestic beasts. But, as Herr Stamm said to Herr Rohrbach, 'For shit mit the whole tam peesness.'"

Theirs is a strong friendship and it's obvious they enjoy testing the limits of both their word play and their friendship. However, cracks are beginning to appear in their relationship as they begin to badger each other about their differences. Even their lives are going in different directions: Ferd Coleman is becoming the young Rotarian, while Piper is more and more the rebel and bohemian. This next letter where Piper tries to woo the pacifist Ferd Coleman with his views on violence marks the beginning of the end of their early friendship.

Coleman has met his to-be wife and his side of the correspondence is missing; however, Piper's reply survives in this letter of April 6th, 1928. "I received your letter and if brevity really were the soul of wit, then by my codpiece, your epistle was truly witty. This, however, I do not hold against you, knowing as I do that you are bowed 'neath the Atlas burden of your weekly (not monthly) rag. So I will, from time to time, favor you with such pearls of wisdom as I have to let drop, what time I am not engaged in wrestling with the Muse.

"Some ideas concerning violence have occurred to me, and I will set them down, hoping to tempt you into an attempt at refutation."

This next passage is very interesting as it shows the younger Piper's view of civilization and warfare. The same views he would display throughout his life and writing career. "Violence, you know, is the foundation of civilized society. When a man enters a house to steal, by stealth and in the absence of its tenants, that is *not* violence. But, should the policeman on the beat observe him in the act and, by clubbing him over the head, subdue him and drag him to the calabozo [sic], that decidedly is violence. It is only by violence and by armed force that civilization is possible.

"In the beginning, certain tribes of savages became more proficient in the application of violence, that is, in the art of war, than others. In this way, they were able to gain surcease from the molestation of wild beasts and of other savages, and they were able to capture prisoners, who they put to useful work. Thus began chattel-slavery, the forerunner of capitalism. These tribes, having leisure, due to the fact that they were no longer molested by wild beasts or by other savages, and likewise to the fact that the 'dirty work' was done by slaves, were thus able to cultivate the arts and sciences, such as they then were; in other words, were able to develop a more perfect civilization.

"All great civilizations of antiquity owed their superiority to armed force, and decayed only when they ceased to be warlike. Egypt succumbed to the more warlike Persians. Persia went under only after the simple and soldierly virtues of her people were destroyed by luxury. Greece went by the same path, and Rome only ceased to resist the barbarians after she had fallen victim to Christianity, then a purely pacifist religion—'and if any smite you on the right cheek, turn him also the left.'

"Now, after owing its origin to violence, civilization likewise owes its continued existence to force of arms. By force of arms alone are its rulers secure in their thrones and its unruly element held in check. Force is the sole arbiter of every question, saving only purely academic ones. That is, force will not prove the truth or falsity of the Doctrine of the Transubstantiation, or the Nebular Hypothesis or—the Tennessee Legislature to the contrary notwithstanding—the Darwinian Theory of Evolution. It will, however, determine whether Alsace and Lorraine belong to France or Germany, or whether Senor Hijo de Puta will be dictator of Honduras or not, or, for that matter, whether or not Slim Clancey will rescue the girl.

"I mention this last because of some objections I thought I heard somebody down around Williamsport make. These are decisions of more practical worth, to the disputants, at least, than whether a priest can turn blood into wine, I mean wine into blood, or whether an ape can turn into a man. Violence, I think, once decided who should own a Pontiac car, if I remember rightly. But then, in the words of Eve, Why bring that up?

"Now, having proved, to my own satisfaction if not yours, that violence is a benign thing—you will certainly agree with me that war is better than religion—I will pass on to other and more pertinent matters."

Throughout his entire recorded life, from his twenties until his death at 60, H. Beam Piper had financial difficulties, bad enough that several times in the 1960s he faced starvation. There is no doubt that Piper had an appetite for the finer things in life, yet he only earned a meager living off his part-time job at the Pennsy and his spotty story sales. He spent money as quickly as it arrived: on his growing weapons collection, dinners out, top-shelf alcohol, bar-hopping—and later on tailored suits. Piper was an astute antique gun and sword collector, often trading weapons or selling them to buy better ones, allowing him to put together a firearms collection that today would be worth a small fortune.

In the long run, Piper's reckless attitude toward money would cause him no end of grief and was probably instrumental in his taking his life by his own hand. For one, he usually spent everything he had as soon as he got it; he seemed to operate on the basis of "more will come when I most need it." Unfortunately, more money was not always forthcoming, but that never deterred Piper from spending any windfall as soon as it arrived!

In "PIPER," Mike Knerr says, "Somewhere along the way, Beam developed a taste for 'the finer things' in life and his pursuit of such items was often just plain crazy. A man who constantly wore suits and ties [at home to write, no less—jfc], with a rather paltry income, he spared no expense. Little, if any, of his attire came from Sears Roebuck or J.C. Penny and his suits were always custom made. His shirts came from the better stores of Williamsport and he usually bought his shoes in New York City. All of this *could* have stemmed from his early home life. A lack of money in the household, perhaps a heckling by his young friends about it, could well have given him a taste for good things later in life. One thing is certain. He never learned the value of a dollar."

Later in life, Piper was very reticent about borrowing money from his friends—no matter how desperate the situation he found himself in. Don Coleman, in a July 20th, 2001 letter, had this to say: "Sister Syl repeated the same words to me that I had written you some time ago, about the fact that our mother always felt that if she would have remained in Williamsport, this tragedy could have been avoided. The financial aid was there, but Beam was just too proud to ask or accept from family (us). And Ma, if she had been there, would have insisted upon covering his overhead. I know this for a fact, because I am her son! But that was yesterday and today we can only 'guess' how things may have turned out."

In his twenties, the young H. Beam Piper was much more flexible; at least, in regards to his close friend Ferd Coleman. When it appears that Piper will be unable to attend one of their camping conclaves, Ferd offers him a $5.00 loan with a 90-day grace period. As Don Coleman puts it, "A hefty sum, considering it was quite capable of filling a week's grocery bill."

Piper wrote, "I got your letter. Damnably sorry, but conditions are no better and will not be until the end of the month, so I can't by any means go camping now. Thanks awfully for the offered loan, but it won't be any help, aside from the fact that it is against my principles to borrow money from a friend."

By August of 1927, interestingly, that attitude of his had changed: "I'm evacuating the cabin tomorrow on the 7.56 train, for Altoona. As you will not be down before then, I will take the knives, forks and spoons, the canned-heat stove and your map with me to Altoona, and mail them back to you. I will also mail you the dollar bill that you loaned me* (*When I get one. Damned near broke again.), and which I am damned glad I accepted."

This is a notable departure of Piper's typical unwillingness to accept help from anyone, especially friends, and to my mind shows that Piper's relationship to Ferd Coleman is unique and 'above' his other friendships. In all his letters, early and late, Piper consistently had problems with money, almost always the lack of it. It would be no exaggeration to say he lived most of his life (even with his parents) in genteel poverty, and was almost always broke. He would make plans, then have to back out for lack of wherewithal, as this letter to Ferd Coleman demonstrates: "I find, after consulting my department of exchequer, that I will be able to pay you a visit during the week following Christmas (Christ's Mass, as it was originally spelled), that is to say, the week between the aforementioned fiesta and New Year's Day. If this will suit you, let me know, and tell me what day would be most convenient to you for my advent into your midst. I want, of course, to have a good wind-session with you, and I also want to stop at McElhattan and see the Colonel if he will be there and see the erstwhile Belle of Bellefonte at the Jersey Shore.... I regret writing you on such cursed short notice, just as I regret my delay in writing you anent my coming down in deer season, but my affairs, financial and otherwise, are in such a damnable tangle at present that I never know, more than a few days in advance, just what I am going to be able to do, and as it is not my custom to make promises and then turn again and break them, I can't help it."

Piper's gun collection was, generally speaking, his spare cash and he would sell pieces from time to time when money was late in arriving or when he was flat broke. He figured he could always buy more when he was flush. He was very canny about it, not letting his friends (even Mike Knerr) know that he was selling his guns off piecemeal because he was short of cash and in a bad way. As far as his fellow gun cranks were concerned, he knew that if they realized he was in dire straits, he would never get a fair price for them. His diary is peppered with his schemes to sell a gun or two, or why he couldn't part with them at the price offered—even when he was down to eating table scraps.

Furthermore, Piper always figured he could buy them back or get more when he was flush. Unfortunately, whenever Piper got a significant story or novel payment he would typically make a big purchase, either a new pistol or two, a rifle, a sword, or a new tailored suit. As long as he lived under his parents' roof, he could afford these extravagant expenditures. However, after his mother's death, these extravagances would play an increasingly important part in his financial meltdown and premature demise.

CHAPTER SIX

Moment of Greatness

Other than comments about different titles and the name of short stories Piper is working on, there is very little known about his early fiction writing. None of the stories have survived his passing. However, amongst "The Early Letters" survives Ferd's critique of "Moment of Greatness," one of H. Beam Piper's early works, as well as Piper's replies. Here is Piper discussing the bare bones and flesh of this never published 'lost' short story in a late 1927 letter.

"By the way, I am on a story now, and I got my inspiration from a passage in Nietzsche.

> "When he judgeth himself—that was his supreme moment; let not the exalted one relapse again into his low estate!
> "There is no salvation for him who hath thus suffered from himself, unless it be speedy death."

"How does that sound? Promising? Or crappy? But I'll read the first draft of it to you when I see you. Then you can judge.... Your brother in Christ, BEAM"

On January 4th, 1928, Piper noted: "I am getting along with that short story about the gangster who gives his life for the girl. I am somewhat at a loss for a fitting title, however. To date I have thought of the following; Paid in Full, Judgment, Atonement and The Flame Burns

Bright—flame of courage and honor and all that, y'know. I am not exactly satisfied with any of them, and as I intend to send a carbon copy of it to you, perhaps you may be able to suggest something more fitting."

By February 21st, 1928, he had decided on a title, "Moment of Greatness," and was ready to send it off for editorial review. "Now as to the story which I was writing. I have finished and this day it goes...three guesses whither. To *Black Mask*? Wrong! To the Street & Smith gang? Wronger! "To...can it be...The *Saturday Evening Post*? Key-rect as hell! I have decided that I will no longer debase my brilliant...nay, by the spear of Odin, resplendent...genius to the penny-dreadfuls. I'm out for big game this time. One does not strain his gun-barrel more by aiming at eagles than at 'shitepokes.' Fear not. Your copy will reach you as soon as I can sort out the earlier drafts to accompany it. I want you to read the finished product first, to get the full effect, and then check up with the three tentative versions. Then, I prithee, spare time enow from pandering to the base-born rabble to let me have your opinion on it.

"Does the story sell—and you can judge what the *Post* will, if at all, pay for it—my summer on the West Branch is a dead cert. You, best of all, perhaps, understand fully what that will mean to me. Not that I'll not be on the spot anyhow, if I have to turn cut-throat or, worse, evangelist, to get the money. Pray, then, for me, perform novenas and burn candles, not forgetting to kill a horse for Odin and a goat for Thor, so as to be on the safe side with the Old Gods. And leave not Aphrodite out of it, for on her aid I reckon much. (Don't know why all the mythology, tonight. A Cabell hangover, like as not.)

On February 22th, 1928, Ferd replies: "I marvel—at your unseemly—unchristly nerve. *The Saturday Evening Post*. Not that they are above you or your literary efforts. Quite the contrary—in justice to the true merit of your creative art; and, in a sense that's why I marvel. *The Post*, of course, is often the standard of your loathful penny-dreadfuls. But be this as it may your nerve to my understanding arises from the fact that *The Post* is practically a closed market, about as tight, for real functional purposes as the erring filles-de-joie after the fourth month. Likewise *Cosmopolitan*, *Pictorial Review*, *Ladies Home Journal* and the *Literary Digest*—just as indifferent to budding toys as the scenario field. I challenge you to ask these various institutions whether it be not so. This I do say: Things have been bartered unto them, and if you are one of the favored, a genius you are, indeed, according to their standard. This particular brain-child you have befriended as excessively and frequently within my notice that I tell you truthfully I anticipate the perusal of the MS, with keen interest. Please send it along, and I promise to devote adequate time to the stuff, both from critical, friendly, and literary angles."

Here's an interesting aside by Ferd Coleman as to why he admires Piper, not only for his literary gifts and fearless toil, but for his willingness to live as an artist—that is, starve for his art! "I have flattered you before with the equivalent of, 'By the gods, I envy you, would that my standards, practices and habits were such that I might struggle as economic' as yourself."

Piper wrote back: "I am not unmindful of my promise to send you a carbon copy of the story. I will do more. Do you remember how, when you were last in Altoona, we stopped in front of a window display of products made in the P.R.R. (Pennsy Rail Road) shops, a display that interested you as much as it pained me? Well, do you recall an exhibit showing various articles in all the stages of their manufacture? That's the sort of thing I'm going to send you, two versions of the story in pencil and the third and final one in type, showing how I actually wrote it. Then, perhaps, observing my method, you will see why I use the typewriter only to put my stuff in presentable form."

In those halcyon days, at least as far as the Post Office was concerned, mail was delivered twice a day and it was not unusual to send off a letter in the morning mail and receive your reply that afternoon. Three days after sending "Moment of Greatness" to *The Saturday Evening Post* Piper wrote, "When you marveled at my ungodly nerve, you marveled well. The story is back, together with a politely insincere but personally written note of rejection. I shot at the eagle and missed, but beyond the waste of two rounds of postage stamps nothing has been lost by it, and if I plague these sons of priests enough, they may buy to be quit of me. I will hold the story until I hear from you, so mention such magazines as you think may lend an ear to it."

Later in his letter, he added, "The story is under separate cover. Owing to the bulk of all four drafts, I am sending only the final one at present, but as I will be in the West Branch Valley before this time next month, I will give you the others. Beam"

Here is Ferd's analysis, mailed on February 29th, in whole:

Dear Beam:--

I am enclosing herewith your MS. Moment of Greatness, and out of my intense love for a comrade I purloin herewith a full hour from business in which to declare the following criticism of it.

I consider the work from three angles: a) As the work of a friend; b) As a product of literature; c) From a general critical view.

a) *As usual, and frequently have I so informed you—your diction is very good, and lends the quality of easy reading to the story. If ever (and this is a foreboding of what is to follow under "c") you do strike the splendid combination of writing a story which best aligns itself to your nature and truest thought, it is going to be excellently done indeed.*

b) *As literature, I can only pass sentence, Beam: it isn't. It has in some measure the ingredients of deep human motives, but they are so shallowly presented that one could not entrust himself to the fair belief that the story could live.*

c) *And, now, from the technical viewpoint: well, I'm sorry, Beam, and a bottle of Florida Farm to prove the maintenance of my friendship to you, but the story can scarcely sell. In spite of many fair qualities, it is in my opinion not commensurate to the established standards that a popular short story should have. I cannot, and there is no need, in this short space, enumerate faults or merit in the order of their appearance in the story, but here are some of the things I have thought of for the past two days.*

Somebody, perhaps you yourself many years later, could make a most excellent psychological portrait of the reaction of a hardened criminal toward a woman who had once befriended him—similar to the legend of the terrible lion who in a moment of desired vengeance did not fall upon his prey when remembering that in infant years the prey had removed a large splinter from his paw. But to involve your thought into a story of your dimensions, and treat it in the crude manner that you have done (crude, as to thematic treatment) leaves the story flat. I have not given considerable thought to recommendations, but I believe if in some manner the story (if not entirely psychologically portrayed as above suggested) were more physical, more moving, more active in its plot, with scarce any mental opinionating whatever by Clancey, just blind instinct brought into play because of the girl's early act, the tone of the story would ring truer.

Certainly by an orthodox editor, or reader, a story headed with a passage from the infamous (to many) Nietzsche, would at once stamp it with the atmosphere of "Scrutinize most carefully what this author has to write, in order that the conventions be not violated." I would recommend its removal. A competent author need not resort to the presentation of another's thought, and then incorporate it as a theme for his own story.

In a 7,000-word story, you consume 1,000 before you have Clancey speak to the girl, and they are the two "exhibitory" characters in the story. This is too large a proportion. The problem is eventually to portray Clancey's mode of action when destiny calls upon him to "be himself" in his conduct toward the girl in her dilemma; and since this is the problem, and a short story technically should have but one major problem, everything should be hastened to this climax.

Your language is excellent, Beam, and thus it is at fault. This is a hard story, and while of course you are good enough not to force your personal scholarship before the reader, you are not good enough deliberately to refrain from high-minded wordings when common expressions in this above-dubbed "hard" story should be the ruling. I have told you this before.

Akin to this complaint, is the tone of dialogue. I simply don't always like it, Beam. (In this respect, of dialogue, I am anticipating keenly how well you shall translate the German hill-hawk dialect in your forthcoming "Tiadaghton" novels.)

Par. 2, p. 5, far-fetched. A hardened, strong criminal if he could get into a chest at all, no matter how tight, would not be in agony "soon."

Pages 11-17, inclusive, well done as a whole.

The meeting with the girl, p. 18, too abrupt.

P. 20, "Oh, God," paragraph—too soft, for Clancey, even in this moment of emotional greatness.

Now, then damnit, it isn't, I assure you, because I frown upon violence, but for purely technical grounds: in god's name, need there be all that gore which followed. Why must all be killed. Is death to others the logical manner in working out one's moment of greatness?

Surely even the editor of a magazine, entitled "Blood and Thunder" would shudder at the swift, repeated murders Clancey commits. I don't see how the story can sell with this modus operandi in it, Beam. Though as to all the other details I do not insist on revisions (after all they are merely opinions) on this latter suggestion I insist on a change. I know if I were the writer I should not change a damned thing. I'm that beautifully temperamental, and you know it; but as a sober would-be commercial project, one must face the facts embodied in short story technique as is.

I like your last hundred words beautifully, Beam. Splendidly done, but of course a "Stickful" of art doesn't redeem the quality of the whole. I like your use of the word, gallant, Beam. And somehow that's how

I think of you, in real life—a gallant gentleman; and, having the temperament of a gallant gentleman, one cannot live the lives of crooks, for one must fully know his characters. I think some of your story projects are coarser than your thoughts really are, and since this is the cheerful circumstance it follows that you cannot best express yourself in this type of writing. In this connection of gallantry I well can understand your predilection to violence in its relation to knighthood and the adventures thereto, and precisely as a result of this feeling of mine toward you I am confident that your historical novels narrating the days that were in the Susquehanna Valley will be beautiful, indeed, and actual literature.

I regret that in this department, Beam, I cannot give a more favorable report, but so it is. However, you know I wish you all dame fortune has to offer in your future work. Even were this story very good, I have so fallen from the literary market-ways, what with my grossly material business, that I am afraid I could not competently suggest a selling point.

May I ask your purpose in visiting the West Branch the latter part of March? I trust to hear from you soon.

Coleman

Unfortunately, even as rich as this correspondence is between the two friends, a lot of what was said about "Moment of Greatness" is lost because many things were discussed, argued and settled in telephone conversations and meetings. Still, a small sample of the twenty-four year old Piper's immediate reaction to Ferd's critique survives in Piper's letter of March 1st, 1928: "I received the manuscript and your appended commentary. While there are some things in it from which I dissent, I value it highly. One has few friends who will be so honest. As to the criticism, I make no answer. That must hold until we meet."

Right after his stay in the hospital for appendicitis, Piper was confined to bed for several weeks; typical of the medical practices of the 1920s, when long stays in bed were *de rigueur*. With all this time hanging over him, he had lots of time to stew over Ferd Coleman's critique of "Moment of Greatness." His appendectomy was a fortunate accident in a historical sense, since otherwise he would have discussed his plans with Ferd in person at their proposed get-together. Therefore, this look into the workings of Piper's mind and how he approached the craft of writing would not exist. Near the end of the letter, Piper loses his 'clinical' detachment and it's easy to see that Coleman's criticism pricked more than flesh—and struck bone.

On March 28th, Piper replied with the following:

> *I am going to take your advice on the story, in part. I will rewrite it changing the first part of it so as to speed up the meeting of Slim Clancey and the Girl. I think I will start the story with Clancey entering the room where the Girl is writing—by-the-bye, did the description of that room and of the girl herself cause you to think of something?—and I will let the things that have gone before, the robbery and the pursuit, be brought out in conversation. I will also adopt a more skillful method of bringing out Clancey's past life and his service in the Army, together with his regrets for his present mode of life.*
>
> *As to the dialogue—it was on purpose that I had the girl talk in the high-toned manner in which she did. There is a small touch of symbolism to the business, and I wished to make clear that she was everything that Clancey was not, that she was something far above him. Hence, I had Clancey speak in thieves' argot and she in the purest poetic English, by way of striking as sharp a contrast as possible.*
>
> *As to Nietzsche, I may let him go by the board. You will recall, when someone brought Napoleon the sword of Fredrick the Great and suggested that he wear it, the Little Corporal replied, "Oh, as to that, I have a sword of my own."*
>
> *As to the massacre, that was, in the first place, even more necessary to*

Slim Clancey, the gunman, than it was to Beam Piper, the author. How in blue hell could he get that girl out otherwise—by holding a gospel meeting and converting the others to Jesus? He had to kill all of them. Besides, in killing all he wiped out the outward symbols of his old life. There is another phase to it, too. While I was writing that, I was killing those men, myself. Subjectively—in my imagination—of course, but I was killing them none the less. Slim became himself. The Girl became—well, another Girl you know of.

Those men menaced her. And, as I would shoot down or dirk her enemies and glory in it, so Slim Clancey dirked and shot and took no small delight in his shooting and dirking, for I was, briefly, Slim Clancey, and I tell you, Fernando, it gave me great joy to see those men go down to the floor writhing in pain of collapse like lengths of chain that may have been held up and dropped or simply sag and fall like toy balloons with the air let out of them.

I regret, somewhat, that is was only in my imagination. Even Slim's death was such a death as I greatly hope the Old Gods send me, when I am ready for Valhalla. And, as to Valkyries—but perhaps I'd best haul up. I've wasted enough ribbon and paper on this already, and you, I recall, are a busy business man, not a carefree convalescent."

Piper's next comments on "Moment of Greatness" come in his letter of April 18th, 1928: "I have finished the re-writing of the short story, 'Moment of Greatness,' and, as I have omitted the quotation at the beginning and the old title is hence without point, I have re-christened it 'Exit, A Gentleman.' Other changes that have been made are: some toning down of the dialogue, particularly the alleged 'highfalutin' talk of the girl, a hastening of the meeting of Clancey and the girl, and—this will please you, 'passivest'—I have made the killing of Nick the Greek a little less atrocious. No changes, however, were made in the casualty list. At the end of the story, the girl alone was left alive to tell the tale."

He then goes on to tell about another yarn he's working on and that's the last time "Moment of Greatness" is mentioned in the collected letters—by any of its titles. However, Ferd Coleman's criticism of this yarn would stick in Beam's craw like a fishbone.

On February 9th, 1931, Piper wrote: "I had meant to write you much earlier, but every time I sat down to my desk I was confronted by a pile of manuscript of my present attempt at pot-boiling, and the number at the head of the last page was always too low to suit me, so my prostitute Muse is to blame rather than myself."

As in Williamsport, Piper did his writing in the gunroom. On May 24th, he wrote, "For another thing, we have been completely renovating the gunroom, and things have been torn up pretty badly, what with painting, papering and so on, and the desk to which my typewriter is permanently attached has been buried under the wreckage."

From 1931 on their correspondence diminishes to a small trickle with just a few notes such as this: "A trip into the woods with my father, the unbearable heat in this room, where my typewriter is permanently fixed, and my natural laziness, have conspired to delay my writing you until now." Most of their conversations from here on out are either on the telephone or in person. Meanwhile, his visits to the Coleman household dwindle as the years pass.

There are no more comments or critiques of Piper's writing throughout the rest of the 1930s and early 1940s. Ferd Coleman's criticism of "A Moment of Greatness," even more than his marriage and children, distances the two men and leaves their relationship less than it had been before.

CHAPTER SEVEN

The Unholy Trinity

It's almost a cliché in our society that married people shed their single friends shortly after marriage. This tendency accelerates even faster after children arrive. Ferd Coleman was aware of this deplorable 'custom' and attempted to convince Piper that his impending matrimony would not end their special bond of friendship.... Piper's been down this road before with other friends and remained skeptical.

As the big day approached, Ferd wrote: "I surely have been something of a cad in delaying this greeting, but god what a truly fascinating experience this acclimation to domestication is; and what sundry details in other endeavors have arisen the past ten days to engage my time, which seems briefly accorded me, indeed.

"I marry at 10 a.m. on Saturday, June 23rd, 1928 in the rectory of St. Boniface church. My best man is our own beloved Edward, who, when approached by me with the assignment registered a rather sickly smile, and consented to be present at the obsequies."

The remainder of the letter discusses an antique auction at Glosser's and a meeting with Ed Morrell, as well as various stratagems for the two of them to meet—and a final drunk—before Ferd leaves on his honeymoon. At this point Ferd knows things are changing in his life, will change even more, but wants desperately to keep his old friendships intact. Piper is standoffish.

In his reply of June 14th, he attempts to make the best of seeing another comrade fall by the wayside. Piper wrote, "I have a big bag of talk to open with you, and I want to see you for about an hour before you go away on your honeymoon."

Don Coleman, who knew H. Beam Piper before he learned to walk, had this to say: "And so it was; H. Beam Piper's innermost compadre, pal-confidant, procurer of prohibitive necessities, and mutual lover of earth's inherent beauties—became espoused to a fair maiden from the woods and farmlands of Cogan House Township. The marriage of Coleman to a country girl named Freida Baumgartner was surely a gain, not just for the obvious compatibility of each, but for the eventual unselfish (and unique) acknowledgement of H. Beam Piper—who welcomed another hiker to the mountaineer group, "even though she be female!"

Letters between the two friends drop off from this point on, as Don Coleman points out, "For nearly two months, written communication ceased between Piper and Coleman, due to the growing addiction to telephones and the prevalence of actual meetings along the Susquehanna."

In his letter of November 24th, 1928 Piper uncharacteristically apologizes: "I don't know whether or not my last letter might have sounded like giving you the cold shoulder, but if I did, be assured that it was certainly not so intended. You and Fritz [Piper—for reasons only a psychologist might dwell on—always used this variation of Freida's name or misspelled it Frieda--jfc] are always welcome at my home, but under the present circumstances [Piper's mother fell into an unmarked roadside hazard and injured herself—jfc], it simply can't be. However, some time toward the middle of next month or, better, the early part of January would do very nicely." He ends the letter with this, "With best wishes to the sir brothers Ranck, Coleman, Lenhard and Bardo, Beam."

Piper, as one can see, during this period of his life had an active social life with lots of friends who shared his many interests, Pennsylvania history, guns, antiques, books, writing, history and alcohol.

Freida Coleman was most accommodating in regards to her husband and Piper's friendship, and by all accounts (in the letters and from Don Coleman's remembrances) she and Piper became friends, too. She knew when to leave the men alone and enjoyed Piper's companionship.

Unfortunately, Ferd Coleman's marriage wasn't the only strain affecting their friendship: his paper, the *Shopper's Guide*, was becoming successful. His editorship of the paper was giving him a good income as well as stature within the community of Williamsport, while Piper was still marching along his Bohemian pathway, working late at night at the Juniata Yards, writing at all hours, drinking and horsing around with friends and taking long hikes along the Appalachian trails.

Still, there was a part of Ferd Coleman that wished he had the courage (or recklessness) to do as Piper was doing and he always admired him for taking the road less traveled.

H. Beam Piper's first love—after literature—was antique weaponry. While he had a lot of books, he was just as happy to check them out from the Brown Library as to purchase them and there's little evidence he collected them per se. His gun collection, of course, was the pride of the Piper household; every place he lived had a gunroom, which also served as his writing room or office. However, spurred on by Ferd Coleman—an avid collector of spinning wheels and Colonial antiques—Piper also began to collect antiques: "I received the diary [unknown Englishman visiting the Muncy Valley—jfc], and found it most interesting and amusing. I thank you for the (gift) (loan) of it, and the Brown Library is to be congratulated on obtaining such a treasure."

The few surviving 1930s letters between the two friends are less personal and more formal. True, the formal Piper/Coleman friendship survived for another twenty odd years, but its 'transcendent' quality was lost. There was a fundamental shift in their relationship as well: Beam, the irresponsible child-man, versus Ferd, the responsible family man.

Ferd Coleman notices the 'change' himself as early as August 19th, 1930, "Beam:—Now, I feel better, that you have written. For not in recent years have you cast me aside so lengthily, and I pray of you never, never do it again. I am busy as you know with the commercial ills of this world, and must betimes need be excused, but though you have wrought a piece of undying literature, I consider you have meditated upon and lived with it solidly for six weeks, the period since I last heard from you, to the exclusion of all else."

What's changed in Piper's world, I suspect, is not the amount of time he's spending writing "undying literature," but the absence of those thoughts on his busy friend Ferd Coleman. There are more changes ahead at the Coleman household. On October 15th, 1931, Piper wrote: "Sorry to have delayed so long in felicitating you on your male heir, but I've been a bit under the weather…

"You know, the friend with whom I mentioned playing chess between trains in Harrisburg was expecting an heir at any moment when I was down there, and he became a father of a daughter about six hours before your son arrived. I had been waiting for reports from both of you with some interest.

"Well, anyhow, congratulations—or commiserations, however you prefer. This, I suppose, means another rattle. My honorary nephews and nieces are increasing in number." This December 13th, 1931 letter, as Don Coleman puts it, "Closes out the written correspondence for the year 1931, and also brings to an end some six years of near-consistent exchange of outlook, opinions and personal happenstances of life among friends."

In Piper's final missive of 1931, he says "Give my best 'reguards' [sic] to all brethren, to Freida, to Sylvia May and to the infant." As Don Coleman says, "The man from Altoona knew not the moniker (Don) given to the male newborn, and this newborn had yet to realize the existence of a man named H. Beam Piper."

Ferd Coleman survived the worst of the Depression and his *Shopper's Guide* began to prosper. Unfortunately, there is no information on how Ferd went from borderline insolvency and firing employees in 1931 to prosperity by 1936—during the Depression yet! Don Coleman has no recollection, since he was very young at the time, of how his father went from near bankruptcy and shutting down *The Shopper* to sudden success all within a few years. Don was nonplussed when I brought it to his attention during a phone call. The only key I could find was the addition of Ferd Coleman's father to the staff, after he retired from his post as sheriff of Williamsburg, just as Ferd was laying off staff and telling Piper he was about to shut down the little newspaper. I suspect that local business and shop owners found it easier to place inexpensive ads in *The Shopper* than gaining the enmity of the former sheriff and his friends in the department.

In 1936 the Coleman family moved to "a brand-spanking-new-house" in an expensive suburb in the north of Williamsport, an area called Vallamont. As Don Coleman recounts, "The most revered space within this house was the den located on the basement floor and flaunting a wall-to-wall and floor-to-ceiling bookcase. The remaining three walls were blessed with natural knotty-pine wood paneling. Opposite the bookshelves, a variety of mounted antique weaponry....

"This lair became Piper's living quarters whenever he visited Williamsport.... In 1939...Coleman purchased a 'Guest Log,' to be inscribed by one and all. Beam auspiciously holds the timely honor of being the second individual to autograph said log.

DATE: 4/13/'39
NAME: H. Beam Piper
ADDRESS: 407 Wordsworth Ave. Altoona, PA
REMARKS:
In the past five months
I have written some 100,000
words, and I cannot think of
a goddam thing to say except:
this man, Ferd Coleman, is my
friend.

"The majority of Beam's visits were generally but a single night, depending upon his security instructions aboard the railroad. Whenever the schedule permitted him two or three days—which was unusual but not rare—he serviced Coleman's flintlocks and affiliated paraphernalia, always accompanied by a can of fine machine oil, gun blue, and a good bottle of whiskey. And when he made it in, meeting between himself, Coleman, and Ted Ranck (the 'silent' member of the triad) would continue through the night with their muffled voices reverberating through the maze of air vents within the walls, until almost dawn. There were many gatherings inside this den.... We kids who lived in this house on the terrace could hear the repetitious repertoire of these three lost sheep linger into the night."

Because of his graveyard shift at the yards, Beam had picked up strange sleeping habits. Don Coleman recounts his stay in the Coleman den: "This lair became Beam's living quarters whenever he visited Williamsport. A magnificent antique cherry wood table, completely *nailed* with wooden pegs, acted as his desk and workbench. And nestled against the main wall of flintlocks and pistols, powder horns and powder flasks, bullet molds and rapiers—there was a cushioned and elongated couch for rest. Although never an admitted insomniac, Piper's assessed time of slumber would be minimal—not enough for this humble but sublime piece of furniture to get warm. As a bona-fide outdoorsman, Beam traveled as if the night were to be dealt in the woods; the trees and moss and streams. Even though the comforts of warmth and shelter were afforded him whenever dropping into the neighborhood, he habitually carried his sleeping bag, whether he used it or not."

The first mention of the "Unholy Trinity" (H. Beam Piper, Ferd Coleman and Ted Ranck) occurred on May 10th, 1930 when the three had their picture taken; most likely during H. Beam Piper's birthday. On March 22nd in Altoona, Piper wrote: "I received the pictures, which I thought were very good, particularly the one of the 'Unholy Trinity.' When I get the ones in my camera developed, I'll send them on."

Don Coleman noted, "Correspondence between friends tends to drop off as Piper becomes endlessly involved with his stories and inundated with the hated and ever predictable rejection 'slips.' It's amazing how the railroad security man, after extensive hours in the yards, was capable of pressing out so many more units of time in sleepless persistence—for his devotion to writing.

"Ferd Coleman, in the meantime, has found that a great deal of legwork is required in obtaining local advertising quotas and maintaining enough column inches of area babble and syndicated news—in order to keep the weekly *Shopper's Guide* kicking. For a time—a very short time—he would wonder if such a profession was worth a lifetime's endurance. Of course! He was as Piper…devoted to his calling."

In 1951, Ferd Coleman wrote the following penciled addendum to the preface of the collected letters:

And now, Sept. 1951 at 47, almost 20 years after, the friendship has endured thru these two screaming decades. The relentless requirements of living have limited our time and frequency in letter writing, but several times annually Piper and I (and Ted Ranck) meet. Piper now has of the past 4 years finally arrived on the professional author's pedestal while for me participation in active literature remains a wistful hope.

Don Coleman wrote, "Less than six month after writing this addendum, Ferd W. Coleman met with such an untimely death that the shocking news could not be digested by his friends and associates, many of whom he had just seen at a Miami convention two weeks earlier. He had been vacationing as well as writing of his experiences in the Yucatan for publication in his beloved Williamsport *Shoppers' Guide*. While en route from the Isle of Cozumel to the capital of Merida, where he would then return home—the plane's engines began malfunctioning and the aircraft literally 'fell apart' at an altitude of about 6,000 feet. One American and nine Mexican citizens perished near Hoctun, Yucatan, just forty miles east of their destination. The date was Saturday, March 15th, 1952.

"The Piper-Coleman friendship did not dissolve at this point. Both Piper and Ted Ranck were two of the six pall-bearers participating at the funeral rites over two weeks later. Actually, this friendship would never dissolve. Later on, down the footpaths of time, H. Beam Piper would move lock, stock and barrel (how ironically true, this cliché) to Williamsport."

PART TWO

Published at Last!

CHAPTER EIGHT

Time and Time Again

It took over twenty-five years of hard work and perseverance before his first sale, *Time and Time Again*, on September 25th, 1946 to John W. Campbell, the legendary editor of *Astounding Science Fiction* to materialize. The story was published in the April 1947 issue of *Astounding* and was later adapted for the radio program *Dimension X* and was first broadcast in 1951. *Time and Time Again* is an interesting tale about a forty-something year old man who dies in a future war and awakens in his thirteen-year old self. The man/boy looks for an explanation of why this has happened and decides it's up to him to change the future. There is a realistic and close relationship between father and son that's unlike anything else in Piper's body of work.

There are no existing letters from either Piper or John Campbell regarding this story, but it's a good example of the kind of stories Campbell was publishing in *Astounding* during the 1940s. It was a huge sale for Piper who had spent most of his life trying to be a writer and when he arrived, he made the most of it. He loved to go to writer's workshops, conclaves, meetings (he was a member of both the Mystery Writers of America and the Hydra Club, the science fiction and mystery writers' group—precursor to the Science Fiction Writers of America) and science fiction conventions. He was a true character, even before his first story sold, but afterwards he 'worked' at being distinctive—even fabricating a life that was fascinating in and of itself. And succeeded, I suspect, beyond his wildest expectations; it's unfortunate that he wasn't around for the Piper revival of the late 1970s and early 1980s. He would have loved the attention! A lot more than Robert Heinlein, who *appeared* embarrassed by his fame.

This first sale was quite a coup for Piper, as he made his debut in the premier science fiction magazine of the era, *Astounding Science Fiction*. Campbell was a well-established author before he turned his hand to editing. He is widely considered the originator of modern science fiction and was almost single-handedly responsible for pulling the genre up by the bootstraps and out of the pulp quagmire it had originated in the beginning with Hugo Gernsback's *Amazing Stories*, which published its first issue in April 1926.

John W. Campbell's "Competent man" was very similar to Piper's own self-reliant characters, almost to the point where some readers and critics thought Piper was 'pitching' his story ideas to what he thought Campbell would buy, as indicated in his *Astounding* editorials. This was not as farfetched as it sounds, since several authors, such as Randall Garret, admittedly did just that—and made a good living off it, too! Campbell, like H. Beam Piper, was a man who knew what he liked, said what he thought and believed every word. And, had a stubborn streak that matched Piper's own; for example, he told Robert Heinlein that he would buy everything he wrote as long as he didn't sell to any other magazines. Heinlein went along with that until the early 1950s when his agent, Lurton Blassingame, convinced him to try to sell to the *Saturday Evening Post*—the flagship of slick magazines before television thinned the ranks. He sold "The Green Hills of Earth" and some other stories to the *Post* and Campbell wrote him off for almost a decade.

Years later after the success of Heinlein's juveniles, Campbell began to buy the serial rights to novels, like *Starship Troopers*. However, Heinlein, still angry with Campbell, refused to write him any more short stories. Piper fit right in with this crew.

John W. Campbell was the man who'd fostered the careers of most of the early science fiction masters, Robert A. Heinlein, Arthur C. Clarke, Isaac Asimov, Poul Anderson, Gordon R. Dickson, L. Sprague de Camp, Lester Del Rey, H. Beam Piper, Jerry Pournelle and his final discovery—John Dalmas.

Campbell was considered by many to be a bit of a crackpot, as he was one of the first boosters of L. Ron Hubbard (another *Astounding* writer) and his new 'psychology/religion' of Dianetics and later Scientology. Campbell became disillusioned with Scientology fairly quickly, but a number of his readers and authors, such as A.E. Van Vogt, got caught up in that quagmire and stopped writing or became estranged from family and friends.

In the late 1950s and early 1960s, Campbell became a proponent of psi phenomenon, psychic abilities and powers, and featured many such stories in *Astounding*. Later on, a favorite of Campbell's was the inertialless drive, or the Dean Drive—another panacea that would prove to be a cropper. Campbell would have loved cold fusion....

While his *fame* as a science fiction author spread, Piper began to tailor his life more along those lines, paying more attention to scientific events and their effects on the future. He went so far as to present himself as an engineer "of the 'slide rule' variety" to his fellow science fiction authors, such as fellow writer, Fletcher Pratt. Somehow he convinced John W. Campbell, who was nobody's fool, into believing that Piper was a railroad detective!

Probably the best description of Piper's personal view of his science fiction writing—mostly aimed at John W. Campbell's *Astounding*, which was the quickest and highest paid SF story market and where Piper was a frequent contributor—is contained in this excerpt from *Murder in the Gunroom* made by Pierre Jarret. In answer to the question: "What are you writing?" Jarret, a science-fiction writer, gives the following reply: "Science fiction. I do a lot of stories for the pulps...*Space Trails*, and *Other Worlds* and *Wonder Stories*: mags like that. Most of it's standardized formula-stuff; what's known in the trade as space-operas. My best stuff goes to *Astonishing* [a barely disguised Astounding—jfc]. Parenthetically, you mustn't judge any of these magazines by their names. It seems to be a convention to use hyperbolic names for science fiction magazines; a heritage from an earlier and ruder day. What I do for *Astonishing* is really hard work, and I enjoy it. I'm working now on one of them, based on J.W. Dunne's time-theories [Piper's Paratime series was based on Dunne's time theories—jfc], if you know what they are."

In this passage, Piper provides an accurate assessment of the early 1950's science fiction magazines as well as a rare look at Piper's writing from his perspective. In *Astounding* Editor John W. Campbell, H. Beam Piper found a kindred spirit; plus, an editor who highly admired his writing and wrote him detailed letters on how to improve or strengthen—as determined by Campbell, of course—those stories. And, in a few cases, ideas for more stories in "that future history of yours." To Piper, who had wandered in the wilderness of rejection and dismissal for over thirty years, he must have felt like Moses finding the burning bush!

Who exactly was legendary science fiction editor, John W. Campbell? Lester del Rey, noted writer, book reviewer and editor and founder of Del Rey Books, had this to say in *The John W. Campbell Letters, Volume I*:

> *Back in the early days [1930s] of science fiction, everyone knew it was impossible to make a living in the field. There were only two SF magazines being published each paying somewhere around $200.00 for a long novelette and perhaps $25.00 for an unusually good short story. Even when a story was accepted, a writer might have to wait months after publication before he was finally paid for his work. Furthermore, no science fiction books were being published; so once a story appeared in a magazine, there would be no further income from it.*
>
> *Writing science fiction was a hobby, not a career and nobody questioned that obvious fact—nobody but John W. Campbell! Against all logic, he was not only determined to make science fiction his life's work, but he succeeded. It took three careers to achieve his goal, during which he became almost single-handedly the creator of modern science fiction. And eventually, others with less genius or less folly found it possible to follow the trail he blazed.*
>
> *Campbell's first sale was made while he was still in college, studying for his science degree. (Later, he used to joke about it, saying that he only graduated because his English professor couldn't flunk anyone who was already selling to a professional magazine.) It appeared in January 1930, six months before his twentieth birthday. Within a year, he had become one of the best-liked writers in the field.*

In only ten years, John Campbell had become two of the greatest writers (under two different names) of science fiction. And then both careers came to an end, as he began a third which was to be even more influential than any amount of writing could have been—so influential, indeed, that a crater on Mars has now been named Campbell to honor him.

Toward the end of 1937, he was asked to be the editor of Astounding Stories *(soon to be renamed* Astounding Science Fiction *and later* Analog Science Fact/Fiction). *He continued as its editor until his death in 1971. As a writer under either pen name, Campbell had been one of the best; but as an editor, he quickly became the greatest. If that is a personal judgment, it is one shared by most writers and editors in the field.*

When he took over as editor, the magazine had settled into a dull routine; and other magazines were folding or turning to blood-and-thunder stories. Old authors were leaving the field and few new ones of any talent were coming in. There seemed no new hope that science fiction would ever become a generally accepted category.

Campbell rapidly changed all that. He had a clear vision of what science fiction should become, and he began teaching that vision to all the established writers capable of learning it. He also discovered a host of new writers within the first few years of his editorship. Most of the leading science-fiction writers today are ones he discovered and trained: Asimov, de Camp, Heinlein, Sturgeon, van Vogt, and many others.

Writers were developed, too, not merely discovered. Faulty stories went back with pages of detailed criticism of plot and technique that meant more than any dozen courses on how to write. Ideas for stories poured out from Campbell to his writers, and many of the best-loved stories in the field came from those ideas. He had the marvelous talent of suggesting just the right idea to a writer and putting it into a form that a writer could best handle.

Even when a story was not right for him, Campbell was generous with his help in improving it for submission elsewhere. The result was the so-called Golden Age of science fiction—the beginning of modern science fiction, which was capable of reaching beyond a small readership of gadget-loving hobbyists and science buffs. When the book publishers finally began turning to this new category, it was only because there was already a body of respectable novels waiting in the back issues of Astounding. *Without him, the current acceptance of science fiction would almost certainly have been impossible.*

To my surprise, many of the writers and fans seemed to consider Campbell a hard man to know well. He was held in some awe and in a measure of affection; but most people complained that he lectured at them, rather than talking to them. This was probably true in most cases. Campbell was somewhat shy, particularly about his personal feelings; and he hated to make conversation, something most people do automatically to fill time. He had no fund of small talk. He was a man passionately in love with ideas, who wanted to chase such ideas back to their beginnings and forward to the furthest possible extension. To him, that meant an all-out, no-holds-barred argument.

His mind was like a rapier, darting out instantly to find any unprotected spot in an opponent's thinking. He was a quick master of the fundamentals of any area of knowledge and he came armed with an amazing fund of information. Apparently he was intimidating to many. But to those who would return his passionate love of argument as a mental exercise, he was a wonderful human being.

Over the years there were many areas where he and I remained in total opposition. His eternal quest for undiscovered fields of knowledge led him into what I considered cultist beliefs, and I fought against those both privately and publicly. But our clash of ideological attitudes didn't matter. I always found him a warm and generous friend, whose loyalty was unshakable.

At first glance, it might appear that for H. Beam Piper, who grew up in rural Pennsylvania working as a railroad night watchman and dreamed of literary success, writing science fiction stories was quite a stretch. However, by his own admission, Piper was an early science fiction fan and most likely tried his hand at writing it, although he didn't start selling science-fiction stories until the mid-1940s. Plus, as evident from "The

Early Letters," he was already writing pulp adventure stories in the 1920s and was a fan of historical adventure romances, such as those penned by Rafael Sabatini.

Science fiction only really came into its own in the late twenties with the first of the Hugo Gernsback pulps, *Amazing Stores*. Within a few years, science fiction magazines were multiplying like rabbits and Piper most likely got his introduction at the local newsstand or drug store.

Mike Knerr, a friend of Piper's and author of the unpublished biography, "PIPER," wrote, "It is obvious the 'pulps' nourished him mentally and taught him much of how writing was accomplished. The so-called pulps, for those too young to remember, were the pulp paper magazines that were largely the training ground for aspiring writers. These were the markets, *Black Mask*, *Weird Tales*, etc., that Beam had been pitching stories to back in the 1920s and 1930s. The pulps cost twenty or twenty-five cents and were a modern version of the 1880 dime novels. By the end of the 1950s they were all gone, victims of rising paper costs and declining sales—mostly due to television and changing tastes."

Unfortunately, Piper's letter where he notifies the Coleman clan that he's made his first sale is among a number of 'missing' letters. However, it doesn't take much imagination to guess that he was literally floating on air—he was a published author, by Odin and by Thor! And, he did it all by himself. I can't recall any other prominent science-fiction writer who labored and toiled as long as H. Beam Piper did before his first sale and publication. I dare say it was the happiest day of his life.

As Don Coleman puts it, "Piper continued with his gumshoe writing but had really put the manuscripts aside for concentration on outer space. Detective stories he had attempted from Day-One, and detective stories he witnessed as round-trip disappointments. So, with probably a sleuthing potboiler in reserve, two or three extraterrestrial thrillers were in the making—manufactured by a mind that could expose several such creations at the same time."

CHAPTER NINE

He Walked Around Horses

H. Beam Piper's second science-fiction sale was "He Walked Around the Horses" to John W. Campbell, which was mailed on June 5th, 1947, and accepted (according to Piper's Story Log: see Appendix II) on July 11th of that year. It first appeared in the July, 1948, issue of *Astounding*. This story is considered by many to be the first Paratime story and is based on the true story of the mysterious disappearance of Benjamin Bathhurst, a British diplomatic envoy in Germany, in 1809 during the Napoleonic Wars. It's an epistolary story written as a series of documents, reports and statement by the various officials involved in Bathhurst's mysterious disappearance.

This story supposes that Benjamin Bathurst slipped into a parallel universe. The point where this time-line splits off from recorded history is the Battle of Quebec on December 31st, 1775 in which Benedict Arnold is killed instead of merely wounded, leading to the victory of British General John Burgoyne over his American counterpart Horatio Gates at the Battle of Saratoga. The end result is the failure of the American Revolution—and consequently there is no French Revolution; thus no Napoleon or the Napoleonic wars. Bathurst's abduction is also referred to in the Piper Paratime story "Police Operation," published later in the same year, tying "He Walked Around the Horses" into the Paratime series, even though no Paratimers are directly involved in the story.

In his "The Way of the Future Blog," Frederik Pohl reported, "For a while, H. Beam Piper was one of the clients of my literary agency....

He had first attracted attention with his story 'He Walked Around the Horses,' about a man who…disappeared into another reality." Having Frederik Pohl, who was both well-known as a writer and editor, represent him was quite a feather in Beam's cap. "With things like that," Pohl continues, "and the better prices I was able to negotiate for his science fiction, Beam was enjoying a modest prosperity. He formed the habit of coming to New York once or twice a month. His first stop was usually at my literary agency office on Fifth Avenue just across from Madison Square, where we would usually pick up a few other writers and go out to dinner.

"Beam had had little experience with exotic eats—high cuisine was not apparently popular in Altoona at the time—and so loved to experiment with menu items. Not always happily. When he ordered a dish that was meant to contain uncooked Italian ham, he sent it back to be properly fried. He wasn't deep into nutrition, either…."

Piper was one of the founding members of the Hydra Club which later spawned both the Mystery Writers of America and The Science Fiction Writers of America.

Fred Pohl, in his "The Way the Future Blogs," wrote his own personal reminiscences about the Hydra Club: "What postwar New York had lacked was a gathering point for the area's SF brethren (and sistren), so Lester del Rey and I created one. I invited a few of my SF friends to come and discuss the subject at my apartment at 28 Grove Street in the Village, Lester showed up with some of his, and we constituted ourselves a sort of roving gentlemen's (and ladies') club for people interested in science fiction, especially if professionally.

"There were nine of us. The mythological Hydra was said to have nine heads. That was good enough, so we called it The Hydra Club and began beating the brush for members. In the process of inviting all the area's sf writers and editors whose addresses we could locate, Fletcher Pratt was one of the first we reeled in. He was a key recruit. We original nine of course knew all the book and magazine editors, and most of the writers, in the area. Fletcher knew everybody else—Basil Davenport, editor (and later judge) for the Book-of-the-Month Club; Bernard De Voto, authority on my personal hero, Mark Twain, and editor of The Saturday Review of Literature and eternally the author of its most popular regular column, "The Easy Chair;" Hans Stefan Santesson, editor of a couple of small book clubs which now and then did science-fiction books and so on," Pohl wrote.

"The cut was between the people who primarily did science-fiction, all of whom we knew, and the people who did all kinds of works, but sometime did or sometimes might do a little science fiction as well. And those latter were the ones with whom Fletcher was our strongest link.

"I have to admit that at first I wasn't entirely easy with the idea of Fletcher Pratt, considered as friendship material for me. There was a generation gap. I didn't have any other friends anywhere near that old. Fletcher was pushing fifty, and almost all my other friends were within at least approximate lying distance of my own age, which was then in my late twenties. Even Jack Williamson's age was not much more than halfway to Fletcher's. Fletcher was also famous—that is, famous in wider circles than just those of science fiction."

Piper memorabilia collector and researcher Tom Rogers uncovered another early SF New York group called The Spectator Club. Piper did a two-part article ("Precognition and a Theory of Time") in the 1947 (Number 4) and 1948 (Number 5) issues of the club's official publication, *Amateur Spectator*. According to David Johnson, "Piper was invited to join after his first story was published in *Astounding*, and he took the opportunity to write about his [and Dunne's—jfc] ideas on time travel and General Semantics. It is fairly dry stuff, but it shows Piper's use of Dunne's time theories as a basis for his own stories." This is the first mention of Piper's interest in the time theories of J.W. Dunne, an Irish aeronautical engineer, which were first proposed in Dunne's essay, "An Experiment in Time."

The Spectator Club, another author invitation only club, was headed by Doc Lowndes, along with Fred Pohl, and Phillip Klass (another Pennsylvania SF author who wrote under the name William Tenn). Tom Rogers thoughtfully provided scans of the Piper article and a 1951 membership flyer from the Hydra Club with caricatures of most of the then members, including H. Beam Piper at the Zarthani.net website.

According to the post from David Johnson, "Piper contributed some letters to the prozine along with his article. Issue Number 5 also states that he helped to collate and staple some other magazines that were sent out to members along with *Amateur Spectator* (each mailing had a number of different zines included). This group formed the nucleus of what became the Hydra Club in 1948/'49, of which Piper was an early member.

H. Beam Piper's next sale to John W. Campbell was his first Paratime story, "Police Operation." According to Piper's Story Log, he mailed it on January 2nd, 1948 and it was accepted by Campbell on the 16th. It was published in the April edition of *Astounding*. Little did he know that the Paratime concept would be one of his most important contributions to SF field.

"Police Operation" was Piper's first story about the Paratime Police, whose primary mission is to protect the secret of Paratime travel. This first Paratime Police story is a police procedural wherein Verkan Vall (the Paratime Police Chief's Special Assistant) is charged with investigating the death of a First Level noble who was killed in an auto accident on a time-line very similar to our own time-line. Normally, nothing would have happened, but the Paratimer had brought a Venusian Nighthound with him—a vicious beast which was killing farm animals in the vicinity. It is against Paratime regulations for Paratimers to introduce non-native species to time-lines they visit because the appearance might raise suspicion that "outsiders" are doing mischief. When the local game wardens and State Police are called in to track the Nighthound, Verkan Vall gets involved to protect the Paratime secret. He hunts and kills the beast and then reports back to Paratime Police Chief Tortha Karf.

Both "He Walked Around Horses" and "Police Operation" were well-received and Piper began to get noticed within the small field of science fiction.

One of Piper's influences was Fletcher Pratt, who had success both in the science fiction and mystery fields, as well as with historical romances and non-fiction. He is also considered one of the fathers of modern war gaming. His *Great Battlefields of History* is considered by Jerry Pournelle to be one of the great historical works, and one Piper was quite familiar with. Fletcher Pratt, writer, editor, and seminal war gamer, wrote the introduction to one of the first science fiction anthologies, *World of Wonder*, published by Twayne in 1951. This anthology contains two Piper stories, "He Walked Around the Horses" and "Operation R.S.V.P."

In his introduction to "He Walked Around the Horses," Pratt provides a good look at what Piper's fellow science fiction authors of the late-1940s thought about him: "When the name of H. Beam Piper appeared for the first time on the contents page of *Astounding*, there was considerable speculation as to which of the well-known writers of science fiction was using this pseudonym. It seemed all too obviously the sort of disguise that would be employed to cover ventures into fiction by some scientist or engineer whose primary concern was with electronics. Also, there was the fact that the writing had the indescribable professional atmosphere which is the result of long experience with exactly how many words are needed to give the illusion of reality to an imagined emotion or scene.

"Of course the speculators did not know that the Beams and the Pipers are two of the oldest families in that curious little enclave of northeastern Pennsylvania which lives so much by itself. Neither were they aware that this particular scion of the stems had cut his literary teeth on solid and rather learned work in history. Born in 1903, Mr. Piper is an engineer on the Pennsylvania Railroad—not the train driving kind, but the type who stays in a shop and operates a slide rule.

"It is worth noting that the singular disappearance of Mr. Benjamin Bathurst is a recorded historical incident."

Once again, there is biographical misinformation—most likely instigated by Piper himself—about his occupation. An engineer had more of a caveat in the SF author circles of the forties and fifties than a night watchman at the rail yards. However, this introduction shows that Piper's first stories made a good-sized splash in the small puddle of science fiction.

No new Piper stories appeared in print in 1949; his only story sale in 1949 was "The Mercenaries," which was mailed to John W. Campbell on January 10th, 1949. A payment of $200.00 was received on April 4th, 1949. However, "The Mercenaries" would not see publication until the following year in the March 1950 issue of *Astounding Science Fiction*. This passage of over a year between story acceptance and publication was not unusual as most magazines liked to have stories on file. What was unusual was how quickly Piper's first two stories appeared in print.

"The Mercenaries" takes place in 1965 in a future similar to the one Piper used in his first published short story, "Time and Time Again." The world is now divided into four major blocs, the Western Union, the Ibero-American Confederation, the Fourth Komintern and the Islamic Caliphate. All four power blocs are in a race to build a moon rocket in order to annex the Moon as a rocket-launching base, thereby gaining world domination.

"The Mercenaries" is about a group of Free Scientists, who don't owe allegiance to any government and are working on their own moon project for the Western Union. Their existence is threatened when Duncan MacLeod discovers that one of their team is leaking secrets to the Fourth Komintern. Duncan MacLeod investigates, finds the traitor and then executes him to preserve the Free Scientists' independence.

The Free Scientists were an interesting group and one Piper could have used as the basis for more stories. But "The Mercenaries" is the last we hear of them. What is even more surprising is how few stories Piper published after his twenty-five years of fruitless labor. Of course, at that time he was still employed by the Pennsy and wasn't dependent upon his writing income. If anything, according to Anne McGuire—the wife of J.J. McGuire—Piper treated his writing money like lottery winnings. Still, one would imagine his first sale, after such a long wait and torturous trail, would have ignited a creative explosion.

CHAPTER TEN

Rebel Raider

In L. Sprague de Camp's 1996 autobiography, *Time and Chance*, he records his impressions of Piper after a meeting circa 1950. "In Altoona we got in touch with a science-fictional colleague, H. Beam Piper. He came to our hotel and later showed me his collection of weapons. Piper had a defect of speech like that of the hard of hearing, giving his voice a loud, harsh timbre. Moreover, while he seemed glad to see me, women made him so ill at ease that he almost ignored Catherine [de Camp's wife—jfc] while she was in the room."

Piper was rarely at ease with respectable women until he got to know them. Prostitutes and bar pick-ups were a completely different matter. While almost twenty years older, he did make quite an impression on Ferd Coleman's 'Gal Friday,' Eleanor Border, whom he got to know while visiting Coleman's office. In a letter to Miss Border, he mentions "another Piper masterpiece on the newsstands" ("Flight From Tomorrow"), with "Last Enemy" due out in a month and three more hanging fire." At that point in time he believed he was on the fast track. According to the entries in his Story Log, things would never again look as rosy as they did in July of 1950.

The period from 1947 to 1955 was the most fulfilling and rewarding period of Piper's life—a time when all things were possible and new surprises were on the horizon, as Don Coleman recounts. "Without a doubt, Beam was quite capable of having several irons in the fire simultaneously. The following month...a nonfiction chronicle emerged. Maintaining a vast knowledge of the Civil War era, it was incredible what weapons of those battles he could sketch from the smallest insignificant fitting, to the enormity of a complete cannon.

"However, when it came to drawing, small arms were his forté. And he could run off the chronology of a complete battle. One would merely mention a specific date between 1861 and 1865 and Beam would muse for a moment, then quite narrowly pinpoint the action that was taking place on that date. His expertise in telling the stories of history was superb and his verbal illustration of the situation at hand was visually transmitted to within the listener's mind with ease; much more readily than the complexities involved with...science fiction.

"So, when a short (piece) entitled 'Rebel Raider' sold to *True Magazine*...Beam's reaction was exhilaration...that he had become one of the proud contributors to such a reputable publication."

In actuality, it was his agent, science fiction editor and author, Frederick Pohl who made the sale to *True Magazine*. "That man," Piper exclaimed in a letter, "could sell snow to Eskimos!"

In "The Way the Future Blogs," his former agent Pohl reports: "Piper was a railroad man from birth. He lived in the Western Pennsylvania rail center of those great continent-spanning lines that appeared after the Civil War. That war was important to Beam. He had strong feelings about such concepts as heroism and personal honor, and he took sides. The side he favored was the slaveholding but militarily exciting Confederacy. Mostly self-educated, Beam was thrilled by the exploits of those dashing Rebel commanders, in particular by John Mosby, the Southern cavalry officer who made parts of Virginia uninhabitable by Federal troops or sympathizers.

"When Beam mentioned to me that he had, on his own time and just for the fun of it, written a lengthy work about his hero, I reminded him of my Basic Maxim No. 1: 'Writers write mostly for the fun of it. Agents exist to see they get money for having fun.' So he turned the finished piece over to me, and I promptly sold 'Rebel Raider' for a decent amount of money."

Fred Pohl sold the story to *True: The Men's Magazine* on March 23rd, 1950, for $1,200 making it Piper's biggest non-novel sale. It was published in the December, 1950, issue of *True* with interior illustrations by Mario Cooper. The article portrayed the Confederate Army Colonel John Mosby and his behind-the-lines exploits with the Union forces. In most cases, this colorful cavalry unit, known as Mosby's Rangers, was successful. H. Beam Piper was intrigued by Mosby, who would gamble with consequences of high risk and peril. He had decided to present just a small episode of a very costly and bloody war and as a result of this factual adventure, the author's credibility continued to rise among his peers.

As Don Coleman noted, "With the telling of this story, another facet of Beam's character surfaced in his delight over a fan letter he had received after the article's publication. It was from a reader in Virginia who insisted that Beam had to be a southerner. He cackled happily every time he told the story. He truly loved that kind of feedback and personally felt that the people of the Shenandoah Valley, after July 1876, should have built a monument to Crazy Horse and the Sioux Nation for having knocked off George Armstrong Custer at the Little Big Horn.

"Soon after publication [June 6th, 1951—jfc], Ferd Coleman received an elated telegram from Piper, advising that Walt Disney Productions had offered a price for movie rights to the article. Beam, of course, agreed to the negotiations… However, some years passed without any indication of this particular story coming to the silver screen. But finally, a series began on television called *The Gray Ghost*, the only ingredient taken from Beam was Colonel John Mosby and Mosby's Rangers." Very little of Piper's original article appeared in the TV show.

No earlier commitments had been instituted regarding television rights or royalties—so Piper received nothing other than the original dispensation ($1,200.00 minus the $200.00 agent fee). Piper had this to say about the film sale in *The Pennsy* article "Typewriter Killer:" "Why Walt Disney bought the movie rights to that article, I've never figured out. Will Colonel Mosby be played by Mickey Mouse, and General Phil Sheridan by Donald Duck? It's baffling. However, I was glad to get the check."

Coleman noted: "When 'Rebel Raider' originally appeared in December, 1950, the television medium in the home was in its infancy, and so…un-thought of (on Beam's behalf) during the initial transaction with Disney."

Nineteen fifty was a busy year for Piper; in addition to "Rebel Raider" he sold four other short stories. His second Paratime story, "Last Enemy," was mailed on January 17th, 1950 and sold to John W. Campbell on April 8th, 1950. It appeared very quickly in the August 1950 issue of *Astounding*. It's obvious that the Paratime series struck a nerve with Campbell and Piper could have done quite well had he continued to write them. Fred Pohl became Piper's agent in February or March of 1950 as "Last Enemy" was Piper's last sale without a 10% agent's commission.

"Last Enemy" is considered by many to be the best of Paratime stories until the Lord Kalvan stories were published in 1964. For a change, the main protagonist in "Last Enemy" is the lovely and impetuous Dalla Hadron, Verkan Vall's wife. This story is the only Paratime story set on the Second Level where Piper introduces us to the fascinating Akor-Neb civilization and its Society of Assassins. While reincarnation is an accepted scientific fact on this time-line, no one is prepared for the consequences of communication with the reincarnated dead—reverberations of which reach even to Home Time Line and threaten the Paratime Secret. This story provides a fascinating look at how reincarnation—once proven to be fact—can have overwhelming major implications throughout a society.

Piper's next sale was "Dearest" to *Weird Tales*, which was sold on August 8th, 1950, and later appeared in the March, 1951, issue. "Dearest" is one of Piper's strangest stories and his only fantasy. For a life-long atheist, he wrote a number of stories about life after death and reincarnation. I suspect Piper longed for some greater purpose to life, than material existence and survival, but never found a religion or belief system that he could believe in. Or one that would measure up to his rigorous intellect. In "Dearest," his protagonist communicates with the spirit of a dead girl a hundred and seventy-five years gone.

While Piper had a strong interest in both the supernatural and the afterlife, as represented in these stories, he had little toleration for do-gooders and professional religionists. Appalachia in the 1920s and '30s was considered part of the Bible Belt and there was a lot of social pressure to be a church goin' and God fearin' man. H. Beam Piper and

Ferd Coleman, to a lesser extent, reveled in their war against mindless Christianity. Nothing incensed Piper more than when one of these Bible thumpers would take his platform into the public arena of politics.

In a September 19th, 1926, letter to Ferd Coleman, he wrote:

Have you had any more tilts with those holy orders lately? If so, let me hear the latest news from the battlefront. I devoutly wish that you were here in Altoona, to take a fall out of some of our pulpit thumpers. God wot, they need it. They have just succeeded in a long and bitter jihad against the local filles de joi and our bordello district is now given over to the bat and owl, a circumstance causing deep and widespread regret. Crucifixion is too mild, by far, a fate for such friends incarnate.

This despicable victory has made the men of God hereabout big-bellied and stiff-necked. They are quite puffed up about it. Weekly they rant to the gaping throngs of morons, telling them all about the New Jerusalem and the Lake of Fire and Brimstone, while the poor whores are hard put to get three square meals and a flop. A hell of a note!

At the risk of being mistaken for a high-toned English butler I subscribe myself,

> *Your brother in Christ,*
> *H. Beam Piper*
> *Long Live the Royalist Party!*

Ferd, a devout Catholic, was having his own problems with the local Newberry ministry and received his friend's wholehearted support: "...I was considerably amused at the account of your war with the local Jesus-brokers, who seem to be a rather swinish lot."

In another letter dated November 13th, 1926, Piper added, "I'm glad to hear that you have enlarged your great organ of public opinion. Evidently the local Jesus-brokers and salvation-smiths didn't fulfill their threat of putting the curse on you after all. Keep up the good fight and double-charge your guns with grapeshot. I sincerely wish you were here to engage our Altoona prelates in battle. They are a rotten bunch, all in all. As bad or worse than that gang in Williamsport."

In this March 29th, 1927, letter to Ferd Coleman, Piper re-evaluates his religious stand: "I begin to doubt that 'agnostic' is my proper designation instead of 'atheist.' Not that my opinions are changing, but that I am beginning to understand the two terms better. An atheist, as I see it is a man who denies the existence of a personal and personified God. This I do deny, and with all vigor. Whether or not there is a central creative force, I cannot say. If that be agnosticism, then I am an agnostic, but I don't think it is. An agnostic, again my idea of it, is a man who neither denies nor affirms the existence of a personified God...."

In a later letter, Piper noted: "Can't some folks discover that atheism is a state of the mind, like pragmatism, romanticism, hedonism or a preference for blondes, is not a sect or a party, like Catholicism, Socialism, Presbyterianism, Royalism, Communism or Republicanism? But, at that, for a man of violence, the post of missionary to the wilds of Arkansas or Texas for this Flking [sic] Dung Tong appeals to me. Those lads, skipping through the backwoods, fighting Fundamentalist mobs, passing from town to town between suns and just ahead of the Ku Klux Klan, being fired upon and showered with garbage by the godly, must have an interesting time of it."

Piper's next sale was that of "Immunity" to *Future Stories*. "Immunity" is Piper's own title for "Flight From Tomorrow," which appeared in the September/October 1950 issue of *Future* (a minor SF magazine and a salvage market for stories that wouldn't sell to one the major magazines such as *Astounding* or *Galaxy*). In those days, as it is now, it was not unusual for an editor to change a story title to one he believed was more "commercial." Interestingly, Piper didn't bother to note the change of title in his Story Log. It was undoubtedly part of the unsold story inventory that Piper gave to Fred Pohl when he joined Pohl's literary agency. (Neither "Operation RSVP" and "Dearest" had mailing dates.) "Flight From Tomorrow" is definitely a minor effort and was not well-known until its publication in *The Worlds of H. Beam Piper*.

The story is about Hradzka, a vicious dictator in the far future, who takes the only existing time machine and makes a one-way journey into ancient times to establish a new empire. The theme of the story is atomic destruction—a theme that runs throughout Piper's work. The scientific premise that man could adapt to radiation may seem quaint today, but at the time Piper wrote this story it was much more plausible. The destruction of Nagasaki and Hiroshima in 1945 put the image of an atomic holocaust front and forward in the public consciousness. However, the ruthless ambition and treachery that form the basis of this yarn are as contemporary as the latest headlines.

"Flight From Tomorrow" is also noted for the first mention of Atomic Era dating—a dating system based upon the date the first uranium pile went into operation; later A.E. dating was used throughout Piper's Terro-Human Future History. It demonstrates how once Piper got his teeth around a good idea or concept he would use it again and again, like his collapsed matter which appears in both the Paratime and Terro-Human Future History series.

Piper's last sale for 1950 was another Paratime yarn, "Temple Trouble," which Fred Pohl sold to *Astounding* on October 19th. It first appeared in the April, 1951, issue of *Astounding Science Fiction*. In this story, the First Level parasite culture is manipulating local religions to divert the natives into extracting uranium ore. When a gang of Paratime criminals begin to con the locals with a cult of human sacrifice, the Paratime Police are called into action.

All in all, 1950 was one of Piper's most productive years in terms of both production and sales. He was no longer a journeyman writer, but an established science-fiction author and an accepted member of the SF clan.

CHAPTER ELEVEN

Day of the Morons

Piper's first sale of 1951 was "Day of the Morons" to John W. Campbell of *Astounding Science Fiction*. According to Piper's Story Log, "Day of the Morons," was first mailed on June 6th, 1947, to John W. Campbell, the day after he mailed "Police Operation." For reasons that will become apparent shortly, Campbell did not buy this story when it was first presented. It wasn't published for another four years, after Fred Pohl resubmitted it to Campbell and sold it on April 14th, 1951.

The story revolves around trouble at a nuclear power plan which stems from a labor/management shutdown. In light of the Three-Mile Island incident the story is as current today as it was when Piper wrote it. The story premise is that with the centralization of power (and all utilities) the effects of careless errors are magnified a thousand fold. As we are beginning to learn in a centralized civilization such as our own, we can no longer tolerate the mistakes of blunderers and half-wits—or nature in terms of a major solar electro-magnetic pulse which would shut down most of our computer/electrical devices. To Piper the average working man was a creature of minimal competence at best, a prejudice I expected he picked up on the job while working with the laborers at the Pennsylvania Railroad.

As Piper puts it in "Day of the Morons:" "The moron I'm afraid of can go on for years, doing routine work under supervision, and nothing'll happen. Then, some day, he does something on his own lame-brained initiative, and when he does, it's only at the whim of whatever gods there be that the result isn't a wholesale catastrophe. And people like that are the most serious threat facing our civilization today, atomic war not excepted." One can't help but think of Homer Simpson and his travails at the nuclear plant he works at in Springfield. The Marching Morons theme is one that Piper will amplify in his short novel *Null ABC* several years later.

* * *

Piper's most important writing relationship was the one he had with the legendary John W. Campbell, the editor who bought Piper's first and last stories. Piper's heroes were self-reliant men, who often read as if they had stepped right out of one of Campbell's editorials, leaving many fans and readers curious as to exactly what his relationship with Campbell was really like. Was Piper just a Campbell puppet, like many other writers, who echoed John's editorials for a quick sale? Or did they share the same ideas and philosophies?

In this June 18th, 1951, letter from Campbell to Piper's agent, Frederick Pohl, [regarding the short story "Day of the Morons"] we see a different side of the legendary editor:

Dear Pohl:

Please tell Piper that this one, as set up, is too hot for us to handle. It'll have to be changed slightly. As set up, it's enough to make most union men ready to chaw the handiest publisher's representative; this we consider an unhealthy phenomenon, as we need publisher's representatives.

The thing to do is to make it clear that the Union officials <u>have been misled</u> by misinformation from the two discharges, and are equally aware of the necessity, once they get the true picture. In other words, the <u>union</u> isn't to blame, but the individuals are.

...And it could be done fairly readily by installing a scene in which the union leader confers with the fired shop steward and organizer, and is given deliberately misleading information.

Point is—we got unions too, you know.

Regards,
John W. Campbell, Jr.
Editor

He made the necessary changes and "Day of the Morons" appeared in the September issue of *Astounding*. Piper was always willing to listen to editorial suggestions, especially if it meant a sale; a sound practice for a budding author. What's unusual about this letter is watching the legendary John W. Campbell back away from a fight—although, New York unions in the fifties were easy to rile and he was probably right to be wary of putting his hand in that particular lion's cage. Especially since most of the magazine distributors were Teamsters and could have easily refused to ship the magazine. Still, it's a side of Campbell rarely seen in personal anecdotes or in print.

While most of the Piper/Campbell correspondence could be described as pleasant and mutually respectful, it's obvious from the tone and words of Piper's letters that he was no 'yes man.' In this 1951 letter, in which Piper is discussing the pros and cons of dealing with agented story submissions, he says to Campbell: "I'm afraid, though, that your suggested solution would do more harm than good, by angering authors; it could easily be reflected in author's instructions to agents: 'Send it to anybody but that s.o.b. at *Astounding*.'

"Another solution, that of refusing to buy from anybody but agents, would result in shutting off the manuscripts from new authors—if you'd had a policy like that in 1946, I'd never have gotten published anywhere. It would leave you with a dwindling staff of old-timers, while the new writers were all going to Sam Merwin or Horace Gold."

While Piper is respectful of Campbell's feelings, he's not afraid to speak the truth—even if it's to the man who made his writing career a reality. Piper, still a night watchman for the Pennsy, makes light of his economic dependence upon Campbell and Street & Smith [*Astounding's* publisher] in his letter's closing comments: "Sorry I can't think of an answer that wouldn't cost money, or lay me open to the accusation of scheming to bore a hole in Street & Smith's money-box to my own advantage and enrichment."

* * *

Piper's only other sale for 1951 was the short story "Genesis," which was sold to *Future* by Frederik Pohl on October 11th, 1951. There is no indication of when it was written and I suspect it was part of the group of manuscripts he gave Pohl when he signed up for the Pohl literary agency. "Genesis" was published in *Future*, another salvage market, in the September 1951 issue.

This short story is one of the most unusual yarns in the Piper canon, since it bridges both his Paratime and Terro-Human Future History series with its human Martian origin story. In his Paratime series, Piper divided the Paratime alternate probabilities into five different levels, based on the Martians' various degrees of success in their attempts to colonize Earth when their own world dried up. For example, the Martians were completely successful in colonizing Earth, seventy-five thousand to a hundred thousand years ago, on First Level—the only level possessing the secret of Paratime transposition.

The Europo-American Sector—which contains our own time-line—is located on the maximum probability level—the Fourth Level. It is on this level that a disaster occurred of such magnitude that all Martian technology and civilization were completely lost. Thus, Fourth Level inhabitants believe they are an indigenous race with a long history of savagery. "Genesis" is the story of the disaster that struck those Martian colonists, and their fight for survival.

However, there is evidence in "Omnilingual" (an early Piper Terro-Human Future History story) that once there was an advanced civilization on Mars and that may well have been the origin of "humanity" on Earth. "Genesis" has been seen by some Piper scholars as the bridge between Piper's Paratime series and his future history. Either way, Piper had a fascination with Mars that was shared by a number of pre-1960's writers.

Piper scholar John Anderson has this to say on the subject: "There is indeed much evidence for the Martian origin of Terro-Humanity in the Future History. Of course, it's a bit circumstantial, because as usual with Piper, one must read between the lines. But I believe his title 'Omnilingual' itself contains a hidden twist; the omnilingual of science enables Martha Dane to translate Old Martian, which is the ancient common language, or 'omnilingual,' of Martian and Terran humanity. Kalvar Dard and the Martians bring *it* to Terra in "Genesis," and so all Terran tongues, including the English of the Cyrano Expedition in 'Omnilingual,' are descended from Old Martian. Martha Dane, among the first Terrans on Mars, is therefore simply translating the language of Kalvar Dard and the first Martians on Terra, who are her own ancestors.

"There also seems to be a subtle connection between the near future story "Omnilingual" and the far future story "The Keeper." In the first story, the Terrans return to Mars, the origin world, and begin learning about its ancient languages and culture among the History Department murals, which is really their own history. In the latter story, Salsalvadran and Dranigrastan return to Terra, the Mother-World, 'to learn about the long-ago times' of the planet, which is really *their* own history. Thus, near the beginning and the end of the Terro-Human Future History, Beam has mankind take a historical look at itself, among its own ancient ruins."

CHAPTER TWELVE

Murder in the Gunroom

Finally, after multiple drafts and over a decade's work, H. Beam Piper's agent sold his first novel, *Murder in the Gunroom*. As Don Coleman recounts in "The Early Letters," during a visit to the Coleman domicile, Piper roared "GREAT CLAPS OF THUNDER! I cannot determine whether Great Thor, son of Odin, is the true benefactor of my pleadings, but whosoever it be, 'Jeff Rand' is about to meet the masses!"

Back in January of 1941, Piper had presented Ferd with "a hard-bound double-spaced 339-page carbon edition of the original manuscript entitled 'Murder Bereaves Hattie.'" At that time, Piper used the pseudonym of Herbert Orr—his father's name! He penned in the following entry on February 12th, 1941: "To Ferd Coleman, who read this in two weeks, which is, for Ferd, a feat comparable to reading the Bible, Shakespeare and the *Encyclopedia Britannica* in forty eight hours. H. Beam Piper, alias HERBERT ORR 2/12/41."

Piper wrote and rewrote endlessly. Not to editorial prescription, but to his own—sometimes flawed—view of the market place. Partially, it was because once he got a good idea, if it didn't sell, it wasn't poor editorial taste or the idea. In his mind it was his execution of the story that was at fault; thus, he would rewrite, often before the book was rejected—or even finished! The Piper process was long and laborious, whether it be short story or novel, it made no difference; both got the full 'Piper Treatment.'

One of "Heinlein's Rules for Writers"—the one that is probably the most misinterpreted, is rule "Number Three: You must refrain from rewriting, except to editorial order." A lot of lazy writers have used this as an excuse for turning out sloppy first drafts and calling them finished. What he meant was, once the story/novel is finished—which may entail considerable rewriting—don't keep going back and rewriting every time it comes back from a publisher or agent, unless someone offers to buy it if certain 'changes' are made. Piper's output would have gone through the roof had he listened to this simple advice; on the other hand in his letters and diaries, Piper was always moaning about being bereft of ideas and abandoning unfinished yarns. Obviously, for a writer, it's better to endlessly rewrite than to write nothing at all.

One of Piper's biggest complaints about Heinlein was that he gave away plot ideas in his novels. For Piper, story ideas and coming up with good plots were always big headaches and he suffered endlessly trying to make his stories work. Yet, once he had a good idea or a plot going, he could write like a house on fire and run with the best writers in the field.

Don Coleman noted: "In 1946, after rewriting and renaming this mystery novel and chipping it down to 250 double-spaced pages, he presented a new bound carbon edition to Ferd Coleman, bearing its new title, 'No Cash Drawers in Coffins.' Again, in a matter of weeks, the manuscript was renounced and thus set aside for more important things as probing into the worlds of the unknown; the stampede of sci-fi competition. Then, in 1952, when Beam had eventually proved that this many-times-worked-over manuscript dating back over ten years, was worth reading—it was long-last convincingly sold."

In Piper's Story Log, in which he kept a record of his story sales and income, the Jefferson Rand mystery is titled *Pistols for Everybody* with (*Murder in the Gunroom*) in parentheses underneath. The book earned $750.00 (minus a 10% agent's cut to Fred Pohl) for a total of $675.00 in Piper's pocket! Using an inflation calculator, the $675.00 is the equivalent of $5,933.00 in 2014 dollars. There is no further mention of any royalties so it's doubtful the book ever earned out its meager advance; although, the amount was typical of the time for a 'new' mystery author. In retrospect, even after sixty plus years of inflation, $750.00 was a piddling sum for a book involving years of labor and at least four different rewrites.

The 1953 *Pennsy* article has this to say about the book: "Mr. Piper's first mystery novel, published by Alfred A. Knopf last March, was *Murder in the Gunroom*, a story of intrigue and violence among firearms collectors. This book gave him a chance to make use of his extensive knowledge of antique weapons, another interest of his that goes back a long way.

"'I was 14, and the Fourth of July was coming up,' Mr. Piper recalls. 'I wanted to make as much noise as I could for my money, and I decided that percussion caps and powder were better than ordinary blanks, so I got the catalogue of a New York gun dealer and bought a .44 caliber Civil War percussion revolver for $4.85.'

"This not only made a satisfying noise, but started him reading about old weapons, buying them and trading them."

The most likely reason Knopf wasn't interested in a sequel was that the first volume never earned out its small advance, despite a good review from the *New York Times*, since there is no record of any royalties in Piper's meticulously kept sales book. That, of course, didn't stop Piper from writing at least two different (and no telling how many rewrites) sequels—"Murder in the Conference Room" and "Murder Frozen Over." However, *Murder in the Gunroom* was his first novel sale and as such represented a big step up in the world of professional writing.

"The next time the author was in Williamsport—unknown to all—he taxied up to the white house at the top of Highland Terrace, waving the cabbie off with adios," wrote Don Coleman. "With small satchel in hand, he made it up to the front door stoop, entered the unlocked house unannounced and directed himself to the den. Knowing every inch of the late Ferd Coleman's lair, he pulled the '46 bound manuscript of *No Cash Drawers in Coffins* from the shelf and quickly laid it open on the cherry wood table. He bent down and made an inked entry on the title page:

Final Title
MURDER IN THE GUNROOM

"He then turned to Freida Coleman who had followed the unseen noises to the den and now faced him from the doorway, awestruck. He closed the old bound edition, walked over to Freida and handed her a pre-autographed fresh copy of the new published book, which read:

'For Freida Coleman
with years of friendship
behind us, and, I hope
many ahead
    H. Beam Piper'

"Suddenly he performed a rarity. With outstretched arms, he flat outright hugged her!

"'I miss Ferd, Freida,' he resounded with guttural delivery. 'I must return home tomorrow but would like to spend an evening of nostalgia within this room. These walls know me well and I can speak to them without equivocation. After all, it may be the last.'"

Piper's had a lifelong passion for firearms. After his move from Altoona to Williamsport, he would go to the abandoned stone quarry outside of town to shoot. In the late 1950s Don Coleman would sometimes join him. "He was an expert, not only firing each [pistol—jfc] with meticulous perfection, but virtually able to sketch the complete works of any of his antique rifles and handguns. I was employed with a local radio station across the river and had considerable free time.... He would telephone me and within minutes, I could be standing before him at his desk."

One of the most difficult things Piper had to do, after moving to Williamsport was to slowly sell off his collection of guns, one, two and three at a time, to supplement his meager writing income.

Piper's literary trilogy "Tiadaghton" was lost in the mists of time, although not forgotten. He alludes to it in the Colonel Shoemaker dedication in *Murder in the Gunroom*. There he says: "...an old and valued friend, who was promised this dedication, with an entirely different novel in mind, twenty-two years ago."

CHAPTER THIRTEEN

New Friends

John J. McGuire, H. Beam Piper's only collaborator, was a very interesting man in his own right. John McGuire (or Jack as Piper and the family called him) was a graduate of Shippensburg State College. Shortly after graduation he joined the Army and fought in Germany during World War II; there he won a Silver Star and other decorations. For a while, he worked for Wild Bill Donovan in the intelligence service; part of his work was going behind enemy lines where he robbed German banks in an attempt to disrupt the Nazi economy and damage enemy morale.

His wife, Anne McGuire, once told his eldest daughter Terry—when she was asking about her father as a young man—that before the War he had been studying English; they'd both had dreams of acting and writing. "In those days "he was quiet and very gentle." Terry McGuire was shocked; this was not a description of the man she knew as her father. While of average height, in most ways he was a larger than life figure; he was handsome, a hard drinker, had a radio announcer's voice and unpredictable mood swings due to post-traumatic shock disorder—or shell shock as it was called in the post-World War II era.

As John Jr. told me, "Father was a battle-hardened soldier with flashbacks. He was never able to sleep an entire night—"Don't ask, don't tell!" was his motto." Jack was also an out of control drinker who by the mid-fifties was well on the road to alcoholism. After the war, the McGuires stayed in Germany, where Jack worked as a criminal prosecutor and investigator with the Adjutant General's office. John Jr. reported, "When Jack arrived in Bavaria in November of 1946, he had to shoot and kill a Nazi sympathizer who came to assassinate him. He wore the assassin's jacket home when they returned to the States in the late forties and settled in Altoona.

"But nobody would have guessed his past from looking at him. My father could be in a room with fifty people and they all had one thing in common—they all liked my father! He was outgoing and interested in people. He used to say, 'Everyone has a story. Even if it isn't true!' He was also a science fiction fan, read *Astounding* and was a fan of John W. Campbell's."

John McGuire got a job teaching English at Keith Jr. High School in Altoona and according to his son, "As a new teacher at Keith, dad was stuck mostly teaching children with learning disabilities. He didn't like it much there at Keith since his specialty was speed reading. Dad would teach for nine months out of the year, and then give private lessons as a tutor for children with reading problems during the summer."

"My mother was very naïve, a small town girl and a good prose stylist. She had her own writing and acting dreams," Terry reported. "In the family, Jack was the author, while she kept the family together."

John Jr. paints a vivid picture of small town Appalachia: "Altoona was poor and it was dirty. Bishop's Cathedral was based on St. Peter's, but was gray from all the soot in the air, from the car yards. Everyone worked in the mines or the railroad yards and there were lots of lay-offs. It was a lot like Victorian England; the yards ran the whole length of Altoona and even the snow was gray in the daylight—a good place to commit suicide!"

Piper not only worked the graveyard shift for the Pennsy Railroad, but he worked over the weekends, too. In this January 12th, 1953 letter to Allan Howard, of the Eastern Science Fiction Association, he apologizes for not being able to attend a meeting he's been invited to give a talk at. "I'm really sorry that I won't be able, in the foreseeable future, to attend one of your meetings; I am not writing full time, but I am also working for the Pennsylvania Railroad Company, in their shops here, and it happens that weekends off are practically an impossibility for me. My equivalent of a weekend is Wednesday and Thursday, and on Sunday I am tightly chained to my galley-oar."

One of John J. McGuire's dreams was to be a writer. As his daughter Terry tells it, "Jack read all the 'pulp fiction.' He was honing his skills by reading other writers." John Jr. added, "Dad had been writing since 1948, but he was a very slow writer, and would agonize over his prose. He was writing poetry, some science fiction and an occasional mystery story; he never sold anything before he met Beam. We could all see he was getting discouraged. He was convinced that working with a successful author such as H. Beam Piper would be his entry into the world of writing." From all the internal evidence, Jack took working with Piper very seriously. Probably a lot more seriously than Piper did.

"Beam always dressed impeccably, even wore a cloak. He was a striking figure and could look quite sinister—but he was generous and courtly to a fault. He had a deep, crackly voice that was a little scary—almost theatrical. Like my dad, he knew how to put on a part. One thing about Beam though; he knew the damndest things—look it up, Piper was right! He read a lot, too.

"Piper grew up locally and was not known in Altoona as an SF author, but as an employee of the Pennsy Railroad. His family had deep roots in that part of Appalachia. He knew everybody and their family and they knew him—the small town mentality.

"Beam always addressed my dad as Jack, and in many ways they were like older and younger brothers. Beam was moody, but he always listened very closely to everyone. He asked great questions, and would have made a great defense attorney."

As Terry tells it, "When Jack found out Beam lived in Altoona, he mentioned to his doctor (Dr. Jack Strassman), who was also a close friend that he wanted to meet Beam. This doctor was also a friend of Piper's, and arranged a meeting at our house. The three men had a roundtable discussion about science fiction and began to discuss fantasy. Beam had lots of 'is it possible medically' story ideas. The next week they were joined by another friend (Sam Parks) who worked in the pharmaceutical business as 'drummer' [traveling salesman—jfc], who could answer questions about medications and their effects. The Roundtable began."

John Jr., the oldest of the McGuire children, has a different view of how Beam and Jack got together: "Dr. Strassman purposely brought the two men together, because he knew Beam was a writer, while Jack was a dandy and college graduate. Science fiction was not that big in working class Altoona. He thought they'd get along famously—and they did. Neither father nor Beam had much money and Dr. Strassman offered to pay for the postage costs for sending out their finished manuscripts."

"Originally, the game plan was that Beam was there as father's advisor. He was direct and logical in person and he talked like he wrote. Beam had a very dry, ironic wit, and a slightly ironic way of talking. Beam wouldn't seek out social affairs, but he was having a great time and he soon went from advisor to collaborator. The four of them would sit around the table drinking and pitching ideas—it was a wonderful atmosphere to grow up in. Even then, I knew I was very fortunate to witness their collaboration and to be a small part of this great group of men."

They would soon call themselves the "Unholy Four" an obviously Piper influenced name and reminiscent of the "Unholy Trinity" of H. Beam Piper, Ferd Coleman and Ted Ranck. As Terry put it, "Every occasion was an opportunity for drinking. And every celebration a cause for another drink!

"Jack and Beam would brainstorm ideas, and bounce them off their friends. Occasionally, outsiders—like Fletcher Pratt or the local music teacher—would join in. Other people would visit, bringing their personal exploits and life experiences. The Unholy Four just soaked it all up. They were all very passionate with their views, whether it be about politics or music. Once you were a part of the gang, such as friends like Fletcher Pratt, you could come and go as you pleased.

"However, they were like southern gentlemen—prickly about points of honor."

"Beam became a constant visitor to the McGuire household in the early fifties and was soon more than a visitor—almost a family member, eating many meals with us," John Jr. remembered. "Beam lived within walking distance of our house on 214 Willow Avenue. He often came over to watch the weekly fights on our television. Mother would make popcorn and the whole family would watch the fights, while Beam and Jack would score each round!"

In a sense, Piper 'adopted' the McGuire family just as he had adopted the Colemans twenty years earlier. He might never have had his *own* family, but he was certainly a *big* part of several families. As Terry told it, "Beam had the run of the house. Holidays, Beam celebrated with us—he always made a big deal out of July 4th!"

In the beginning, Piper and McGuire had a lot of fun together, but they were serious about their writing. It helped that Piper was represented by a major literary agent. According to Anne McGuire, they would meet several times a week at the McGuire residence to work on different writing projects. Terry McGuire described how they worked: "Jack and Beam would sit at the table until they agreed on a basic plot. They would call my mother into the room and give her the plot and storyline. She would type it up, then Jack would write the first draft. Beam would read the first draft, add and revise. Back to my mother to retype; both Jack and Beam would read it, making any final corrections. Beam would then 'polish' the manuscript, making sure there were no 'dangling' plot lines, conflicts in events and overall continuity. Back to Anne for the last typing, then off to the agent.

"Beam was still working for the railroad and writing his own stories. No one in the family can remember the date when Beam was introduced to Jack, but I suspect it was sometime in 1951 [about a year before Ferd Coleman's death—jfc]." According to Anne McGuire, Piper and McGuire wrote a number of stories together before they sold "Null-ABC" to John W. Campbell at *Astounding*. According to Piper's Story Log the short novel *Null-ABC* was finished on October 17th, 1952 and was serialized in the March and April 1953 issues of *Astounding*. Less agency commission, Piper made $498.22.

Null-ABC was a sharp satire about the public school system, undoubtedly inspired by McGuire's actual experiences as a Keith Junior High School English teacher in Altoona. The story is an "if this goes on" yarn, where after a number of wars and nuclear attacks the public becomes increasingly illiterate and suspicious of "learnin'" and books. While most "Illiterates" are content to watch TV and listen to audio recordings, a few "Literate" people are needed to keep things running. Some of the power brokers approve of the general illiteracy and are forced to take action when an important anti-Literate politician is revealed to have taught his children in secret how to read.

Terry has this to say about their first sale: "Beam and Jack finally did it! They sold their first story. My mother may still have a copy of their first check. Beam lived with his partially blind mother in an apartment. She kept house and cooked for him. Beam kept a small cannon there, and had a tradition of firing it when he sold a story. This was where the huge production of Beam loading the gunpowder took place. Mother and I covered our ears, expecting a huge **BANG**. Instead it was a very small bang. But everyone was delighted.

"From then on Beam became a constant presence in our house. My mother stated she was very naïve then, and would sometimes invite Beam for dinner, and he would say, 'No, Anne, tonight I'm going out to beat the bushes.' My mother later understood that to mean he was going out to meet women." John Jr. reiterated, "Beam was always a ladies' man. Sometimes Beam would take us [Jack and Terry] along with him—"we called him 'Uncle Beam,' while he trolled for women at the local taverns."

As John Jr. tells it in our telephone interview, "Beam and Jack loved to talk even more than they loved to write. They would talk their stories out, with inflections and feeling. I always believed the stories were better before they were written down; they lost some of their flair when put to paper. They were both great verbal storytellers. Mom would take shorthand notes and write the dialogue down. Sometimes they would argue over every word of the stories after they were written down, but Beam always had the last say. Their goal was to write simply and concisely. The problem was that some of their best prose was sacrificed for clarity.

"Both men wanted to be acknowledged as writers, wanted to be known for what they were. The 'day job' allowed them to control things. Beam, especially, liked to be in control. They never talked about being full-time writers. Beam used to say 'In their own times, ninety-nine percent of all great authors and artists were always out of fashion!'"

This last statement supplies some insight into how Piper was able to keep writing for twenty-five years in the face of constant rejection.

"Story money," according to John, "was not real money to them. They wanted to sell their stories and re-sell them, to anthologies. More to get them into print than for the money. Mother never heard Beam or Jack talk about mundane things, such as bills. When the money arrived—'Oh Goody!' Then they'd spend it all up."

John Jr. added, "Beam and Jack both considered John W. Campbell and Anthony Boucher as the best editors in the business. They would talk to Campbell on the phone; John was always trying to get them to write stories 'he could use.' Campbell's complaint was, 'They didn't write enough.' These guys were very much individualists and wrote what they wanted to.

"They both were very much into the Elizabethans, especially William Shakespeare. Beam loved how Shakespeare wrote both for the highborn and the pit. They looked for plots in his plays and sometimes their stories would be titled with Shakespearian quotes. They both also loved Sherlock Holmes; I remember them listening to the Holmes radio shows.

"Jack also did some radio work at Station WFHA announcing in Williamsport and local game commentary. He had a wonderful voice. He worked off and on at the local radio station. A lot of the smaller stations during the fifties made use of radio transcripts that they would have read over the air featuring local announcers. Jack did a lot of that and sometimes read from the teletype and did the news. Occasionally, he would do a special show; once he actually interviewed the 'Unholy Four.' Another time he interviewed Beam about his writing. Great fun was had by all!"

Terry had this to say, "Later, my father had a radio show on WFHA in Red Bank, New Jersey. He did shows on science fiction (Fred Pohl occasionally appeared) and other literary efforts."

"A lot of ideas were germinated at these sessions," John Jr. said. "I remember them talking about Fuzzies. Sam Parks drew pictures of what the Fuzzies would look like on his yellow pads! It never went anywhere until Beam wrote *Little Fuzzy*.

"They were really good writers and they knew it. They usually wrote in the dining room. My father had the furniture specially made. Beam brought Jack that final level of craftsmanship to his writing—the shimmer of gold. Beam was out at the house four or five times a week; they did most of their work in the summer time, when dad was off.

"We'll never know how many stories they wrote together. If a story didn't sell after making the rounds of the science-fiction magazines, Beam and Jack would get drunk and 'celebrate' by burning the offending manuscript and rejection letters in a big drum trashcan." Terry added, "Mother would often hide the carbons so they wouldn't burn everything. They got very drunk and exuberant. It was their 'letting go' ceremony, I guess. Sometimes, when they sobered up the next morning, they'd regret burning their stories—not that they'd ever admit it!"

CHAPTER FOURTEEN

Uller Uprising

Piper's only sale in 1953 was his first science-fiction novel, *Uller Uprising*, which was also the first true Terro-Human Future History tale. Piper was never a hard science fiction author, i.e., one whose primary interest is in technology and science. While he was fascinated by scientific progress, he was more interested in human beings and how they related to larger historical forces. Thus it was that he created his Terro-Human Future History, the framework for most of his stories from *Uller Uprising* to *Space Viking*, his last major future history work.

Uller Uprising was written especially for *The Petrified Planet*, an anthology of three original short science-fiction novels (with an introduction by John D. Clark), including *The Uller Uprising* by H. Beam Piper, *The Long View* by Fletcher Pratt and *Daughters of Earth* by Judith Merril. The idea behind the series was to publish three science-fiction short novels around a common theme. The resulting books were published by Twayne Books and were to called Twayne Triplets, being they were based the joint efforts of a scientist and three authors. There was a strong Frederick Pohl connection since he represented both Piper and Judith Merril, his then wife.

The scientist involved in the project was John D. Clark, a chemist and rocket fuel developer, former science fiction author and fan. He was a former college roommate with L. Sprague de Camp and was instrumental in convincing de Camp to write full time. He was also close friends with another of Piper's friends, Fletcher Pratt. Clark was also instrumental in the Conan revival and later introduced de Camp to Fletcher Pratt and other influential New York SF writers such as John W. Campbell, Henry Kuttner, Jack Williamson and H. Beam Piper.

Science fiction was still considered a niche market in the early 1950s and the only SF books appearing in hardcover were from small publishers (usually founded by fans) such as Gnome Press, Shasta Publishers and Arkham House. All three of the Twayne stories were based on a science-fact introduction written by John D. Clark.

Two versions of the *Uller Uprising* appeared in print. Since both advances, from Twayne and *Space* magazine, arrived on the February 26th, 1953, it appears to have been a combined sale. Interestingly enough, the Twayne Triplets' version—which was the longer piece—was published in 1952, while the edited and shorter version of *Uller Uprising* was published in the February and March issues of *Space* magazine in 1953. This is a bit unusual as typically an author sells the first serial rights to a magazine which publishes the story first. Still, during the early fifties, very few science fiction novels were published except by small specialty publishers like Twayne, which catered to the fanatical SF fans who pretty much bought everything that was published as science fiction.

Unfortunately, *The Petrified Planet* did not sell well; Twayne Books only published one more triplet, a fantasy trio titled *Witches Three*. A third science-fiction book was planned in 1953. Again, a scientist would create the world and the book would contain three novellas by Isaac Asimov, Poul Anderson and James Blish. Asimov finished a story entitled "Sucker Bait," while Poul Anderson did one titled "Question and Answer." James Blish never completed his story and the project was stalled. According to the *Wonder Timeline: SF & F Retrospective* a fourth Twayne volume was planned in 1953 containing the following stories "Get Out of My Sky" by James Blish, "Second Landing" by Murray Leinster and *First Cycle* by H. Beam Piper. Piper wrote his short novel, but after the Twayne Triplets publishing venture went under his agent was unable to resell it.

First Cycle was later discovered among Piper's surviving files by Jim Baen when he purchased the Piper literary estate for Ace Books. It was a complete work, but derivative and flawed in its execution. The premise is about a solar system with twin planets, Hetaira and Thalassa, where one world got all the water resources and the other had a very limited supply. Despite its short length, *First Cycle* chronicles the two planets' development and their different societies (with a political background roughly based on the American/Soviet Cold War) and the conflicts that result from this imbalance of resources and the prejudices between the two races.

A Federation spaceship frames the story and places it within the Terro-Human Future History, but many readers and critics see it as a deeply flawed work. Ace hired Michael Kurland to rewrite it. He made some minor changes and additions, but for the most part they are hardly noticeable when compared to the original manuscript (which resides in the Pennsylvania State University: H. Beam Piper, Special Collections).

The majority of Piper's writings (mostly short stories) were unpublished; there were many of them, but only two works, *First Cycle* and "When in the Course…," have turned up and been published since Piper's death. Both works have serious problems which may help explain why Piper had such a difficult time getting published and selling his work. Other than "When in the Course…" (circa 1960), most of them were early works. Piper sold most of his later science-fiction stories; although, after *Murder in the Gunroom*, Piper was never able to sell any of the many mystery novels and short stories he had written.

* * *

Piper didn't always have the best luck with agents, which was one reason Kenneth White—a man he both liked and respected—was to play such a pivotal role in Beam's life. Piper's relationship with the Frederik Pohl Literary Agency came to an end around 1951, as indicated by the letter below. At this time, Fredrick Pohl was having troubles with his third wife, Judith Merril. They divorced in 1952, but the money problems began before then. Pohl began to withhold payments to authors and H. Beam Piper was not one to take that lying down. In this 1951 letter, Piper wrote to John Campbell about the situation.

Dear John:

I've been having a bit of trouble about some money due me from my former agent, Fred Pohl. In fact, I'm having trouble finding out just how much money he owes me. It occurred to me that you might be able to help me check on one minor item.

I notice that your Who Goes There? appears, under the title <u>Wer Da?</u> in the Karl Rauch anthology ÜBERWINDUNG VON RAUM UND ZEIT, along with my Time and Time Again (Zeit und Wieder Zeit). Did you ever get any money from Karl Rauch for that, and if so, how much? Pohl never paid me a goddamned cent—exchange difficulties he said. I realize that this is a very small item, but I want to check up on everything, no matter how small. If you got paid, that blows the exchange difficulties story.

H. Beam Piper

On July 21st, 1951, Campbell fired back:

Dear Piper,

My friend, I had trouble with Fred Pohl years before you did. You are indeed having exchange difficulties with him: I know enough of the story of the Pohl Agency to understand that. But in the case of the German translation, I think you're not out much: the German public wasn't as ripe for science fiction as Gotthard Guther thought they were.

But I can't help you on the <u>Wer Da?</u> problem. I have my difficulties, too, you see—and my difficulty is that Shasta Publishers handled "Who Goes There?" They may be somewhat better than the Fred Pohl's agency, but believe me, not much. I haven't had an accounting from them in nearly two years; Korshak sold pocket book rights to "Who Goes There?" despite the fact that he didn't have a right to, and then neglected to inform me that he had done so—particularly, he neglected to send me any of the $1500 proceeds that he owed me.

> *You think I know what royalties Karl Rauch paid? Hell, I wasn't even informed that Dell had paid $1500!*
>
> *Regards, John W. Campbell, Jr.*

As these letters indicate, it was one thing to sell a story in the 1950s, but another to actually collect payment for it. Another reason why John W. Campbell was such an important figure in the field, since he not only paid upon acceptance, but he paid the highest rates.

Due to earlier stories that Pohl had sent out for submission, it was not a clean break-up and Pohl continued to sell Piper's stories as late as 1959, when "Hunter Patrol" (a collaboration with J.J. McGuire) was finally published. Interestingly enough, this story was never listed in Piper's Story Log.

Frederik Pohl has this to say in "The Way the Future Blogs:" "That happy state [working as Piper's agent—jfc] continued for some time, and then I closed the literary agency down and plunged into the line of work God (or Somebody) had obviously intended for me all along, the telling of stories. I saw less of a lot of writers who had been clients, especially out-of-towners like Beam.

"Stories floated in from Western Pennsylvania, first astoundingly that he had quit his job. That was a little worrying, in the case of a life-long old railroad man like Beam, but it indicated good news. I had fixed him up with a new agent, my old friend (and one time boss at Popular Publications) Rogers Terrill. I was glad to see that things were working out for both of them...."

Pohl's memory may have been cloudy, or Rogers Terrill didn't work out, because Piper's next agent was Harry Altshuler, whom he mentions visiting with Betty in the 1955 diary. Science-fiction writer and historical novelist, Michael Shaara, who was also represented by the Fred Pohl Literary Agency from 1952 to 1953, also went with the Harry Altshuler Agency in 1953. That didn't work out so well either, because Piper replaced him in 1956 with Kenneth White.

CHAPTER FIFTEEN

The Collaborators

On May 10th, 2001, John McGuire, Jr. and I talked on the phone for several hours about his father and H. Beam Piper. John is two years older than his sister Terry and was more aware of what was going on in the McGuire household. He also spent a lot of time over at Piper's apartment in the gunroom, where Piper did most of his writing and kept his weapons.

It was a fascinating conversation about Piper, his father and the "Unholy Four" as they called themselves! I got a chill up and down my spine when John Jr. mentioned the "Unholy Four," as it brought back memories of the "The Unholy Trinity"— Piper, Ferd Coleman and Ted Ranck. The "Unholy Four" consisted of H. Beam Piper, John McGuire, Sam Parks (a friend and prescription drug salesman) and Dr. Jack Strassman.

"These four men were bigger than life. There was an air of mystery about them—I was in awe of them," John told me. "They lived large, talked large and kept their word. They detested those who blabbed before Joseph McCarthy's House Un-American Activities Committee—to a man they were with Dashiell Hammett. They were all very well read and connoisseurs of everything—boxing, vintage weapons, politics, literature. They looked, acted and drank like film stars—I felt privileged as a boy to be in their company. The four of them loved life and didn't try to blend in.

"Beam reminded me of Sherlock Holmes, his incisive intelligence, deductive reasoning and decisive mannerisms. Beam was the low-key member of the 'Unholy Four,' but everyone listened when he spoke; he was like a hero from the 1930's movies, very witty, picked and chose his moments carefully—a great showman. I had a lot of great times with Beam; he absolutely molded our character as children.

"They all loved boxing, especially Beam. The Unholy Four used to come to our house to watch the fights on our TV. There was always lots of drinking, and then talking and autopsies of the fights.

"I met Fletcher Pratt, too. My mother used to let me go with my father when he went to Beam's apartment; she trusted Beam and saw me as father's chaperone. They were all in the gunroom drinking and telling tall tales, Beam, Fletcher Pratt, my father and Sam Parks, who was a big man, taller than Beam, a hulking Viking, but bald.

"Beam had a display case, larger than the average windowsill, where he kept some of his weapons. Parks and Pratt were fooling around, suddenly words were said—they both yanked out swords and started swinging. They weren't paying much attention to us bystanders and suddenly steel was clanging.

"Beam grabbed me and pushed me under the table, while my father picked up the brandy bottle, as Parks and Pratt crossed swords right in the gunroom—lots of slashing steel and war cries. It was a miracle no one got hurt and afterwards everyone was laughing so hard they were teary-eyed.

"All these men, but Beam, had pasts—hard pasts, dealing with death and destruction. Parks was a World War II veteran and drug drummer, the doctor dealt with death every day and my father was a highly decorated World War II veteran; he used to work for Wild Bill Donovan. One of his jobs was to rob German banks behind enemy lines—very dangerous and his 'work' left some bad scars.

"I think the only thing Beam regretted was that he didn't have his own dark past. These men had done the things Beam only wrote about—saving lives, dodging death, shooting guns at real people and taking lives. He loved to draw them out and hear their stories. I got a hell of an education from those gunroom conversations."

In 1954 the Piper/McGuire team published their second story, *The Return*, a Sherlock Holmes pastiche of sorts. It's one of the two stories not listed in Piper's Story Log so there is no proof of when it was written, probably in 1953. The story was later expanded for its appearance in *The Science Fictional Sherlock Holmes* hardcover book in 1960. The story takes place two hundred years after a nuclear war devastated the world. Finally, scouts from Ft. Ridgeway (in what had once been Arizona) are advanced enough to search out other functioning communities. On their way to Pittsburgh to dig up a lost cache of microfilmed books, the expedition encounters what appears to be a civilized community. The inhabitants are the survivors of a long lost platoon and have managed to retain much of their organization and civilization; however, the "Toon," as they call themselves, began to believe that the expedition leader is either their long-awaited god or his adversary.

"The Return" was one of the team's best works and was snapped up by John W. Campbell and published in the January 1954 issue of *Astounding Science Fiction*.

Piper's only solo sale in 1954 was a new Paratime novella, "Time Crime," which his new agent sold to Campbell on August 13th, 1954. This was Piper's longest Paratime story to date and first appeared in the *Astounding Science Fiction* in the February and March issues.

* * *

H. Beam Piper was a long-time mystery buff and was always unhappy that he was unable to sell any other stories to the mystery market. In 1954, he wrote the first of two sequels to *Murder in the Gunroom*—"Murder at the Conference." Unfortunately, he was never able to sell it. Years later, he wrote another sequel, "Murder Frozen Over." Mike Knerr, his friend and protégé, thought that Piper's inability to sell his sequel to the Jefferson Davis Rand novel, *Murder in the Gunroom*, was among his greatest literary disappointments.

As Mike Knerr pointed out, "Here was Beam Piper writing drawing room mysteries, when all the New York publishers were looking for hard-boiled mysteries—Mike Hammer, stories featuring that kind of anti-hero. Even with his mysteries, Beam was out of step and out of time. He really did want to be a successful mystery author—it was more respectable."

Despite his deepest wishes, neither the mystery field, nor his other love, the historical novel, were the genres upon which Beam was destined to make his mark. Science fiction became his bread and butter and he was able to adapt his historical adventure style to the young field. Whatever he wrote, Beam put a lot of himself into his work, but mostly his hard-eyed historical view of the world based on extensive reading and an eye for detail.

Mike Knerr noted: "A craftsman in the science fiction field of writing, his primary love was history, a subject in which he was an exceptional scholar. While he totally enjoyed science fiction, his secret yearning was to write historical novel. Beam's knowledge of history usually influenced his science fiction tales. He was firmly convinced that the events of the past were cyclic and would become current events in the future, given a proper set of circumstances. Hardly a Pollyanna, Beam doubted that mankind had become more intelligent over the ages—just technologically more capable of destroying the race with greater efficiency."

In editor John W. Campbell, Piper found a kindred spirit; plus, an editor who liked, sometimes even loved, his writing and wrote him detailed letters on how to improve or strengthen—as determined by Campbell, of course—those stories. And, in a few cases, ideas for more stories in "that future history of yours."

Despite his professional status and growing acclaim, H. Beam Piper had just as much trouble generating good story ideas and finishing them in the 1950s as he did in the 1920s and 1930s, as detailed in the Piper/Coleman letters. Mike Knerr tells us, "While Beam wasn't getting rich at the machine, he was establishing himself as an up and coming writer on the science fiction scene. He was writing in longhand during his shifts at the car shops and on his off hours adapted it to typing paper. The 1955 diary, as are the others, is poignant with frustration. 'The whole day was about as total a loss as it could be. Did get the equivalent of about 6-7 typescript done this evening at work.' And again: 'Working on story in evening. Typed three rather shaky pages, and doodled on outlining ahead. Story's in a hell of a mess.'" On March 6th, Piper wrote: "Started work on 'The Young Immortals,' again—The damned thing is in a hopeless mess—will have to start the final draft from what I have and worm out the ending from that."

The creation of stories is seldom easy for any writer, and Piper struggled far more than most. Piper never had a problem "writing" a story once he knew where it was going; his biggest problem was coming up with good story ideas and workable plots. However, even after considerable success, the writing and plotting never got any easier for Piper. The diaries that record the last nine years of his life are filled with all the troubles he experienced in trying to write and come up with salable story ideas.

CHAPTER SIXTEEN

On Writing

In 1962 Bill Bowers and his friend Bill Mallardi joined together to create a new fanzine they named "Double: Bill." The new fanzine was the usual mixture of fan speculation and in-group humor mixed with serious examinations of science fiction, the field they loved. In 1962 they came up with the "Double: Bill Symposium," in which they interviewed some 94 writers and editors—among them the biggest names in science fiction. The idea behind the Symposium was that each of the writers and editors would answer questions about writing and the science fiction field. For an accomplishment of this size, it took them almost a decade to assemble material (remember these were unpaid submissions) from all the writers, which include everyone from Isaac Asimov to Roger Zelazny, a veritable Who's Who of the field. The only major author of this era the "Double: Bill Symposium" doesn't include is Robert A. Heinlein, but the rest of the guild is there, including Arthur C. Clarke, Philip K. Dick and Harlan Ellison.

Only one issue of this unique fanzine was ever published, and it came out in 1969. H. Beam Piper rarely discussed his writing techniques, and certainly not in person. While he might have discussed such things at writers conclaves, like the Bread Loaf Writers' Conference, he otherwise kept his opinions to himself. In the early sixties, Piper was contacted by Bill Bowers and Bill Mallardi about answering some questions regarding writing for the "The Double: Bill Symposium." He always had a soft spot for fans and, if possible, acceded to their reasonable requests. Once he learned about the other celebrated authors who were participating, it probably made it easier to fill out the questionnaire.

These questions were answered about a year before Piper's death, and are his last recorded words on the subject of writing.

Here are the eleven questions and Piper's replies:

1. **For what reason or reasons do you write Science Fiction in preference to other classes of literature?**

H. Beam Piper: In my 'teens, which would be the early '20's, I decided that what I really wanted to do was write; I wasn't quite sure what, but I was going to write something. About the same time, I became aware of science fiction, such as it was then, mostly H.G. Wells, and fantasy, Bram Stoker, H. Rider Haggard, and then I began reading the newer science (more or less) fiction—Burroughs, Merritt, Ralph Milne Farley, Ray Cummings, *et al.* This was the Neolithic, or Hugo Gernsback Period of science fiction, and by this time I was a real 200-proof fan.

This first enthusiasm waned slightly after a while. I got interested in history and historical fiction, and for some time read little else in the way of fiction, and every historical novel I read started me reading up on the history of the period involved. I wanted to know who this guy Richelieu was and why D'Artagnan & Co. had such a down on him. Then the Prohibition period was in full swing, and I became interested in Chicago gangsters for a while. All the time, I was scribbling stories, few of which ever got finished, thank God! And gradually, I found myself returning to my first love, science fiction.

Well, along the line somewhere I bought a second-hand typewriter and for years I squandered my money on paper, ribbons and two-way postage on manuscripts, and I sent stuff to everything from *American Boy* to the *American Mercury*, and finally, lo and behold, instead of a returned manuscript, I got a check from *Astounding*. And then I began getting more checks instead of bounces, all for science fiction stories.

So I found that science fiction was easier to write and easier to sell, and it was simply a matter of knowing what I was best at and doing it. For the last few years, in between science fiction stories, I've been tinkering with a historical novel, and to some extent I am applying science fiction methods to it. After all, the influence of the invention of gunpowder and the development of the arquebus on the politics and warfare of the Sixteenth Century is just as much a science fiction theme as the development of the spaceship on Twenty-Sixth Century society.

2. **What do you consider the *raison d'être*, the chief value of science fiction?**

H. Beam Piper: The same *raison d'être* of any other form of fiction, the entertainment of the reader. The term entertainment labels any activity for pleasure rather than necessity. It covers everything people do because it's fun. Science fiction entertains the type of reader who enjoys speculation on different hypothetical, philosophical, scientific, sociological, political, military, economic, technological etc. possibilities. This type of reader is not inferior or superior to others, but he is *different*.

3. **What is your appraisal of the relationship of science fiction to the 'Mainstream' of Literature?**

H. Beam Piper: I deplore this term 'mainstream.' It is currently used, in fiction, to label novels, etc., of psychological characterization, and nothing else. As stated above [question #2], difference does not imply superiority or inferiority, but only difference. However, a certain clique of critics, pretending to intellectual superiority (Orville Prescott will do as a specimen), prefer fiction of this genre and refuse to give works of any other kind serious consideration. It might be noted that most of this critical clique are themselves non-scientific if not actually anti-scientific in orientation. It might also be noted that most of the characters delineated in such fiction are immature, semantically disoriented, bewildered, complex-ridden, unhappy and often neurotic if not psychotic. (I do not claim this as an original discovery: Reginald Bretnor pointed it out ten years ago.) It might also be noted the 'mainstream' writers who experiment with science fiction themes usually butcher them atrociously.

4. **Do you believe that participating in fandom, fanzines and conventions would be a benefit or a hindrance to would-be-writers?**

H. Beam Piper: If nothing else, fan-activities give the would-be writer an opportunity of learning what his potential customers want and of familiarizing himself with the medium in which he intends to work. I have heard it argued that fandom tends to make a sort of cult of science fiction, restricted to a narrow circle of the initiated. This I seriously question. The people who contribute to fanzines and attend conventions are merely the most articulate of the class enumerated in [Question #2], and I have never attended a convention at which I did not hear all sorts of opinions, often quite contradictory, vigorously maintained.

5. **What source or sources would you recommend to beginning writers as having been, in your experience, the most productive of ideas for science fiction?**

H. Beam Piper: Now, I won't attempt to answer this. Ideas for science fiction stories like ideas for anything else, are where you find them, usually in the most unlikely places. The only reliable source is a mind which asks itself questions like, "What would happen if—?" or, "Now what would this develop into, in a few centuries? Or, "How could so-and-so happen?" Anything at all, can trigger such a question, in your field if not in mine.

6. **Do you feel that a beginning science fiction writer should concentrate on short stories?**

xx [Not answered, or edited out.—jfc]

7. **What suggestion can you offer to the beginning writer concerning the development of 'realistic' characters and writing effective dialogue?**

H. Beam Piper: Know your characters intimately. Plan them just as carefully as you plan the action of the story, and let them develop in your first draft, and by the time you are ready to start on the final draft know their background, past life, education, experience, etc., and understand how they will react to any situation.

This, of course, is most important with the means-of-perception character, the 'viewpoint' character as the old technique writers called him, through whom the reader experiences the story, because not only what he experiences but his reactions and attitudes will be a part of the narrative. You don't include the thoughts, as such, of other characters, but you have to make their overt behavior *plausible and consistent.*

And don't break means of perception. Switch it from one character to another in different scenes if you can't get the story across with a single means of perception, but never change means of perception in a single scene or action-sequence.

Name your means of perception character in the first paragraph, if possible, and don't name him thereafter unless someone addressed him by name, or something like that. You're giving his thoughts along with his experiences and actions. You don't think of yourself by name; not often, anyhow.

In dialogue, know your character, think how he would express himself. Everybody has individualities of speech; make use of that, but don't overdo it. (Don't overdo anything, of course.) Dialogue, of course, is people talking; they talk to convey information (or misinformation) to one another. In a story, dialogue can also be used to convey information to the reader. This, of course, can be overdone, too. I recall a movie, *The Iron Curtain*, I believe, in which two Communist spies in American went into a five minute dialogue about basic Communist doctrine and Soviet policy, a terrible false note, because they were fundamentals to which they both subscribed, and would have no business to discuss with each other.

Just have your characters do and say what you think people of their sort would do and say, under the circumstances.

8. **Do you believe that an effective novel requires a message or moral? Please comment?**

H. Beam Piper: Absolutely not. If kept within decent limits, and not advanced with any Hyde Park soapboxary [sic], a 'message' or 'moral' doesn't do any particular harm. It is not, however, the business of an author of fiction to improve or inspire or educate his reader, or to save the world from fascism, communism, racism, capitalism, socialism, or anything else. As stated above, his main objective is to purvey entertainment of the sort his reader wants. If he has done this, by writing interestingly about interesting people, human or otherwise, doing interesting things, he has discharged his duty and earned his check.

9. **To what extent do you think it possible to detect a writer's viewpoints as to politics, religion or moral problems through examination of his stories?**

H. Beam Piper: To a very large extent. The story comes out of the author's mind; it will, inescapably, drag at least some of the author's attitudes out after it. This will be most evident in authors who are most careful to cling to their means-of-perception. They will be much more likely to endow their means-of-perception character with their own attitudes than take the trouble to adapt themselves to his. Considering the one author about whom I am uniquely qualified to speak, I question if any reader of H. Beam Piper will long labor under the misunderstanding that he is a pious Christian, a left-wing liberal, a Gandhian pacifist, or a teetotaler. Although he really tries to avoid it, there are times when I suspect him of climbing onto a soapbox under the Marble Arch himself.

10. During your formative writings, what one author influenced you the most? What other factors such as background, education, etc. were important influences?

H. Beam Piper: "My formative writings go back a long time, and one tends to forget. I am sure, however, that their name is legion. In the early days, as soon as I'd discover a new favorite, I'd decide that I was going to write like him. I was going to write like James Branch Cabell, which would have taken a lot of doing. Before that, I was going to write like Rafael Sabatini, and like Talbot Mundy, and like Rider Haggard, and even, God help us all, like Edgar Rice Burroughs. I never wanted to write like H.G. Wells; he spent entirely too much of his time on a soapbox. Eventually I decided to write like H. Beam Piper, only a little better. I am still trying.

As my stories all have a political and social slant instead of a physical-science slant, I think the one author who influenced me most was Nicco Machiavelli, with H.L. Mencken placing and Karl von Clausewitz showing.

11. What do you consider the greatest weakness of science fiction today?

H. Beam Piper: Not enough people read it, and there doesn't seem to be much of anything to do about it. I remember, years ago, Fletcher Pratt was bemoaning this situation and saying that we must enlarge our readership. I said then that it couldn't be done, and I still think so. It's like the attempt of Charles VII of France to create a French archery to compete with the English long bowman. He found he couldn't grab a lot of peasants out of the fields, give them bows, expect them to stand up to the English, who trained an archer by starting with his grandfather. We wouldn't have to go back quite that far to make science fiction readers, but the type of inquisitive and speculative mind needed for the enjoyment of what we know as science fiction must be developed rather early, and our present school system seems to be doing little to help.

When Charles VII found that he couldn't train French long bowmen, he settled for training crossbowmen. They weren't as good on the battlefield, but they were the best he could do. What I'm afraid of is that the publishers who decide which stories will be bought and which bounced back will buy stuff suited to the mentality of a large mass readership, a readership that will accept as science fiction anything that casually mentions a spaceship or a World Government, without any confusing egghead stuff about what the planets the spaceship goes to are really like, or what a World Government would have to do.

Then we'd be back where we started, only it wouldn't be nearly as much fun. Instead of Ol' Space Ranger doubling for Hopalong Cassidy and the cattle-rustlers all in the space-pirate business, we'd have psychological stories with robot psychologists, and Boy meets Girl—or maybe Boy meets Boy, to judge from some of the recent mainstream stuff—on a spaceship to Mars instead of a Caribbean cruise, and sagas of ad-agencies, in which thought transmitters take the place of TV.

And the only real science fiction writing left will be in the fanzines.

I am almost sixty now. It gives me the most inexpressible pleasure to reflect that by the time this has happened, I shall be dead.

PART THREE

Big Changes

CHAPTER SEVENTEEN

The Lovebirds

In his early fifties, H. Beam Piper finally fell in love with a woman who reciprocated those feelings, Elizabeth (Betty) Hirst, formerly of Carmel, California. Nothing is known about Betty's early life and background, except that Carmel, even in the early part of the Twentieth Century, was an expensive upper-middle class beachfront area just north of San Francisco. It's a place people usually migrate to, not move away from. Also, Betty was a divorcée, had money and traveled frequently to Europe, as part of her work. According to L. Sprague de Camp, it was Inga Pratt who played matchmaker. "On Inga Pratt's advice, he married an attractive school teacher of about his own middle age."

Mike Knerr wrote: "Beam did have other things on his mind than stories—he was in love. His lady, Betty Hirst, lived in New York where she worked for a student travel service called the Council of Student Travel. Beam used his free pass on the trains to commute to her on his days off. In the interim, he spent his off hours from work writing, listening to the *Sherlock Holmes* radio show with Sir John Gielgud in the title role and conversing with John McGuire, his collaborator on 'Lone Star Planet' and other stories."

Most of Piper's visits to Betty and his friends took place in the middle of the week. The only information in the diaries post-1955 is that she was working at the Paris office of the Council of Student Travel until 1954. Fletcher Pratt's wife Inga introduced them to each other, but there is no hard evidence as to where or when in 1954 they met. Unfortunately,

Piper burned his pre-1955 diaries in a bonfire as soon as he began to have serious feelings for Betty. He told Mike Knerr that he burned them to cover his tracks, that is, the other women in his life—mostly bar pick-ups and prostitutes, one of the reasons he was later so worried about the state-required Wasserman test for syphilis. Fortunately, he never got around to destroying his post-1955 diaries.

In the novel, *Little Fuzzy*, Jack Holloway, the protagonist in his books most reminiscent of Piper, keeps a diary just like Piper: "…then went to the kitchen, poured himself a drink and brought it in to the big table, where he lit his pipe and began writing up his diary for the day." I'm convinced this is exactly how Piper wrote in his own diaries right down to the drink and pipe smoking ritual.

Piper's surviving diaries begin on January 1st, 1955. There is little mention of Betty until January 17th when he wrote: "A nice long letter from Betty, how she just read 'Last Enemy.' Science fiction seems to be a fascinating new world for her." "Last Enemy" was published in the August 1950 issue of *Astounding Science Fiction* so it had been out for a few years. If Betty is just now reading Piper's stories and getting introduced to science fiction, I doubt if at this time they had known each other for more than a few months. Her reading of his stories was part of the 'getting to know you' phase of a relationship. The next story the diary mentions that she's reading was a more current yarn, "Time Crime," which was serialized in the February and March 1955 issues of *Astounding*.

"Time Crime" was the last of the Paratime stories (other than the Lord Kalvan stories) that feature Verkan Vall as the protagonist. It's a rip-roaring yarn about a secret cabal of Home Time Line criminals who call themselves the Wizard Traders and engage in outtime slavery and other nefarious deeds. They have intertwined their tentacles throughout most of the Home Time Line institutions and pose a great danger not only to out-timers but First Level civilization as well. When the Paratime Police get word of their goings on, Verkan Vall steps into the fray and tries to locate them among the uncountable number of time-lines where they could be hiding. It is Piper's deepest exploration of the Home Time Line culture and he shows it from top to bottom, warts and all. It many ways "Time

Crime" reads like an unfinished novel, stopping with only the first two-thirds of the story done. I was always surprised that it was never snapped up by Ace Books for one of their Ace Doubles, like "Null ABC" (retitled *Crisis in 2140*).

In a January 27th entry, Piper reveals something of his growing romantic feelings for Betty as well as his fear of involvement. "Up 0900. Working on story A.M. Started a letter to Betty, tore it up. I'm beginning to be afraid that we're beginning to become emotionally involved with each other beyond the safety-point."

Only making around $50.00 per week at the Pennsy, according to Mike Knerr, Piper was already experiencing financial difficulties with his bi-city romance. His Strategic Reserve was his savings account, which he was beginning to hit fairly regularly. Piper, who was still living with his mother, was not only traveling to New York once a week, which was oftentimes free since he got occasional free railroad passes at work. However, he and Betty were eating out a lot, often at expensive nightspots like the Stork Club.

On February 7th, he wrote. "Up town shopping P.M. Bought a valentine, an amusing thing with a couple of affectionate cats." This romantic Piper, buying 'cute' valentines is so completely at odds with our cynical young bachelor of "The Early Letters" that it's somewhat disconcerting. He's beginning to act like a teenager in love. Piper's infatuation with Betty is becoming a raging romance. Three days later he writes, "Letter from Betty. Now she's three letters up on me; will have to get one off to her."

Mike Knerr wrote, "In early February of 1955 there lurked not a wisp of storm clouds in the blue sky of their romance. Marriage was just around the corner and Beam was as giddy as a schoolboy, his feet usually about six inches off the pavement."

"Another of Betty's lovely letters," Piper wrote in his diary. "How I hope things work out for us all right and nothing gets in our way!"

He was wallowing in a romantic mist and his writing, of course, suffered accordingly. In the hours he had free from his job at the car shops he would hammer out a few pages on "The Young Immortals;" the next day he would tear them up and start over. He couldn't sit still. He took walks, ate dinner at the Penn Alto or the Dutch Kitchen, or went over to John and Anne McGuire's house to watch the fights.

The one thing that is certain: Piper didn't write a salable story the entire year of 1955. Nor did he receive any writing income, other than a bonus from Campbell (1 cent a word) for the first part of "Time Crime." Fortunately, he was still working for the Pennsy, although change was in the wind as the railroad shops across the nation closed as the age of the steam-engine locomotive came to an end. All the new locomotive engines were now running on diesel fuel and made in Detroit, not in Altoona, Pennsylvania. The Pennsy RR did not change with the times and the railroad town of Altoona was about to be turned upside down.

As Mike Knerr noted: "Even with the prospect of a rosy future before him the Piper disgust of stupidity rose glowingly to the fore. He drew money from his bank account in preparation for 'the Federal shakedown,' as he called the IRS, and 'Find that I only owed Public Enemy #1 the sum of $16.62.'"

Interestingly, Piper had still not introduced Betty to his mother. On Saturday, February 19th, 1955, she comes for a visit. "It [train] got in at 1725, Betty on board, and we went to the Dutch Kitchen for dinner, stayed there for a while, and to the Penn Alto for a Katinka, one of Piper's signature vodka cocktails. *Betty likes Katinkas.* Saw her to the train and then home at 2110. Hydra meeting on 24th…so we'll see each other again soon." Here Betty was in Altoona—for the first time—and he never introduced her to his mother.

True, it might have been a shock to his ninety-year old mother, but it's surprising that Betty didn't make more of a fuss to meet the reclusive Mrs. Piper. Piper must have spun a fanciful tale to get out of this jam. Perhaps he was protecting his mother from the shock learning that her fifty-year-old bachelor son was in a serious relationship.

He met up with Betty later in the week, visited with friends and then went out to dinner. Then to Brooklyn to visit a friend of Betty's, also named Betty. "Stabbed myself in finger very painfully while cracking ice with a big kitchen-fork."

The next day Piper had breakfast at the hotel, took a walk up 5th

Avenue and had lunch at the Press Box with *Astounding* editor, John Campbell. "Got away from him at 1600, had to run like hell to change shirts and shave, to keep date with Betty. Mad rush down town by cab, the driver breaking every law of God, man, and the City of New York, and landing me at 179 Broadway at exactly 1700. A drink with my dearest at a Childs' [Restaurant], then up town for dinner at St. Dennis and then up 5th Avenue and to Fletcher Pratt's for a Hydra Meeting—very jolly affair, lasted until 2400."

March 3rd is the first time the word "marriage" comes up. "Another letter from Betty. She has the same idea I have—let's get married now. The only thing I'm afraid of is that I may fail Wassermann-Test positive."

The next day: "To Altoona Hospital to get a Wassermann; couldn't. Have to have a request from a physician—Goddamned bureaucratic stupidity!" For a committed bachelor, it's surprising how fast Piper gets in over his head. Obviously, the two lovers have been making plans that aren't reported in the diary.

Behind the scenes, already straining their unraveling relationship, Piper's friend and collaborator, John McGuire and his wife, Anne, were trying to talk him out of his marriage plans. John Jr. related, "My parents were skating on thin ice the moment they expressed their concerns about the marriage. They thought Beam was acting out of character and didn't trust Betty's motives. Beam, when it came to relationships, was an innocent. They had no idea of the depth of his feeling for Betty or they would have kept quiet."

On March 11th: "Up at noon. Letter from Betty, with enclosure re New York marriage license procedures. My God, if anybody had told me, a year ago, that I would be rushing into wedlock, I'd have told him to get back in his padded cell before the doctors missed him!" Here is further corroboration that Piper didn't meet Betty until sometime in 1954.

On the 17th, Piper noted, "Her mother is coming to New York? Without saying when. Must be troubled about the latter." Next day two more letters from Betty. "I still don't know what the trouble is, or when her mother is coming to New York. I wish I dared to telephone her from here." He has still not told his mother about his impending marriage or fiancée. On Saturday, "A letter—very short one, this time—from Betty. Nothing about the crisis, which may have been a mare's nest."

What's surprising is how fast this romance unfolds. Piper goes straight from wondering if he's growing too emotionally involved, to making marriage plans. It's very likely that Betty was the one making the plans; she'd been married before. There were no children.

Betty was obviously romantically attracted to H. Beam Piper the man; he had no money, although with his custom suits and courtly ways he may have initially given her that impression. Once Betty learned that he worked as night watchman at the Juniata car yards and lived at home with his mother—so much for any fantasies about wealth or family position. It had to be a love match and, with Beam so set in his ways and conservative, Betty had to be the dynamo behind the marriage plans.

On the 21st of March, he wrote: "Two more letters, on arrangements for Wednesday and Thursday. I'm going to have to be a lot gentler, and very patient—she isn't quite as tough-minded as I am. Up town in evening. Got proofs of pictures at Schaeffer's, and the blood test certificate at Strassman's. Wrote Betty a hasty letter in the bar at the Legion and mailed it."

Piper goes to a local photography shop to see about getting a picture of himself for Betty. "Started two letters to Betty—Isn't there anything to write about but Betty? *No, there isn't.*" He has hit the wall with his fiction writing, "The Young Immortals" completely stalled—and he doesn't care.

The next day he wrote, "Am worried like the devil about that Wassermann Test. Maybe I'm imagining symptoms. I hope so. Monday will tell." His trysts with prostitutes and bar pick-ups were coming back to haunt him. In his defense, in those puritanical times sex without marriage was difficult, and prostitution was a quasi-acceptable outlet.

But there were other benefits as well. Betty wrote that she enjoyed "Time Crime" and in March of 1955 he reported, "Over to library with autographed copy of "Murder in the Gunroom." He must have enjoyed adding one of his own to the local library. Still, Piper was having a hard time concentrating on his writing, especially as the marriage approached. On March 16th, shortly after passing the Wassermann, he wrote, "Tried to do a little writing—couldn't get concentrated on it."

Piper's agent at the time was Henry Altshuler and he wasn't selling his stories. "Letter from Harry Altshuler; optimistic about MATC ["Murder at the Conference"], but not holding my breath waiting. Tried to get some story planning done, but no soap. Hope I can get my mind on my work after Betty and I are safely married."

On the 21st of March, "Sat up till about 2100, re-reading Betty's letters, which seems to have become my chief form of literature. Can't seem to write anything but letters to Betty, either." The wedding would be on the 25th of March, but he's back home in Altoona, sans bride, and the next night he's trying to 'fix' "The Young Immortals" again.

"Slept till 1800. Breakfast and dinner in one. Cleared up my desk, and then tried to get the story back into order again. Heavy going." The next night Piper wrote, "A very bad night, cold and high winds. Home 0700, and not a drop of rum in the house. Up, 1700—another breakfast merging into dinner: Spent evening trying to get a letter out to Betty. McGuire in about 2055, just in time for the *Sherlock Holmes* broadcast—*Silver Blaze*, this time."

On Saturday, Piper's back to the beginning: "Got started on an entirely new version of 'The Young Immortals,' worked on it all late P.M. and evening." The next morning he wrote, "Slept till 1500. Working P.M. on story, got a letter off to Betty, and up town to mail it before dinner." And another evening spent listening to *Sherlock Holmes* on the radio with John McGuire, a repeat of *A Scandal in Bohemia*.

Friday, March 25th—wedding day. "Up 0500. Betty and I breakfasted at Piccadilly and started on foot for the Pratts', but decided to take the 5th Avenue bus; arrived 1005. Inga with us by cab to be our witness. A ghastly ceremony, performed by a low-county political apparatchik. Then up to the Piccadilly to get our luggage, and to Penn Station for lunch. Inga left us about 1300; at 1400, took #23 [train] home, leaving my lawful bride of three hours behind."

So it was, Piper's wedding—a low-rent comedy ceremony with a dashing bridegroom, dashing back home to mother! Betty must have truly loved him to put up with this kind of nonsense. It's apparent from his diary entries that Piper feels a little sheepish about it, but clearly not enough to do anything.

Piper doesn't see Betty the next Wednesday, the usual date of his New York trips, instead he spends the day taking his mother to Dr. Cooper's for her lower plate to be fixed. He writes a couple of letters to Betty and finally gets around to telling John McGuire that he's a married man. The next day he's reading a book, *Faithful Are the Wounds* and watching the fights that evening over at the McGuires!

On Monday, "Two letters from Betty, mostly on details about our new home at the Roger Williams, and plans for next midweek." Obviously, Piper was not happy about the separation. The next day he wrote, "Napped in evening after dinner, 1900-2100; still sleepy and feeling like hell. 2300 Juanita II. Back to work at the car yards."

Wednesday, "Caught #32 for New York, slept all the way, getting in late. Went directly on foot to the Roger Williams and was there when Betty arrived. Dinner at the apartment by Betty…called Betty's mother in California—she seemed to bear up well under the news." This is more of Piper's understatement. Although, I suspect that Betty's mother was told in advance about the wedding—unlike Harriett Piper. Later that evening they go to a MWA (Mystery Writers of America) meeting at the Press Club with a talk on legal procedures.

"Up 0700, and got breakfast while Betty was dressing (bacon & omelets). Betty off for work 0800; I dressed more leisurely, and out shopping. Bought can-opener, and electric extension cord for kitchen, and a card-table, a horribly expensive ($15.50) thing, but wonderfully well-made, for a dining-table."

That afternoon he took Betty to meet his agent, Harry Altshuler, and met Mrs. Altshuler—probably for the first time. "Home at 1830, had dinner, and to see *Teahouse of the August Moon*. Home early and to bed about midnight."

As Mike Knerr noted, "Beam had never done such a thing before, nor ever would again, and he wore his wedding ring until the day he died. Later in the evening he tried to nap, but gave it up to write a letter to

Betty. 'Isn't there anything to write about but Betty? *No, there isn't.*'

"Beam's love for Betty is apparent throughout all of his diaries, and it was glaringly obvious to me in our conversations, yet it was scarcely the kind of love most people would opt for. It is, I believe, safe to say that Betty undoubtedly found it less than to her liking. Most things, it would appear, had to go Beam's way or, like the rigid person he was, he would pick up his marbles and go home.

"In attempting to understand the relationship between Beam and Betty, and, of course, the eventual breakup, it is necessary to not only use the journals but to read between the lines. It was even more important to watch his eyes and listen to the sound of his voice when he spoke of her. In the end, one gets the strong feeling that Betty was a woman who made the mistake of marrying a man too old, too set in his ways and too uncompromising in his beliefs."

CHAPTER EIGHTEEN

The Case of the Missing Gun

Neither John McGuire nor his wife were happy with Piper's plan to marry Betty Hirst; first of all, everything about it was shrouded in secrecy. Secondly, they thought that Piper, a confirmed bachelor of fifty-one, was just too set in his ways and too much a loner to adjust to all the compromises and shared time of a committed relationship. Jack tried to tell this to Piper in early 1955, but he wasn't listening, and grew quite angry at Jack for what he considered interference in his 'personal life.'

"Piper was in love—a goner." John McGuire Jr. told me, "Father and mother warned Beam about Betty. Told him, 'he was not going down a good road.' Beam did not take it well."

The split between the two friends clearly began sometime during the previous year, in 1954. It wasn't all about Betty, either. The collaboration was not working out; certainly, they weren't selling stories any more. The stories they did have out, making the editorial rounds, were collecting rejection slips for their agent; two of them would later sell, but not for several years. Piper and McGuire were still discussing 'story ideas,' but not doing much writing. On top of that, Piper's own writing was stalled as well—his only sales for 1953 were "The Return" and the novel, *Uller Uprising*. Nineteen fifty-four was just as bad: the only story of his that sold that year was "Time Crime."

There's also an interesting anomaly in Piper's Story Log—there is no listing among the 1953 entries for "The Return," their most recent story sale which appeared in the January 1954 issue of *Astounding*. This is not a case where the title was changed by editorial direction, nor was it a minor sale.

So why wasn't there an entry for "The Return" in Piper's Sales Journal?

Piper was very meticulous about listing his sales and money earned. Was there a dispute between the two men over writing credit or the monies? I doubt it was an oversight since there's no entry on the 1960 page for the sale of the anthology rights in 1960 to *The Science-Fictional Sherlock Holmes*, either. Yet, McGuire is credited as co-author on both works. Could this have something to do with his growing animosity towards John McGuire?

As mentioned previously, McGuire's drinking was out of control. His English classes at Keith Junior High were for teenagers (many of them delinquents) with reading problems and he was under a lot of pressure at work. Some of the boys were acting out and McGuire had a short fuse. After his experiences in the OSS, it must have taken all is self-control not to resort to harsh discipline. A few smashed heads and broken limbs might have solved his discipline problems, but they would have ended his employment, as well.

The Piper/McGuire team was not selling many stories; I suspect McGuire had expected more success from his collaboration with Piper. I'm certain that Piper never informed him of the dearth of sales during his writing early years, or how long it took him to get published. To the McGuire family Piper was an internationally published author. Both Terry and John McGuire Jr. admit that their father's drinking started to accelerate at this time.

H. Beam Piper, who was an intensely private man, was certainly beginning to feel crowded by McGuire, who visited at all hours without invitation or calling ahead. On January 8th, 1955, Beam wrote: "McGuire hasn't been here, at least to my knowledge, since the lock went on the door. A chance that he came here, tried to get in, couldn't, and went away offended." He put the lock on the apartment door because of McGuire's unannounced visits, and because Piper wasn't home much, either working at the car yards or spending time in New York courting Betty and attending writers' meetings.

Four days later, Piper noted: "McGuire dropped in about 0700. Don't know whether he'd been here before—suspect he had. He was griping about the lock on door. Got a couple of pages typed after dinner. Over to McGuire's in evening to see fight on TV." Again Piper is talking about the lock he had put on the door to keep McGuire out of his apartment. In the next entry he talks about being entitled to privacy. "McGuire called in, saying that he and Sam Park were coming over. I believe that I am beginning to make it understood that I have some rights to privacy. They arrived about 2300, and I rode to Juniata [the car shops] with them. McGuire has finally taken the hint, he left here around the end of last night."

Still, Piper continued to be a regular visitor to the McGuire household. "Over to John McGuire's. His TV out of order, so he, Sam Park and I saw the fight at Nick's, and back to his place afterward for a mess of *oeufs a chervil*, cooked by Anne and I."

The next day, "Up to Keith Junior High—John, Sam (Parks) and I fired fifty rounds in the basement range, and then over to the Dutch Kitchen for a few drinks." Since John McGuire was an English teacher at Keith Junior High, they had access to the basement range any time they wanted to use it.

After a mid-week 'weekend' in New York for a Mystery Writers of America meeting and two evenings with Betty, Piper returned to Altoona on Friday. "Got in about 1650. Home, and napped after dinner until 2000, when John McGuire put in an appearance, pissed off about some trouble at school—his prize monster…again. He stayed 'till time to go to work, 2300."

On February 10th, Piper wrote: "Up town 0300. Lunch at Penn Alto; did a little shopping, and to Keith Junior High for pistol practice, all double action, on the…profile target. Sam Park disgraced both John and me by beating us roundly. Then to Dutch Kitchen for a few drinks. In evening, John and I went to Legion Home. Only five boys—I talked on Colt revolver: showing examples. To McGuire's afterward. Home by midnight." Piper is still spending considerable time, while in Altoona, with Jack and Sam Parks, but there's little talk about writing. Their last sale had been *The Return* in January of 1954, over a year ago, and *Lone Star Planet* was still making the rounds.

On the 13th he mentions, "John McGuire and Sam Parks in about 2050, in time for the Gielgud-Richardson broadcast of Sherlock Holmes, this time *The Adventures of the Dying Detective*; wonderfully well done. Had some amusement afterward with a Mobius Strip."

This diary entry from Tuesday, February 15th, signals a major turning point in their friendship: "John McGuire showed up, plastered to the walls, insisting that he is going mad, and that I call the Veterans' Hospital to come and get him. I called a cab for him and he left about 2100, presumably for that destination. He has been under considerable mental strain—probably needs hospitalization." According to John Jr., his dad's drinking was steadily growing worse as was his insomnia. He was haunted by flashbacks and a growing sense of paranoia. McGuire had taken to wandering through the house late at night.

Piper was a hard drinker; no doubt about it. So it took something pretty significant for him to suggest "hospitalization." With Piper spending all his free time in New York and having trouble concentrating on his own writing, his focus was no longer on John and their collaboration, or with the McGuire family as it had been for the past several years. His growing love for Betty was unsettling all his relationships, not only with all the McGuires, but with his mother, too.

The next day he wrote, "Worked P.M. on story, and early evening. Called Anne McGuire and found that John was at home, laid up with a cold and fever. Up to see him, and saw remarkable fight on TV—Bobo Olson vs. Tiger Jones."

McGuire starts to fade out of Piper's life after the February 15th bender. On the 21st, he noted: "John McGuire sent his son, John Jr., for some manuscript he'd left here." It sounds like McGuire was too embarrassed to show his face.

There's no mention of McGuire again in the diaries until the 26th, when Piper wrote: "John and Anne McGuire in about 2130, for a short while." He is steadily formalizing McGuire's name, an indication of their growing estrangement. Piper is freezing Jack out of his life. McGuire's helping him by clinging, drinking too much and acting out.

On March 1st Piper noted: "John McGuire in just at dinner time. Gave him some of my curried rice and chicken, whereupon he was delighted." After a long night at the yards, "home 0655. Stayed up almost 0945, writing a letter to Betty. I took it down and mailed it, and then to bed. Got up around noon, and back to bed—seemed to have forgotten what day it was. Next thing I know it was 1700, and John McGuire was in to see me slightly potted. Pissed off about trouble at school. He went away after a while."

The next day "Was writing a letter to Betty when John McGuire and Joyce B. [a friend of McGuire's—jfc] showed up—we sat in the middle room and talked and doodled until 1700. John and I stopped for drinks… and talked over a story idea for a while." They were still working on stories at this point; although, their collaboration had taken a distant second place to his trips to New York to see Betty.

A few days later, "Was going to get to work on story, didn't get around to it before dinner, wrote a letter to Betty, and then John and Anne McGuire in for a long session on a short [story] John and I have cooking (Wait till I have my secretary with me, too!)." Here he's referring to their practice of dictating their stories to Anne and having her type them up. I sense that being his secretary is not going to go over well with Betty….

On March 10th, "Sent Betty a card and over to Dutch Kitchen, where I had lunch (lobster tails, excellent) and to work on the dueling talk I was scheduled to give the Sons of the Legion this evening. When John and Joyce B. arrived. John informed me that the talk is postponed to next Thursday, at which I am not at all disappointed."

March 13th, Piper wrote: "Worked on story; got a couple of pages typed. John McGuire in about 2050. Pulled up the Iron Curtain enough to let him in on my impending marriage. Hope that wasn't a mistake.* [At the bottom of the page—'*I suspect that it was.']" There were a couple of reasons behind this: 1. Piper couldn't count on John McGuire keeping his mouth shut, especially if he'd been drinking. 2. Both John and Anne had attempted to talk him out of his upcoming nuptials. The most compelling reason was that Piper was afraid that John might accidentally tell his mother about the impending marriage. Overall, however, this lack of trust in either John's character or his sobriety doesn't bode well for the future of their writing relationship.

Things are not looking up, as this March 17th, 1955 diary entry shows, "Had photos taken at Schaeffer's (for Betty) and then over to Dutch Kitchen. McGuire and Joyce arrived a little later: the pistol lecture is again postponed. Up to the Legion for a devilish boring affair—bargain-basement style show and St. Patrick's Day party. McGuire won the first door prize, a lady's handbag. Drinking with McGuire afterward. Had to get firm with him when he tried to interfere in my personal affairs."

I suspect there's a lot hidden beneath the line "Had to get firm with him." The personal affair was no doubt Betty and their upcoming marriage. Jack was on very thin ice and appears oblivious to Piper's growing distance.

The next week is the wedding, not to be shared with the McGuires who oppose it. He doesn't see John McGuire again until Sunday, the 27th, when John comes over to listen to the radio and Sherlock Holmes. He doesn't tell McGuire about the marriage until Tuesday, "Didn't get a damn thing done, this evening. McGuire in about 2100—told him about marriage." The following evening: "To McGuire's 2100, saw a hell of a good lightweight fight; some newcomer who won (split decision) over Willie Pep, which took some doing. To Nick's, afterward, for a while. Home 0045."

On Sunday, "John McGuire in, 2100, with his son's battery radio, which was fortunate, since mine wasn't working very well." They listened to the repeat of an earlier *Sherlock Holmes* broadcast.

On Monday the 11th of April, he wrote: "Got a little work done before McGuire put in an appearance at 2100." Thanks to John's persistence, they are spending a lot of time together, but are doing very little work on their writing. Mostly, they're drinking at the Dutch Kitchen, listening to *Sherlock Holmes* on the radio or watching the fights on TV. This continues through all of April.

On Sunday, John drops by and Piper noted, "Told him about the declassification of the marriage subject." Piper doesn't provide McGuire's reaction, in fact, rarely does, but then drops a bombshell. "John says he has stopped drinking and joined Alcoholics Anonymous, which seems like an excellent idea for him." For Piper to welcome AA for a friend is surprising, he surely must have thought that John's drinking was completely out of hand. This is verified by conversations with John McGuire's oldest children, Terry and John Jr.

Piper's decision to spend more time in New York with his new wife had unexpected ramifications. This one was profound enough to sever his bonds with John McGuire for good. On Friday, May 13th, after spending Thursday and Friday morning in New York, he wrote the following: "On getting home, found that John McGuire had been here on Thursday evening; Mother let him into the gunroom and he took the 9mm Browning pistol and left a wrist-watch on my desk. Tried to call him at 1400, but his wife told me he was out."

Piper doesn't articulate his fury here, but shortly he will begin to refer to John McGuire only by his last name, later just his initials—even in conversation with Mike Knerr! According to John Jr., "Dad was the kind of guy who would give his right arm for a buddy and expected the same in return. I don't believe he really understood—or believed— Piper's rigid code of honor. Jack was much more flexible; he expected to be forgiven—he'd just 'borrowed Beam's gun.' I don't know whether he pawned it, or just went shooting. He left his watch as a sign of good faith; he meant to return it sometime. Beam wouldn't listen to him; when wronged, he was a hard man.

"They talked on the phone one night and were going to fight a duel over this situation. Sam Parks was going to be dad's second. Jack even went target practicing at the range. It was like something out of *High Noon*.

"The duel fizzled out when Dr. Strassman refused to be Beam's second."

On the 14th, Piper noted, "Packed McGuire's watch for mailing, and wrote a letter to accompany it. Am leaving no room for doubt that he is through as far as I am concerned. I wish I'd done this long ago."

The next evening he wrote, "Wrote a letter to Betty; after dinner (pork and sauerkraut) took it up and mailed it, also the letter to McGuire and his god damned wrist-watch. Spent rest of evening on 'The Young Immortals' and got out two pages."

On May 16th, "Up town in evening and withdrew $50.00 from my dwindling bank account, now down to $84.00. On my return home, about 2000, found the stuff I had left on the landing gone." I suspect this "stuff" was McGuire's objects, old jackets, pipes and such; he was over a lot—and maybe even unfinished stories. "A few minutes later, McGuire tried to talk to me on the phone, I hung up on him at once. At 2100, the doorbell rang, and I found him sitting on the doorstop, apparently quite drunk. I had to shout at him and curse at him to get him away. Finished packing lunch. Hope this is the last I hear of him."

According to Terry and John Jr. the aftermath of this breakup was horrendous for the McGuire family. The children loved Beam and because of their father, they didn't lose a friend—they lost a beloved 'Uncle.' For the older McGuire children this was the beginning of the end of their childhood; for their father, a descent into the dark depths of acute alcoholism. As John Jr. said, "Jack loved Beam! When he couldn't make a reconciliation—he was never the same."

On Friday, June 3rd, Piper wrote after arriving home from New York, "Home and napped after dinner. Sam Park in about 2100. Told him about excommunication of John J. McGuire. Park has also dropped McGuire, for approximately similar reasons." I suspect their "reasons" have to do with John's advancing alcoholism and to his growing mental instability. If things were that bad with McGuire's friends, they were absolutely hell at home for the family....

It's over two weeks before Piper hears from John McGuire again. According to Anne McGuire, John was awfully broken up about Piper freezing him out of his life. "John called in the evening; Beam just cut him off."

Piper was now watching the fights alone at the William Penn bar—"Archie Moore knocked out Bobo Olsen in 19 seconds of 3rd round."

There is no mention of McGuire in the diary until Saturday, July 30th, "Letter from Ivan Washebeugh, wondering what happened to McGuire.

Will probably have to give him details."

Piper's "excommunication" of John McGuire completely devastated the McGuire family and cut them off from most of Jack's friends. The Unholy Four were no more; there were no more TV fights with Piper in attendance, no more trips to the hotel bar with him, no more writing sessions, no more hope.... John Jr. says, "After the split, dad started drinking much more heavily, he almost stopped writing. In 1956 we moved to New Jersey where dad taught English. They were going to let him teach speed-reading; he liked that. He had a miserable time at Keith Junior High. But he started drinking and started smoking more—he developed emphysema in the early sixties from too much smoking. He began to get very frail. The years in Altoona with Beam were the best times of our childhood...."

Piper's last mention of John J. McGuire in the diaries is over a year later, on August, 9, 1956. "Met Jim Beaty.... Find that he has heard from Sam Park the story of the 9mm Browning. He also says McGuire has teaching job in New Jersey." In an interesting coincidence, the McGuires were moving to Red Hook, the same town where Fred Pohl—science fiction writer, editor and Piper's former agent lived. Pohl at this time was well known in science fiction circles as a former fan, pulp magazine editor, agent and rising star of the SF field. Pohl's *Space Merchants* is still regarded as one of the 1950's classic science-fiction stories. In the early sixties Pohl would take over the helm of *Galaxy Magazine* and as editor buy "Graveyard of Dreams" from Piper's agent, Ken White.

CHAPTER NINETEEN

Harriett Piper R.I.P.

It turns out that 1955 was the pivotal year in the life of H. Beam Piper. It was the year of his courtship and marriage to Betty, the end of his working relationship with John J. McGuire and the death of his beloved mother. If these weren't enough troubles for one year, Piper was unable to finish a single story or novel the entire year. I suspect his preoccupation with romancing Betty made it difficult for him to find the alone time he needed to plot out his stories.

As Mike Knerr noted: "True to his peculiar form of being closed mouthed about his personal life, Beam never told his mother that he was married until May 7th, 1955; although he had 'lifted the iron curtain, as he called it, to tell John McGuire of his intentions some days before the actual event. Even then he was cautious, noting in his diary that he hoped 'it was not a mistake.'

"The couple fell into a 'weekend' marriage—his wife working in New York and Piper in Altoona. On his off-days he grabbed a train into the Big City and played the role of husband. At the end of his weekend he would take the train back to Altoona and his job as guard in the car shops."

On April 11th, 1955, Piper wrote: "Letter from Betty, enclosing copy of a letter she sent her mother. I tremble to think of the edifice of mendacity that girl is erecting about me." On Wednesday, April 20th, Piper is back in New York in their apartment at the Roger Williams. "Spent all evening at home—great triumph—we completed the *Times* crossword puzzle together.... Betty gave me a lovely trench-coat, albeit a little large.

Will have to get it exchanged for sure tomorrow."

Finally the big day arrives, Saturday: "After I got back (from the market), had a couple of drinks and told mother about Betty. Quite a jolt to her, but she seemed more pleased than otherwise. Sat up talking to about 1100, and then to bed. A great relief that I can wear my ring, and that I don't need to maintain security—whole business de-classified." H. Beam Piper was fifty-one at this point, which put his mother at about ninety. I think he really believed she would take the news of his marriage badly. Later in the day, he wrote, "Wrote a letter to Betty, telling her the news of my revelation of our marriage. Will go to New York Thursday, and more frequently in the future." Having her mother visit may have been a gentle nudge in Piper's direction saying, "It's time for you to tell your mother."

He visits Betty again on the 18th of May, writing, "Home 0655; changed, and up town to get #70 for New York, by day-coach to save money. (45 minutes late out of Altoona; into New York about 1500.)... Arrived home about 1530. ...spent rest of evening working a double-crossword and just being in love."

Piper is still having trouble coming up with ideas for stories, but he's enjoying his new marriage. "After dinner (pork chops, mashed potatoes, gravy, peas); damned good; by Betty. We worked 2, repeat TWO, double crostics. And so to bed. DIDN'T HAVE TO SET THE GOD DAMNED ALARM! (For first time in our married life.)"

On Friday, as usual, he returns home to difficulties. "Mother becoming a bit difficult; however, still balking when asked to consider the question of Betty coming to Altoona." This is just for a visit since Betty is still working full time at the Council for Student Travel and not about to leave New York. After accepting the marriage, it's hard to fathom why Harriett Piper refused to meet the bride. Perhaps Harriett felt betrayed by her son, since she was the last to know of his marriage.

Next he wrote, "The news of my marriage is out at the Penn Alto; congratulations from everybody." They probably were all shocked. If anyone was a 'born' bachelor; it was Piper, even by his own admission.

On his next trip to New York, the Pipers attended the MWA meeting, and on Thursday they had their first cocktail party. "Betty arrived at

1700. By 1730, guests began arriving. Party lasted till past 2000."

By June Piper's weekly visits have become routine. Betty seemed to accept this 'bi-city' living arrangement, but there may have been trouble brewing under the surface. Piper rarely put emotional matters to paper, and when he did it's when they have come to a head, as in the McGuire fiasco. For a reputed isolate, Beam and Betty have a very active social life, visiting New York friends, like Bill and Nancy Boylan. Plus lots of dinners at New York City hot spots and various writers' gatherings, such as the Mystery Writers of America and the Hydra Club.

On June 14th, he wrote, "Another letter from Betty, written on Sunday—we don't answer each other's letters any more—we just fire them off at each other and let them cross in the mail." Another visit to Betty at the apartment and another cocktail party—very William Powell and Myrna Loy.

One of the 'problems' between Beam and Betty was that she had money. In Betty's obituary in 1990, it states that she left half a million dollars to the US Government. An interesting development, revealing there were no close relatives and that she stayed single after her divorce. Piper, on the other hand, needed money desperately most of his life; a real incongruity and certainly an issue in their marriage. Which makes Piper's unkind comments about his wife only having married him for a 'French vacation' ring with irony.

This July 11th diary entry is the first inkling of money problems: "Letter from Betty—serious crisis at Council of Student Travel, much money needed; she wanted advice on lending them some money. Called her up and advised her—I hope, rather without much conviction—to do so."

Later in the same day another trouble spot pops up, "Up town to bank money and cash check for Mother in evening. Call from Betty while I was out—she and Mother had a little talk." Piper was decidedly uncomfortable about being in the middle between the two women he loved. It must have been an interesting conversation, to say the least!

Piper was in New York on Thursday, July 21st, preparing for their trip to Bread Loaf Writers Convention. He loved going to writers' meetings, conclaves, workshops and conventions which makes sense since he had such a long road to take before getting published. "Got plane tickets, bought scrap-book for the Beam-and-Betty letters, did some miscellaneous shopping, and back to Roger Williams 1130…and up to Central Park. Visited our friends at zoo—didn't see the eland, but saw some nice monkeys and chimpanzees and one seal. Dinner at Tavern on the Green (which was Oomph!) and had our picture taken by camera girl. We're a hell of a good looking couple."

The next day back in Altoona, Piper received official notification from Bread Loaf. "We are in 'Brick' at $125.00 per capita." On the 23rd, "Letter from Betty, very happy and full of love." The following day he wrote, "Up town shopping P.M. Bought three pair of colored shorts." This is definitely a 'new' H. Beam Piper. The "Honeymoon Stage" is still in force.

"Had dinner—mostly a mixture of Heinz potato hash and rice—and then up to Central Park, stopping on the way at New York Public Library, where we looked up some 'crossword-puzzle words. Home about 2300." Next day, "Put in A.M. on "Allergy' [a new short story he was working on] and made some progress. Up town on foot—got chair for return tomorrow, bought shirt at Lunine's, lunch at Astor, and on foot downtown—bought tinned foods. Got back to work on plotting, with time out for a nap 1430-1600."

On August 4th, "At 1700, Mrs. MacGrew called from Altoona, telling me that Mother had fallen and injured, presumably fractured her knee, and is in hospital. Looks as though Bread Loaf is out the window. Phoned, got non-committal answer…. Park in evening, saw our animal friends at zoo."

The next day, "Left hotel about 0930, took #75 to Altoona. Read *Penguin Island* on the way home. Arrived Altoona 1745, and directly to hospital. Found Mother in much better spirits than I had expected. Got her comb and Kleenex at hospital cantina. Home, spent about three-quarters of an hour resting and enjoying a rum highball, and back to hospital. Mrs. McGrew took my laundry, yesterday, and paid for it—paid her— Good fences may or may not make good neighbors, but good neighbors are damn useful. Didn't get any sleep."

The next day, August 6th, Piper takes care of the household chores usually done by his Mother. "Up town about 1700, dinner at Penn Alto, and to see Mother 1900-1930." Then off to work and "Home 0700; slept till 1500. Had breakfast, wrote a letter, and up town to mail it. Had a pint of ice cream for dinner—didn't feel up to cooking anything. To see Mother at hospital in evening. Still don't know what's wrong with her or how long she will be there, or anything, and worrying like the devil about whether Betty and I can make it to Bread Loaf. Managed to get three pages of story typed."

On Monday, August 8th, "Took a short nap to 1100, and up to hospital. Talked to Dr. Hull. Mother's knee-cap is fractured, and that she will be in hospital until I return, so Betty and I will not be defrauded of our vacation and honeymoon. Back to the apartment, wrote Betty a letter giving her the news, wrote checks for rent and telephone, and up town to banks. Transferred $200.00 from Mother's account to mine to meet hospital bills. Did some shopping, and then up to hospital to see Mother. Mother has a very pleasant bed-neighbor…who talks to her and keeps her company." The next evening, "Dinner at Penn Alto. To hospital in evening to see Mother."

Piper leaves for New York on Wednesday, the 10th, "Dinner at home and up to Park, our friends the animals are feeling the cooler weather… very playful. Polar bear more comfortable and their yak (incredible) out. Sat on our bench by the lake—sky was spectacular on account of low ceiling. Light rain as we were leaving about 2100." The Pipers now have their own rituals; out to dinner, usually, a nightcap or off to the Central Park zoo. In the morning, acrostics or the crossword puzzles. With friends coming over for cocktail parties or just to visit, this is not the H. Beam Piper who used to live with his mother and wander the streets of Altoona wearing a slouch cap and black overcoat at all hours of the day or night.

On Friday, "Up at 0700. For a change, Betty got breakfast. Don't think much of idea—breakfast was wonderful, but timing unsatisfactory.… In about 1810, home, had a drink and up to hospital to see Mother, who was operated on and has leg in cast. Visited the MacGrews, had a couple of drinks with them, till 2145." He woke the next morning to "The edge of Hurricane Connie, which came up as far as Chesapeake Bay, killing at least 19 and doing $5 million damage. Completely soaked from knees down, boots full of water." Piper had to work all night at the car yards—good weather, bad weather. Very little writing was done during this period. "Up to hospital in evening to see Mother. Spent rest of evening packing lunch, straightening up a little around the apartment."

He is still planning his trip to the Bread Loaf Conference. On Sunday, he wrote, "Dinner up town at Crist's (everything else closed) which was just barely edible; and to hospital to see Mother. Spent the rest of the evening trying to think of what I have to do before I leave—" Piper spends most of Monday packing and getting ready for Bread Loaf. "…dinner at Penn Alto, and then up to see Mother; left the little radio and a lot of extra batteries with her. Home again by 2000, and continued packing."

The next day it's off to New York. He reads and finishes Sir Leonard Wooley's *Digging Up the Past* on the train. Dinner out at Stoeffer's and off to Central Park to see "our friends the animals." Afterwards, the new couple, "Walked all the way home, stopping to re-fuel at the Whaler."

On Wednesday the 17th, they take a flight out of LaGuardia to Burlington, from there a bus to Bread Loaf just in time for the opening session. A lot of time was spent with friends (Fletcher Pratt for one, who lectured on "the short story'), going to talks on different aspects of writing and lots of dining and drinking—lectures, and short story and novel clinics. Fun was had by all. On Saturday, the 20th, "Robert Frost read poetry and lectured in evening. Even found time for a square dance on the 23rd, in which Betty and I participated much against our better judgment. Good fun, but rather exhausting." The dapper Mr. Piper square dancing—that must have been a sight!

Leave it to Piper. He found a deserted stone quarry and on the 24th, "Out target shooting at the stone quarry, in the afternoon." The next day he reports on a little fracas started by their friend Fletcher Pratt who gave the evening lecture on 'Mass Media.' "A stupid Catholic woman indignant about something Pratt said about the Legion of Decency; going around denouncing him as a Communist. Out for drinks afterwards at the local tavern."

Next morning, "Betty slightly provoked at me for waking her when I came home drunk last night." That's a first. "Breakfast at the Inn—Non-Fiction Clinic Magazine article subjects. Short story clinic—a very bad homosexual opus." On the 27th, it appears Betty—who was not a writer—was growing restive. "Betty proposed that we leave Conference and go to Canada for the week and the first part of next week. We therefore cut classes for the morning, packed and said our goodbyes, at pre-lunch cocktails at Tremen and elsewhere. By taxi to Middlebury for the bus to Montreal, with an hour for dinner at Burlington."

Piper's mother's medical situation deteriorated while he was in Canada and she was in serious condition when he arrived back in Altoona in early September with a bottle of wine. "Found her looking very badly, breathing with difficulty. At about 1940, called a nurse, who became alarmed, called head nurse and an intern. Some fumbling attempts to take blood pressure. Mother was given an injection, and an oxygen tent was called for, but before it could be rigged, she died. Brought home her few effects, but left the wine I had brought." According to the Certificate of Death, Harriett Piper died on September 3rd, 1955 of bilateral thrombosis/pulmonary emboli.

At ninety-one, her death couldn't have been a great shock to Piper. Nor did he appear overly broken up at the funeral. "I thought it was going to be rough as hell, but it wasn't really bad. Hicky did a fine job on Mother, considering that the goddamned blockheads at the hospital lost her false teeth."

Mike Knerr has this to say about Harriett's death, "The death of Beam's mother upset him, although he never mentioned it in the diaries. One had to read between the lines, and know the man, to understand his true feelings. The truth surfaces in his entries, such as on September 11th: 'At 1700, started to get dinner. Baked pork chops (burned) mashed potatoes (not very good) gravy (frightful). Definitely not one of my better meals.'"

It was Betty who lifted his spirits. "Letter from Betty, full of plans for a Christmas trip to Bermuda, with which I am most heartily in accord."

While awaiting this sojourn to the world's most northern coral reefs, he busied himself with cleaning up finances and his apartment. Through it all he attempted to write, but had little success. On the weekends he, at first, horrified Betty when she discovered the tinned wild boar he had bought at Altman's, and later charmed her with how good it tasted.

Mike Knerr wrote, "By himself, in Altoona, his cooking was a disaster and he often ate out. In New York, with Betty, he became somewhat of a chef and they whiled away their time working double acrostics at home or wandering up to the Central Park Zoo to feed the animals and pull the eland's horns."

The death of his mother threw his writing into a tailspin. He couldn't focus and wasn't happy with anything. Piper was not an emotionally expressive person and usually kept his feelings bottled up.

He continued working on "Allergy," which never came together; later a short story called "Two Hours," which was also never finished. Lots of wastepaper produced, but nothing even remotely salable. September 24th, "Started to do the story over again.... Will have to get away from this sort of thing—get a story firmly in hand before starting, and then carry through to the end. I used to be able to do that. Will have to rediscipline myself."

By November, Piper was looking around for someone to blame for his lack of sales; despite his zero output for the year his agent Harry Altshuler still had a number of unsold stories, including his *Murder in the Gunroom* sequel. On November 15th, he wrote: "'Plausible Motive' back from Harry Altshuler, with a note alleging it to be un-salable, an admission Fred Pohl, for all his faults, would never have made. Have decided to get rid of Altshuler." Later in the day he did. "Wrote letter to Altshuler, firing him."

His own vacation from the car shops started on December the 12th and, while he waited, Beam busied himself around the apartment at the Roger Williams, in New York, hanging up Christmas cards and playing housefrau. His own cards to friends he usually signed by drawing a piper on an H-Beam. This year, of course, there was another piper on the H-beam.

Knerr wrote, "The weekend the Piper newlyweds spent at the Hamilton was a bit like a belated honeymoon and they both relaxed in the warm sun of the Gulf Stream. Years later, in Williamsport, Beam looked back fondly at his memories of the islands. They returned to New York and he spent the remainder of his vacation being the typical husband until he returned to the car shops on December 30th."

With all his traveling back and forth to New York City and his marriage to Betty, there seemed to be no way Piper could get a handle on his writing in 1955. Mike Knerr wrote: "…Beam doodled at writing while he and Betty made plans for the Bermuda trip on December 24th, 1955. His total story sales for the year—zero, his stories written for the year—zero. On the writing side it was a total disaster and as he went into 1956 things didn't look like they were going to improve any time soon."

"Am still worried what in hell has become of *Lone Star Planet* and 'Hunter Patrol;' a simply deafening silence about both of them," Piper noted. Along with the short story, "The Return," these were the last of the un-sold Piper/McGuire collaborations; not only did they represent dearly needed revenue, but an end to an era he'd rather forget. Knerr noted: "This sort of frustration carried over into his job. He would forget to turn in his keys, then have to take them back to the railroad office. Once he locked himself out of his apartment and had to climb over a neighbor's roof and through a kitchen window to get in."

Piper sums up the year: "This has, in spite of everything bad that happened, been a pretty wonderful year. Betty is what makes the difference. It would have been a horrible year without her."

CHAPTER TWENTY

The Dark Side

It was quite obvious that H. Beam Piper appeared to others as an eccentric individual far beyond the most distant galaxies, always mumbling inaudible comments to himself and giving one the impression that he was conversing with other worlds—and of course he was in a sense doing just that—eventually discharging a barrage of thoughts radiating from these bodies in outer space. Yet, during his earlier life, while anticipating the pursuit of novel writing—a commodity that contains a good measure of life itself—he was particularly dubious of any goings-on hereafter as proclaimed in the Holy Scriptures. I recall him once saying quite raspingly, something to the effect, "When you're DEAD, you're DEAD! There is no more—just a large black and very deep hole."

Don Coleman,
"The Early Letters"

Piper, who was known to play with the truth in regards to his own biography and life, often did the same in his writing, as Piper scholar John Anderson pointed out: "Conn Maxwell and his father Rodney 'play with the truth' [in *The Cosmic Computer*—jfc] about the existence of Merlin to their fellow Poictesmians (they say it exists when they believe it doesn't). General Travis and General Shanlee lie to the Maxwells on the same topic (they tell them it doesn't exist when they know it really does) and, at the end of the story, the Cosmic Computer itself become a liar, falsifying the truth about the breakup of the Federation to all of Terro-humanity....

"Beam mentions the Big Lie in several palaces, most notably in *Space Viking*. On Tanith, Lucas Trask lies to the Back-to-Gram and Raid-Xochitl parties [telling them] Andray Dunnan is on Marduk, when he believes he is not—because Trask wants their support to liberate Marduk, a much better course than their partisan ones. But in both, *The Cosmic Computer* and *Space Viking*, the Big Lie actually turns out to be the truth. Merlin really does exist, and Andray Dunnan really is on Marduk…

"As he has Dearest [in the short story "Dearest"] think to Colonel Hampton, 'When bigger and better lies are told, we tell them, don't we, Popsy?' That may well reflect some of Piper's own internal dialog, with Col. Hampton representing Beam himself, and Dearest representing his conscience (although I'm sure he didn't call himself 'Popsy')."

In the only known tape recording of H. Beam Piper, provided by Don Coleman, of a "meeting" of the Unholy Trinity (Piper, Ferd Coleman and Ted Ranck) in the early 1950s, Piper talks quite amusingly about putting on a lady at the train depot by giving her a number of fabrications, which all three of the men find hilarious. The tape is quite fascinating as it provides a glimpse into the 'world' of these three good friends and how they relate to each other.

Piper was quite theatrical and aware of his unconventional appearance, often times reveling in it. His Victorian dress and aura made him a notable figure at science-fiction conventions as well as in his hometown of Altoona. Fans were intimidated by him and he wasn't really close to many of the science-writers since their contact was limited by attendance at the various conventions.

He could also be very stubborn and unforgiving; once he wrote John J. McGuire out of his life there was no coming back.

"Piper habitually rejected most of the world he lived in and felt much more comfortable with the Fourteenth and Fifteenth Centuries," Mike Knerr noted, "and he was rather disenchanted with government. Politics, he felt, seemed largely a matter of blundering through a series of difficult social problems that faced a particular nation, and hoping against hope that someone would do something right. Still, he always voted, in spite of this flat statement: "What this country needs is a damned good king!"

Piper had a strong interest in both national and local politics. This started early in life and his political views are scattered through his correspondence with Ferd Coleman, especially in regards to the Herbert T. Ames, the Prohibitionist mayor of Williamsport. On August 18th, 1930, he wrote: "You deserve the Croix de Guerre, with palm, for your gallant conduct in the field against that enemy of civilization, Herbert T. Ames. I herewith confer it upon you, kissing you on both cheeks. May your shadow never grow less and may you keep it up. Your idea about dumping the signs in the river is a good one. Maybe on my next visit I will take some action on it."

As Don Coleman wrote in this November 2nd, 2003, letter: "Dad's paper was 'Advertising supplemented with news!' He would tell it the way it was, of the politicians of those days. Dad was no dummy! He'd bring out the facts and apparently the truth really teed some of those guys off! There may have been those who didn't care about receiving the *Shopper's Guide*, but at the same time, many looked forward to the political views brought forth in the publication…and all for free! As you can surmise from the 'Letters,' Piper always had an emphatic comment or two to interject about politicians—or by any other name, for that matter."

Other than the anti-alcohol crowd, Piper saved his strongest venom for the Jesus mongers. In a letter to Ferd he wrote: "This station (WFBG) is said to be in a bad way financially. Finally, I would say that it is used by the worst type of Elmer Gantries in town. One of these became so abusive during a recent political campaign that his mike was turned off and he spoke for some time without knowing it."

Mike Knerr noted: "A notation on his political attitudes lies in his entry of Sunday, January 30th, 1962, which commemorates the birth of Franklin D. Roosevelt in 1882. Beam blacked it in and wrote above it: "Day of Ill Omen." I once asked him how he reacted when FDR died, since it seemed to have convulsed the whole nation. He grinned. 'I said: Ding Dong, the wicked witch is dead!' Not being too well versed in politics, I asked him how you could tell a Democrat from a Republican. 'Oh,' he said, 'that's easy. Republicans have halos and Democrats have horns.'

"I thought, on November 22nd, 1963, that he would have something terrible to say about the Kennedy assassination so I called him and gave him the news. He didn't disappoint me. He said, 'Now that's taking your politics too damned serious.' He also thought it remarkable that an Italian Carcano rifle could shoot that well. When Jack Ruby killed Lee Harvey Oswald a few days later, Piper dourly wrote in his diary: '…to keep him from talking?'"

Piper appears to have seen himself as some sort of vigilante enforcer for the sake of his friends, as indicated by this excerpt from a March 15th, 1929, letter to Ferd: "I heard from Shoemaker today. He says that this H.T. Smith, as he signs himself, has given him no end of bother in the past with threatening and abusive letters and he seems pleased that I stepped on the fellow so promptly." It's not clear just what "stepped on the fellow" refers to, but it may indicate he gave the man a bad beating.

In a July 23th, 1929 letter, he wrote: "…I had a first-class souse and, I am informed, I was under the impression that I was the devil and was laughing at the rest of the crowd because they were all damned. A good time was had by all."

Piper was a lifelong hard drinker and booze aficionado. Whether or not he was an alcoholic is a matter of conjecture; if he hadn't crossed the line, he was certainly straddling it. There is little mention of his alcohol in his diary, when his money problems went from serious to catastrophic; regardless, alcohol was as much a part of Piper's life as gunpowder, pipe tobacco and typewriter ribbons.

Don Coleman reflects on Piper's expertise of alcoholic beverages. "Actually, when it came down to the subject of booze, Beam was a real judge of the stuff, as affirmed in 'The Early Letters.' No one around today seems to know or recall his 'rookie' year…. Truly, in the 1950s he could be considered a connoisseur; he would orate the origin of, as well as savor any type or classification of whiskey known to man…black rum continued to be his working-at-desk favorite. He also improved a concoction that proved to be a standout with the imbibing bunch, when relaxing with 'family' and friends. He called it the 'Katinka.'

"In my asking for the ingredients, Beam (would) pull his multi-colored ink pen and a small scratch pad from his inside coat pocket. (As anyone knows who is familiar with the late H. Beam Piper, he was never without paper. And this particular pen he possessed, regardless of its worth, was one of his most valued treasures—less the antiques.) In giving me the recipe, he printed four lines of instructions, each with a different color…black, blue, red and green:

> 3 parts Vodka
> 2 parts Apricot Brandy
> 1 part Grenadine
> STIR over ice…<u>DO NOT SHAKE</u>!

"This conglomeration would then be strained into a brandy snifter. For years, this 'Technicolor' recipe was a part of my wallet. I have gone through many billfolds, just as new automobiles, and somewhere along the way, this folded-up little slip of paper has passed into oblivion. But the memory of the recipe lives on.

"On one occasion, I dropped into the City Hotel lounge with Beam in downtown Williamsport, and becoming comfortable at the recently renovated bar—with the cork of his cane hanging over his forearm—he would ask for a 'Katinka.' I remember turning to him dubiously and remarking, 'This guy wouldn't know a 'Katinka' any more than he'd know what he had for supper last Tuesday!'

"'Oh HELL!' Beam burst. 'Tommy's been mixin' 'em for some time now!'"

"The year was 1957 and Beam would properly appraise the going rate of his creation 'in the vicinity of seventy-five cents' among his favorite haunts about town."

Like a lot of the writing crowd in the 1950s and 1960s, including the science fiction crew, Piper was a hard drinker, favoring Jim Beam (his signature drink) at science-fiction conventions, but at home drank Myers' Rum almost exclusively. A number of those hard drinkers later died of alcoholism, Randall Garrett and Bill Tuning come to mind, both acquaintances of Piper's. The diary shows that Piper suffered from depression—or the blue devils, his code word—and loved to imbibe—Myers' Rum when working, Bacardi for highballs, Vodka and Apricot Brandy for Katinkas, and Jim Beam whiskey. We also know he got plastered with some regularity and enjoyed a 'good drunk' now and again.

Jerry Pournelle, in those days no slouch in the drinking department, mentioned the two of them getting drunk at ChiCon, where they first met in 1962. At a Washington DC science fiction con, the two of them went out for more liquor when a mugger approached them with a knife. He turned and ran when Piper pulled the sword out of his sword-cane and flourished it menacingly.

In a few cases, Piper's binges got completely out of hand, for example. For example, John McGuire, Jr. tells a story when his father was called by the Altoona police and told that his help was needed at the Piper residence. Since Anne was not at home, John Sr. elected to take the boy with him. They rode over and found a small crowd.

"Beam had barricaded the first floor of the apartment stairway with chairs, furniture and boxes. His small brass cannon was mounted on top of the barricade. A group of policemen were trying to keep a growing crowd back and out of range of the cannon. One of the policemen who knew Beam and John told him that Beam claimed he was a Confederate officer making a last stand.

"My father arrived with me in tow.

"Beam asked, 'What are you doing here, Johnny?'

"'Tryin' to talk you down, Cap'n.'

"'What for?'

"'The War's over, Cap'n. Time to go home.'

"'It was a good fight. Damn Lee and Roundtree!'

"Eventually, my dad was able to talk him down and took Beam and his small cannon back to the apartment."

They had a few drinks and the McGuires left when Piper passed out in the writing room. He always had a lot of sympathy for the underdog and the nobility of the Confederacy won his heart. Piper's only published non-fiction piece was about the Gray Ghost, a Confederate partisan the Union could never capture.

As far as his drinking was concerned, few alcoholics will stay away from the bottle for more than a few weeks. Alcohol addiction is an obsession of the mind and an allergy of the body, and once in its grip an alcoholic will do damn near anything to get his next drink. Piper was quite aware of the pitfalls as evidenced by these comments by the protagonist, Jack Holloway—who comes closest to mirroring Piper of any of his characters—in *Little Fuzzy* after Little Fuzzy (a small furry alien) leaves Jack to find his family:

Maybe the little fellow ran into something too big for him, even with his fine new weapon—a hobthrush, or a bush-goblin, or another harpy. Or maybe he'd just gotten tired staying in one place, and had moved on.

No; he'd liked it here. He'd had fun, and been happy. He shook his head sadly. Once he, too, had lived in a pleasant place, where he'd had fun, and could have been happy if he hadn't thought there was something he'd had to do. So he had gone away, leaving grieved people behind him....

He started for the kitchen to get a drink, and checked himself. Take a drink because you pity yourself, and then the drink pities you and has a drink, and then two good drinks get together and that calls for drinks all around. No; he'd have one drink, maybe a little bigger than usual, before he went to bed.

There's another telling quote from the sequel, *Fuzzy Sapiens*, in which Victor Grego has come up with a great idea and Jack Holloway thinks: "He forgot about the drink he was going to have with Mr. Victor Grego. You had a drink when the work was done, and there was still work to do."

While low on the folding stuff, he wasn't completely broke, not like in 1964. The next day Piper received a check from Ken for "The Answer," sold to *Fantastic Universe* months before. It added $41.00 to his bank account. 'Lunch at Heylmun's, got haircut, bought diary for next year, which I hope to live to complete. Also first bottle of rum since I can't remember when.'

Piper is now on the wagon, not because of his drinking problem but because of financial difficulties. This will plague him from now (1959) up until the end. Upon cleaning out Piper's apartment after his suicide, Mike Knerr said he ran across an entire hall closet filled with empty bottles of Myers' Rum. Mike, another hard drinker, said it took him back. He admitted. "Yes, we used to toss 'em back in those days when we'd hit the local joints in Altoona. I didn't think anything of it, though. Hell, I like a good drink or two myself."

Was Piper an alcoholic? He clearly skirted the line, but he recognized when his writing partner stepped over it and recommended Alcoholics Anonymous. There is no indication in his diary that Piper thought he personally had a drinking problem, but few alcoholics do. Many alcoholics use drink to stave off depression, a malady from which Piper certainly suffered. Had he lived another decade or two, he very well might have turned into a full-blown alcoholic, or died of liver failure.

* * *

Piper saw incredible technological changes come about through his lifetime. World War I produced fighter planes, poison gas, the first armored vehicles and the trench warfare. Word War II accelerated these changes with bombers, V rockets and jet fighters—and, finally, the atomic bomb. Mike Knerr wrote, "And there was something else to intrigue him—the Manhattan Project. The beginning of the Atomic Age whose birthday would be December 2th, 1942. No longer would Dr. Robert H. Goddard's rockets be toys. They were the future engines of space, and there would be no more of Jules Verne's gun cotton.

"With the Atomic Age, came the fear of atomic war and this Piper took more seriously with every passing year. His first published story concerned itself with it, and it was a subject he never stopped believing in. 'There has never been a weapon of war designed,' he said, 'that wasn't tested in war.' He meant a full-scale war and he never really gave up the idea that we'd have one in 1990.

Like many realists during the peak of the Cold War, Piper fully expected a nuclear war to break out. He touches on this fear in many of his later letters, such as this one written on July 2, 1963 to Charlie (the founder of the *Locus* SF fanzine in 1968) and Marcia Brown: "You will undoubtedly see me at the Discon, if we are all alive by then, and Washington hasn't been H-bombed in the meantime."

In a March 22th, 1963 letter to Jerry Pournelle, he wrote: "You know it must have been lovely, living in an era when the Clausewitzian "extension of politics by other means" was accomplished by nothing more lethal or expensive, especially expensive, than black powder…Well, see you in Washington over the Labor Day week-end, if there still is a Washington then."

* * *

Terry McGuire noted in a telephone interview: "Beam used to have a human "skull" he kept on his desk in his Altoona gunroom. He'd often turn it upside down and use it as an ashtray. When we were 'acting' out Shakespeare, Beam would sometimes give us the skull to talk to. Beam had us act out *Romeo and Juliet* and we had to know our parts!

"Beam had a dark side as well. Because of his penchant for dark clothing, capes and slouch caps and working all evening as a night watchman, he would come home late at night. Some people, mostly kids, thought he was a vampire; Beam encouraged this kind of speculation. He would laugh in that deep voice of his; he enjoyed terrifying children.

"I had terrible nightmares at one point, and no one could figure out why. Finally, Jack mentioned it to Beam. He asked me what I was dreaming about. I said, 'A big monster comes up from the ocean and cuts me open with a long claw and eats me while I'm alive!'

"Beam looked around the room they used to write in and said, 'Where is your bedroom.'

"My room was directly over the room they used to write in and the radiator pipes went up to my room. Beam found a large opening there, went upstairs and moved my bed to another wall. 'I think your nightmares will stop now.'

"And they did."

It doesn't take much imagination to see Piper—with a slouch cap and black overcoat—wandering the deserted car shops in downtown Altoona, where they kept the boxcars, locomotives and railroad flatcars, late at night in a light drizzle like some wraith, talking out the story complications of his latest yarn. Woe to the bum or wrongdoer who ran into Mr. Piper, for—if needed—he could dispense Billy club justice with nether sentimentality nor rancor—just the firm application of *force majeure*.

CHAPTER TWENTY-ONE

Knife Edge

In late 1955 Piper wrote one of the seminal works in his Terro-Human Future History, which he called "The Knife Edge" (it was later re-titled by the editor as "The Edge of the Knife") which tells the story of a history teacher who can "see" into the future—sometimes with disastrous results. He not only *sees* into the near future but the far future and the First Empire.

During the mid-fifties, Piper was often in New York and while there he would have luncheons with various editors, often Campbell. On November 7th, 1956, he noted in his diary: "Lunch with John W. Campbell—he is not buying 'Knife Edge' because it conflicts with the strategy he has adopted in trying to boost psionics." That's a very strange reason to bounce a story, but if Campbell hadn't liked it—he would have let Piper know. Campbell, however great an editor, had his hobby horses that he liked to push on his reading audience: "Dianetics" in the late 1940s, "psionics" in the 1950s and the perpetual motion machine, the "Dean Drive," in the late 1960s.

As Mike Knerr noted, "Shot down on this tack, Beam did what all writers do—turned it all over to his agent and began scribbling notes for a new SF novelette (the poor fisherman who sold the holy relic). Beam had, of course, long ago learned the most important lesson a writer can learn—pay no attention to rejections. Most scribes can paper their den with those odd little slips of paper that say, 'Thank you for your submission, but we regret to return your manuscript as it is just not right for our needs at this time.'"

In Mike Ashley's analysis of the Analytic Lab (a feature in which readers' votes for their favorite stories were tallied and the authors given a monetary bonus) in his *Complete Index to Astounding/Analog*, Piper ranked third in overall cumulative Analytic Lab voting, which is amazing considering he didn't publish all that many stories and novels in the magazine—only behind C.L. Moore and number one vote getter, Robert A. Heinlein.

It has been said that John W. Campbell confided in a few associates that very few fans actually sent in Analytic Lab votes for their favorite stories, so Campbell picked the winners himself, and used it as a means to up the word rate for those authors whose work he most valued. In Campbell's letter to Ken White, about wanting Piper to rewrite the novelette, "Gunpowder God," Campbell wrote: "If Beam can cut this to 18,500, I'll give him the full 4 cents bonus rate on acceptance." [Now, if this isn't clear evidence that Campbell cooked the AnLab bonuses, I don't know what more in the way of a 'smoking gun' would be needed.—jfc]

It also shows how highly Campbell valued Piper writing, since many of the *Astounding* regulars published two or three times more fiction in the Street & Smith publication as H. Beam Piper.

Piper's reaction to Campbell's remarks about "A Slave is a Slave" was quite positive as reflected in this November 8th, 1961, diary entry: "Called John Campbell, first at his office, and then at his home—he is quite delighted with it, John is almost as big a fascist sonofabitch as I am—but wants a couple of points hammered home a little harder." He assured Campbell that he would get right on it as soon as he got back to Williamsport. Then Piper went down to Robert Abels [a New York antique weapons' dealer] and "bought a sword, late XIV or XV century for $125.00."

There were some things about Piper's writing that Campbell did not like, for example this May 13th, 1959, rejection letter regarding *Little Fuzzy*:

Dear Piper:

First, I'm drowning in novels, four times more than I can use.

The thesis of this one is one that I'm keenly interested in, but I feel that you've somewhat ducked the central issue which you established. That is, the "talk and build a fire" rule is shown to be no proper test; in the end you have the Fuzzy's speech picked up and understood. Remember Hal Clement's starfish people who had no sonic communication—but wig-wagged with several thousand tendrils over their body surface. "Look, Ma...no speech!" Also no telepathy.

But the basic problem of "whaddaya mean... 'human'?" is an enormously important one. You've made it 'sapient,' which is an excellent idea.

But I feel this novel isn't as strong as it could have been. You, in your detective experience, found that life is in fact made up of a most awful confusion of too many people who might be involved. You must have learned how to mentally juggle two dozen relevant characters at once in your work.

The average reader hasn't. Your story would be more effective for John Q. Public if you trimmed the cast of characters to about six individuals, plus assorted off-stage stooges who don't have to be remembered. Detective stories are fun; sure. But this isn't a detective story; it's a philosophical problem story. The problem has some tendency to get lost, strayed, or forgotten under the deluge of characters.

Regards,
John W. Campbell

Piper may have juggled more characters than Campbell liked; regardless, John Campbell thought very highly of Piper's work. This June 5th, 1962 letter from Campbell says it best:

Dear Mr. Piper:

> *I don't know what plans you have for the next story project, but the world-picture you've been building up in the Sword World stories, or Space Viking stories, or whatever you designate the series offers some lovely possibilities. Space Viking itself is, I think, one of the classics-a yarn that will be cited, years hence, as one of the science-fiction classics. It's got solid philosophy for the mature thinker, and bang-bang-chop-'em-up action for the space-pirate fans. As a truly good yarn should have.*

> *One of the beauties of the set-up you've got is that it allows the exploration of cultures of almost all conceivable levels of complexity and technology. They can be examined either internally or externally-i.e., either by a native, or by a visitor.*

Campbell goes on with one of his legendary three-page giveaway story synopses—interestingly enough one that Piper never followed up on. John Campbell was well known for buying stories based on the story synopses he tossed out to fellow writers. In fact, Randall Garrett made a living doing just that. Here, Piper, who was always having difficulty generating story ideas—according to his own diary entries—had a good plot thrown his way by a man known to buy such self-propagated stories, and he never followed up on it or mentioned it again in his diaries! Yet, here's a writer who is constantly on the search for salable ideas and when one is thrown at him, he ignores it.

Independence is nice, if you can afford it; but Piper took his intransigence to a level that bordered on self-defeating. Writing three or four stories a year for Mr. Campbell would have solved most of Piper's financial problems as well as made his editor happy. There's no indication in their correspondence that Piper is intimidated by Campbell so that's not the issue. Maybe Piper felt his independence would be compromised by working on one of Campbell's story ideas. If so, it was a miscalculation that would haunt him in the future.

PART FOUR

From New York to Paris

CHAPTER TWENTY-TWO

The Big Move

In 1956, "the New Year came in with a whimper in Altoona," Mike Knerr wrote in "PIPER": "No whistles blown, and a faint scatter of shots up in Fairview as the years changed guard. Piper busied himself in cleaning up the aftermath of his mother's death and, naturally, found himself eating sauerkraut and frankfurters for New Year's dinner; pork would probably have been more traditional, but it was still the custom."

It was around New Year's when Betty dropped a bombshell: the Council of Student Travel was considering transferring her to the Paris office. Betty had worked there previously from 1951 to 1954. Obviously, Betty was in a position of some importance (Piper never provides in the diaries any information on what she did or what her position was with the Council), plus she just had "loaned" them some money. It will probably never be known whether or not it was her employer's idea, or her own that she be transferred to Paris.

Maybe part of his hostility towards their stay in Paris and his "she married me for an expensive Paris honeymoon" story was fueled in part by his resentment of her transfer to France. Certainly, with the railroad industry in big trouble—closings, mergers and outright bankruptcy in some cases—his own job at the Pennsy Railroad was not secure. And his writing income for 1955 was pitiful—by any standards.

On top of this, in 1956 the railroads started making major cutbacks—everyone was driving cars and the railroads were losing money every which way. Furthermore, the main product of the Altoona shops, steam locomotives, were now obsolete. In one of many wrong-headed moves, the Pennsylvania Railroad did not invest in the new diesel fuel engine technology; instead, they left that market to Detroit. General Electric was a pioneer in developing the diesel-electric locomotive, where during the 1920's they were mostly confined to switching yards. It wasn't until World War II that the Electro Motive Division of General Motors made diesel-electric locomotives powerful enough to replace their steam-power counterparts in heavy-duty service. By the end of the 1950s, steam engines were out of service and Altoona was turned into a ghost town.

Mike Knerr noted, "In past years, writing had been something of a hobby and the railroad check came in with a regularity that publishing would never match. The world, however, was changing. Suddenly the booming troop trains of the 1940s were gone and the freight of the 1950s was in its death throes. Railroads were merging with one another just to keep their heads above the current of progress. The iron horse was fading into the same murky twilight that had swallowed up the village blacksmith and Beam was caught up in the shuffle. The embryonic beginning of a slogan was starting: 'If you have it, a truck brought it.'

"On May 23rd, the axe had fallen at the car shops and Beam drew a small guillotine on the page for that day. 'To police HQ to get my check *and learned that the positions and functions of watchmen have been abolished*. After Friday I don't have any more job than a jackrabbit unless I bid onto the Stores Department or something like that.' The following day he went back and talked to 'Corporal Yost and Sergeant Gutchell,' then scribbled something in his diary about going on relief, or getting another job. By May 28th he had made up his mind: 'Went directly to Police Office, where I announced my decision to quit, and turned in my pass and wrote out my resignation.'"

Piper went back to his apartment and hammered out another four pages of 'final first draft' of 'Omnilingual,' with a break for supper. There's no mention of Betty or what she thought about him losing his job at the railroad; however, it would soon tilt the balance of their new relationship in ways that Piper would not find to his liking.

* * *

On question that bothered me for years was: Why did Piper resign from the Pennsy Railroad, rather than wait until they laid him off—at which time he *might* have been eligible for retirement? After all, Piper had worked for the Pennsy for close to 40 years.

Kurt R. Bell, an archivist with the Pennsylvania Historical and Museum Commission, was able to authoritatively answer that question. "The maximum age for employment or re-employment was 45, and retirement age 70, so the minimum service to get a pension was 25 years. Persons who were 65 and disabled could get a pension if they had 30 years of service, so that was probably considered the time required to keep the system solvent. Most people were expected to begin in their teens or twenties, so some people would put in over 40 to 45 years before being pensioned."

Since Piper was 56 years old when he left his job, he was 14 years shy of being eligible for retirement benefits which explains why it was not addressed. It's unfortunate, since even a small pension would have gone a long way to help smooth out the bumps in the road of his freelance writing career—kept him in food if nothing else.

* * *

The trip to France was now scheduled and Piper was forced to settle his mother's affairs in Altoona. That's when he learned from Louis Walton, the estate attorney, that his mother's estate would not be settled until October; thus "H. Beam Piper, Administrator, had to advance H. Beam Piper, Heir, a grand for Europe'" At the time, $1,000.00 equaled about 350,000 francs and represented a considerable sum of money.

Knerr noted: "Armed with cash, he fell into the mess of getting his gun collection loaned out [to the Lycoming Historical Museum—jfc], and the apartment furnishings were sold, given away or thrown out. By the last of May, he was working at a feverish pace to get things done—making boxes for his pistols, swords and daggers."

Of course, one wonders—had Piper not lost his job—what he might have done had Betty chosen to leave for Europe while he was working and living in Altoona? It's quite possible that Betty was the impetus behind his resignation; she had her own agenda and it didn't include living in the US—not for long, anyway. For a newly married couple, they were under a lot of pressure.

In retrospect it appears that the Pipers were both lost in a romantic fog. They were both middle-aged and used to living alone. She had been married before, but it hadn't worked out. Piper, by all indications, had never been involved in a serious relationship, nor does it appear he had much tolerance for other people's foibles. Betty's plan was to return to Europe and live abroad; this with a man who has spent his entire life in a small town—and who did not like change. Piper, on the other hand, was living beyond his means and marrying a woman he didn't have the means to support—even if he hadn't lost his low-paying job! A good recipe for a disaster.

Betty had a good job and a good deal of her own money, while he was making a precarious living even while he was employed. Yet, they were in 'love' like a couple of teenagers, with no parental interference. Inga Pratt couldn't be objective; she was the matchmaker. The poor McGuires, who were having their own problems and knew and understood what marriage meant and the troubles that came when two people shared their lives, were the only ones it appears who objected—since Piper didn't tell anyone else! For this, they earned his unending enmity.

Piper was now a full-time writer and not by his own choice. He was a self-proclaimed gentleman writer—an auteur, as he told the McGuires. John McGuire, Jr. said, "Beam and my dad never entertained the concept of writing as a way of making a *living*. Not because Beam wasn't good enough, but because he felt like this was not his 'time.' He was a Victorian, not a cosmopolitan."

Adding to the stress, he not only had a wife to support but had to pay his way to Europe! With all the headaches of the previous year—his marriage to Betty, not a single story sale, the split between him and John McGuire and the death of his mother—he was in a tough spot.

* * *

On the writing front, Piper was still worried about "Hunter Patrol" and "Lone Star Planet." He needed money and couldn't understand why they hadn't sold. His concern about "Hunter Patrol" solved itself on February 27th, when it was bounced by *Fantastic Universe*, "With a nice but non-negotiable letter." By March 15th, he was working on "the—let us devoutly pray—final first draft of 'Omnilingual.'"

"Lone Star Planet" was rejected on March 30th, 1956. Mike Knerr noted, "Beam continued to work on his pet project, around which his stories would revolve and from which they would evolve. It was called, in his words, 'Piper's History of the Future' and it was an outline of what he thought the future would be. The story he was presently laboring over, 'Omnilingual,' was to be about the first expedition to Mars which he felt would take place in 1996, or A.E. 54. He was also fascinated with time travel. It was scarcely a new idea, since it had been dabbled in by nearly everyone—including H.G. Wells. Piper added his own variations by creating parallel time levels and a police force to keep everything under control."

Time travel was important to Piper and it's hard to tell how seriously he took it. During a discussion about Piper, Jerry Pournelle said, "Piper once admitted to me that 'He Walked Around the Horses'—a Paratime travel tale—was a true story. 'I know,' Piper said, 'I was born on another time-line.'" Even now Jerry can only say, "Beam looked me right in the eyes when he said it. And if there was a twinkle in his eye, I couldn't find it." Pournelle's still not sure whether he believes in it, but he's almost certain Piper did.

Mike Knerr noted: "Piper was an expert at confusing the issues and extremely careful how he did it. He started the same sort of story with me that he had sprung on Jerry but hastily backtracked verbally when I told him that I had read the books of Charles Fort and knew about Benjamin Bathurst. It is no coincidence that his second story 'Police Operation' begins with a quote from Fort's book *Lo!*

"The fun, where Piper was concerned, was keeping people off balance. It worked nicely on him, too. He had me pegged as a gun-totin' militarist until one night we were having an argument with Bill Stroup, a pacifist.

Years later, I mentioned the incident to him and he slammed his palm on the desk. 'Yes,' he roared, 'that was the night you were giving aid and comfort to the enemy!'

"To try to dupe me, he shifted to reincarnation rather than the timeline bit. He once asked to read a manuscript I had written based on the so-called 'Great Runaway of the Susquehanna River in 1778.' I was reluctant at first, but I finally relented.

"'It's good,' he told me after reading it. 'You stayed with the history and your hero solved his own problems.'

"'What about the runaway? History doesn't mention Indians attacking the flotilla of rafts.'"

"Beam's eyes squinted a little. 'I once had a dream in which I was dressed in buckskin on a raft. We were shooting at the shore of a river. Yes, I think you wrote it right.'

"He was lying, of course, but this was how he taught people to write. What he was saying, in effect, was that the scene I had written carried the story and, since history made no mention of attacks, my guess was as good as anyone's.

"Beam was a natural writer with very little training in the trade. Most of his creative ability had been picked up by reading. He was always a voracious reader with extremely catholic tastes in books. Although he knew about narrative hooks and plot development, I doubt that his study of writing mechanics taught him about the wave formula or other such tactics."

Mike Knerr knew Piper well, but there was a lot he didn't know. As his letters to Ferd confirm, Piper was very aware of literary conventions, though maybe not in a formal way; he wouldn't have been caught dead taking a 'course' in writing at a local university. However, he spent a lot of time at writers' meetings and talked 'shop' with other writers. Piper wrote a lot—and re-wrote even more. This is why his stories 'feel' so solid; reading a Piper story is like reading a non-fiction account because it's that *real*.

For all of Piper's knowledge of writing and thirty-six years of putting his words to paper, he had always been a part-time writer; the 'other job' paid the rent and put food on the table. On May 23rd, 1956, he knocked out four pages of the "final first draft" of "Omnilingual." The next day he wrote a letter to James Blish about getting Blish's agent, Kenneth S. White, to "handle my end of 'The Heavenly Twins.'" Apparently this reference was to *First Cycle* which was to appear in the doomed fourth issue of the Twayne Triples. This was another story that had its seeds sown in barren ground, but it began his association with Ken White, a one-time editor of *Adventure* magazine turned author's representative.

Knerr noted, "Ken White and Beam really clicked. Ken could sell Beam's work better than anyone else." Later Piper recommended White's agency to Mike Knerr.

Bill McMorris, Piper's editor at G.P. Putnam's Sons, had this to say about Ken White: "When I knew Ken in 1958, he was small, slender and slightly stooped. He wore a gray-blond moustache tinged with nicotine and I recall him as always squinting through a haze of tobacco smoke. He and I both loved Martinis and tobacco and if could repeat one of our lengthy luncheons today, I believe it would kill me.

"I did not know him beyond our business contacts, but he was an amusing luncheon companion and had a pretty good sense of what kind of material I was looking for, a not very common attribute of literary agents at that time. I had known Ken before I came to Putnam, because he had sold short stories and articles to *Boy's Life* magazine, where I worked as an editor before I entered the book publishing business. We did not have any contact through the magazine, but I was aware of his accurate sense of what was publishable for the readers of the magazine.

"When I was hired by Walter Minton at Putnam (1958) to take over the juvenile department, Ken White was one of the first agents I contacted. His description of Piper, who Ken claimed was living at the YMCA in Altoona at that time, was delivered with a combination of admiration and puzzlement: 'He's a One.'"

Even taking inflation into account, H. Beam Piper was not making much money writing science fiction—his best year's income was only a little over $3,000.00. Nor, at that time, was anyone else in science fiction making a lot of money, other than Robert Heinlein who was making most of his income from story sales to *The Saturday Evening Post* [the *Post* was a very lucrative market and would pay several thousand dollars for a single story—jfc] and his juvenile science fiction novels. Paperback sales were few and far between, but a revolution—thanks to television—was going on that would undermine the entire field, starting with the death of the pulps.

By the mid-1950s—thanks to television and higher paper costs—the pulp magazines were in trouble, many disappearing like mayflies. Most SF authors made the bulk of their income from the ½ cent to 4 cent rates paid by the magazines. Each had its own appeal, but, for example, a Campbell author could rarely sell more than two or three stories a year to *Astounding*. The other good paying markets were the more adventurous (emphasis on sociological SF versus *Astounding's* more realistic/scientific SF) *Galaxy* under Horace Gold, or the more 'literary' *Fantasy & Science Fiction* magazine; few writers could sell to all three. To make a living a writer needed to sell stories to the secondary magazine markets, like *Future*, *Weird Tales* and *Amazing Stories*—even though they paid poorly.

The young Robert Silverberg made a good living in the mid-fifties pounding out adventure SF tales, sometimes filling entire issues of small circulation pulps with stories and short novels under different pseudonyms. However, even Silverberg was having problems with finding markets and in the early 1960s turned to writing juvenile non-fiction books on archaeology and other such subjects.

Anthology sales were few and paid poorly: for example, Piper, who was paid $147.00 for "Time and Time Again" by John W. Campbell, only received $37.80 for the anthology rights' sale a year later to *A Treasury of Science Fiction*. He made twice that selling a short story, "Immunity" ("Flight From Tomorrow") to *Future Stories* in 1950, which was a salvage market. For the first half of 1956, his only writing income was $45.00 for anthology rights for "Police Operation" and $5.69 for the German anthology rights for "Time and Time Again." Hardly a significant source of income, even to H. Beam Piper.

During the same time frame, Philip K. Dick was starving in Berkeley,

California, eating dog food when times were bad. Theodore Sturgeon, another writer who managed his finances about as well as Piper, was living in hovels and eating over at friends' to keep from starving. Almost everyone else in the SF field had a day job; many were engineers—or living like grad students. Or like Reginald Bretnor—another character—living off his wife's earnings and the occasional story sale.

As Mike Knerr, who published enough men's adventure, crime stories and soft porn during the late 1950s and 1960s to support himself, puts it: "If beginning writers, as a rule, do not make large amounts of money, the scribes of the sci-fi genera during that period made even less. To the 'Gee, I could write a book' crowd who every year graduates...to arm themselves with a ream of typing paper and a typewriter, the cold hard facts of the business are enough to make one cry. Yet, as with Piper, the heady wine of that first sale spurs them on to write another story, and another, until somewhere in the maze of their lives it is *all* they can do. When that point is reached, the writer becomes a sort of blend of emotions and feelings that has taken over the original entity and the typewriter (or computer keyboard) becomes a hungry maw that insists on swallowing enormous amounts of paper.

"There are few trades in the world which might require up to ten years of study and finally, when graduation comes, produce less money per year than is made by the average laborer. A rather well known sci-fi writer, at one of Forrest J. Ackerman's parties in Los Angeles, confided that he probably had made 3 cents per hour for his work on the typewriter.

"Beam's troubles were to grow in late spring (1956) in the form of the railroad cutting back on its workers. As Shakespeare wrote: 'When troubles come, they come not in single spies, but in battalions.' With all the problems of the past year, Beam was to face a new conflict with his job and he was not a young man. Writing, naturally, was to play a fateful part in his final decision."

After the death of his mother, Piper had to deal with burial and estate expenses: "Find that between one thing and another, the money in the bank—$1,850.50—will be wiped out in settling estate, and will probably have to sell the Pennsylvania Railroad stock." On September 20th, he added, "…turned Pennroad stock over to be sold, and wrote checks for damn near the whole of the bank balance. Have I ever mentioned what a damned expensive thing it is to die?"

All in all 1955 was a financial debacle for Piper —no writing income to speak of and no new stories to sell, no agent to represent the unsold stories and no new ideas on the horizon. Combined with a marriage, the death of his mother (who supplemented his apartment rental and utilities expenses) and having to wipe out his mother's estate for funeral, burial and estate expenses, we have a very worried H. Beam Piper.

Added to this, Betty's employer was considering sending her to the Paris office since she had been there from 1951 to 1954 and spoke rather fluent French.

The relocation to France is a possibility that Piper never brings up in his diaries. He may have been in a state of denial; if I don't believe it will happen, it won't happen. Unfortunately, with the upcoming loss of his job and his lack of sales, there were no other alternatives for Piper. He and Betty were still in the honeymoon stage and he did what he had to, for as long as he could, to keep their marriage a reality.

Even at the Roger Williams apartment things were in a state. A fuel strike had complicated the couple's lifestyle and had 'cooled off' the city. "Effects of fuel strike," Piper wrote, "being felt here at Roger Williams— we are running the tub full of hot water to heat the rooms."

In early February Piper had not only bought a map of Paris but picked up passport applications. Knerr noted, "The handwriting was taking shape on the wall. He began making notations in his diaries in the form of doodles on the corner of the page. On February 24th he drew a red dollar sign in the center of a magnifying glass—$5.69 from Karl Rauch of Dusseldorf as payment for a German anthology which used 'Time and Time Again.' He also listed the weather for the day and had, naturally, declared the Christian Era obsolete. Nineteen fifty-six, he wrote, was actually Atomic Era 13…"

Piper's Atomic Era is reckoned as beginning on the 2nd December 1942 Christian Era, with the first self-sustaining nuclear reactor, put into operation by Enrico Fermi at the University of Chicago. He often added this addendum to notations on the Atomic Era dating: "The dating of the Atomic Age will be numerically correct, and not based on the life of some upstart, Jewish carpenter."

* * *

That spring Piper was attempting to learn French. "The dictionary has definite limitations," he wrote on May 9th, 1956. The trip to France was by now a fact; Piper's last 'excuse'—his job—was no longer part of the equation. There was no way—although he was not at all eager to go abroad—he could refuse. After all, it was a job-related decision by Betty; and he no longer had a *real job*. For Piper, after the disaster of 1955 with no new sales or stories, it would have been impossible to mount a counter-offensive to the change in address, especially "when a writer can work anywhere that he has a typewriter and paper."

On June 2nd, Hans Santesson, editor of *Fantastic Universe*, bounced "Plausible Motive," but mentioned that he liked "Lone Star Planet." He wanted to talk about paring it down; however, Piper wasn't exactly happy about that. He would have to do all the work himself since he was no longer talking—or in contact—with John McGuire who was now teaching and living in Red Hook, New Jersey. Just another delay, with no guarantee that even if he did make the recommended cuts—without gutting the story—the sale would go through. On top of that *Fantastic Universe* was a salvage market, paying about a cent a word.

Then, on top of all this turmoil, another friend died. "Letter from Betty; news of death of Fletcher Pratt. A great loss to all of us." Pratt was only fifty-nine years old when he died of cancer at Monmouth Memorial Hospital, New Jersey, and the news had a profound impact upon Piper, just seven years younger. They had been good friends, both members of the same clubs, and he had been an admirer of Pratt's historical works for years. He spent the evening in writing a letter to Betty, with one of condolences to Inga Pratt.

Fletcher Pratt's death was especially devastating to Piper since Pratt was in many ways, according to Mike Knerr, Piper's role model as an author. He sold fiction of almost every stripe, including mysteries and science fiction, as well as non-fiction and—best of all—both historical novels and historical non-fiction. Everything Piper himself wanted to do and more.

Knerr wrote, "Amid all the hustle of getting everything ready for the voyage on the *Arosa Star*, Beam wrote: 'saw Ken White—think I have a good agent lined up in him.' He continued his writing of 'Omnilingual,' which was beginning to hang together in a way that was suitable to the author's critical eye."

However, not even their friend's death would get in the way of their French vacation. Knerr wrote: "With the help of Freida Coleman, a friend who drove down from Williamsport, Piper managed to get things arranged and packed by June 21st and made it to the Coleman residence that evening, finally having dinner at the Hillside Restaurant. The party also included Ted Ranck, a long time hunting and drinking buddy. The next day he took a plane to New York to get ready for the trip to Paris.

"He and Betty managed a last Hydra Club meeting at Jeff Markell's house and left by plane for Wolfe's Cove and their ship for Paris—not, however, without confusion. For all his courtly, meticulous ways, Piper never seemed to get anything done 'by the numbers.' The ninety-five minute plane flight from New York to Montreal was uneventful, but the flight into Quebec was a snafu. He found himself on one flight and Betty on another. Confusion reigned in the shipping as well, Beam wrote, 'After some phoning, and general hell-raising, Betty's suitcase arrived; hat-box still overdue 2345.' Eventually even that surfaced and the day ended well.

The next day, July 3rd, they boarded the *Arosa Star* and Betty spent most of the day embarking three hundred, sixty-three students. The ship got under way from Wolfe's Cove at 1800 sharp and they headed across the Atlantic. While Betty babysat her students, he worked on "Omnilingual." As his diary indicates, Piper had mixed feelings about this working "vacation."

Piper was eager to see some of the historical spots he'd read so much about and looking forward to visiting museums and battlefields. Despite all this, Piper was a homebody and traveling in Europe would soon grow tiresome and weary despite the company.

CHAPTER TWENTY-THREE

Graveyard of Dreams

The Atlantic crossing on their first trip to France was rough and Betty suffered almost constantly from seasickness. Piper seemed immune and was still grumbling about Campbell's rejection of his latest Future History yarn, "The Knife Edge" [published in *Amazing* as "Edge of the Knife"]. Ken White appeared pleased with it and even tried to sell it to the top market of the day, *The Saturday Evening Post*; a sale there would have been quite a feather in Piper's cap—but alas, it was not to be.

The boat trip was uneventful, other than Betty's seasickness, and Piper went back to work on "Omnilingual." After their arrival, the Pipers settled into the Hotel Raspail in France. Betty tended to her job with the Council while he wrote and made friends with numerous French cats.

For the first time, Piper was *on* the soil that he had been studying about for most of his life and he took full advantage of the opportunity, beginning with the Louvre where he inspected the crown jewels and the state swords of monarchy. He added a trip to Napoleon's tomb… "(tombs of Vauban, Roch thrown in gratis)," but he was also getting a taste for Europe that would eventually rub him the wrong way. Many parts of Europe, France and England included, were still recovering from the damage of World War II and Piper was not accustomed to many common inconveniences. "Hot water," he wrote on July 17th, "still not-existent. Non-bathing situation critical."

In Paris, living in the Hotel Raspail, Piper had nothing to occupy his time but sightseeing and writing. He got right down to work on

"Omnilingual" without any of the false starts, stops and rewrites that plagued his writing throughout all of 1955. While he worked on "the final final draft' of 'Omnilingual,'" he managed to see the palace at Versailles, noting dryly in his diary that the main attraction in the Hall of Mirrors needed cleaning. Naturally, he 'did' the Champs Elysees and the Arc de Triomphe and on the 23rd wrote happily that the *eau chaud*, the hot water, was finally running. Of his more practical discoveries in Paris, he was delighted to locate the Gastinne–Renette firing range on Avenue Franklin D. Roosevelt where he kept his shooting eye in shape by firing a dueling pistol.

Piper spent the next month, August, taking walks, working on "Omnilingual" and shooting pistols. The Pipers were scheduled to return to the States in October, leaving October 3rd from London. It's never made clear in the diaries if this trip was the prequel to their relocation to Paris, or a chance for Betty to oversee the French end of the Council for Student Travel. I believe that Piper's appetite for travel was more than appeased by their European jaunt. He was lonely most of the time they were in Europe, and missed his familiar haunts and Altoona friends.

Piper completed "Omnilingual" in early August and mailed the manuscript out to Ken White on August 6th. He received a note from Ken White on August 31st, telling him that Campbell had purchased "Omnilingual" for $630.00. "Omnilingual" is probably Piper's most anthologized story, most recently in 2005, and is considered by many to be his finest work. The story takes place in the early days of interplanetary exploration of the Sol System. An expedition is sent to Mars where the ruins of an ancient city are discovered. When the team discovers books and documents that have survived the millennia, despite internal strife, they make a determined effort to decipher them.

That sale gave Piper a temporary lift of spirits. After a short celebration without the cannon, he began to work on the new story and Betty left for work at the Council. They were already packing their things to be shipped to London, their point of departure for their return to New York.

Mike Knerr noted: "The trip to London and their embarkation on the *Arosa Sun* from Cowes was not exactly in a straight line. The couple spent the month of September touring a great deal of Europe; their itinerary included Geneva, Montreux, Zermatt, Zurich, Heidelberg, Mainz, Cologne, Brussels, Bruges and London. Beam took in every museum he could manage, was properly impressed with the Matterhorn and was introduced to Betty's old friends and places in Geneva. Betty had been there in 1954 and even located an old acquaintance in a cat named 'Lucrezia.' On the 19th they took a boat to Dover and a train into London, checking in at the Regent Palace hotel.

"Although Beam played tourist at parks, museums and various art galleries, he did manage a side trip that stunned him. 'Went to Baker Street, found 221 occupied by a big office building, learned that the Sherlock Holmes Museum *is now in New York*!' To soothe his outraged Holmes-fan-ego he took a train as far as Salisbury to visit Stonehenge. Even at this he was annoyed by English problems. He got a bus to Amesbury, but couldn't find transportation 'of any sort' to Stonehenge. He ended up walking the last 'two miles each way.'"

It was the minor inconveniences, not understanding the language, the difficulties of travel (since Piper did not drive), the lack of hot water and the strangeness of a foreign culture that really got under his skin. While he enjoyed the sightseeing and visiting museums and battlefields, it was quickly getting old. He missed his Pennsylvania friends and gun enthusiasts. He was anxious to get home, but he was under the knife so to speak; Betty was already making plans for her return and clearly wasn't interested in living in Altoona or even New York. Piper was caught between two loves, and at this time his love for Betty was the stronger of the two.

Mike Knerr noted, "Getting back to New York wasn't as easy as leaving had been. The *Arosa Sun* found a mess with Canadian customs, the passengers being held for two hours on 'B' deck, 'a horrible experience,' Beam wrote. In New York, there were no apartments available at the Roger Williams, but they were given a temporary room until one became vacant. To top off a somewhat lousy trip when they returned to their room they found the key wouldn't work. The next day, Betty left for the office and Beam had lunch with Ken White and Kelly Freas who had just finished the *Astounding* illustrations for 'Omnilingual.'"

Piper continued with his writing finishing the never-sold "The Little King of Lagash" in late November 1956. Just before Thanksgiving he and Betty flew to Williamsport and were met by Freida Coleman who took them to the Lycoming Historical Museum. There he unpacked part of his pistol collection and set them out to be displayed.

Betty didn't stay; she took a bus back to New York and work, while Piper returned to Altoona to settle his Mother's estate and buy a marker for her grave. Altoona seemed much smaller and shabbier since his return from Europe. His diary comments were harsh: "This town is dying on its feet." He took a train the next day to New York and Betty.

Actually, it was Piper who was changing the most, becoming more cosmopolitan; travel and living in New York and Paris had changed his perspective. The Pennsy Railroad was still in business, but things were slow at the car yards. Altoona looked the same as always; it was Piper's eye that was different.

Back in New York, Piper got to work again on a new story, "The Keeper." Meanwhile, on December 20th, 1956, he learned that the *Lone Star Planet* novel had finally sold for the princely sum of $110.00 (as he notes in his Story Log: "half of sale price shared with J.J. McG."). It was sold to *Fantastic Universe Science Fiction*, edited by Hans Stefan Santesson, a salvage market and one of the last of the pulps; its last issue was published on March, 1960.

Lone Star Planet was later reprinted by Ace Books as half of one of their Ace Doubles in 1958 and retitled *Planet For Texans*. It's a political satire of Texans and red-necks; Piper's only attempt at humorous satire. On the planet, New Texas, the Solar League ambassador to the Lone Star Planet has to convince the locals that an alien attack is imminent and that the dog-like *s'Strauff's* are dangerous. Based on the political views of H. L. Mencken's essay, "The Malevolent Jobholder," mayhem, buffoonery and misguided tomfoolery are the result. *Lone Star Planet* won the Prometheus Hall of Fame Award in 1999 for Best Classic Libertarian SF novel. Those who like it, like it a lot.

It was during this interlude that Piper finished "The Keeper" and sent it off to Ken White. "The Keeper" is set in Piper's Terro-Human Future History, but thousands—not hundreds—of years in the future in the 301st Century. In this story, the Keeper, whose job is to protect a precious relic, learns that the planet he is living on (Earth) is the birthplace of man and that off-world there is a great empire that rules the stars.

On January 4th, 1957, Piper picked up a copy of "Omnilingual" and liked the *Astounding* version, particularly the Kelly Freas illustration with a pun on the periodic 'tables.' The words were coming easier and this was shown both by his increased production and the upswing in story sales.

He received a call from Donald Wollheim of Ace Books, who wanted to make a paperback of *NULL-ABC*. Wollheim retitled it *Crisis in 2140* and put it out as one half of an Ace Double (D-227) later in the year. There's no mention of the sale in Piper's Story Log (typical of his McGuire collaborations after the split), but Piper probably got the usual $500.00 (which was split in half) advance less Ken White's ten percent.

Piper was also engaging a tailor to make him a new suit. By the 25th of January, he was outlining "Graveyard of Dreams" and commented: "looks as though it's going to develop into a real story."

Betty wanted to visit her mother in Carmel; Piper's reaction says it all: "After dinner, did some packing for the (gulp!) trip to California...." The Pipers stayed a couple of days in Carmel, then returned to San Francisco to tour the town, including helping to push a cable car around on the turntable. They returned to New York on February 12th. It would appear, although he doesn't say so in the diaries, that this trip was a kind of farewell to the States and Betty's mother.

The Pipers got back to New York in time to learn that *Astounding* had bounced "The Keeper." Piper went back to work on "Graveyard of Dreams." This short story showed a deepening of his panoramic outline of the future. "Graveyard of Dreams" would lay the groundwork for *The Cosmic Computer*, a juvenile story he would write after reading Robert Heinlein's *Space Cadet* and *Tunnel in the Sky*. Prior to "Graveyard in the Sky," Piper's stories were somewhat isolated—even though they dealt with his Terro-Human Future History—they were unique stories that just happened to be based on *his* future history. Now he was beginning to get a handle on something that would influence him in the coming years, the Terran Federation.

At the moment, nothing was coming out of the typewriter without a great deal of literary sweat. Dissatisfied with the way "Graveyard of Dreams" was going, Piper scrapped it all on February 8th, and started over. Left with just the embryo of a story, he doggedly returned to the machine to begin again.

Meanwhile, plans for the big move continue. While Piper appears in denial about the trip, no employer ships someone overseas for the fun of it. Therefore, the relocation to France had to have been in the works for some time; I suspect Piper thought if he didn't think about the move, it would go away, since there are no comments about living in France in the diaries prior to the move itself.

Obviously, Piper, who wasn't thrilled with the previous trip to France, was dreading this more 'permanent' move. Probably writing about it in his diary would have made it more *real* in his mind.

On February 21st, he wrote, "Council of Student Travel office a madhouse, getting new shipping schedule out, everybody sick." Betty had been having a time of it during the past year, suffering what appears to have been stomach trouble. Maybe Betty was beginning to realize that their marriage was a mistake. Her stomach pains would continue to plague her during their remaining time together.

Events were swirling around the Pipers as they prepared for their return to France. It was during this period that Piper 'discovered' a little dachshund puppy, a new addition to the Piper household. While they tried to figure out where to keep the puppy before they left for France, the story "Graveyard of Dreams" was suffering. Piper wrote "…have come to the conclusion that the story needs a lot of pruning—needless characters and situations to be ejected."

The pet shop owner agreed to board the new addition to the Piper household until they were ready to sail for France. "On Betty's suggestion, we are calling him Verkan Vall…." Although Piper might have had some initial doubts, he soon found himself captivated by Vall, or 'little squiggle,' as he often called him. Over the next few days the Pipers visited the pet shop whenever they could, while he wrote notes like this in his diary, "Up town to visit Vall at the pet shop."

In a February 18th, 1981, letter, Paul Schuchart relays: "The next to last time I saw Beam was in New York. I was there to attend some kind of meeting and called Beam. It was when he was having problems with his wife; all because he (Beam) had got his wife's dog drunk on 'very dry' martinis, served in a dish. That Beam even married-up surprised me. Beam and I had a few drinks before the evening was over. I do not remember meeting his wife."

Early in March the Pipers began packing for the voyage to Paris on the 27th. Just before departure, Piper learns that Ken has sold "The Keeper" to *Venture Science Fiction*, a new digest-sized SF magazine. His share, less commission, is $175.50.

The day before they're scheduled to leave, he finally opens up about the move. "Betty finished her packing while Beam cowered in bed." Betty was seeing a local doctor about her stomach trouble while he was disturbed about the upcoming move. Piper was in a terrible spot forced to move to a foreign country he disdained (if not hated) to save their marriage.

What is unclear is why Betty was so determined to live abroad; she could have stayed in New York at Council headquarters—after all, she was loaning the organization money. Therefore, she was in a position to call the shots. I'm sure she realized that her husband was too proud to be supported by his wife, but a pretense could have been kept up that he was "supporting them" had they stayed in New York where he had friends and connections in the publishing business.

She had to know that he hadn't really enjoyed their previous visit. Why would things change now? It seems they were both stepping around the elephant in the parlor.

He didn't speak French and there's no indication he ever intended to learn so it's obvious, even before they left New York, that things were not going to work out. From the evidence in Piper's remaining diaries it appears that Betty never left France except to obtain his signature for the divorce papers. Therefore, it looks as though this move was not meant to be a temporary change of venue. France was to be the Pipers' new home. He hadn't minded the visit—or at least, the tourist part, trips to museums and libraries—but had not at all *enjoyed* the living conditions, or the language problems. Plus, without his railroad job, he was completely dependent upon his writing for money. And, while there had been more sales and less stops and starts in 1956 than there had been in 1955, Piper was a long way from having a financially stable writing career.

If Piper had still been working at the Pennsy car shops, I doubt that he would have *allowed* this move to happen. Of course, Betty may have had her say in which case the split might have happened in early 1956. From Piper's "cowering under the bed" notation in his diary before they left for France, it's obvious the two of them were not really discussing the move; if they had, Beam might never have left New York. There's evidence later in the diaries that he thought they might live part-time in New York, but Betty never gave in. For two people so much in love, they were as hardheaded as a couple of rocks.

"Finally packed, they checked out of the Roger Williams just before noon and boarded the *Queen Mary*," Piper noted on March 27th. The Pipers, with little Verkan Vall, left for France with a less than enthusiastic H. Beam Piper. Mike Knerr noted: "While the ship sailed Beam worked on 'Graveyard of Dreams' and, with all the traveling he had been doing since leaving the Altoona locomotive yards, it was probably just as well that he was not writing historical novels or stories that required a great deal of research."

The sea journey was rough—March not being the best time to cross the Atlantic—and things got bad enough for a few days that Piper had to forego his writing and Betty retired with a case of seasickness. The weather settled itself the next day, however, and he went back to work and soon they were back on French soil. In early April they moved into the Chambre Dix hotel in Paris and settled into their new *home*.

It was while he was working on "Graveyard of Dreams" that he met one of his neighbors. "The little girl in the next room has a pet hamster—saw it today. Cute little fuzzy." This is the first recorded usage of the term in Piper's diaries.

While he continued working, in fits and stops, generally thrashing his way on "Graveyard of Dreams," Betty began her job with the Council of Student Travel. Betty, while she continued to work, was not feeling very well—her stomach continued acting up a good bit of the time. Vall was also having health problems, but being a puppy and full of energy kept bouncing back. He had developed an infection in his ears which his adopted parents tried to correct, and he was being taken to a local vet for shots. On April 16th, Piper mentioned that Vall was listless "showing symptoms of ill health" which he attributed to the shots he had been given. This was not the case and the little dog's sickness was to get worse.

Unable, or unwilling, to express his feelings, Piper's emotions come to the surface over little things, such as the price of cigarettes, after buying a couple of packs for Betty. He mentions the "price outrageous" and these kinds of discontentment, signs of the emotional struggle buried much deeper, were to grow. Mike Knerr noted: "Betty was, quite naturally, conscious of spending money, but Beam was not. He always regarded foreign currency with a kind of contempt: 'I never thought of French money as anything but wallpaper,' he said, years later."

* * *

More aggravation: for the next several weeks, in addition to writing, Piper traveled back and forth to a Paris dentist getting impressions made for a new plate, after breaking his previous one shortly after their arrival. He picked up the new set of false teeth on June 1st, but they were uncomfortable and he continued to go back again and again to have them ground down. He continued to get lost on his walks around town, suffered with his dentures and punched away at the creation "of wastepaper." To add to his problems he worried because he had heard nothing from Ken White about the stories he had out making the rounds.

Knerr noted: "While writing 'Graveyard of Dreams,' Beam was also doodling on a detective novel, namely 'Murder Frozen Over,' and perhaps the germ of the *Little Fuzzy* novel was also starting to take shape in his mind. He was, during this period, filled with ideas for stories, but the never-ending problem of getting them down on paper to suit him was always difficult. For some reason writing a goodly amount of pages on one day would be followed by a dry period on the next.

"One also has to take into account that this move from Altoona and the change from part-time writer to 'writer' had to have had a major effect on Beam's writing. No longer could he sit at the car shops and write first drafts longhand, or walk through the shops searching for and discarding or accepting new story ideas or plot developments. This was a man who was born and bred in the Pennsylvania soil and 'loved' to write its history, had youthful dreams of writing a literary trilogy on the area. Now he was in a completely foreign environment and all his guns were back in Williamsport, along with his hunting and drinking buddies. Beam's long cultivated weapons collecting network was abandoned, and no more writer's meetings, editorial lunches, award dinners at the Stork Club and science fiction conventions...."

But the work must go on and Piper finished "Graveyard of Dreams" on April 19th, 1957, after "doing over" several pages. "That's usual," he comments in his diary, "after a burst of production like yesterday's." The interesting part is that he put almost as much work into an eight thousand word short story as he did to a novel and damn near the same amount of time. With the rise of television and the disappearance of the magazine market, the late 1950s was the beginning of a radical ground shift in science fiction and genre fiction in general, away from short stories to novels. This allowed writers more freedom to put the 'odd' scene and extra character in a novel, whereas in a short story everything had to be concise and pertinent to the theme, or at least, plot.

Piper mailed "Graveyard of Dreams" to Ken White on the 23rd, and began the plotting of a new story the following day. "Betty to office, Beam to work on story," he wrote. Almost every page of the diary opens this way. He was a dedicated writer and was used to working late into the night trying to get a storyline straight in his mind. Although Piper's, or any writer's, work day has no fixed hours, he usually spent more than an eight-hour session at the typewriter. This, of course, would be interspersed with breaks—shopping, smoking or taking Vall for a walk. It wasn't Piper's work ethic that was at the bottom of his writing problems; it was difficulty in generating salable story ideas and workable plots that caused him so much grief and mental anguish. Piper was one stubborn and bull-headed man to stick to his art decade after decade with so much frustration and so little success.

And worst of all, coming up with good stories never got any easier. He might get on a run with a story or novel, but as soon as it was done he was back to creating wastepaper and banging his head against the wall looking for something inspiring to write about.

On June 17th, Piper wrote, "Lots of mail, including letter from Ken White—both Campbell and Mills bounced 'Graveyard of Dreams', H. L. Gold has it now." Later in July, Piper went to *Chien Elegant* for Vall's dog food and found that he owed them 2000 francs on the previous purchase. He paid it and went back to the hotel to find "copy of 'Null-ABC' re-titled *Crisis in 2140*, God only knows why—in mail, but no word of check." Piper wouldn't receive the check, for the second half of the advance from Ace—a whopping $225.00 less 10% commission—until August 19th.

He received a letter from an English agent, E.J. Carnell, who wanted to use "He Walked Around the Horses" for a British anthology. Beam agreed, writing letters to Carnell and Ken White, then worked on notes, "trying to get story back on the track. Still not doing enough work in advance, starting to write with story unclear."

With all the weekend trips, from a writing standpoint, "Murder Frozen Over" was into heavy going.

Mike Knerr wrote: "On the last day of April he made reservations for the London World Science Fiction Convention, slated for September 6th, and began to think about what he and Betty would wear to the masquerade party.... They finally decided that Beam would go as a fan magazine editor and Betty would be a fan. Piper had all kinds of problems with this bit of costuming, but that was typical of life in Europe for him. He spent five days searching for an eyeshade and finally found one in a bicycle shop! On the following day, the Pipers left for London.

"In London, Beam took in the Tower and its arms collection as well as the Convention, but noted that he and Betty had to leave in the middle of John Campbell's talk on psionics to catch their plane back to Paris."

Knerr further noted: "While Betty was…settling into European life, Beam was fretting over the whole thing. Beam got his raincoat back from cleaners, all the buttons off. The weekend of June 15th, 1957, began what Beam would come to call 'another of those weekend trips.' Whether or not they were connected to Betty's job isn't quite clear, but they came to annoy Beam who would probably rather have kept writing on 'Murder Frozen Over.' The novel was 'coming along' albeit not with any great speed."

This is the third Jeff Rand mystery and one has to wonder why Piper was wasting his time on another sequel to *Murder in the Gunroom* when he'd been unable to interest a publisher in "Murder at the Conference." On the other hand, there is a euphoria that some writers experience when they have, or believe they have a great story idea and that they are working on an important work—even if they're the only one who believes in it. It's this kind of blind faith that keeps many writers toiling over their "masterpieces" and writing new stories in the face of editorial indifference and, in some cases, outright hostility.

This "belief" will often overcome any rational thinking on the writers' part and they will continue writing, even in the face of constant rejection, knowing that "once the world recognizes what I'm doing" sales will follow. It was this blind faith which kept Piper writing in the face of 25 years of constant rejection, as well as the rejection he faced even after being published.

Knerr noted, "This trip was to Luxembourg, where they stopped at the Alpha Hotel. The highlight of the journey appears to have been that they 'Reveled in real tub baths' and took a tour of the American cemetery where they saw the grave of General George S. Patton. Having gotten their fill of tub baths…the couple took the train back to Paris on Sunday."

The month of July was, "infernally hot," Piper wrote, and all three Pipers suffered from it. Without a refrigerator, a luxury in France at this time, their food spoiled and their bathing situation was limited. Betty was forced to take her shampoo to the office in order to wash her hair. As Knerr noted: "The only plus to the hot weather was that Beam could move their tub out on the balcony and let the sun heat the water. He wasn't exactly bubbling over with joy about this, but then he could generally 'make do' in such situations."

Piper was actually quite resilient when it came to *camping out,* even if it was in a French hotel! What bothered him most was being away from America—his home and his friends—writers, hunters, campers and fellow patrons of the bottle. He was unhappy living in France, which must have been obvious to Betty. Like a branch after a heavy snowfall, he was about to break; it was only a matter of time.

CHAPTER TWENTY-FOUR

Back in the USA

As the Pipers settled into life on the continent, H. Beam Piper's dissatisfaction with living abroad grew, while Betty, on the other hand, was settling into the life she loved. There were continual problems with the water and heating at their Paris hotel. "Water leak developed at our sink," he reports, "much fussing on part of Monsieur the Landlord, and now we have hot water but no cold water." The following day a plumber came to fix it. A day or so later, at a restaurant there were problems. "Uproar caused by drunken or demented character shouting insults at customers from the sidewalk."

There is a growing litany of complaints in the diary: on their next daytrip, another misunderstanding about breakfast at the hotel—which wasn't served in their room, but available in the main dining area. Little things, but indicative of a groundswell of frustrations at living abroad. Beam loved Betty, there is no doubt about it, but he was growing very tired of France. Knerr noted: "Perhaps as an indication of his state of mind, at this time, on July 31st, Beam records: 'Lost a day—Tuesday's entry for today.' This is the only time he 'missed' a day in his diaries. His displeasure with France was growing. The following weekend they went to Tours. On Monday, back in Paris, Erich [one of Betty's coworkers jfc] had a run-in with a truck in her new VW resulting in both right side fenders bashed in. Betty took it for repairs, probably at the Pipers' expense."

On September 13th, Piper scribbled: "Spent evening packing for another weekend trip, this time Deauville." But trouble develops the next evening when they went out to dinner. "Out for dinner 1930," he wrote. "We went to a rather expensive (1,200 fr.) restaurant. Betty wanted to run as soon as she saw the menu—I insisted on staying." Once again, we see Piper's indifference to price, while Betty, who had money, was more of a penny-pincher.

Piper added, "She became furious, and as a result, words were exchanged when we left, ending in my getting my things out of the hotel and, after paying the bill, leaving. Found the station closed and no train to Paris before 0645 tomorrow. Put up at a hotel for the night and was given an alarm clock to wake myself at six."

Any further hints about the blowup in the diary are subtle. Piper rarely expressed his deep feelings, other than in a few letters to Ferd Coleman, and now to Betty; but never in his own diaries. One has to read between the lines: the storm clouds had begun during their previous "French vacation" or scouting trip. They flared up again in New York before departure with Piper "cowering under the bed" while Betty packed. The real issue was Betty's work, or rather where she worked. She must have had enough clout—after all, she was an "investor"—to remain in New York at the main offices of the Council of Student Travel, but she had lived in Europe before and was determined to do so again—despite her husband's wishes.

There's no doubt that H. Beam Piper in his mid-fifties was not an easy man to live with. Charming, gracious, learned; he was. But he was as stubborn as a jackass, and he had been pampered for 55 years by a doting Mother. The Prince wanted it all his way, but so did the Princess—and she had the bigger dowry. Piper was as hard as the flint of his Kentucky smoothbores when it came to sticking to his guns.

Had Piper kept his job at the Pennsy, things might have turned out differently. He might have had more say concerning their future residence. When he lost that job—as unglamorous as it was—he lost most of his earning power and the marriage dynamics shifted. Betty was now the wage earner and it's obvious she was no shrinking violet. She was a career woman, as well as a divorcée living by herself in New York City. Betty had no problem with living in France—with or without him.

As Mike Knerr noted: "The restaurant at Deauville, and the incident that followed, appears trivial in the extreme. Piper puts it in a more direct light in his last entry for the day: 'I am going to miss both Betty and the little dog like the devil. I think Vall is going to miss me, too. But, at last, I can go back to my own country! I needn't be in exile anymore.' And, that, is the crux of the breakup: Beam wasn't happy in France; Betty was. Beam didn't like their living quarters; Betty did. Beam wanted to go home: Betty didn't.

"Before he could leave France, however, Betty located him and attempted to patch things up. Beam had caught a morning train back to Paris, managed to get his belongings into shape for leaving and had checked into the Hotel Unic.

"Betty found him on Tuesday, September 17th, and was waiting for him in his room when he returned from shopping. 'Seems she'd put in a couple of busy days trying to trace me, and put a French private eye on me—he probably located me by some corrupt tie-up with the cops.' They went back to her hotel room, picked up Vall, and had dinner at a Chinese restaurant. Neutral territory.

"Betty's idea—I go back to U.S., join her here in November for a trip south. My reaction—negative. I've had Europe."

Over breakfast the next morning, Piper tried thinking things out over coffee, but felt that his decision was the only one he could follow. "It won't do any good for me to go on that trip with Betty in the winter—we'd both be at each other's throats inside a month. Will try to persuade her to come back to the States with me when her vacation starts." He was obviously unhappy living abroad and probably felt hornswoggled when Betty 'maneuvered' them into living in France. Betty wouldn't, or couldn't, leave her job. But she could have agreed to vacation in the States, but when she didn't it showed her commitment to the marriage was not rock solid. They were both stubborn, and they'd pay dearly for it in the following years.

In this letter to Freida Coleman, Piper gives the "official story" on why he left France on September 20th:

Dear Freida,

I am returning to the States immediately, sailing on the Ile de France from Le Havre tomorrow. I will be in New York for a few days, and then will come to Williamsport. I wonder if it would be too much to ask you to put me up for a day or so, until I can get an apartment. I am coming back alone, but I have every hope that when I can get established Betty will come to join me. I'll explain all about it when I see you; at the moment it is rather painful for me to go into. The worst of it is that we still love each other; if we had parted spitting curses at one another it would be much easier on both of us.

Even coming home alone, however, will be better than staying here any longer, and it will be very good to be in Williamsport again, and I hope I may be able to remain there for the rest of my life. I always wanted to live in Williamsport, you know.

This seems like a very incomplete sort of letter, under the circumstances, but there is so much that I haven't space or time to write about now, and I can't seem to think of what to select. In less than two weeks, I should be talking to you, and can tell you all about it then.

My very best wishes to you and everybody in Williamsport. I'm writing Ted Ranck also.

Beam

It's obvious that this was not an easy letter to write, and it's hard to believe after what they went through in France that he *really* expected Betty to join him back in the States—in Williamsport of all places! She was going to give up her job, leave her friends in New York and live in the wilderness of central Pennsylvania—not likely. I think Piper knew he was just whistling up a blind alley.

Piper not only lost Betty when he fled France, but his dog, too. Don Coleman wrote, "He loved and idolized his dachshund Vall, and leaving the dog was a trying experience—especially for a tough guy like Beam who was so hypnotized with adoration.... Somewhere, some place, is a small black and white photo of Vall tugging at a slipper intact aboard the author's foot, while he sat back in a recliner perusing a manuscript. Why in such a short time, had this photo been so manhandled? Obviously, Beam showed off this jewel to everyone—knowing the critter probably considered itself *this* man's only friend abroad."

In his letter to Freida, he had written, "I always wanted to live in Williamsport, you know." He was through with Altoona; on his last visit he had been repulsed by how small and shabby his hometown had become. He had always loved the beauty of the West Branch Valley and the James V. Brown Library was first class—a good library was a necessity for Piper. After the split with John J. McGuire, his 'forced' retirement from the Pennsy, his mother's death and impending divorce with Betty, there were no longer any ties—other than personal memories and a few old friends—to keep him in Altoona. Thus, it was no surprise that Piper decided to move to Williamsport in 1957 and make a new life for himself.

Aboard the liner on the way home Piper worked on the 'new' Jeff Rand mystery "Murder Frozen Over" and finished Chapter Two. Once docked, he checked into the Plymouth Hotel and called Ken White who told him that Horace Gold had bought "Graveyard of Dreams" for $210—the author's share being $189.00. On October 1st, he flew back to Williamsport, where he was met by Don Coleman. He spent the night with the Colemans and the next day he went out apartment hunting. He settled on a shotgun apartment at 330 East Third Street.

A few days later the Soviets shot up the equivalent of the first atomic bomb: they put an orbiter in space, Sputnik—accomplishing the impossible. The Space Race was on. Like most American science fiction writers of the time, Piper was chagrined that it wasn't an American craft orbiting the Earth and at the same time in awe of this 'new' miracle of science.

As Don Coleman remembers: "In early October 1957, Beam was enjoying a 'Katinka' cocktail at Freida Coleman's den bar when a news bulletin broke over TV, announcing the launching of the Russian satellite

'Sputnik' that was gloriously circling the earth. It had to be a severe blow to US technology, learning that the Soviets had fired off an orbiting satellite that would circle about the globe....

"'DAMN!' Beam growled. 'If only Odin had given me a clue. And Thor himself must have surely known!'

"Shaking his head in anger," Piper continued, 'They got the jump on us. And the DAMN thing is no bigger around than a boxcar wheel; and only a mere 25 pounds heavier than yours truly!'

"He turned to the bar, pulled the ever-existent pad of paper from his breast pocket, and taking his multi-color pen to hand, began to draw 'Sputnik.' Beam utilized the four colors of ink on the small sheet of paper, telling us all the details of how it worked, how it was built and how it was launched. He was so excited because this was something he excelled at! He would sketch what he termed as a 'simple spherical space-oriented vehicular orbiter.'"

"Diane Coleman Simpson, Don's sister, continues: 'An amazing thing happened the next day; the newspaper had a full account of it, including a staff drawing. It was astoundingly similar to the picture Beam had drawn the night before!'

"Far from crude, the likeness by Piper was undeniable in fact, and as sound as his own logic in his conception of space.... In little more than two months, it burnt up returning to earth, but another had been launched (with a dog) just thirty days after the first launching. This irritated Beam further, not only because the United States of America had yet to get a satellite successfully of the pad—but it 'interfered' with his own space 'program.'"

Piper had good reason to be irritated, other than sheer unapologetic American patriotism. This orbiter had just invalidated his own near-time Future History in which he had invested a good deal of work and a number of recent stories. Never again would he write any story closer in time to the present age than several hundred years.

In a letter to a British fan—in answer to a question asked for his fanzine—Piper wrote a short piece titled, "The Future History of H. Beam Piper," which includes the following addendum: "Beyond this, with the exception of one story, 'The Keeper,' (*Venture*) about 30,000 years in the future when the Fifth Empire was at the height of its power, and Terra was in the middle of another glacial age, I have not gone. Nothing else, with the possible exception of a novelette called 'The Edge of the Knife,' *Amazing*, May, 1957, belongs to the History of the Future. This was a story, time 1973 CE (Christian Era), about a history professor who got his past and future confused, and had a lot of trouble as a result. It was written and published shortly before Sputnik I invalidated a lot of my near-future stuff, and made me swear off doing anything within a couple of centuries of now."

Don Coleman noted, "I had approached Beam sometime before this breakthrough, inquiring, 'How in the hell are you ever so far ahead in writing such goings-on in space when, in reality, they are becoming fact every day?'

"'Oh HELL,' he responded quite loudly, waving an arm about. 'I just have to maintain a distance of a few centuries or so, which sometimes, I find difficult to uphold.'"

Piper was true to his word. Most of his pre-Sputnik stories take place in the 'indefinite future' or near future. After Sputnik, almost all of his stories took place several hundred, to several thousand, years in the future.

CHAPTER TWENTY-FIVE

Ministry of Disturbance

It took some time for Piper to get the new Williamsport apartment in shape and most of October was spent buying the usual necessities. It took time, with Freida and Bub Coleman—Don Coleman's younger brother—to clean out the old apartment in Altoona. That he kept this apartment after his mother's death, living in New York and then moving to France, was one of the great anomalies of the Piper story. True, he had been selling more stories since 1956, but his writing income was still under a thousand dollars for 1957 and paying the rent on that apartment must have been a major drain on his financial resources.

Despite setting up the new apartment and clearing out the old one in Altoona, he still continued work on "Murder Frozen Over:" "Finished—very unsatisfactorily Chapter V late P.M. and early morning."

Sunday, October 6th, 1957, was Don Coleman's 26th birthday with Piper in attendance. "…an event which makes me feel *très ancien*. Big celebration, with my favorite dish, leg of lamb, which I loathe, for dinner," Piper noted in his diary.

Knerr noted: "The next few days were a bit on the hectic side as Beam tried to get his gas stove hooked-up, the phone installed and generally suffered at the hands of workmen who didn't show, or came at awkward times. He arranged to travel to Harrisburg, to his cousin Charles' house to pick up his pistols and wrote: 'To bed again, about 0100, mentally fagged out. Hope my subconscious works something on this damned story!'"

His mystery novel, "Murder Frozen Over," was progressing with all the usual Piper blocks and frustrations. He would work all day on it, then end up throwing everything away except a couple of pages the following morning. The hell of it was that after all that work, he would never sell the novel. His diary entries are typical: "Spent evening working on story; like the dinner, not one of my better days. Manufacturing wastepaper at a great rate, ended with two satisfactory pages." Piper would have loved word processors—the ease of rewriting would have saved him endless hours of re-typing the same pages over and over again....

On November 5th, "Letter from Ken White, enclosing letter from J-n McG-e [John McGuire], re *Lone Star Planet*, which Ace wants for another double-back pocket book." Obviously, word had filtered down to McGuire and now he wanted his share of the royalties. The Ace advance of $225 wouldn't arrive until late February 1958.

Once again a publisher arbitrarily re-titled one of Piper's books; of course, during this seminal period of science fiction writing, editors were gods—or had godly powers. Writers didn't see them the same way; Mike Knerr wrote: "All the years of rejection and humiliation in trying to sell his stories, left Beam bitter about the publishing business. Although he had many friends in editorial positions, he used to laugh at them as well—on at least one occasion referring to them as the 'lowest form of animal life in the universe.' He always pointed out that there were not enough desks in the editorial world and 'when the music stops, everyone grabs a desk. It's how,' he would add, 'New York rearranges their editors.'"

Piper plowed his way through "Murder Frozen Over" for the rest of 1957, which he was now describing as "A horrible thing—just saw how story can be much improved by postponing one of the events in it; will have to re-plan, and scrap the last twenty-five pages, painfully rewritten this week." The new *Galaxy* magazine with "Graveyard of Dreams" hit the stands just before Christmas and he picked up a copy. "Was afraid word-age cut would ruin it; it didn't—story reads very well."

By the end of the year, he was still struggling to get the Jeff Rand novel under control. "I hope I am not being optimistic in saying that I think I finally have the story planned the way I want it, but believe I have."

His loneliness for Betty and Vall seemed to grow rather than diminish and his work suffered.... Piper began 1958 with a new resolution: "Never to start a story in manuscript again until I have it *completely* planned." This resolution lasted until April 16th. "I've done it again; started first drafting a story without proper planning."

At a time when he could ill afford it, he was still punching away on "Murder Frozen Over" and was slated to spend nearly an entire year in its writing. As Knerr explains: "In writing mysteries he was creating errors of judgment that eventually would come 'home to roost.' The publication of *Murder in the Gunroom*, by Knopf in 1952, hadn't gained him any real money, nor success as a mystery writer. Yet, he produced three Jeff Rand mysteries—two of which never sold. *Murder at the Conference* had long ago been shelved.

"Beam's mystery novels were as meticulously planned as anything he had ever written, but the publishers and the public were not much interested in them. Perhaps there was too much of the 'Victorian' in them at a time when readers wanted Mickey Spillane, Richard Prather or Fredrick Brown."

Unfortunately, for Piper, drawing room mysteries were passé; a new mystery reading public had emerged along with the Cold War, weaned on the carnage and destruction of World War II and Korea. Mystery readers now wanted hardboiled detectives and mean streets. Beam's mysteries harkened back to a kinder, gentler period of Conan Doyle, Agatha Christie and John Dickson Carr [no relation—jfc], or what are now referred to as cozies in the trade.

Knerr further noted, "On the other hand, Beam's science fiction stories…seldom finished out 'of the money' in the *Astounding/Analog* bonuses. 'He Walked Around the Horses' was anthologized around the world, including a British school reader. *Murder in the Gunroom*, by comparison, fizzled out to the point where…even Beam didn't have a copy of it, except in carbon.

"Still, he doggedly plugged away at it, went for walks and fired his pistols at the YMCA range. During one of these walks, on January 21st, he slipped on an icy sidewalk and hurt his back. 'Have a devilish pain in my side,' he wrote on the 25th. 'Don't know if I hurt something when I fell on ice Tuesday or not.' Whether or not the fall on the ice was the cause, the back problems returned again in November, concerning him enough to write: 'This is really something serious.'"

Piper would suffer from back pain for the rest of his life. Whether he was too poor, or too proud, to see a doctor, we'll never know. It did make it harder for him to work at the typewriter and undoubtedly added to his ongoing depression. Despite the pain, he finished the first draft of "Murder Frozen Over" by the end of January.

As Mike Knerr wrote, "By now, since the novel had been started in France, he had probably gone through several reams of typing paper in his efforts to get it right. The following day, while he girded himself for the final draft battle, he doodled on a science fiction short story. 'This is going to be an idea John Campbell gave me—the practical Romans and the philosophic Greeks, in terms of a Galactic civilization. Beginning to get some ideas.'

"Beam was a little worn out from banging away on the 'revised revised first draft' and not quite ready to launch into the final. '...doodling at nothing much, and just feeling like a spent bullet. Will take it easy for a few days, and then get cracking on final draft.' While he rested up, Ken White wrote him and informed him that 'Ace was publishing *Lone Star Planet* in July or August.'

"When Beam began the final draft of "Murder Frozen Over," a couple of days later, he immediately ran into problems. 'After lunch, started on the final, or white-paper draft. A hell of a job, spent hours on the first paragraph of the first page. Style is something that can't be planned, it has to be revised.' Quite possibly Ernest Hemingway would agree with him, but not all writers. One can become so obsessed with revisions, as Jack Woodford once pointed out, that one couldn't write a note to the milkman without revising it several times.

"He made it to page 131 by February 20th, maintaining an average of 10 pages a day, but typically ran into problems. 'Whole thing sour—typed one page and saw I'd have to re-plan everything. To work on that after dinner, and by 2000 reached decision to scrap the whole thing and rewrite from the beginning. This is a dreadful thing and will set me back at least a month, but may make the difference between sale and no sale.'

"It didn't make a difference in the long run, but writers often cannot tell that. The end result was that 'Murder Frozen Over' wasn't mailed out until April 7th. On February 28th, 1958, he did receive the first check from Ace Books for *Lone Star Planet*, and that helped bolster his sagging finances.

"On March 18th, Piper wrote—'Did a little doodling on a science fiction idea, to be worked on when I finish "Murder Frozen Over".' Such was the birth of *Little Fuzzy*, a book destined to be another novel Beam would agonize over until it had gone through the hands of more than a dozen publishers. When it finally found a home with Avon Books, that company had already rejected it three times.

"In addition to the gun exhibits and his writing, Beam read constantly, and his opinions on writers was as definite as his opinions on writing. And, for all of his reading, the factors that produce a national best seller escaped him. In reading Ayn Rand's *Atlas Shrugged*, he wrote: '—heartbreaking to see a good story idea like that mangled to death.' Again while reading the same book in early April (1958): 'I certainly wish I'd written that story—it would have been about 75 percent shorter.' He couldn't *see* the whole picture and, at times, one would have thought he had tunnel vision. Once, when I mentioned that I liked Robert Heinlein's work, Beam exploded—slammed his tobacco pouch on the desk. 'Heinlein wastes plots,' he roared, although later he admitted that he too liked the man's writing."

Knerr noted, "The Little Fuzzy idea, still in the womb and kicking for birth, seemed to go into false labor early in April when Beam picked up a copy of John Dewey's *Reconstruction in Philosophy* 'and came across an idea ["Ministry of Disturbance"] that looks like something useable. Hope I can get a story out of it.'

"'Ministry of Disturbance' did develop, but not without all the labor pains of a typical Piper brainchild. By April 16th, he was again moaning that his 'proper planning' had been shot by his fervent desire to get it down on paper. In the meantime, Ken wrote that he was 'optimistic about 'Murder Frozen Over' and wanted Beam to send him a carbon for a magazine sale. Piper did so, the next day, and later found a 'lucky' pin, which he always considered better than finding a penny."

"Ministry of Disturbance," like any other Piper story was not without its problems: "I have done the same goddamned thing I always do," he wrote on April 26th, "gotten antsy to start the story before I had it planned. I wonder if I'll ever plan a story properly before I start it." The next day, he confided to his diary that the "whole thing is a bloody mess. I'm doing everything wrong the way I always do it." By the last of the month he had decided, "the whole thing needs drastic revision—maybe I'll have a chance to plan this story as it should be planned." He was concerned as well about the title, toying with the idea of calling it "Last Challenge."

By the first week in May, Piper was wallowing in literary confusion, totally sure of what he *wanted* to write, and just as totally unsure of *how* to do it. He solved the problem by shopping for tobacco and rum, and having "peanut parties" for the squirrels in Brandon Park. He had, by now, switched from Dunhill tobacco to Brindley's Mixture. He decided to "change means of perception" on the story and, as usual, he tore it all up to begin again.

Mike Knerr noted: "Freida and Don Coleman came to his rescue, although they probably didn't know it, and took him for a drive to Cogan Valley (several miles north of Williamsport) which gave him a new perspective on the story—albeit: 'Not saying anything rash.'"

Piper here sums up what in retrospect was the central problem with his writing. "There seems to be a limit to how closely I can plan a story; I can't allow for what my imagination adds to it while working on it." This is a problem many writers experience. Over-plotting can lead to headaches of its own; boredom or writing by the numbers.

Some writers like Philip K. Dick worked like automatic writers, they just pulled words from the ether, or went into a dissociative state. That was one reason why Dick was so prolific and often dealt with philosophical and quasi-religious themes. Other writers over-plot and spend too much time in research and agonizing over story developments.

Dr. Robert A. Howard, a psychology professor at San Diego State University, was a published mystery writer. A former newspaper reporter, Doc Howard had written a number of novels and mystery stories for the mystery magazines, like the *Alfred Hitchcock* and *Ellery Queen* digests in the 1950s. His best known novel was *Murder Takes a Wife*. When he wanted to write a novel, he would spend three or four weeks making detailed character studies of his main characters, sometimes running twenty or thirty pages. Once he was completely done with his character profiles, Doc Howard would go into his writing room and stay there until the book was finished, sometimes three or four days, pausing only for food and bathroom breaks. He would enter what he called a "fugue state" and the writing just poured out of his head and into his typing fingers.

* * *

By June 3rd, 1958, Piper was correcting the final draft of "Ministry of Disturbance," but interrupted his work to fly to New York for a Mystery Writers of America meeting. He mailed off the final story to Ken White on the 7th. He noted sourly that *Cosmopolitan* had bounced "Murder Frozen Over" and started "work on preliminary planning for a bastard science-fiction short (parallel time)."

Knerr noted, "A few days later, after hearing a lecture on the canal days of Pennsylvania, he wrote, 'may work up a historical novel out of the canal pirates.' Instead he finished the 'first-first draft' of the short story, and added that he was planning to call it 'Outsider.'"

"Although Beam had dozens of ideas for stories, he couldn't seem to get them into any kind of usable shape and he spent a considerable amount of time doodling and casting bullets for his .44 cap and ball revolver. When he did get to work on the typewriter, he usually scrapped everything or doodled on a mystery story he'd thought of. The 'Outsider' fell apart on June 27th when he decided, 'I was going at it the wrong way—surprise ending to be reinforced by putting story on another time line, the stranger to come from our world.'"

Piper finished the story on July 3rd, re-titled it "The Other Road" and shipped it off to Ken. While this new story deals with parallel time, it's not a Paratime story; just a one-off. It was later retitled "Crossroads of Destiny" when it was published in the July 1959 issue of *Fantastic Universe*.

Knerr wrote, "While uptown he got his pistol permit renewed and noted that there was a 'remarkable' and laudable absence of chicken-shit about that.' Back at the apartment he was 'thinking of doing a short on the theme of Jack the Ripper killed by an intended victim.' The story got 'sick and died' before it was more than an idea and Beam began to work on the 'negamatter meteor' story which eventually developed into 'The Answer.'"

"Ministry of Disturbance" sold right away to John W. Campbell's *Astounding Science Fiction*. It's a classic wheels within wheels story. Campbell's story blurb went, "Sometimes getting a job is harder than the job after you get it—and sometimes getting out of a job is harder than either." A thousand years after its founding, Emperor Paul XXII found the First Empire's civilization growing stagnant and decadent. He planned to shake it up, creating a Ministry of Disturbance. His plans were successful, at least for a while....

Ken sent him the check for "Ministry of Disturbance," which arrived on July 8th to give Beam's bank balance a badly needed transfusion. Meanwhile, he went back to work on the 'negamatter meteor' story.

PART FIVE

The Science Fiction Novels

CHAPTER TWENTY-SIX

Little Fuzzy

In early July, Piper finished the first draft of "The Answer," which he wrote was, "rough as hell." He promptly put it aside to toy with ideas on the Jack the Ripper story and *Little Fuzzy*. By the middle of July, 1958, he had decided that the Jack the Ripper story was hopeless and started the final draft of "The Answer," which he mailed on the 24th. He began work on *Little Fuzzy* with a first draft start on August 1st.

By the 11th of August, he was in another literary jam. "The *Little Fuzzy* story seems to have gotten very sick; will put it to bed and let it have a nice long rest and maybe it'll get well again." Unable to forget mysteries, Piper started plotting a new Jeff Rand—a fourth!—story hoping by the time he had worked out the details *Little Fuzzy* might be up and about again.

During this period he was depressed, missing Betty and Vall. And, despite the fact that he was actually producing salable copy—instead of 'wastepaper' as he did through most of 1955 and '56—he was angry and frustrated. "I wish it didn't take me so God damned long to get the right slant on a story!" His frustration with writing was beginning to follow a pattern...added to all this Piper had periods of not feeling well, yet somehow he managed to get *Little Fuzzy* up to page 51 by August 17th.

"Soon it will be a year since I left Betty and Vall," Piper wrote on August 19th, 1958, and promptly fell into a depression. "This is about the lowest my morale has been so far, since I came here." In an attempt to beat his depression, he took a train trip to Baltimore and stayed in 'a fleabag' near the train station. The trip didn't do much to lift him out of the dumps and he quickly returned to Williamsport to get back on the stalled *Little Fuzzy*.

Then he scrapped most of it and started over. "I seem to be working like hell and getting nowhere, and am now wondering if I'm not working on a job that won't amount to anything if I ever get it done." By the end of August he was still sweating out the storyline and not doing well at it. Piper was finding it difficult to get a handle on *Little Fuzzy*.

Since he was stalled on *Little Fuzzy* he took off for New York for a Mystery Writers' meeting and a talk with Ken White. Mike Knerr noted, "Beam had recovered enough of his sense of humor by the 9th to write beneath his diary entry, 'Pope died,' and on the next day's page: 'Great consternation in Heaven; Pope long overdue and still unreported.' Back in Williamsport, the story wasn't going any better. 'Can't see to get anything accomplished; just running around in circles.' Beam's health was deteriorating, whether from his back injury or from his older knee injury… and he was having pains in his legs, as well as a stomach ache."

To add to the general run of problems Ken wrote and told him that both 'The Answer' and 'The Other Road' had been rejected by Campbell. On October 21st, Piper learned that his New York and his local bank accounts were together below $1,000.00 so he cancelled plans to go to a Hydra Club meeting in New York City.

Knerr noted: "Toward the end of the month, as a change of pace, Beam helped John Hunsinger, a teacher at Lycoming College, put a canon into shape to be fired at football games. He went along to several and helped with the firing, but his morale didn't get much of a boost. On the 29th, he 'read some old Betty-letters from a year ago—not good for morale.' His copy of *Astounding Science Fiction* arrived on November 7th, 1958, with "Ministry of Disturbance" in it and he found that it 'Looks good in print.'"

Piper's back had started aching again and he told Ted Ranck that he wasn't going deer hunting this year, commenting that "It's getting to where I can't take it anymore." He stopped drinking, but that didn't help his back and by the end of the month it was still bothering him. As suddenly as it began, the pain ceased early in December and he went to a meeting of the Mystery Writers of America in New York. He also learned that "Murder Frozen Over" had been bounced by the Crime Club and that didn't make him too happy.

Knerr observed: "He went back to work, mostly manufacturing wastepaper, and had some domestic troubles with the local birds: 'The pair of pigeons still roosting over the back door, shitting all over everything. Wish I could harden my heart and murder both of them—instead, threw out some dry bread for them.'"

On December 15th, Piper decided to redo his last weeks' work on *Little Fuzzy*: "Better junk a week's work than spend months trying to sell an un-salable story." Even when he rewrote it, he didn't like the results and shortly before Christmas he scribbled, "Don't like what I wrote during the last week; if anything, worse than what I scrapped." He put it aside to begin working on ideas for a 10,000 word mystery story.

December 24th, he wrote, "Spent A.M. doodling and brain racking for ideas, and finally, while I was eating lunch, one emerged. Spent early A.M. developing it—insurance arson; man kills brother, who was responsible for fire in which a dozen factory workers die, because he feels he must be put to death for his crime but family must not be publicly disgraced." He kicked this idea around most of the day, then spent the evening reading his second unsold Jeff Rand novel. Piper noted, "'Murder at the Conference' suffers from same fault as all the others, too many characters, too much bullshitting around." John Campbell would have agreed about Piper's tendency to include too many minor characters and, although, he was aware of this problem, he never did anything about it.

Knerr wrote, "Don Coleman's mother, Freida, called him and invited him to her wedding slated for December 27th, which probably brought back memories of his own marital problems."

Yes, and memories of friends lost, like Ferd and Fletcher Pratt. On Christmas day, not being the slightest bit religious, he took in a movie. "…and then found there wasn't a god-damned restaurant open anywhere, so came home and heated a tin of clam chowder, and then worked more in the evening." As a kind of footnote, he added: "All in all, had a hell of a merry Christmas." The next day he got four pages done on the new mystery story and vowed that, "As soon as I have it done in first draft, will go back to *Little Fuzzy*."

On Saturday, Don Coleman picked him up and took him to church to see Freida become a December bride to…Jim Shannon. Piper had this to say: "Freida and husband, Jim Shannon, off on honeymoon about 1600." From then on parties were the order of the day, and he toured the various clubs of the Williamsport area with Don and friends. He took it easy on the 30th, but was back with the Colemans to see in the New Year, "…a regular old fashioned New Year's Eve."

Don Coleman wrote, "With me leaving town for a career in Cincinnati in 1957, I more or less lost contact as to the comings and goings of Beam. I never knew he had fallen on the ice! When Beam decided to come to Williamsport to live—and surely his closest friends were there—we in the family were ecstatic! It was truly wonderful. And then, eventually Diane and Sylvia left due to their marriages, and finally my mother remarried and left town…. Now, he was alone, except for Ted. His ultimate fate was very sad and my mother would always blame herself…. She talked about the fact many times that things may have been different had she remained in Beam's Billtown [Williamsport—jfc]."

No one knows the future and in retrospect it's hard to blame the Colemans for getting on with their lives; after all, Piper showed himself to the world as this strong, hardy self-reliant man who could damn well take care of himself. With his tailored suits and Victorian ways, he appeared to be a man of means; not many outside the writing game know how poorly it pays—even its better journeymen. The only ones who make a killing selling books—besides the New York publishers—are those few who occupy the top of the bestsellers' lists year-after-year. Piper, sadly, was not of that ilk.

Nineteen fifty-nine started off on a bad note. Knerr noted: "The story [*Little Fuzzy*] wasn't going well, as usual, and he was manufacturing wastepaper at a steady clip. On the other hand, the nesting pigeons on the back porch were producing their own particular brand of 'wastepaper' at about the same rate of speed. Finally, realizing that his waste could be burned, but that of the birds had to be scrubbed, Beam declared war. '...after lunch, up to Dicky Grugan's [a local hardware store—jfc] and bought four feet of 48" chicken netting and used it to block the entrance to back porch, then cleaned up the pigeon shit. Result, a pair of mighty disgusted pigeons.'

"On January 18th, the temperature dropped to minus three degrees and the story dropped with it. Beam scrapped everything as 'utterly worthless' and started feeling 'sick about the whole thing.' The Betty memory was still working on him and a couple of days later he would write: 'A hell of a bad day.' During the period going to gun collector meetings gave him the diversion he needed and friends like Bill and Dick Houser, Lynn Henry, Cliff Breidinger and Louis Conrad were very important to him. They probably, like everyone else, never knew it."

Piper was a master at hiding his emotions and his mask was so good that not even his closest friends like Mike Knerr and Don Coleman could see through it. When Marvin Katz, a writer for *Grit*, invited Piper over for dinner, he greatly enjoyed their time together, but they never invited him again for fear of imposing. With the Colemans gone from Williamsport and his circle of friends growing smaller every year, he was becoming more and more isolated. Other than Mike Knerr, whom he met in 1959, he didn't have any other close friends in the writers' group.

On the other hand, Piper was an introvert and usually liked to work alone and not be social. He enjoyed writing, especially when the words were flowing. When a writer is in the zone there's nothing much better. Unfortunately, his writing didn't always flow and Piper spent as much time fighting for the right ideas and words as he did actual writing. A lot of his isolation may have been by choice. Unfortunately, his circle of friends was closing; he no longer had any one he could talk openly with. Mike Knerr, like Don Coleman, was much younger than Piper, and he always kept them at arm's length. Ted Ranck was more of a hunting buddy, and he never was as close to Piper as Ferd Coleman or Jack McGuire had been.

Piper still had his writing friends in science fiction, like James Blish and Jerry Pournelle. But, unfortunately, he only saw them at conventions or on trips to New York City, when he could afford it. Piper took the train in mid-February for a Hydra Club meeting at Basil Davenport's place. When it broke up Piper, Randall Garrett and Larry Shaw finished it off at a handy pub. He talked to Ken White, heard nothing of interest and headed back to the typewriter. At home, as in Paris, the utilities were not working properly and he had to call his landlord about the heat being off in the apartment. It gets cold in central Pennsylvania and these type of interruptions were not helping his work.

Suddenly, Piper was making real progress on *Little Fuzzy*. On March 7th, he got a call that a party was going on at the Colemans; Freida was back from her honeymoon. It was undoubtedly just what he needed. "Got home sometime late, plastered. Just went to sleep. Maybe I'll get up early tomorrow and take a fresh start."

Mike Knerr wrote, "After finishing *Little Fuzzy*, Beam was at a loss for what to work on next. He went back to trying to think of an idea for a detective story and, for some hare-brained reason, shaved off his moustache the last of April. 'Don't know,' he admitted, 'whether I like me without it or not.' He finally decided he did, and let it grow back. He was still having troubles with the pigeons; now they were invading his peanut parties for the squirrels in Brandon Park. His morale was sagging as low as his bank account and he wasn't happy about it."

"The Answer" finally sold to *Fantastic Universe* for $50.00, $45.00 for Piper. So far, his only sale for 1959. He had high hopes for *Little Fuzzy*. *Astounding* was Piper's primary market, as well as the best paying, and Ken White sent *Little Fuzzy* to John Campbell first thing. The following rejection letter for *Little Fuzzy* from John W. Campbell dated May 13th, 1959, did not help his morale:

Dear Piper:

First, I'm drowning in novels, four times more than I can use.

The thesis of this one is one that I'm keenly interested in, but I feel that you've somewhat ducked the central issue which you established.

That is, the "talk and build a fire" rule is to be shown to be no proper test; in the end you have the Fuzzy's speech picked up and understood. Remember Hal Clement's starfish people who had no sonic communication—but wig-wagged with several thousand tendrils over their body surface? "Look, Ma...no speech!" Also no telepathy.

But the basic problem of "whaddaya mean...'human'?" is an enormously important one. You made it "sapient," which is an excellent idea.

But I feel this novel isn't as strong as it could have been. You, in your detective experience, found that life is-in-fact made up of a most awful confusion of too many people who might be involved. You must have learned how to mentally juggle two dozen relevant characters at once in your work.

The average reader hasn't. Your story would be more effective for John Q. Public if you trimmed the cast of characters to about six individuals, plus assorted off-stage stooges who don't have to be remembered. Detective stories are fun; sure. But this isn't a detective story; it's a philosophical problem story. The problem has some tendency to get lost, strayed, or forgotten under the deluge of characters.

Regards,
John W. Campbell, Jr.

To a degree, Campbell is correct; there are a lot of viewpoint characters in *Little Fuzzy* and sometimes it's easy for even an astute reader to get 'lost.' Part of this can be blamed on Piper's 'technique.' Piper—in the "Double Bill Symposium"—offered this bit of advice on writing from a 'viewpoint' character: "Name your viewpoint character in the first paragraph, if possible, and don't name him thereafter unless someone addressed him by name, or something like that." Piper's reasoning is good: "You're giving his thoughts along with his experiences and actions. You don't think of yourself by name; not often, anyhow." True, but fiction is not quite a mirror of life, as Campbell so astutely points out. Sometimes even the most observant readers need a few signposts as to who is saying what to whom.

The most confusing thing about the large number of viewpoint characters in *Little Fuzzy* is at times it is hard to tell which character *is* the viewpoint character. This is a failure of technique, not Piper's concept. A few more carefully placed character names could have easily cleared up most of the confusion. Something Piper does do in his later works, like *Space Viking* and *Lord Kalvan of Otherwhen*, where the more 'unusual' invented names force him to place more character tags than usual.

After wasting a couple months on a dud title, "Pest Among Men," and a racketeering story that ended up in the incinerator—where all of Piper's duds ended up sooner or later—he began work on a new story in his Terro-Human Future History, "Hot Time on Kwannon," later published as "Oomphel in the Sky." On the Fourth of July he went to feed the squirrels at Brandon Park when he, "Stopped to light a colored-fire flare for some small boys; got home just in time to see fireworks on South Side from back porch."

His financial condition was getting severe enough that he was beginning to sell off more of his pistols in New York, mostly to Robert Abels, a New York antique arms dealer. For Piper, this was going from bad to very bad. But *Little Fuzzy* was bouncing all over New York—1959's major accomplishment book-wise—and his cupboard was growing bare.

In August, after several months of false starts and rewriting, he finished "Oomphel in the Sky" and went back to work on another one of his mystery stories that would go nowhere.

Knerr noted, "On Sunday, August 23rd, he wrote: 'Betty's birthday,' at the top of the page and sketched little red and blue flowers and ribbons around the name. To add to his dismal feelings, the weather clouded in on him with occasional rain. 'Dark and gloomy,' he wrote, as if it mirrored what he felt.

"Although he 'believed' he was getting somewhere with the story, it was heavy going interspersed with days of anger… 'This was a bad-luck day,' he scrawled, on the 28th. 'Got a letter from Ken White—Gold

Medal has bounced *Little Fuzzy*. Lost my Dunhill 4-color pen. The price of rum has gone up another .25 cents—Shit!' He seemed to add the 25-cent rise in the price of rum as the final capper to the whole day."

Things got a little better in August. Campbell bought "Oomphel in the Sky" for *Astounding* and Piper's check, less agent commission, was $513.00. Still, to this point his total income for 1959 was only $558.00.

"Oomphel in the Sky" is a short story set during the "plantation era" in the Ninth Century A.E. It takes place on the planet Kwann, where the Terrans are having problems keeping the local natives under control. In this story, we find a classic Piper conflict: inefficient government versus efficient private enterprise. The story takes place thirty years before the System States War when Terra is a hotbed of Neo-Marxist liberalism, and we get the idea that it's slipping into complete decadence. At this point, it appears that Terra's colonial offspring are all that's keeping the Federation from falling apart.

When Ted Ranck came over to the apartment to invite Piper to go deer hunting in Tioga County, Piper said he would go. Later that evening he wrote, "…wish now that I hadn't. Think I'll call him up and change that—tell him I can't go." He begged off the next day; with the various aches and pains he was having, it was…a wise move. To sit at a desk about fifty-one weeks out of a year, then try to hunt in rugged terrain for even a few days, would tax a much younger man than H. Beam Piper.

Mike Knerr wrote, "On September 21st, both Beam and I (among others) received a call from Ray Young 'who is organizing something called a writers' forum, a meeting on 2 Dec. to which I am invited.' Both of us were gun-shy about any such organization, but when we were invited we thought it over and decided to go. Beam, perhaps, out of loneliness for other scribes."

One of Knerr's old friends, Monty F. Melville, in this May 19th, 2008, letter, provides a wonderful overview on the origin of the Williamsport Creative Writers' Forum, as well as the first meeting between H. Beam Piper and Mike Knerr, who later became Piper's literary protégé and repository of the "Lost Fuzzy" novel and other memorabilia, including the

Piper diaries:

> *It was early autumn of 1959. Mike called me. Said there was an article in the newspaper that a writers' group was starting up. Would I like to go? Sure. We met in some guy's house. There were 7 of us there. Piper, and Bill Stroup, Mike and myself and 3 others. All guys. Piper of course was the main attraction. He was the only one published and had some recognition. He was a quiet, unassuming man. He appeared to be rather gaunt looking and seemed to look a little uneasy with all the attention he was getting and spoke only when asked for his input. Mike and him hit it off immediately.*
>
> *Piper had what Mike wanted—publication and recognition. So Mike gleaned as much off Piper as he could: Do you have an agent? How do I get one? Where do I get one? Should I ignore agents and go directly to publishing houses? What's your writing routine?*
>
> *After we settled down we introduced ourselves and told a little about our writing life. It was a typical writers' club discussion and critiquing. I went back one more time but felt out of place, so I never went back again and I don't know how long the group lasted. I never saw Piper again and once in a while Mike mentioned something about him like he had a great gun collection including some flintlocks. He also showed me one of his books he had bought.*

Here is Mike Knerr's view of their meeting: "On the evening of December 2nd, 1959, the area writers congregated at the Young residence on West Third Street. Piper said of it, in his diary: 'Had dinner at the Day & Night, and then to a meeting of something called the Creative Writers' Forum, the moving spirit of which seems to be a young fellow named Ray Young. It was a rather enjoyable affair at that.'

"At the meeting, I wasn't sure I liked Beam," Knerr wrote. "I'd never met the man, nor had I read anything he'd written. Garbed in a black suit, vest and necktie, he looked like a character out of a Victorian novel. Ray told everyone to introduce themselves, and their line of writing to the group.

"'I'm H. Beam Piper,' Beam said, in turn, 'and I write science fiction.'

"Someone asked, 'Do you sell it?'

"'Yes,' Beam replied, no doubt holding himself in check among these dunderheads.

"'May we touch your hem?' Kathryn Hoover asked.

"'Hem touching,' Beam said, with a twinkle in his eye, "will be at three P.M. tomorrow.'

"I started to like him."

CHAPTER TWENTY-SEVEN

When in the Course...

Piper was already having problems with his latest science fiction yarn, "When in the Course..." and was busy rewriting and reformulating the plot. Meanwhile, he wrote, "the ceiling started to leak and continued throughout the evening." Piper was plagued with periodic losses of heat from the landlord's furnace, inconsiderate pigeons, the inability to get a story planned the way he wanted it—and now water dripping into the gunroom.

He ended 1959 working on a lecture for the Gun Collectors. On New Year's Eve, he fired "the eensy brass cannon' and read until 0300 A.M. "Alone."

Piper was finding it increasingly more difficult to live on his sporadic writing income, but believed he had no other alternative—certainly, not one that he would have chosen or tolerated:

Mike Knerr had his own view of Piper's problems: "It was a confused several years for books during the early nineteen sixties; the ruling in March of 1960, by the US Court of Appeals that D. H. Lawrence's *Lady Chatterley's Lover* was not obscene was a major breakthrough. In and of itself, the ruling had little effect on general reading material, or science fiction, but it served to demonstrate that the times were on the verge of change—as were the reading tastes of the American people. It was a confused several years for books during the early sixties and it was hardly a time for a writer to make mistakes if he or she wanted to remain a selling (eating) professional.

"Beam and I became fairly close friends about this time but it was not until 1961, when I became a selling writer that my opinions really meant much to him. This, of course, is understandable; at 56, and with dozens of published stories to his credit, his attitude was one of—*the student doesn't tell the teacher how to write*—and he stuck to it.

"He lent me a carbon of 'Murder Frozen Over' and I read it. I'd read mysteries for years and was, by then, building quite a collection of Piper's science fiction. That was about the time that he was starting *Four-Day Planet*.

"'Stick to science fiction,' I told him.

"In those days I had no idea why he was selling his guns (gun collectors do this all the time) and I had no idea how broke Beam was, nor how much in love he was with Betty. That information only surfaced after Ken White became my agent."

On January 8th, 1960, Piper was "doodling in evening; a lot of half-assed ideas, none of which go very far." He added that: "The next one will be a detective story. I hope so, anyhow." He was back to beating his brains out on "Pest Among Men" and was totally bogged down again. By the 26th, having torn up all sorts of beginnings, he started over. "This is the same damned thing I've done with every other story I've ever written, but I think in this case it's necessary. In order to get on with the story, I have to get the beginning established, or I'll go on planning and re-planning it and getting no further."

On February 4th, he wrote, "letter from Ken White—Campbell has bounced 'When in the Course…,' and Dell is not going to publish *Little Fuzzy*. This is the worst of all."

Here is John W. Campbell's rejection letter for "When in the Course…," sent to Kenneth White on January 20th, 1960:

Dear Mr. White:

Piper has one, long-standing characteristic in his writing that causes trouble; he personalizes, identifies, <u>all</u> his characters equally. There are too many spear-carriers being treated as stars, which makes it hard for the reader to get the hang of the story. Real life man, indeed, may be this way; but art is not the reproduction of life—that's photography of the snap-shot variety—instead it's an abstraction from and clarification of life.

That's one fault here. The second fault present is that the reader winds up with a vague feeling that nothing much happened. Agreed freely and fully that it's not true; a lot did happen. But the <u>feeling</u> can be there.

The problems are made as diffuse as the cast of characters. (That, too, is true of life…but makes for ineffective art.)

If he had made the Problem the House of Styphon, then, at a particular period, under particular circumstances, the reader would sigh, feel "Ah! Now they've licked the problem," and be able to rest content.

As is…where's the climax in this story?

Regards,

John W. Campbell, Jr.

Ken White would continue to make the rounds—ever smaller each time as one pulp after another disappeared—with "When in the Course…" but the story would fail to be published during Piper's lifetime. Fortunately for posterity, it did turn up among the 'few' surviving unpublished manuscripts when Ace Books took possession of Piper's literary estate from Charles Piper, Beam's cousin. [As editor of Piper's four short story collections, I was able to include it among the stories in *Federation*—the first ever collection of H. Beam Piper stories.—jfc]

Despite the story's flaws, it was quite a coup to be able to publish a "new" Piper short, made even more so by the fact that it was the 'origin' story of the Kalvan stories as well as *Lord Kalvan of Otherwhen*.

Piper often re-used the better elements of his unsold stories and in this case he took the fictional kingdom of Hostigos out of "When in the Course…," transplanting it into the Paratime series as a small princedom in the Great Kingdom of Hos-Harphax in Fourth Level, Europo-American, Aryan-Transpacific.

As Campbell noted, there were several story problems with "When in the Course..:" itself. The story has a meandering plotline and numerous subplots that for the most part go nowhere. The biggest problem was a resolution that solves the major plot problem in a simplistic manner, thereby robbing the reader of satisfaction. Along with *First Cycle*, "When in the Course…" was one of the only two surviving unpublished Piper works. The writing, of course, is fine; it's the plot and the resolutions that are badly flawed. One begins to suspect that these flaws were typical of many of Piper's unpublished and "lost" works.

Yet, there are some great characters in the story; Rylla, Ptosphes and Harmakros make their first appearance and the fascinating gunpowder theocracy of Styphon's House is introduced. It's actually fortuitous that *Fantastic Universe, Amazing Stories* or one of the other Piper salvage markets didn't pick up the story, preventing him from reinventing it as "Gunpowder God"—the first of the Lord Kalvan novelettes.

Piper went back to being frustrated with the way "Pest Among Men" was going, and soon decided to take a break from it and write an article on the Battle of Cerignola. As Mike Knerr points out: "Unless he had planned to sell the article overseas, he would have done better to write about Appomattox or Gettysburg. A European battle fought in the Sixteenth Century wouldn't seem to draw much of an American audience."

Yet, Piper launched into it the same time as he reached insolvency. "Up town to bank—am down to $20.00 now, worst ever—and got something for dinner." It took him about a week to write the article; it is unfortunate there was no real market for it. Writing and selling a nonfiction piece every few months would have solved most of his financial problems. He sent "The Queen Comes Into Her Own," to Ken White on February 15th; it fell victim to editorial flack and didn't sell. He went back to working on "Pest Among Men" and began considering the sale of some of his gun collection.

A letter from Ken on the 16th of March in 1960, added Putnam's to the "list of publishers who didn't want *Little Fuzzy*." On the 19th: "Horace Gold has bounced 'When in the Course...' as expected, with characteristic Goldian comments." Finally, on Piper's birthday... "The whole story ["Pest Among Men"—jfc] fell to pieces on me, and I spent most of the day among the wreckage, wondering how the hell I was ever going to get it put together again."

Mike Knerr explains, "To those who are not familiar with writers and the world of writing, it should be pointed out that authors do not write on one line of subject matter necessarily. Bart Spicer, in the 1950's, wrote a lot of mysteries, but he also wrote historical novels. Francis Van Wyck Mason wrote historical novels, but he also wrote the Hugh North series of espionage—North, of course, being promoted in Army rank every other book. One familiar science fiction writer used to write 'true confessions,' and the list goes on. Writers, by the very nature of their profession, should not be pigeon-holed.

"On the other hand, if a writer yearns to write historical fiction, but knows that it won't sell at the moment, he either shifts to another subject that *will* sell—or he's a damned fool. Piper made a $675.00 advance on *Murder in the Gunroom* and never sold another mystery. While he insisted on writing material that wouldn't be published (when he could have been devoting his time to science fiction that would have sold), he was steadily going broke and constantly suffering from writers' block. After leaving Betty in 1957, his earnings for the next two years totaled a mere $1,624.85, and prices were steadily going up. In 1960, his earnings were just $5.00 short of $1,400.00."

Piper's efforts might have been better served by writing science fiction; however, that wasn't a guaranteed sale, either. He was still getting rejection slips for both *Little Fuzzy* and "When in the Course…" In retrospect, we know that *Little Fuzzy* has become a small classic, while "When in the Course…" was only half-baked. Still, had either sold, he might have focused more on science fiction stories. However, Piper was not writing to the tune of the time clock, but to his inner meter—which is why he stamped his unique personality all over his best works. What he learned writing unsuccessful stories like "Pest Among Men," "When in the Course…" and articles such as "The Queen Comes Into Her Own" was transmuted into his other fiction works, such as *Lord Kalvan of Otherwhen*.

One of the unique aspects of Piper's later writings is that they have a very 'lived in' feel; it's as if the author is a reporter from a different time or dimension. Very believable. His knowledge of history and mankind gave them gravitas and verisimilitude. All of his rewriting and re-casting of his stories gave them a solidity that few stories of that time have. Robert Heinlein during the late 1940's and early 1950's wrote some good novels, but many of the early ones don't hold up today. (His juveniles and later 1950's works like *Starship Troopers* being an exception.) Other than *Citizen of the Galaxy*, *Double Star* and *Beyond This Horizon* (which reads like it could have been written by Beam!), Heinlein's work of this period just doesn't have the 'weight' of Piper's best novels.

I don't believe it's any coincidence that Piper wrote his best work starting after his separation with Betty in 1957. His people are more 'real' and multi-dimensional. Stories like "Omnilingual" rank with the best science fiction tales of the era. His later novels had a believability and emotional depth that his earlier ones, like *First Cycle* and *Uller Uprising* lacked. It's unfortunate that Piper had to go through so much emotional upheaval, but a good case could be made that it did help his writing.

On Monday, April 11th, 1960, Piper wrote, "Up 0830, and tried to work on planning. Money trouble intruded to such an extent that I spent most of the time debating whether or not to shoot myself; proposition defeated by a very narrow vote, and may be brought before the house again if things don't get better. Am going to give 'Pest' a rest for a couple of days and try to cook up another short or novelette."

After reading this diary entry, it's almost surprising that Piper managed to slog along for another three and a half years before shooting himself. Mike Knerr explains: "This was Piper's first decision to use a gun on himself in the diaries, and it is significant in that he isn't really talking about money. He is talking about writing, and his tremendous problems in getting a story down on paper. It may have, at the time, seemed to him that money was the villain—yet he solved this whole 'financial problem' over the coming weeks simply by selling a few guns."

Piper wrote: "Dick Houser dropped in on the 15th: Sold him the .44 Rogers and Spencer for $45.00, which will pay my rent next month and give me $5.00 to live on." Piper was sailing pretty close to the edge, but that didn't stop him from working on mystery stories. He went back to work on "Pest Among Men" just before he died, which shows how much he was floundering in his final days.

It wasn't just the money problems or the frustration he experienced finishing his stories; it was the constant draining, hard-scrabble existence that helped drive him to kill himself. Piper would sell a story, then spin his wheels working on a new story that wouldn't quite gel, or finish another yarn, send it to his agent and have it rejected over and over again. There were no guarantees; he was only as good as his last sale....

Piper wasn't one to write to editorial order, either, or he would have been busy polishing off stories that Campbell oftentimes handed him on a silver platter. Campbell respected him both as a writer and a working detective. Unfortunately, we will never know the tale Piper spun that turned his night watchman job into that of a detective, but I'm sure it would have been fascinating! Certainly, John W. Campbell—not known to have a gullible bone in his body—bought it.

CHAPTER TWENTY-EIGHT

Four-Day Planet

Piper was living very sparingly through April of 1960, hoping that *Little Fuzzy* would sell and take him out of the morass he was in. On May 1st, he was still punching away at a first draft on "Pest Among Men:" "I piously hope, last, attempt at first draft."

On May 7th, he received a letter from an editor at Putnam's named Bill McMorris who wanted to discuss the possibility of having Piper write some science fiction juveniles for Putnam's line. Robert A. Heinlein's success at SF juveniles had every editor in the business looking for his successor now that Heinlein was again writing adult fare. A number of prominent SF writers, including Lester del Rey, Andre Norton and Jack Vance, all wrote for this growing market.

Even to Piper it was becoming obvious that the mystery stories he was working on were not coming together. "Up 0830. Still trying to get story underway, and simply couldn't. The more I work at it, the worse it gets. I can't do a damned thing with it. Afraid it and the other story, 'Pest Among Men,' are both dead ducks, and I have wasted months on the latter and weeks on the short story."

So Piper put away the mysteries and started jotting down ideas for a science fiction juvenile novel. He talked to his agent, Ken White, and decided on the 17th to go to New York. McMorris called him on the 19th and they made a luncheon appointment for May 27th, 1960.

By way of research, he checked out two of Heinlein's juveniles, *Space Cadet* and *Tunnel in the Sky* from the Frederick Brown Library. "Spent all evening reading *Tunnel in the Sky*, and was agreeably surprised at maturity of matter regarded as 'juvenile.' Finished it and to bed 0100." I suspect McMorris was looking to compete with Scribner's since their juvenile division with Robert Heinlein had done so well.

Once again he started writing before he had the story plotted and worked out. On May 21st, he wrote: "Worked on story, started a rough first draft, without much idea of where it was going. Maybe this will work better than spending a couple of months making notes. Kept at it all morning." Some writers can't put a word down to paper unless they know every plot point and climax of the story; others write by the seat of their pants, letting the story go where it will with maybe, or maybe not, an ending in mind. Piper combined the worst aspects of both schools, one of the reasons he found writing to be such a punishing exercise.

Piper picked up a plane ticket for New York on the 24th and went home to pack. He arrived in New York the following day only to learn that Ken was still in Connecticut so, since this was his first visit to New York in some time, he took in the sights. "Great changes since last time, for worse." On the 26th he talked to Ken, had dinner at the Three Crowns and attended a Hydra Club meeting. The next day he saw Hans Santesson, editor of *Fantastic Universe*, then had lunch and a long talk with McMorris, who presumably offered encouragement as he outlined the story he intended to write.

Piper returned to Williamsport and ran into the same old wall: "Spent all day trying to organize story—couldn't seem to get anything done." This went on for the rest of the week and it wasn't until June 1st that he knocked out twenty-two pages of first draft. The next day he wrote: "This wasn't a very productive day, the day after a big day seldom is." He slowed the pace down and by June 10th, he had ninety pages of a first draft.

The same day a letter from his agent arrived, informing him that "Damon Knight, at Berkley Books, likes *Little Fuzzy*." Damon was one of the foremost science fiction critics of the fifties and sixties and was working as an editorial associate at Berkley. This was a good sign.

By June 24th, Piper stopped writing because he was within twenty pages of the end. He wanted to start the final draft before continuing "so that I will have discrepancies cleared out."

As Mike Knerr points out, "The interesting thing to note here is that on *Four-Day Planet* he didn't wallow through the baloney of a first-first draft, a first draft, a second first draft...ad *nauseum*. He had his usual troubles, tore up pages here and there and rewrote them, or bogged down for a day on plotting—but this one was a lot easier to write then, say, 'When in the Course...'—and a damn sight better story.

"By July 17th, at 2330, *Four-Day Planet* was finished, all 224 pages of it. He had only used two drafts and he accomplished it with a minimum of wailing and gnashing of teeth. Not only that, but his writing was interrupted by writers' meetings, gun collectors' meetings and me dropping every now and then to shoot the breeze.

"During this period of time his morale is up, his mind is clear in what he wants to write and he doesn't mention problems of health. Although he doesn't say so in the diaries, he was probably running pretty low on funds. All he states is that on the 19th he had planned to do some house cleaning and didn't get around to it. 'Reaction to the pressure of getting *Four-Day Planet* finished, I suppose.' He also 'Began planning novelette, tentative title, 'Three Came to Asshur.'"

With *Four-Day Planet* wrapped up, Piper's spirits were up. "Worked on planning all morning," he wrote on July 25th. "Seem to be really getting something done on it." A dark note on the day was that "Berkley has bounced *Little Fuzzy*, in spite of Damon Knight's recommendation." He went back to working on the story, with the usual production of scrap paper, but minus a lot of his previous frustration.

Former Putnam's editor Bill McMorris has this to say about *Four-Day Planet*: "The story was lively and would appeal to boys, I felt, but some of the scenes were quite violent and I was afraid the library market—our principal source of sales—would pan it, so I asked the author to make a few revisions and tone it down a bit. Piper's response was, 'You bought it, you do whatever you want with it.'

"So I did some minor trimming of the most violent descriptions—probably a few dozen words—and the book was published with limited success."

Four-Day Planet takes place on the dangerous world of Fenris, notable for its two-thousand hour day/night cycle with four such cycles per Earth-length year. The weather is so harsh during the nights that only an Extreme Environment Suit can preserve anyone who leaves the underground shelters. Fenris' only valuable resource is Tallow-Wax, a substance that comes from the Jarvis' Sea Monster. When the underhanded head of the Hunter's Guild Co-Op tries to make cuts in the income of the Jarvis' Sea Monster hunters, a group of hunters attempts to bypass the Co-Op and sell their wax directly to the interplanetary merchants. There is no recourse locally since they have to deal with a local government so corrupt that they no longer hold elections. These events are narrated as seen by the protagonist, Walter Boyd, a cub reporter for the *Port Sander Times*.

Knerr noted: "In August, Beam was back to his usual problems with his writing and his morale, both of which began giving him trouble. 'Three Came to Asshur' started off the month by '…finally found the story getting completely away from me and began rewriting what I have done so far, a procedure I usually resort to at about this point.' Beam's morale was a bit on the low side and it seems vividly apparent that his writing suffered in direct proportion. Money doesn't really seem to enter into the picture that strongly—there were always the guns. But the low morale and the difficulties in writing seem to go hand-in-glove.

"The contract for *Four-Day Planet* arrived on August 17th, and Beam sold his 1836 U.S. pistol for $125.00. Sunday, August 21st, was a Writers' Club picnic at Anne Winter's house, north of Williamsport, and we all took turns plinking with Beam's .22 Smith and Wesson revolver. None of us would have qualified for the Marine Pistol Team and, unless it was an off day, Beam wasn't that good. When the party broke up, Bill Stroup took Beam home to meet his father, another pistol fan, and then to Richard Frank's house to see his science fiction collection."

In late August, Piper wrote, "scrapped the whole damned story, 'Three Came to Asshur.' Decided to get story back on track and the only way to do it will be start from scratch. Begin anew, and I hope final, first draft." His agent sent him his first half-payment check of $900.00 for *Four-Day*

Planet, which he banked. Then he went back to work on the story that had been giving him fits before he started *Four-Day Planet*.

Mike Knerr wrote, "On August 31st, just before leaving for the Pittsburgh Convention…Beam started to plan another juvenile 'in case Putnam's finds *Four-Day Planet* a success and wants another.' On the 2nd, he took a flight to the Iron City and, after checking into the hotel, took a walk to the Golden Triangle to see old Fort Pitt. He went up to the convention and spent the rest of the night drinking and talking. The next day, Saturday, 'Ran into Fred Pohl, who says he has money for me. If so,' Beam wrote dryly, 'Age of Miracles still in operation.'"

"On the PittCon's last day, Piper wrote: "Had breakfast with a few of the fans and Randy Garrett and Clayton Rawson. Convention gradually burning out—auction, business meeting. Had a couple of drinks with Fred Pohl, Lester del Rey—who looks quite handsome with his grizzled Conquistador's beard—and their wives. They both know J-n McG-e, who is now at Red Bank, N.J.'"

Piper was still angry with John McGuire and continued to use his initials rather than spell out his name. He knew how to nurse a grudge.

While Piper was gone, Ken White was attempting to sell the serial rights to *Four-Day Planet* to *Astounding*. On September 12th, in a letter to White, John W. Campbell wrote: "Putnam is right in feeling this yarn by H. Beam Piper, *Four-Day Planet*, makes an excellent book. But it doesn't make a good serial. And I suspect it's intended as a juvenile. Split into parts it would lose all sense of unity, I fear."

CHAPTER TWENTY-NINE

Junkyard Planet

The next day H. Beam Piper flew back home and he went back to work wracking his brains for another juvenile for Putnam's, but nothing seemed to click and he gave it up. He could not, however, leave the battle of Cerignola alone. His fascination with the Italian Wars and Gonsalo de Cordoba—the Great Captain—never seemed to leave him. Like his friend Fletcher Pratt, who was able to successfully sell historical non-fiction, historical fiction, mysteries and science fiction, he wanted to do it all. Unfortunately, his only real successes were in the science fiction field and all the time Piper wasted writing mysteries and historical works left him exhausted and broke.

Piper spent the next month trying to put together his historical novel: "Worked A.M. on background for historical novel, probable title, 'Only the Arquebus, battle of Cerignola.' Out P.M., did some shopping, got a haircut. Had dinner at Heylmun's, and home about 1930. Got Sabatini's *Life of Cesare Borgia* and, for the fourth time, Prescott's *Ferdinand & Isabella* out of the library. Spent most of the evening on them...."

Off and on during the rest of his life, Piper would continue working on his major historical novel, "Only the Arquebus." Jerry Pournelle still remembers many an evening spent with Piper in his hotel room discussing historical figures and events and how they might apply to the future.

According to Pournelle, Piper had many keen insights into the past and often expressed a longing that he wished he'd been alive in the simpler days of the Christian Era, when Clausewitzian politics and nuclear wars were a faraway nightmare. As Piper wrote to Pournelle in a 1963 letter, "You know, it must have been lovely, living in an era when the Clausewitzian 'extension of politics by other means' was accomplished with nothing more lethal or expensive, especially expensive, then black power."

Unfortunately, he wasted his time trying to work up a plot and "doodling out notes" that didn't work into a story. On September 23rd, 1960, he wrote: "I do have a lot of history, and have the geography of southern Italy in mind, but still no story." When he turned in at midnight on October 2nd, he scribbled, "I wish to Christ I could get something done."

On October 5th, Piper flew to New York for a Mystery Writers of America meeting, then talked to Ken White, who told him that Putnam's wanted another juvenile from him. "The historical novel is going to be set aside for a while," he wrote. "Think I can use the *Galaxy* story 'Graveyard of Dreams' as a starting point." He discussed it with McMorris over lunch, as well as the possibility of other stories in the future. Then went to several bookstores looking for a copy of Heinlein's *Starship Troopers*. He returned to Williamsport on the 8th and found the new *Analog Science Fiction and Fact*, which used to be *Astounding Science Fiction*, in the mailbox. It contained "Oomphel in the Sky," as Piper put it: "...finally published."

The Cosmic Computer, under the title *Junkyard Planet*, was written as a juvenile for Putnam's, but featured a character older than the typical juvenile protagonist. Piper started working on it on October 9th: "spent all day working, which is to say, sitting at my desk smoking and drinking coffee and 'contemplating my navel' and doodling." The story began slowly and it wasn't until the 16th that he started to write on the typewriter; he wrote fourteen pages of first draft of what he was tentatively calling *Junkyard Planet*.

Nineteen sixty may have been the most productive year of his career. True, he had more trouble getting *Junkyard Planet* written than he did with *Four-Day Planet* but it was nothing compared to his usual symphony of agony. November 2nd, Piper stopped the first draft and began a synopsis of the book to send to Putnam; in this as well, he was frustrated: "Story in a hell of a mess, don't know what to do with it." On November 7th, he wrote: "Worked a little on planning, and finished the letters I had started to write, including the god damned questionnaire for Putnam. Up town, lunch at Heylmun's, and had myself photographed—Putnam wants some pictures of me."

By November 18th, Piper had plotted out enough that he was already on the third chapter. "That leaves this god damned synopsis to tinker up, and then I can send it in and get started on first draft proper." He mailed the photos off to Putnam's for the *Four-Day Planet* dust jacket and sent the synopsis on November 21st. He then turned his attention to the main story and began seriously writing on Thanksgiving Day.

Knerr noted: "In the end, *Junkyard Planet* was easier to write than most of his stories, but it still gave him trouble. Piper never wrote anything as easily as *Four-Day Planet* and, oddly enough, it was one of his better novels. Beam was his own worst critic and, while a writer must be careful and critical of what he does, there are definite limits to how far he can go—especially when his bank account is below $100.00, as Beam's was on December 2nd, 1960."

Three days later, Piper received a note from Ken White: "McMorris liked the synopsis, is taking the story, contract will be drawn end of week, should have dough pre-Christmas." Piper didn't get the advance until the 31st. He did get the galley proofs for *Four-Day Planet* and corrected them while sweating over the new novel. He had, during the writing of *Junkyard Planet*, slipped back into his old pattern of writing a first-first draft, first-final draft, etc. and spent more time trying to figure out just where the hell the story was going.

Piper's morale during December had the usual peaks and valleys. On the 13th, he wrote: "Up town after lunch to bank; so horrified at what I discovered my balance to be that I came directly home without getting my haircut as I had intended." Mike Knerr noted: "He wasn't all that disturbed, however; after the evening's writers' meeting, he, Bill Stroup and I found a ridiculously noisy bar and dumped a few during our meeting-after-the-meeting, as usual."

The contract arrived by special delivery on the 17th, together with a bonus check of $85.00 for "Oomphel in the Sky." The contract advance on *Junkyard Planet* called for $500.00 [less 10% agent commission] on signing and another $500 on receipt of the final manuscript. To celebrate, Piper wrote: "Fired the *eensy* brass cannon and then felt too good to go back to work."

Former Putnam's editor Bill McMorris had this to say: "About *Junkyard Planet*: It was published by Putnam's after I left to go to W.W. Norton to start a juvenile division. My good friend Tom MacPherson replaced me (with my enthusiastic support) as editor of children's books at Putnam's. Tom, like so many others associated with Piper at that time, is no longer with us."

Knerr wrote: "For the rest of the month, Piper slugged away at the story and when the check came for the advance on *Junkyard Planet*, it was New Year's Eve and he was unable to cash it. He celebrated the end of the year with Ted and Mary Ranck, and another couple, and fired the *eensy* brass cannon at midnight.

"He worked hard on *Junkyard Planet* without all the usual fits and stops. For Beam, having the story planned out in advance gave the best results with less rewriting and fewer story breakdowns. Even he realized it, but unless prodded by an editor like McMorris of Putnam's, Beam would not do the advance story planning required for him to complete the story—the worst part is that he *knew* he should do it, but still couldn't."

In early January of 1961, Piper's ceiling began to leak and his typewriter began to fail. He put a pan under the leak but bought a new typewriter. "I think I shall have to fix it with a new one," he wrote. Knerr wrote: "He'd had this Smith Corona less than two years, but he'd given it a good workout!" Piper hauled it up to the store and swapped it on "a showy new model" of two-toned plastic and jet-age sleekness. "Writing with a new typewriter is a delight. I didn't realize how much work it was to punch the keys of the old one."

January 20th was a "Very bad day for morale" and he only did two pages, but his blue devils were allayed by attending a party for Freida Shannon (formerly Coleman) who was in town. "Home late, potted, went to bed at once." In the morning he learned that Avon had rejected *Little Fuzzy*. The "ceiling is still leaking," but he lived with it for two more weeks before calling the landlord and getting it fixed.

Junkyard Planet was finished on February 26th, 1961, with a minimum of fuss—for H. Beam Piper. The ceiling started leaking again, only now in the gunroom. He wrote: "stuck a pan under the leak, corrected the manuscript and mailed it off to Ken."

The novel was later retitled *The Cosmic Computer* when Ace Books purchased the reprint rights in 1964. Mike Knerr brought Piper a copy of his latest Ace paperback version of *Junkyard Planet*. Piper hadn't known it was even out. There is no mention of reprint rights (Ace in those days typically paid $500.00 for novel reprints) in Piper's Story Log where he listed all stories sales and their income. It may have been because the Putnam's edition never earned out the advance. Book royalties were low in those days, 4 to 6%, and few genre hardcovers earned any royalties. If the paperback rights were sold, the money often went to the hardcover publisher; the only time the writer received any money was if the original advance had been recouped. Of course, royalty statements from that era often contained as much fiction as truth.

In a June 16th letter to Charles and Marcia Brown, Piper has this to say about the Ace reprint: "I'm glad to hear that the paperback *Junkyard Planet* (*The Cosmic Computer*, for Christ's sake!) is selling well. I will probably be reaping the harvest in six months or so; they got the rights on it from Putnam's, and Putnam's will pay me." Sadly, he didn't live long enough to see that check.

As SF writer Jack Chalker wrote in his memorial to Piper, "When the Lights Go Out": "His juvenile novels for Putnam's, *Four-Day Planet* and *Junkyard Planet*, showed him a master of all levels, perhaps the only man who could equal the gifts of Heinlein and Norton in writing juveniles that did not play down, and were often far superior to the bulk of adult fiction. Beam never wrote for adults or for juveniles—he wrote for everyone."

Like most of his novels, *Cosmic Computer* takes place in Piper's Terro-Human Future History. One of science fiction's earliest future histories, it begins with the formation of the Terran Federation and goes on to span several galactic empires. H. Beam Piper had a lifelong love affair with history.

Another historical analog, the Pacific Cargo cults, was used by Piper as the springboard for the short story, *Graveyard of Dreams*, which was later expanded into the novel, *Cosmic Computer*. After the war in the Pacific during World War II, anthropologists documented a new religion that had taken root among the Polynesian islanders. The Polynesian Cargo Cult members built replicas of airports and airplanes out of twigs and branches, even making the sounds associated with airplanes to try to activate the shipment of cargo.

This new religion was centered on the concept of "cargo" which the islanders believed was the source of the invaders' power and wealth. The vast quantities of goods and military materials both sides parachuted in or airlifted to landing strips to the troops based on these islands made drastic changes to the lifestyle of the Melanesians, many of whom had never seen outsiders before. Manufactured clothing, medicine, canned food, tents, weapons and other goods arrived in vast quantities for the soldiers, who often shared some of it with the islanders who were their guides and hosts. This was true of the Japanese Army as well, at least initially before relations deteriorated in most regions.

The cultists believed that with the proper attitude and ceremonies that shipments of cargo would arrive from their heavenly source. It was all quite reasonable to the Pacific Islanders. They worked hard, but were poor and backward, whereas the invaders did nothing more than write words on paper and in due time shipments of wonderful things arrived from the sky. Some Islanders even believed that the cargoes were being sent by their dead ancestors and somehow the foreigners were intercepting them.

Of course, once the war in the Pacific ended, the allies abandoned many of the Melanesian bases and cargo deliveries dried up. Some Cargo Cult leaders promised their people that if they continued to believe and follow the rituals they would continue to receive gifts of food and goods. In attempts to get cargo to fall by parachute or land in planes or ships again, islanders imitated the same practices they had seen the airmen and soldiers use. Some of their rituals included performing parade drills with replica rifles and mimicking landing signals. There were reports of signal fires and replica lighthouses. Some U.S. national emblems became semi-spiritual icons.

In his novel, *Cosmic Computer*, Piper applied the concept of Cargo Cults to the planet Poictesme, the former headquarters of the Third Terran force during the System States War. During the war Poictesme was a major staging ground for the System States War. Millions of men and uncountable tons of war materials were dropped off on Poictesme for the anticipated invasion by the System States fleets. The invasion never happened when the System States unexpectedly capitulated, bringing the war to a sudden end. Klem Zareff, a former Colonel in the System States Services, had this to say: "'Space attack!' Klem Zareff was indignant. 'There never was a time we could have attacked Poictesme. Even if we'd had the ships, we were fighting a purely defensive war. Aggression was no part of our policy—'"

The System States War was in several ways analogous to our own Civil War, and was fought over economic issues. After the System States War's sudden ending, Poictesme found itself a deserted backwater. Most of those remaining on Poictesme earned their living by salvaging and recycling old army vehicles and stores—a way of life that continued for some time on many of the Pacific atolls and islands after World War II had ended. The survivors created a belief system based on Merlin, the legendary super-computer that was reputed to have won the war for the Federation against the System States, which once discovered would enable Poictesme's economic recovery and allow it to become one of the Federation's major civilized worlds. "But there *was* a computer code-named Merlin," Judge Ledue was insisting, to convince himself more than anybody else. "Its memory-bank contained all human knowledge. It was capable of scanning all its data instantaneously, and combining, and forming associations, and reasoning with absolute accuracy, and extrapolating to produce new facts, and predicting future events, and...."

Most of the inhabitants of Poictesme have as firm a belief in its existence as any Melanesian islander had in the Cargo Cults. Despite all evidence to the contrary, brought by Conn Maxwell who was sent to Earth to learn the whereabouts of Merlin, the Poictesmians continued to believe in the semi-mythical super computer. Conn's father has the following to say about Merlin: "'Merlin's a religion with those people. Merlin's a robot god, something they can shove all their problems onto. As soon as they find Merlin, everybody will be rich and happy, the Government bonds will be redeemed at face value plus interest, the paper money'll be worth a hundred Federation centisols to the sol, and the leaves and wastepaper will be raked off the Mall, all by magic.' He muttered an unprintability and laughed bitterly."

Most of Piper's Terro-Human Federation stories, with the exception of "Graveyard of Dreams" and the novel it inspired, *The Cosmic Computer*, involve the Federation's exploration and subjugation of new planets. *The Cosmic Computer* takes place after the disastrous System States War in the Ninth Century Atomic Era (A.E.), when the Federation has clearly entered its Toynbeean "time of troubles." In the follow-up novel, *Space Viking*, which takes place in the "interregnum," Piper wrote that the System States War led to a period of instability and the eventual dissolution of the Second Federation.

In *Cosmic Computer* Piper chronicles the heroic efforts of Conn Maxwell and his cohorts to push back the rising blood-tide threatening to descend upon the Second Federation and the worlds of man.

CHAPTER THIRTY

Naudsonce

Piper's life had a consistent pattern: he would worry himself to death over a story, which would be accompanied by serious cash flow problems. He'd resolve the story and finish it, or toss it aside and do something else. Meanwhile a check or two would come in, the financial pressure would ease—for a while. At least during the early 1960s he was finishing stories, unlike 1955 and 1959, when he couldn't seem to get anything going right.

There's always been a question among Piper scholars as to why he quit writing in his Paratime alternate-worlds series, since he hadn't written another one since "Time Crime," which appeared in *Astounding* in 1955, a story of which he was quite proud. Some have hypothesized that he lost interest in the subject, or changed his views on alternate probabilities—until, for lack of other ideas, he was forced to recast "When in the Course..." into "Gunpowder God." What we learn in his diaries is that Piper just didn't have any ideas that fit into the Paratime concept.

Some writers spin ideas off their creations, but not Piper. "Spent A.M. thinking about idea for a new story—I think I'll make it a Paratime story." He spent the day occupied with the usual chores while his mind sifted through this new idea. By evening, he had this written, "This is going to be a civilization in which the slaves run everything because the masters have delegated everything to them and allowed them to take over all problems of management." What we have here is the 'germ' of the idea for "A Slave is a Slave," which ended up being cast in the Terro-Human

Future History instead of the Paratime series. It could have gone either way, but this is conclusive proof that Piper still thought there was life left in the Paratime concept.

However, the new idea didn't seem to be going anywhere and was shelved—for the time being—while he went through the usual rigmarole of Piper story generating, with lots of mea culpas and angst. "Seem to be suffering from idea constipation. Still trying get a story put together and getting nowhere on it. Running out of both food and money. Knocked off work about 2100, completely frustrated—story seems no good at all. Hope some kind of idea arrives; don't like to dump the whole thing."

Knerr noted, "He dug out Toynbee's *Study of History*, searching for something to write about. Ken wrote to him that McMorris had received *Junkyard Planet*. 'No idea,' Piper wrote, 'when they'll get around to mailing the check, or even if they will without wanting a lot of revisions.'"

By the 23rd of March, 1961, "A Slave is a Slave" had "gotten sick and died." However, he had a new idea: "...think I have something for a short novelette—a race who feel rather than hear sounds; effect of new mechanical noises introduced by Terrans."

Piper was having the usual trouble starting off: "Started first draft of story. Worked on it all morning; wrote a few pages, scrapped them, wrote a few more and scrapped them. Usual thing for beginning—have a fair idea of what I want to do, having trouble with how I'm going to do it."

The Williamsport Writers' Forum was beginning to break up. Beam had a lot of fun at these affairs, according to Mike Knerr, and was one of the more faithful members of the group. After the meeting, most of the club went for a meeting-after-the-meeting, usually at a handy tavern, or Piper's apartment. Gradually, most of the males left the club. When Mike Knerr came back from a visit to California, Piper responded with, "Gawd," he said laughing, "the writers' club has been like Piper and his harem!"

In April of 1961, Piper was having problems plotting out his latest yarn, "Naudsonce," which like almost everything else he ever wrote was not coming together in the idea department. "Don't know why I can't do anything anymore," he wrote. This was two stories in a row he was stuck on. His bank account was below the $100.00 level again, which for Piper was the signal that it was time to start worrying. On April 10th, it was tax time and he drew a dark cloud around the date, writing "Day of Disaster." He was still having trouble with the first first draft of "Naudsonce." "Out P.M. to get my Income Tax fixed up—this time it cost me $40.00, counting Social Security, the latter a damned piece of extortion."

Another roof leak the next day, "Snow on roof melting and leaking through badly into gunroom. At a little after 2200, a piece of ceiling plaster came down, about a square yard of it. Made some clearance of rubble, nothing else I could do, and then back to work on story planning. Whole gunroom in a hell of a mess." He called Wetzel and Rider, the landlord's property managers, and they patched the leaks.

By April 26th, Piper was up to his usual tricks and tossed out everything he had written so far on "Naudsonce." "Read back on yesterday's work, very much dissatisfied. Out to get second sheet paper. Home a little before noon, and after lunch began manufacturing wastepaper again, and realized that the story is both badly planned and badly written. By late P.M. came to the conclusion that everything so far will have to be done over. Started on it after dinner, and kept at it till almost midnight, got 15 pages done." The money situation was getting desperate again, below $100.00 in his account, and he was determined to get "Naudsonce" done and out the door.

Piper kept doing his usual corrections, throwing away a dozen pages, then rewriting them. On May 2nd, he wrote, "Looked at the stuff I did today—terrible—will have to do it over." Somehow he managed to finish another rewrite and still get it into the mail by May 4th, 1961. At the same time, the cavalry arrived, in the form of a check from John W. Campbell for reprint rights to "Omnilingual" in an *Analog* anthology. He was paid $127.50, and fortuitously the check arrived the same day he finished "Naudsonce"—on May 3rd.

"Naudsonce" takes place in the Seventh Century A.E., some six hundred years after "Omnilingual." The Terran Federation Colonial Office has sent an expedition out to find new planets suitable for colonization.

Although the Federation bureaucracy is more and more making its weight felt, its explorers and researchers are now receiving "extraterrestrial bonuses" for their off-Terra duty. The local aliens, the Svants, both hear and feel and experience the "invaders" sounds as painful. In order to keep the Svants from rioting in the presence of Terrans, the explorers have to discover what's causing them so much distress. "Naudsonce" is another of Piper's anthropological detective stories that Campbell liked so much.

Ken White sent Piper's new story to John W. Campbell and he quickly bought "Naudsonce." for $502.20 (less 10%) on May 23rd; Piper celebrated with dinner at the Lycoming Hotel. Afterwards, he went back to work on his historical novel. On May 31st, he wrote: "The whole thing is a hopeless clutter of characters, historic events, fictional incidents, situations. Sometimes it looks as though I have too much story, and sometimes I don't have enough. Beginning to think that I should take a long rest from the Great Wars of Italy and do something else for a while. Detective story?"

He started work fiddling with ideas for his new mystery-detective story, "Juvenile Specialist." On the 6th of June, 1961, he went to New York for a Mystery Writers of America meeting. While in New York, he had lunch with his agent and McMorris. He wrote, "Nothing much came of it, but it lasted most all afternoon." It's unfortunate that Piper hadn't worked up another juvenile for Knopf in the weeks before the meeting; the two novels, *Four-Day Planet* and *Junkyard Planet*, he wrote for them were among his best books and the writing went smoother than anything else he wrote during this period. A juvenile novel a year, like Heinlein did in the 1950s, would have been money in the bank and built up a core of young fans who might well have bought Piper's other novels. Heinlein worked that strategy to perfection and Piper's juveniles were of the same caliber.

Mike Knerr was getting ready to leave for California to write books: "By the time we'd organized Bill's [Stroup] and my farewell party on June 14th, Beam had gotten himself into the first draft of his story. He'd managed, in spite of heavy-wastepaper work, to get a half dozen pages put together. Bill and I were slated to head west on Saturday, June 17th, and

Bill had Piper autograph his copy of *Four-Day Planet*. 'For Bill Stroup. Off to Californy with his banjo on his knee. Hope the Injuns don't git him acrossin' the plains. H. Beam Piper.' It was a fun party, with large amounts of Myers' rum consumed and it didn't break up until 4:00 A.M."

Rather than write another science-fiction yarn, Piper immediately went to work on "Juvenile Specialist," a new detective story that never sold. On July 3rd, 1961, he wrote: "Ernest Hemingway reported killed 'while cleaning a shotgun'—a suicide?" This is the first time the term suicide pops up in the diaries. Hemingway, like Piper, was a heavy drinker and had a strong personality with a theatrical flair.

More typewriter trouble, this time with the new two-toned Smith Corona. "Trouble with typewriter—this machine is no damned good." On July 10th, Piper noted, "Still stumped on final scene. This is no way to make money writing stories!" He went back to work on the mystery story and after a week's work came up with "Juvenile Specialist," which he finished on July 12th. It never sold. He was back to selling his pistols to Dick Houser for rent and food money. With "Naudsonce" and "Juvenile Specialist" out of the way, Piper went back to work on his historical novel, "Only the Arquebus." On July 19th, he sold his 1860 Colt, with the mould and flask, for $120.00, writing: "This relieves financial situation slightly; out of immediate danger for another month."

Piper put "Only the Arquebus" aside and tried his hand at another mystery but the story idea was too complicated for a short and not weighty enough for a novel; after a week of frustration, it was abandoned and he went back to work on "A Slave Is a Slave" at the end of July.

The new story, "A Slave is a Slave," was a touchy one and he went through the usual ups and downs. On September 12th, 1961, Piper wrote, "Started reading back—story finished to page twenty-seven in first draft, a mess. Morale very low. By noon, decided that present form is hopeless—scrapped the whole thing and started over." He spent the next month fighting with the first draft. But one thing about Piper, as much as he might fight a story out, once he had it fixed in his mind and a complete first draft—he just ran with it.

CHAPTER THIRTY-ONE

Little Fuzzy Sold At Last!

On May 2nd, 1961, Piper wrote: "Ken White says (cross fingers) that there may be a chance for a sale on *Little Fuzzy*. This has happened so many times before, though." It appears Ken had a lot of faith in *Little Fuzzy*, since he had long since stopped trying to sell Piper's mystery novel, and several mystery and science fiction short stories. Ken's faith was well placed, considering the story has since become one of the most beloved tales in science fiction. Ken delivered it to Bill McMorris, hoping that Putnam's could use it for their juvenile line.

Putnam's former editor Bill McMorris remembered: "Ken brought me *Little Fuzzy*. I really liked the book, but it was too adult for the teenage market of those years and of no interest to the adult trade department at Putnam's. However, Janet Carse (*née* Wood), wife of Bob Carse, one of the writers on our juvenile list, was newly employed as an editor at Avon and was looking for science fiction. With Ken White's permission, I sent *Little Fuzzy* to her, she loved it and got it published."

The wheels of the publishing industry move slowly, so it wasn't until the 18th of September, 1961—while Piper was well into the final draft of "A Slave is A Slave"—when he was interrupted by telephone call from his agent. Piper wrote, "*Little Fuzzy* sold, after all these years to Avon. Will have to be some work done cutting it down at end, don't know what." At the bottom of his diary page he drew in red a fuzzy jumping up and down going, "Yeeeek!"

"A Slave Is a Slave" was set aside while he worked on the *Little Fuzzy* revisions. "Called Janet Wood, at Avon, in New York," he wrote on September 19th: "She wants the last eighth or tenth of story compacted and a lot of the end-tying eliminated. Sat around for a while wondering what the hell to do next. Decided to use last half of version II and splice it to beginning of version I."

We know, since Piper wrote the *Little Fuzzy* sequel, *Fuzzy Sapiens*, for Avon at Janet Wood's request, that she liked *Little Fuzzy* enough to see potential for a Fuzzy series, as well as a Fuzzy movie and toys. In the early 1960s science-fiction novels were still establishing a market and sequels were rare. Piper, on the other hand, didn't have a clue about the novel's potential; he had enough trouble finishing one novel without worrying about foreshadowing and setting up *Little Fuzzy* sequels. As desperate as he was in 1955 for salable story ideas, he never thought to do the sequel to "Time Crime," which is as open-ended a tale Piper ever wrote.

It was part of John W. Campbell's 'genius' as an editor that he saw editing, not as an end to his own writing, but as a way to get an entire clan of writers writing *his* stories! Janet Wood saw the Fuzzy story as a great springboard for more tales and, history has proven her right. In fact, even before his death Piper was bedeviled by fans wanting more "of those damn Fuzzies!"—even when he couldn't find a publisher to buy them. An irony, according to Pournelle, not completely lost on Piper himself....

H. Beam Piper spent a couple of days splicing the two versions of *Little Fuzzy* together, coming up with *Little Fuzzy* version III which he then sent off to Ken. He took a holiday for a few days and then went back to work on "A Slave Is a Slave," original title being, "A Slave Is a Slave Is a Slave."

Mike Knerr, who was now living in California, noted: "Most of the young men in the Creative Writing Forum were gone; Altoona is one of those rust belt towns where any youngster with grit and brains leaves as soon as possible."

In his diary Piper wrote, "In evening, to meeting of writer's club at Cynthia Hoover's—now I am the only man among nine women." At the bottom of the page Piper added, "Money dangerously low." The contract for *Little Fuzzy* arrived on September 26th, 1961, but the money situation was getting serious again. When he completed "A Slave Is a Slave," he didn't have enough money to post it to New York. He wrote, "If you can't eat, the next best thing is to sleep." Dinner was "some ice flavored with chili-sauce, and snippets of Vienna sausage. It was sort of good."

He spent a tough two weeks on short rations before the check for *Little Fuzzy* arrived on October 11th. Once his bills were paid and the larder filled, he went right back to work on "Only the Arquebus." Unfortunately, it was going nowhere, although he felt he was getting the background down. He decided he was "Getting the boy-meets-girl angle worked out satisfactorily and the menace-to-girl as well. A lot of work to be done, but direction now visible."

His month of near starvation forgotten, Piper decided he didn't like the gray tweed; instead he had a plain gray suit tailor-made that cost him $260.00! After eating mostly gruel for the past two weeks, it's hard to fathom Piper's extravagant expenditures on new suits. In this case and others, his vanity got in the way of common sense; he could have bought a year's worth of groceries for the price of that suit, or prepaid his rent for four months. It was bad decision-making like this that would make his final years so disastrous.

A few days later he put away the historical novel again and went to work planning *Space Viking*, deciding he had "a good story" in mind. One has to wonder how much of this 'historical science fiction novel' which was to take place in his own Future History was inspired, or even driven, by his work on "Only the Arquebus"…? For most writers, the old cliché—everything and anything is grist for the mill—is a truism, and it certainly was for Piper.

On October 31st, Piper got the second check for *Little Fuzzy* and he "Just loafed around—I never can get any work done the day the money comes."

Along with *Space Viking*, Piper had an idea for an anthology of his Terro-Human Future History stories. According to Knerr, "It was for an anthology of his short stories, with interpolative sections in between explaining them.

The stories he wanted to use were 'The Edge of the Knife,' 'Omnilingual,' 'Naudsonce,' 'Oomphel in the Sky,' 'Ministry of Disturbance' and 'The Keeper.'" Piper had this to say about the project in his diary: "Have doubts about it, both as to merit and salability." It's unfortunate that he never put the proposed collection together as it might have shed a lot more light on the scope of his "history of the future" and how it had developed, but nothing ever came of it. It isn't even known whether or not he even broached the subject to a publisher, or even his agent, at the time, Ken White.

Piper went to New York in early November to meet with Ken and John W. Campbell about "A Slave Is a Slave" and the revisions Campbell wanted him to make.

In a December 6th, 1961, letter to Piper's agent, Kenneth White, Campbell wrote:

Dear Mr. White:

> *Beam Piper's "Slave" yarn is a lovely thing; he's got some lovely lines in it—and some very sound philosophical points."*

> *There is, however, one that belongs here so solidly that I'd like to have Beam insert it, in his words, where he thinks it fits, if he agrees it fits—and I believe he will!*

> *St. Augustine, nearly 1500 years ago, made a very interesting point. The fabled 'innocence of a babe,' he pointed out, has nothing whatever to do with innocence of intent, but innocence of opportunity and power. A lamb isn't a sweet, kindly, inoffensive creature—it's just weak. It's actually, a mean-tempered, stupid, and remarkably nasty little batch of protoplasm.*

> *Much of the oh-so-liberal love for the Common Man is based on comparing his "gentleness" with the ruthless, aggressive behavior of the uncommon man. The common man is, in fact, like the lamb and the babe—innocent of deed only because he is incompetent, but anything but innocent of intent.*

The massacre at the end simply represents precisely what the common man wanted and intended all along.

St. Augustine's point, I think, belongs. One should not mistake inability to carry out vicious desires for innocent intent.

The check for the manuscript—$750.00—will be along shortly.

Regards,

*John W. Campbell
Editor*

Before leaving for the airport, Piper visited Janet Wood at Avon, who showed him the cover for *Little Fuzzy*. "The people at Avon full of plans for pictorization, Little Fuzzy dolls. My fingers determinedly crossed on all this," he wrote. Sadly, none of it worked out, but not before Janet asked him to do a sequel.

Little Fuzzy is the story of Jack Holloway, a prospector for sunstones on the planet Zarathustra, which is owned by the Chartered Zarathustra Company under the rule of boss man Victor Grego. Jack Holloway befriends a small alien critter he nicknames Little Fuzzy. Jack quickly takes note of the cute alien's intelligence and, when he begins to discover that Little Fuzzy may be sapient, he finds himself at odds with Victor Grego and the Chartered Company, which owns the rights to discoveries on Zarathustra. If it is proven that the "Fuzzies" are sentient the Federation will declare the planet a protected zone under Federation control and the Zarathustra Chartered Company will lose rights to most of the resources there, including the sunstones. When one of Grego's underlings, Leonard Kellogg, kills a Fuzzy; it provokes a court case to determine whether or not the Fuzzies are sentient beings.

CHAPTER THIRTY-TWO

Space Viking

Piper took time out from planning *Space Viking* to give a lecture on the Battle of Cerignola to John Hunsinger's students at Lycoming College, one of the 50 oldest colleges in America in December 1961. Ironically, Piper was the man who was thrown out of high school, now giving a lecture on history at the local college. Piper scholar David Hines has this to say about Piper's connection to Lycoming College:

.... You mentioned the sentry cannon Beam fired off at Lycoming College football games; John Hunsinger, who'd been the president of the Phi Alpha Theta honor society, told me that Beam started doing that after the Grand Army of the Republic Hall moved a bunch of material to Lycoming College. The college didn't know what to make of the stuff, so they looked for an expert on old guns, and somebody said, "Hey, how about Beam Piper?"

So Beam was helping clean and identify the guns. In the collection, they came across a sentry cannon, circa 1850, in the collection, and while they were cleaning it Beam got a gleam in his eyes and said, "You know, there's no reason this couldn't be fired."

Naturally, this sounded like a fine idea, so they got some black power and took the cannon outside. They loaded the cannon up, using Kleenex for wadding, and then nervously looked at each other as they realized that now one of them had to actually light the damn thing. The prospect of an unfortunate explosion had them scared shitless.

And up strode Beam Piper, gleefully, match in hand....

After that he became the designated cannon-firer at home games, when the Lycoming team scored a touchdown.

Best,
David Hines

On December 6th, he gave the talk and thought it was "a very poor performance, but the customers seemed to like it." More Piper understatement.

"Letter from Bill Stroup—he wants to get Ken White as his agent. Not in favor of idea myself; don't think Ken White would want to handle him." Bill was a member of the writers' club, trying to 'break-in' to a writing career.

Piper went to work on the Campbell requested revisions for "A Slave Is a Slave." "Finally finished—I hope I've made the point, without over-making it, that the proletariat aren't good and virtuous, only stupid, weak and incompetent." It went into the mail on the 13th and he went right back to *Space Viking*, one of his finest novels.

Piper spent the next couple of days working on *Space Viking*, "writing and tearing up beginnings..." He also got the new *Analog* which featured "Naudsonce" and noted: "Also review, brief but very favorable, by Schuyler Miller of *Four-Day Planet*. Started reading the latter over to see if it's really as good as Miller says—I think it is—and didn't get to bed till 0500, which really sets a record."

He was down to writing the first chapter of *Space Viking* when he got a letter from Ken telling him that he had the check for "A Slave Is a Slave." Piper noted in his diary: "He is also separated from his wife and in financial straits—wanted to borrow a hundred from me till the first of March. I agreed. Hope this doesn't turn out like Fred Pohl's divorce."

Piper received the check for "A Slave Is a Slave" on December 22nd, 1961. He was having problems with *Space Viking* so he put it aside and celebrated Christmas dinner with Ted and Mary Ranck and, of course, a good drunk.

The novella, "A Slave is a Slave," takes place during the expansionist period of the First Galactic Empire and revolves around Aditya, a former Federation planet which had gone into decline during the interregnum after the fall of the Old Federation. The current government is an oligarchy run by the descendants of Space Vikings, who had conquered the planet and used it as a base world to attack and loot nearby planets. Similar to the Chinese Imperial governments run by eunuchs, Aditya is actually controlled by slave bureaucrats. The story is a cynical look at how the slaves try to maintain their current "status" when threatened by an Imperial government that deplores and denounces slavery.

It is quite likely that "A Slave is a Slave" sparked the idea behind *Space Viking*, when Piper decided to explore the period following the fall of the former Terran Federation. On the 27th, Ted Ranck (Ted was one of the original Unholy Trinity back when Ferd was alive) picked Piper up and they went to the Colemans' house to celebrate Freida's third wedding anniversary. He had reached chapter two of *Space Viking* on New Year's Eve and he knocked off writing, "…and made ready to greet the New Year—a better one than 1961, I hope not too optimistically—with three shots from the 'eensy' brass cannon."

Piper started New Year's Day 1962 writing and plotting *Space Viking* and later working double acrostics. "Had a couple of drinks at the Lycoming and home to a dinner of pork and sauerkraut, which I had been boiling all day." The new novel was in the agonizing period and he was still beating his brains to work out plot and character complications.

He flew to New York on January 18th to meet with Ken White and attend a Hydra Club meeting. Piper had reason to feel good about himself, money in the bank and a new novel, *Little Fuzzy*, coming out. Also, he was selling all his new short stories to John W. Campbell without having to shop them around in a drastically reduced magazine market. There were now less than half a dozen science fiction magazines still standing and most of the 'pulp' writers were out of business.

He had graduated into writing novels for the growing paperback business. He was not so fortunate with his mystery stories, and from now on they play a less and less significant role in his life. On January 24th,

1962, he learned that *Little Fuzzy* was on the stands. "Letter from Ray Young—he says *Little Fuzzy* out—why haven't *I* heard about this?—and he says he enjoyed it. Hope millions of others do." Most publishers routinely send author's copies to the writer, but sometimes they get delayed or misappropriated.

In early February, Piper was still working out the complications of *Space Viking*, including removing unnecessary characters, "who didn't seem to be doing much for the story." *Space Viking* is a complex work with a lot of time and location shifts to even complicate it further and—not surprisingly—it was giving him considerable grief.

He received a letter from Ken White on Valentine's Day with a fan letter and a note to the effect that—no surprise here—Janet Wood, at Avon Books, wanted a Fuzzy sequel. For someone who wrote in two distinct 'universes,' it's odd that he didn't do more sequels; after all, his projected history of Pennsylvania was to be a trilogy. "Don't know what this could be," he wrote, "but can try."

He drew a red heart at the top of the diary page and filled it with, "Beam Still Loves Betty."

All through February and March, Piper was still having troubles working out the plot and construction of *Space Viking*. On March 7th, he wrote, "Worked all morning planning what I most devoutly hope is the final form of the story. Intended getting to work after dinner, but didn't. Just slumped and dozed and read. Felt like hell."

Fan mail was trickling in from *Little Fuzzy*. On March 10, he wrote, "A letter today, forwarded by Janet Wood, from a little girl in New Mexico, who wants me to send her a Fuzzy. Will have to write her—yes, Virginia, there are Fuzzies. Don't know exactly how." A welcome distraction from the typical plot morass a Piper story fell into before magically coming together in a rush of work. "Wrote a letter to the little girl—yes, there are Fuzzies, but we don't have any here."

As Mike Knerr told it, "The little girl's name was Margaret Ward, and she couldn't have picked a better time to write him. Beam was dragging himself through *Space Viking*, fighting to get the novel firm in his mind and even more firmly on paper. The letter made him laugh and melted his heart as well. It was the only piece of fan mail he ever framed. 'By Gawd,' he chuckled, when he told me about it, 'I wish to hell I *had* a Fuzzy to send her!'"

Piper was still having trouble "getting narrative worked out, action sequence," but he was making progress. By April 1st, he had 211 pages of the first draft: "Believe I will start final drafting tomorrow and do the last 50 or so pages of first draft when I get to it. May save me more work than it will make." For the next few days he worked from 9:00 A.M. to after midnight and rarely left his typewriter. He managed to reach 77 pages in the final. Again, money problems: "Things are back where they were last fall—the money has run out again. Things are worse than they were last fall; much worse. No money due me except $100.00 from Ken White."

Piper's writing income for the 1961 had been way over average. His Income Tax was $73.55: "Not as bad as I expected."

By April 17th, he had reached page 185 and was getting close to the end of his word budget. The wordage for genre novels in the 1950s and 1960s was ideally 55,000 words—up to 60,000 if your editor liked it a lot. From his comments, it appears that many of Piper's problems with his novel-length works revolved around writing to such tight strictures. He complained, "Don't know what to do with story. Want to keep ending originally planned, but it will make story too long—want to work up some kind of a slam-bang ending in the 70-odd pages I have left, and can't think of one."

On April 29th, 1962, Piper wrote: "Worked on story all day—wasn't out at all. Finished to page 223—too much wordage, and too much story left to tell. Don't know how I'm going to get it finished up in 50 more pages and that's the most I can allow myself."

Knerr noted, "Apparently he set limits on himself, where wordage was concerned—unless this was something John Campbell had laid out. Most book publishers have a minimum word limit…In 1962 that limit was 50,000 words, since then it has risen in direct proportion to the cover price."

Piper's target market for most the science fiction he wrote was John W. Campbell's *Astounding/Analog* since Campbell paid the highest rates and had the quickest pay-off time in the magazine business. For Piper, who was always broke, Campbell was the first and best market; plus he would almost always get the AnLab bonus payment. In addition, the pay rates Beam was getting from Ace and Avon were far less than Campbell was paying. The best deal was to sell the First North American Serial Rights (for magazine publication) to *Analog* and then turn around and sell the paperback rights to Ace, which was the primary salvage market and bought most of their inventory from magazine sales—one reason for the Ace Doubles; they'd put two magazine novellas of 30,000 to 40,000 words out as an Ace Double paperback.

Of course, Campbell didn't like filling his monthly magazines with long novelettes, or worse a novel that would have to be serialized over three or four issues, like *Space Viking*. He had to *really* like a yarn to serialize it; plus, he had more stories and novels on tap than he could use. This became a real problem with the Kalvan novelettes, since Campbell's inventory was so flush that he really wasn't interested in 20,000 word novelettes from anyone—not even one of his favorite authors.

Somehow, some way, he managed to finish *Space Viking* by May 8th, and was already thinking of the Fuzzy sequel on the 9th: "After dinner started re-reading *Little Fuzzy*. At it all evening till 0200, and off to bed. Feel just plain bushed after finishing *Space Viking*."

Piper had never planned for a *Little Fuzzy* sequel; in conversations with Jerry Pournelle he mentioned he thought *Little Fuzzy* was one of his lesser works, probably meaning less rigorous in its view of the future and its overly-cute alien critter. According to Pournelle, Piper wanted to write at least one story in every century of his Terran Federation, not do sequels to already finished books. To have to go back and force out a sequel was painful, and it shows: "Spent A.M. doodling on story. Ideas don't seem to be arriving in any great numbers."

Piper's wry wit was still intact, though. On May 11th, he wrote: "Money situation becoming very critical." This probably helped motivate him to work out the plot tangles for the *Little Fuzzy* sequel: for once, this novel has an eager editor waiting for it. He now had a title, *Fuzzy Sapiens*.

Then some good news: "Campbell is taking *Space Viking* as a four-part serial, wants me to indicate installment breaks and write synopsis up for last three sections. Avon doesn't want it—Janet Wood doesn't think it is in keeping with *Little Fuzzy*." Mike Knerr has this to say about Wood's comment: "I invite anyone to try and figure *that* kind of logic out. *Space Viking*, in my not so humble opinion, stands as one of the best novels Beam ever wrote—and just what the hell did the book have to do with the Fuzzy thing? If Janet Wood thought that Piper was just going to sit in Williamsport and crank out Little Fuzzy adventures just for Avon, she had another think coming.

"We laughed about it a lot, while Beam struggled to find a decent plot for the sequel. 'Hell, yes, We'll do 'Little Fuzzy and the Jewels of Opar;' 'Little Fuzzy and the Golden Lion' and 'Little Fuzzy at the Earth's Core'… How's your drink? I'll get us a refill.'

"It was fun, but it never happened that way. The only way the Fuzzy series came about was through sheer struggle. Beam would have been the last person to admit it, but the Fuzzy books would eventually drive him up the wall."

Piper's financial problems were solved when on May 25th, he received a $500.00 advance from Campbell for *Space Viking*. He went to work on the synopsis for John Campbell and sent it out on the 28th. The balance of $1,714.00 for *Space Viking* arrived on May 30th, and he put $500.00 into a savings account in case money became scarce again. From the *Analog* magazine first serial rights, Piper made more than twice the amount he got from Avon Books for the original novel, *Little Fuzzy*, and he was free to sell the paperback rights to another publisher.

Piper was in high spirits and on June 5th, he wrote: "to Writer's Club meeting at Katherine Hoover's—I took three bottles of champagne, treat on *Little Fuzzy*, who promised drinks for the crowd when he got published." The following day *Analog* featured "a rave review of *Little Fuzzy*" and Piper was as happy as he was ever going to be.

In early June *Space Viking* was rejected by New American Library and on June 7th, Piper decided to go to New York to talk to Ken and John Campbell about future stories after receiving this very generous letter dated June 5th, 1962:

Dear Mr. Piper:

"I don't know what plans you have for a next story project, but the world-picture you've been building up in the Sword World stories, or Space Viking stories, or whatever you designate the series, offers some lovely possibilities.

Space Viking *itself is*, I think, one of the classics—a yarn that will be cited, years hence, as one of the science-fiction classics. It's got solid philosophy for the mature thinker, and bang-bang-chop-'em-up action for the space-pirate fans. As a truly good yarn should have!

One of the beauties of the set-up you've got is that it allows the exploration of cultures of almost all conceivable levels of complexity and technology. They can be examined either internally or externally—i.e., either by a native, or by a visitor.

Try this concept on for possibilities:

If one of the old Federation techniques they've preserved was a genetic technique of the order of Heinlein's "Beyond This Horizon," their Utopia would really be stable. The rulers would be just as much locked in the cultural system as the workers—as the queen is locked in the bee-culture. But they'd be good rulers—by imposed choice!

What could—or should!—the Organization of Civilized Worlds do about such a planet? Why shouldn't a real, functioning Utopia be allowed to continue operations?

Regards
John W. Campbell

Piper met with Campbell and Ken White in New York for lunch, but he never pursued the Campbell story idea. While there, he talked with Janet Wood and showed her the *Analog* review of *Little Fuzzy*. At a Mystery Writers of America cocktail party he "met Cornell Woolrich [a noted mystery author—jfc]; we continued drinking at a couple of bars afterward. Finally got back to the hotel around 0300."

CHAPTER THIRTY-THREE

Fuzzy Sapiens

Back at the typewriter, H. Beam Piper was finding the *Little Fuzzy* sequel tough going. "Still having trouble; can't get beyond the beginning." On July 1st, he wrote, "Think I'm getting somewhere—dumping a lot of story complications that had been giving me trouble."

Piper didn't start on the first draft until July 6, 1962. "Will send in a few chapters and synopsis for an advance—swore I'd never do that again, but need money and so does Ken White." Mike Knerr wrote, "Besides Beam, Kenneth White's only other major client was James Blish and he was never prolific. Ken was still having financial difficulties due to his divorce. Beam, no matter how much he made, seemed unable to budget his finances. It just dribbled away within a few months...." Ken White must have been in bad shape for Piper to have felt responsible for his well-being. Unfortunately, their fates were linked in ways that neither man could have foreseen.

Piper continued work on *Fuzzy Sapiens* but had to curtail his working hours; he was having trouble working nights, in part due to his lingering back problems from his slip and fall on the streets of Williamsport. "Didn't get back to work after dinner—why can't I work in the evenings anymore? Will have to get back to it." He received a bonus check for $112.50 for "A Slave Is a Slave" along with a rejection of *Space Viking* from Monarch Books, which shows that Ken White was trying all possible publishing markets before shopping the book to Ace Books.

He was having all the usual plotting and runaway character problems with *Fuzzy Sapiens* and it took him a month and a half—till August 15th—to get the synopsis and the first few chapters done and mailed off to Janet Wood at Avon. He continued trying to plot out the story as he wrote it and was in a constant state of agitation. Knerr wrote: "Beam would have rather cut his own throat then let any of us (the Writers' club) know that he was having so damned much trouble setting up a plot line."

On August 29th, Piper wrote: "Spent most of the day being frustrated. By evening I had given up hope of accomplishing anything." Ken White wrote to tell him that *Little Fuzzy* had been sold to the Italian market for $270.00 and that Avon had approved the chapters and synopsis; contract and advance to follow.

On August 31st, he flew to Chicago for ChiCon, the annual Chicago World Science Fiction Convention and third one held in Chicago. This is the convention where Piper first met Jerry Pournelle. In his blog, "Chaos Manor," on June 3rd, 2012—in answer to a reader's questions about whether Piper and Heinlein knew each other—Pournelle replied: "I know they met, because at ChiCon III I met H. Beam Piper and we became friends; and Saturday night, late, there was a party in Robert Heinlein's suite. I was invited because Mr. Heinlein and I had been corresponding about aerospace matters and had become friends.

"Beam and I went to the party together. I don't remember if they had known each other before although I rather think they did, but they certainly would have met then. Beam, was a bit under the weather and left early. Ginny Heinlein was stuck in an airport somewhere in the Midwest. The party lasted until dawn and ended with watching the Sun rise over the lake. I have no idea whether they read each other's works, but they were both fairly close friends and two of my favorite people, but I don't recall either commenting on the other. Mr. Heinlein was very successful at that time, and Beam was having financial difficulties."

Piper had this to say about the convention, "To hotel, and fell in at once with friends—partying started early P.M. and kept up all night literally. Got to be about 0600." The next day, "Up 1100. To Coffee Shop for breakfast, and then panel discussion, talks, auction sale. Masquerade party in evening and more parties—details rather vague—Jerry Pournelle and I singing? Lasted until 0600 again."

At the bottom of the page he put: "SECOND COMING OF CHRIST AT HAND—FRED POHL PAID ME."

September 2nd, more partying. The next day, "Managed to get in on tail end of lecture by Willy Ley and then a muster of the Hyborean Legion, and lecture by Jerry Pournelle on warfare 1962 - 2000 and political discussion which was adjourned from 1530 to 1730. Out for dinner, very tough shish kabobs. Partying resumed, first in my room and then in Robert Heinlein's. This time I fell out at 0400."

After his return to Williamsport, the eye problems started up again. "Bought a pair of eyeglasses at Woolworth's for a dollar and a half; amazed at the improvement in reading. They are reading glasses only—range up to 24"—but print looks clearer than I can remember it looking. Eyes don't get tired, either." Mike Knerr reports, "The Piper vanity, however, kept the glasses in secret. I never saw him wear them—"

On September 14th, the contract for *Fuzzy Sapiens* arrived and Piper signed it and sent it back. However, he was only on page 14 of the new book. He was still unable to work evenings, his most productive period of the day. "Wish I could get back to work in evening—used to be able to work in evenings, that used to be my best time."

He was spending money on non-essentials again, buying a new overcoat for $140.00. On October 1st, 1962, the advance arrived: "Check from Ken White, advance of $875.00, less 10%, $787.50 arrived. Now I have to get the goddamned thing done." This Fuzzy novel was as slow going as the first one. He'd only reached page 58 by October 8th. Not much enthusiasm for it, either. Piper was lucky to bang out five or six pages on a good day. He was outside a lot, reading or just loafing. The lack of progress and plot frustration—"Trouble seems to be, too much story; can't keep it simple"—kept him from enjoying his off hours. He was back to reading Prescott's three volume *Ferdinand and Isabella*; research for "Only the Arquebus," which wasn't helping the new book.

In early December 1962, Piper continued with the first draft of what he had so far, but he wasn't pleased with the 17 or so pages he wrote of *Fuzzy Sapiens*. He was only up to page 40 by the 9th.

On December 19th, 1962, he wrote the following letter to Pournelle about his problems with the *Little Fuzzy* sequel:

Dear Jerry,

Yours of September 17—this is a record for neglect, even for me!—got onto my desk to be answered in a day or so, got snowed under,

I got home from the convention alive, sort of, and have been working on this infernal Little Fuzzy *sequel ever since; wrote more or less completely, and scrapped, at least three versions of it, and am now half done in final draft with what will be the final version. I had hoped to finish by the end of the year; now fear it will run me into the middle of January. There must be easier ways of making a living then this.*

Was at another convention at Philadelphia the early part of last month; a lot of our drinking comrades of Chicago were there, and remembered Bonnie Dundee, so if we're both at Washington next Labor Day, we can give them a repeat performance.

Toast for the Christmas season:

To that great and wise man, scorned by his contemporaries, vilified shamefully by his only biographer, and unjustly execrated by posterity – Ebenezer Scrooge!

I drink to it about this time, every year; I shall stop, on my way from mailing this batch of Christmas cards, at my favorite bar, and perform the ritual.

Beam

Piper's lack of progress is confirmed by his diary entry of the 21st, "Worked on story—finished another short chapter XVI to page 150, nine pages. Had to transfer $200.00 from savings to checking account. Can't let this happen again till the former is filled in some more."

Then it all went to hell again; on December 24th, Piper scrapped everything he'd written. "This is a horrible thing to have happen at any time, let alone the day before Christmas." He began at the beginning, trying to form coherent ideas that would work; he didn't have much luck. On the 31st, he wrote, "Up 0930. Gunroom too cold to work in. I moved into dining room. A day of frustration—after almost eight months, I still have nothing that even looks like a story. This was one of my worst days.

"Up town 1700, dinner at Lycoming. Ted Ranck's in evening, 2000—to his place for New Year's Eve party; much to drink, a goodly crowd. Home at 0300, and to bed. Happy New Year!"

Piper started the 1963 New Year with a bang: "Up 1100. Had breakfast in dining room, but by noon the gunroom was inhabitable and moved into it. Working on an attempt to reconcile all the different Fuzzy stories I have put together in the last eight months and discarded. I don't like to mar this page with bragging or over-optimism, but this time it looks good. Mary Ranck called about 1430, inviting me to dinner—almost as big a crowd as last night, and sauerkraut was excellent. Didn't leave till 2011, and by the time I was home, felt too drowsy to do anything—read till about midnight, and to bed."

This was another false start and when the holidays were over he was back to fiddling "with story detail work, doodling and note scrawling." On the 6th of January 1963, he tore up everything he'd done to date. As Mike Knerr noted, "The only thing that kept him banging away at this book and the one he would write in the future was the knowledge that Avon Books wanted them. He felt that this was more of a sure thing than the speculation he usually wrote under—and both he and Ken White needed the money. Ken, in addition to his domestic troubles, was having eye problems."

Finally, on February 13th, the paperback rights to *Space Viking* sold to Ace Books for a whopping $1,500 in two installments—it also came out as a 'novel' not one-half of an Ace Double, as his previous stories had been packaged. As Mike Knerr observed, "This wasn't much money, considering the amount of work that had gone into the book, yet that was the going rate. One of the sad, but real truths of creative writing is that advances and royalties have never kept pace with inflation..." Still, Piper had already been paid over two thousand dollars in 1962 for the *Space Viking* serial version in *Analog* so this was just frosting on the cake, making it—by far—his most profitable book.

Then, after all his struggles, *Fuzzy Sapiens* came together with a bang; he finished the novel on February 22nd. "Don't know what life without Fuzzies will be like, now, or what I will do next. Clean house, for one thing, I suppose." Exhausted from *Fuzzy Sapiens*, he went back to doodling notes on "Only the Arquebus:" "Still trying to work up a fiction-story, with love interest, to match history." Piper was still working out the mechanics of the story when the first Ace check for *Space Viking* arrived on March 11th. For the time being, he was flush.

With *Fuzzy Sapiens* finished, Piper was back to trying to work out the plot problems of "Only the Arquebus:" "Still trying to get story planned—no progress. Devoted most of time to trying to avoid working at all."

On March 22nd, 1963, he wrote: "Debby Crawford called me and wants me to help her in 'establishing a fictitious residence' in Pennsylvania. Divorce?" He had completely misunderstood the conversation. "I was April-Fooled today but good! The phone call, on the 22nd, wasn't from Debby but from Betty—it didn't come from New York, but from France, and while I did hear something about 'fictitious residence' what it was about was that she is divorcing me. All this was explained in a letter from her today, with enclosures of some letters for me to sign, to be used as evidence.

"They were typed on French paper; I copied them on American paper and sent them off to her by airmail. Well I'd been expecting something like this, even if I had been trying to make myself believe we could get together again. Now I can stop kidding myself.

"Glad I didn't know it was Betty when I was talking to her—would have gotten emotional."

At the top of the page was a broken wedding band with a lightning streak through it and the words "All Fool's Day" beneath. It's sad to think of Piper, still lonely after five long years, mooning after his wife—the love of his life. The both of them were as stubborn as pit bulls; neither willing to compromise.

As Mike Knerr noted: "The divorce wasn't over easily and it dragged on into 1964; and Beam didn't stop kidding himself at all. Like a drowning man clutching at a twig, he hung onto the idea that they would still get back together. He even sold a bunch of guns to have the money to meet her in New York while she was en route from California to Paris on February 16th, 1964. It was to be the last time they saw each other and the effect upon Beam was a great deal heavier than the diaries let on. His cast-iron refusal to compromise was beginning to have a tremendous effect on him and his career."

On March 22nd, 1963, he wrote the following in a letter to Pournelle: "Yours of the 15th found me just having finished the sequel to *Little Fuzzy*, on which I had told you about in September. After I got that off, I simply sat around for a couple of days doing nothing whatever, and then went into a convulsion of house-cleaning; my place gets cleaned regularly every time I finish a story. Now I am getting at my unanswered-letter file (correction; pile) and since yours of January 15th is at the bottom and yours of March 15th is on the top, I am starting with both...."

"Just felt washed out today," Piper wrote on April 4th, and comments on weariness begin to crop up more and more frequently in his diary. Four days later, he wrote, "Spent most of morning and early afternoon writing letters to Betty, tearing them up, and finally managed to get one written more or less to my satisfaction." The separation was one thing, but divorce was something else—an end to all his fantasies about the two of them getting back together again. The divorce from Betty was sapping his strength and keeping him from his writing.

There was some good news: Ken White wrote, "the movie possibility for *Little Fuzzy* has become a reality—something simply called Moving

Pictures Corporation (actually, the Motion Picture Company of America) is taking it, paying generously." He wasn't so pleased when he learned the same day that he was hit with an Income Tax payment of $344.00. His reaction: "Jesus!"

He continued his fruitless doodling on "Only the Arquebus," getting nowhere fast. On the 17th of April, he flew to New York to sign contracts for the *Little Fuzzy* movie deal and attend a dinner of the Mystery Writers of America. "Saw Janet Wood at Avon—everybody there delighted at movie of *Little Fuzzy*, and pleased with *Fuzzy Sapiens*." He and Ken White had lunch at Jansson's where they signed the contract.

Piper was back in Williamsport on April, 21st, 1963 and writing another letter to Betty, which took several days. He tossed ideas around on "Only the Arquebus" until May 3rd, when he *finally* began a rough draft.

He was still waiting for the movie rights check, but it was slow in arriving. Instead he got a surprise, "one for $226.41 from Mondadori in Milan for Italian rights on *Little Fuzzy*." The historical novel wasn't coming together and he wrote, "worked on story, all morning on one page, must have done it over six times."

CHAPTER THIRTY-FOUR

Fuzzies and Other People

On June 15th, Ken called to inform him that the rest of the Ace advance, $675.00, for *Space Viking* was in the mail, but the movie money was not forthcoming. "It seems MPC is undergoing re-organization…going bust?" The final note was bad news indeed: "Janet Wood has been sacked at Avon—another of those publishing-house revolutions." This was bad news since Janet had been the in-house champion of *Little Fuzzy* and the sequels.

All of June was wasted, flailing about with the historical novel, but no real progress. On June 29th, 1963, Piper received the *Analog* bonus check for *Space Viking* from Ken White and the surprising news that Avon wanted another Fuzzy book. He put away "Only the Arquebus" and began to work through ideas for another sequel—the working title was *Fuzzies and Other People*.

Then Betty wrote again to tell him that the divorce had been postponed until October 4th and that they were still married. He was now mired in the new Fuzzy novel and totally frustrated. He received a letter from *This Week* magazine stating that they wanted 2,000 word mystery and suspense short stories. Piper went into his trunk and pulled out "Juvenile Specialist," "Precaution" and "Negative Pattern" and cut them down to the 2,000-word count and mailed them out on August 8th.

In a July 2nd, 1963 letter to Charlie and Marcia Brown he wrote:

Dear Charlie and Marcia Almost:

"*I discover, on rooting into my file-cabinet in the course of one of my periodic clean-up campaigns here, that your letter of January 15, on the back of a Charles Addams Christmas card, is still unanswered. I am answering herewith.*

In answer to your questions, which seem to be based on the situation as of our last meeting in Philly:

Space Viking is being book-published by Ace sometime in August; a book all by itself, not an Ace Double-Barrel.

The sequel to Little Fuzzy, (Fuzzy Sapiens) *will be published by Avon probably about the same time. I hope it is out by the time of the convention, which may stimulate sales.*

For the last three months, I have been working on the historical novel, "Only the Arquebus." I have the story all plotted, and a good start made on the first draft. It is now shelved, however, since I have just had a letter from my agent telling me that Avon wants a sequel to the sequel to Little Fuzzy, *and I want that finished and accepted as soon as possible, so the arquebus has been hung up temporarily. Inasmuch as this story is going to run to about 100-150,000 words, I never had any expectation of getting it all finished at one uninterrupted writing. If I have it finished in another two years, I will feel that I've done very well.*

Little Fuzzy is also going to be a movie; I have already signed contracts on that. Beyond that, I don't know when or anything about it, except there is talk that it will be filmed in Europe, either Yugoslavia or Greece.

I am now in the process of being divorced, if my future-ex-wife can ever get her French lawyers to get all the red-tape untangled. I suspect that she just doesn't know who to bribe. We are writing to each other again, in a very cordial and friendly manner. She reports that our red dachshund, Verkan Vall, of whom she retained custody when we split up, was in a movie along with Brigitte Bardot and Jean Gabin, a couple of years ago.

I seem to be getting to the bottom of the page. Well, best wishes, and am looking forward to seeing you both in Washington.

Beam

Piper purchased a brass key from which to make an "eensy brass bombard" to go with the eensy brass cannon. Then went back to work on the new Fuzzy novel, "getting nowhere at the speed of light." He wrote a letter to the court at Nice, France telling why he would not show up for Betty's divorce case on October 4th. Then, began to make preparations for the Washington D.C. Labor Day science fiction World Convention where *Little Fuzzy* was a nominee for a Hugo Award for Best Novel.

This was Piper's first Hugo nomination and a big deal, although he downplayed it to friends and the world in general. Winning the Hugo for Best Novel would have changed his life significantly, although it would not have solved his financial situation in the short run. However, the celebrity from a Hugo award might have helped Ken White sell some of his older works, like "Time Crime," and the Paratime and future history collections he mentioned in his diary. Plus, it would have done wonders for his morale.

Piper flew to Washington and spent most of his time talking and drinking with fellow science-fiction professionals. On August 31st, he wrote, "Costume ball in evening, followed by party in Randy Garrett's room to 0500." Banquet and Hugo Award presentation was September 1st. "Disappointed that *Little Fuzzy* didn't make it."

The following morning, "Met Fritz Leiber, Randy Garrett, Judy Merrill at breakfast, and immediately became involved in a skit which was to be put on at end of convention. We put it on about 1530—it was a 'catastrophy' [sic]. Afterward the convention started coming apart." He had to "chase like hell" to get his plane back to Williamsport the next day.

"Still groping, the more sequels you pile on, the harder they come, it seems," Piper noted, "...at this all morning, and gave it up after lunch." It was until September 14th, that Piper appeared "to have 'groped' up something that looks like an idea." He continued with his usual stop and go production of wastepaper and over the next week wrote twelve pages. "Read in evening—seems I can't seem to force myself back to work in the evening."

As Mike Knerr noted, "D-day, as Beam called it, was October 4th: "This is the day Betty's divorce action is supposed to come up in Nice." Very little writing was done during and after the 4th. On October 7th, he heard again from Betty: "Letter from Betty—the divorce went through, at 1117 Friday. Got nothing written, but think I have finally gotten something to use for a story."

Both his ideas and page production for *Fuzzies and Other People* was stalled throughout October. "Tore up what I did yesterday and started over again—think I have a couple of pages that will do. Out for a short walk P.M. Wrote to Ken White to find out what's wrong about the movie check." He was only to page 64 of the first draft by October 18th, 1963.

On the 21st, he learned, "Letter from Betty—it seems we aren't divorced at all. All this business in court she reported in her last letter was just preliminary—there will have to be some delay before the actual decree is granted." On top of this he lost a five dollar bill: "a dreadful disaster now."

Piper tore up what he'd written, discarded material and characters he no longer needed. Money was tight and like a captain he battened down the hatches, laying in supplies for the coming storm—"coffee and tobacco enough to last awhile. Wrote a very strong letter to Ken White." Things were going from bad to worse. On November 12th, he wrote, "Up 1000. Worked on final draft most of morning and early P.M., out for walk late P.M. First draft in unholy mess. Decided to do some final-draft to pull it back into order—this is always an act of desperation."

On November 16th, he received the movie advance of $900.00 for *Little Fuzzy*, which must have come as a surprise. And his financial problems were set aside—for a while. New dentures and the usual expenses, rent, utilities, food, rum; now, he was able to concentrate on writing *Fuzzies and Other People* again. He even brought the first part to the writers' club to get some feedback. Mike Knerr noted: "Probably everyone said it was great and, likely, so did I, although I don't remember that particular meeting. Piper didn't like it."

Piper had this to say: "Read some *Fuzzies and Other People*—dissatisfied with how it sounded. Think too much expository matter. Don't want to do all this over again, but think I ought to…am convinced I'll have to go back and do over the first couple of chapters, too windy, too much straight exposition and recapitulation of previous stories."

On November 22nd, 1963, he wrote, "Out late P.M. and had dinner at Rice's. Met an acquaintance who told me that President Kennedy had been shot and killed by an assassin in Dallas, Texas, today. Mike Knerr in this evening with some more news—the assassin probably uncaught, one suspect arrested. Shooting done with a rifle, telescope-sighted Winchester 30-30? From a window, Kennedy and others with him in car shot, several killed."

Knerr had this to say, "I went down to Beam's apartment with very little information, but he had learned that it had been a military rifle. I remember his statement to me that night. 'Now that,' he said flatly, 'is taking your politics too damned seriously.'"

On November 25th, Piper left his apartment and "got lunch, and then up town. Found everything closed, banks, stores and all—mourning for President. Picked up a newspaper—it seems that Lee Oswald, the suspect the Dallas police were holding, was shot and killed by some local character while being transported from one jail to another. To keep him from talking?"

The French dental plate, which had been giving him nothing but trouble since he'd had it made, needed replacing. With money in the bank, he decided to replace his false teeth and take a trip to New York for a Mystery Writers of America dinner on December 4th.

Meanwhile, he was still slogging away on *Fuzzies and Other People*. Knerr noted, "Beam arrived in New York around noon and after checking into a hotel, took his French letters to the consulate, 'where I found out little or nothing. Waiters at St. Denis more helpful. Appears I am not yet divorced. To MWA meeting. Naturally, much talk about the latest and greatest crime.'"

Piper met with Ken White, but didn't find much to his liking. "This is one of the most pointless trips I have ever made to New York." Back at the typewriter, he found the going just as pointless: "Spent A.M. going over the story to date. Don't like it at all. Finally decided it is not good—scrapped it, started over, from the beginning, and worked on it all afternoon and evening. Got 15 pages in—my God, I hope—final, final draft, to end of Chapter II, by 2230, then read till 0200 and to bed. Back where I was a month ago!"

On December 20th, he wrote this short postcard to Charles and Marcia Brown: "I certainly will make the London trip in '65, if still alive and solvent then. I finally got the first advance on the picture rights for *Little Fuzzy*, six months after signing contract, due largely to persistence of Ken White. I'm afraid that is all, no mention of any production date. *Fuzzy Sapiens* won't be out until sometime after the first of the year. Sorry I wasn't able to make it to the PhilCon: were you there? Best wishes for a happy 1964."

On the 24th of December, Piper found his new dentures in especially bad shape. He could barely eat and even had pain when holding his pipe—intolerable! He had the dentist grind them down and then grind them some more. Eventually, they fit well enough that he wasn't in constant misery.

Once again, he spent New Year's Eve with the Rancks and even fired the "eensy brass bombard" at midnight. He celebrated New Year's Day with his usual pork and sauerkraut dinner "slightly burned," but he was still suffering pain from his dentures, which made it impossible for him to eat. "Made tapioca pudding, could eat that all right." Once again, another trip to the dentist's to get his new false teeth to fit right; along the way he discovered he was going broke again. "Drew some more money out of bank—account now below $100.00—what the hell did I spend it all for?"

Piper started the new year working hard on *Fuzzies and Other People* and by January 10th, 1964, he was up to page 135. The book was finally on track and he wrapped it up and mailed it off to his agent on February 3rd.

A call to Ken White on the February 18th only gave him more bad news—Avon, now under a new regime—had decided not to accept

Fuzzies and Other People. Not a surprise to anyone but Piper. The first thing the new Avon editor had done was put the kibosh on *Fuzzy Sapiens*, giving it the ugliest, murkiest black/purple cover in paperback history—as if daring the fans to buy it. To add insult to injury—and guarantee that fans couldn't find it—they changed the title from *Fuzzy Sapiens* to *The Other Human Race*!

When a new editor comes into a house, it's not unusual for he or she to shoot down all the major books of their predecessor—after all, if they do sell, it only vindicates the departed editor. In the industry such books are referred to as "orphans." If the new editor, puts obstacles—read no publicity, few review copies, poor artwork—on her predecessor's works; well, of course, then they were bombs to begin with. Obviously, woe to the writer who gets caught in the crossfire, as Piper did with the Fuzzy sequels.

Avon never had much of a science fiction line, but a Hugo Nomination for *Little Fuzzy* was big news and they should have made a killing on the sequel. But in New York publishing; it's not *always* about the money. Ego is often the biggest coin of the realm. Writers are as indispensable as cabs, there's always another one around the next corner…

Worse, for Piper, was the fact that Avon didn't want the third Fuzzy novel which cast a pall over the book—it was a series orphan since the parent publisher didn't want—or reading between the lines—the previous book didn't sell. Or at least, that's how a competing editor would see it. Few editors have the story certainty and understanding of their readership as John W. Campbell had; most editors only buy what's already selling, not what might sell. The first whiff of failure sends them scurrying like rats off a sinking ship.

Maybe if he could have gotten the rights reverted to the earlier Fuzzy books, Piper could have sold the whole Fuzzy shebang to Don Wollheim over at Ace; Wollheim, a long-time fan, knew the value of a good book, especially a good series. But, while Avon no longer wanted the Fuzzy books, the last thing they'd do was revert them; after all, what if another house was able to sell the hell out of them? That would not look good to the parent company and said editor might shortly find himself in the unemployment line.

It's always easiest to let the writer twist in the wind...

Fuzzies and Other People is now with Ace," Ken wrote, "But Satan only knows whether or when."

CHAPTER THIRTY-FIVE

The Kalvan Saga

With *Fuzzies and Other People* off to Avon, Piper he had a new story idea: "Worked in morning planning a new story, tentative title, "Gunpowder God"—a Paratime story about theocracy with the corner on secret of making gunpowder." In part, the new story was based on the events and setting of "When in the Course...," the 1959 novelette he never could sell. "Will have to write this in three parts, 20-25,000 words apiece, since *Analog* is loaded with serials for the next three years." He began with the usual doodling and planning, but mentioned that his morale was not very high.

Fuzzies and Other People was done and making its way to Avon so this insolvency appeared to be business as normal. Except, he needed cash desperately; Betty was coming to New York on February 13th, 1964.

On the next day he received a letter from Betty; she would be returning to France from California, on Sunday, February 16th. Piper replied, "...and I will go to New York to see her. Ken enthusiastic about *Fuzzies and Other People*. Home 1700, read for a while, worked on future history—I hope that blighter in Birmingham is duly appreciative..." Piper is referring to an English fan, Peter Weston, who had written asking Piper for a chronology of his future history (see Appendix III).

He was in New York at Idlewild Airport on February 16th. "Betty got in 1715, right on schedule—the years show on her a bit. We had a few drinks, Daiquiris, and a delightful chat until her plane for France got in." He stayed in town for a while, then took a return bus to Williamsport.

With the Pennsy down-and-out, no more free train rides to New York for Mr. Piper.

Mike Knerr wrote: "The divorce, of course, went through, but Beam never seemed to give up hope. Although he was apt to make caustic remarks about their relationship, or to make fluff of the whole thing to anyone who might ask, inside he was neither bitter nor flippant about what had happened. His bus left New York at 12:30 A.M., but he couldn't sleep en route. 'Awake all night, couldn't get to sleep at all. Arrived in Williamsport 0730, and home to bed immediately.'"

Betty had this to say in a November 26th, 1964 letter to Freida Coleman: "I cannot believe lack of money could have been the reason [for his suicide—jfc]. He was always broke—and when he got a check—he blew it—and was broke again. There must have been something else. His later letter had been so cheerful, telling of a paperback out and three stories to put together [the Kalvan novelettes]. He was going to make a speech on Columbus day—did he have a bad time at the speech? Or could he have been putting on one of his acts and pretending he was Ernest Hemingway or something? He would get awfully hurt or blue sometimes but his mind always turned around and he came out on top again. When I saw him at Idlewild in February he seemed healthier and steadier than when he was with me."

Despite his comments to Pournelle and *Locus* editor Charlie Brown about how Betty only married him for an expensive European vacation, the divorce settlement left Piper despondent and less able to cope with the upcoming creative and financial difficulties that would plague him in the later part of 1964. The divorce settlement was one of the final breaks that left him alone and feeling adrift.

Not surprisingly, back home in Williamsport, Piper was having trouble concentrating. "Wasted the rest of the day doing nothing at all—reading, working double-crostics and otherwise avoiding work." By the first week of March he was working on three drafts of "Gunpowder God," the first-first draft, the second first draft and the first final draft. On the 6th, he wrote, "A letter from Betty and one from Peter Weston in England thanking me for the future history letter. Started a letter to Betty; it bogged down and I gave it up."

By March 13th, he was making progress, but having problems "mostly because I'm getting too many things in for proper length of story." While things were improving on the writing side, they were not going so well on the financial end. By the 30th, Piper was down to $5.50 in his bank account and was working toward the finish of "Gunpowder God," the first Kalvan novelette, for *Analog*. He did finish it and mail it off to Ken White on April 2nd, and went right to work on "Kalvan Kingmaker," the next novelette in the series.

Ken White wrote the following submission letter to John W. Campbell:

Dear Mr. Campbell:

Here's a new novelette by H. Beam Piper, Gunpowder God, we hope you're going to like. It's one of his Paratime stories and he plans two more of similar length to follow it.

Cordially
Ken White

Once Piper had the plot of a story down and he knew where he was going, he was a hard worker. Before his back injury, during one of his walks, he often wrote all night until early morning; probably a holdover from his years with the Pennsylvania Railroad when he worked the graveyard shift. At sixty, Piper was no longer able to put in 14 to 16 hour stints at the typewriter; another reminder of old age and the increasing frailty of his body.

Mike Knerr wrote, "By the middle of April, 1964, with $173.12 to his name, he ran into an Income Tax problem that even today rankles me more than what I consider his untimely suicide—and I'll be damned if I'll forgive the government for it. That was the estimated income tax writers were supposed to pay in advance for being self-employed. Income tax,

Piper wrote, 'Amounts to $479.04—couldn't pay it—I'd misunderstood quarterly-payment system, that is for advance for *next* year. Don't know what I'll do—that is putting it mildly.'

"The first year I wrote," Knerr noted, "I was told by the Income Tax character that I had to do this estimating sort of thing. Being the hothead that I was, I told him to jam it; that I'd pay my taxes when I got paid and not before. Of course, he told me that I'd go to jail. I never did, and I paid my taxes at the end of the year. Beam, however, for all he bitched about the government, was so damned honest it used to make me mad.

"That same adherence to stupid rules caused Beam to starve, shoot pigeons and suffer. At a time when politicians were writing off bills for $10,000 for paper clips and stationary, not to mention their salaries, he ate tapioca gruel. Without paying those taxes, he could have made it a while longer.... While Beam slaved for pennies, Williamsport had second-generation families on welfare who never missed a meal."

Not Beam, Pournelle said it best: "He was a cavalier."

"At the moment, he was a 'cavalier' in a lot of financial trouble," Knerr wrote. "Besides the income tax, he was two months behind in his rent and he owed gas, water, electricity and telephone bills. Piper found himself $430.30 in the red and commented at the bottom of the page: 'This looks like Piper is in a jam.' He sold a couple more pistols for $100.00, but he was still over $300.00 in the hole.

"This sort of living, by now, was beginning to wear a little thin for Beam, and on several occasions he and I had discussed the idea of becoming 'written out.' It's a possibility that all writers have to consider, and it isn't an easy thing. At the age of twenty-eight, I *thought* about it but it was about in the same abstract way that I thought about death.

"You think you'll ever get written out, Beam?" I asked one evening.

"'Yes,' he said flatly, without hesitating.

"'What'll you do?'"

"He made his right hand into a 'gun' with the index finger representing the barrel and stuck it in his mouth. He laughed.

"Jesus. That's messy."

"The grin stayed on his face. 'Someone else will have to clean up the mess.'

"He was right."

A few days later Piper withdrew the last two dollars in his bank account; he was having troubles again keeping his mind on writing. He sold a couple of pistols and tried to finish "Kalvan Kingmaker." On April 20th, "Worked all morning on first draft for 'Kalvan Kingmaker.' Letter from Ken White—tough shit all around—Ace, as well as Avon, has bounced *Fuzzies and Other People*, and John Campbell wants a rewrite done on 'Gunpowder God.'"

Dear Ken:

We got troubles!

This is a lovely yarn; unlike many of Beam's Paratime series, he doesn't have too many individual characters named and described, until the reader tends to go slightly nuts trying to keep track of 'em.

But he does have too many words for us right now.

The situation is that we've got novels on hand and already scheduled through August 1965. Now when I run a novel installment, that takes about 25,000 words of the magazine; I can't run both a 25,000 word novel installment and a 25,000 word novelette; it wouldn't leave me enough room for the rest of the things I have to get in.

About 18,500 or so is the top length I can manage until sometime late in 1965.

He has a pair of characters in here who really aren't functional—the "blind" minstrel and the "stupid boy"; some wordage could be saved there—and Beam is still somewhat over par for the course on characters, even so.

Readers have objected to Beam's tendency to throw in detailed characterizations of dozens of individuals; the reader expects characterized personnel in a story to be important actors. Beam just enjoys describing personalities—which is fine, but gets readers lost.

If Beam can cut this to 18,500, I'll give him the full 4 cents bonus rate on acceptance. (If this isn't clear evidence that Campbell cooked the AnLab bonuses, what more in the way of a 'smoking gun' would be needed?—jfc]

Regards
John W. Campbell

Piper rewrote "Gunpowder God" and sent it off in five days. Mike Knerr brought him a copy of his latest Ace paperback version of *Junkyard Planet*—only Ace had re-titled it *The Cosmic Computer*. He hadn't known it was out.

He was having the usual troubles with "Kalvan Kingmaker:" "Worked all day on final draft, another re-do; this is getting tiresome, and, looking it over, I think it's going to have to be re-done again. Wasn't out at all, at it all day and typed 22 pages."

On May 19th, a letter from John W. Campbell and a check for $684.00 advance for "Gunpowder God." "Letter from JWC accompanied check—he's enthusiastic about more stories of same sort. Will provide."

Dear Mr. Piper:

Your yarn, as shortened, is fine; check on its way.

Your suggestion for further yarns along the path you've sketched out is also fine. I'm definitely looking for stories with a bit more guts in them than the stuff that's standard American literature these days. The Apotheosis of the Common Jerk, or the Life of the Common Suburbanite, and his trials, tribulations, and insignificant temptations and naughtiness acutely disinterests me. Why authors think the frustrations and eroticisms of insignificant suburbanites is the most important material possible for stories, I don't know.

One thing I am very sure of; no story that's lived for more than a couple of centuries had a central character so vapidly incompetent as the standard "hero" of the standard modern American novel.

Your Aryan-Transpacific paratime line allows for some grand yarns, with men who are damn well MEN, and women who aren't afraid to be different from men, and like it that way. It's a world where insurance hasn't been invented, and every individual is acutely and personally responsible for his own acts and behavior—which, as Bob Heinlein pointed out in Beyond This Horizon, *breeds a race having good manners, clear thinking, and fast reflexes!*

There's very little neurosis in such a culture. The neurotic gets himself killed off too quick to pass on his problem!

Your idea of a series in which the reader can trace the action on the maps of here-and-now is fun, too. But I suggest that Kalvan can, every now and then, come a slight cropper by trying to do just that… and forgetting that the world he's in was made by a different set of probabilities. Like a growing tree that shoved a boulder that deflected a stream that caused what Kalvan knew as a major obstacle to a cavalry charge to be half a mile from where he was counting on it.

Incidentally, the House of Styphon doesn't appear to have discovered the possibilities of blasting powder. (Their motivations being what they were, they wouldn't. That's economically important, but doesn't appear at first glance to have the political impact Styphon's fireseed-as-war-material has.)

I have a hunch Kalvan could raise merry old hell with the opposition by the simple technique of using blasting powder. The stuff is very annoying to defenders of castles, armies trying to cross bridges, or attack through a narrow pass. Also, nitroglycerin is astonishingly easy to make, and a small bottle of the stuff makes a wonderful booby trap for the uninitiated. You just leave a flask of it on the table; he's certain to pick it up to see what-the-hell—and all he has to do is shake it a little, set it down hard, or taste it. The first two eliminate him and the surroundings; the last eliminates him with a heart attack. A simple bottle of nitroglycerin is an elegantly simple booby trap; it's practically certain that it will be a long time before anyone reports to the enemy just what the booby trap is!

And nitroglycerin is so much easier to make than good powder. Literally, it makes itself in just the right proportions. And double-base smokeless powder is reasonably easy too; nitroglycerin and nitrocellulose. Of course, high speed information-handling is a terrific military weapon, too. And you need neither vacuum tube nor transistor technology for radio-telegraphy.

...But most particularly...have fun! The general attitude of the conquerors of that cultural type was rather largely determined by an air of practical jokes, on a large scale, with murder, mayhem, and conquest as a sort of by-product. They had fun!

Regards,
John W. Campbell

"Kalvan Kingmaker" was growing fast and Piper decided to cut it into two stories to fill Campbell's 18,000 words requirement. "Down Styphon!" became the second story of the three proposed novelettes and he worked hard at both until the wee hours. Piper wrote, "A little bat got in somehow; found him snoozing, upside down, at the top of the window frame in hall. With hall light on, he still thought it was still daylight—still there when I went to bed at 0130..." Mike Knerr wrote: "The bat left during the night; anyone else would have clobbered it, but if it would have hung around Piper would have fed it."

Piper finished "Down Styphon!" on June 1st, and went right to work on the third story, "Kalvan Kingmaker." He was hoping for a check, when instead he got a letter from Ken White on June 15th: "Campbell wants rewrite on 'Down Styphon!,' long letter from Campbell enclosed. Hope this doesn't get to be a regular thing. Started re-writing; out 1900 to bank, now only have $8.00 in account."

Dear Beam:

I'm just back from Scotland, where I've been having considerable fun learning the background of Scots history and mine own people. There was an ancestor of mine who, around 1750 or so, was residing with his parents in New Jersey, when an Indian raid on the town practically wiped it out. He saw his mother and father killed and scalped, and he was captured and carried off by the Indians.

Poor Indians! They didn't know Scots history. They'd never heard of the Massacre of Glen Coe. They didn't know why it was that when a Scots clan decided to wipe out a rival clan, they were careful to kill all the children, too.

Anyhow, my seven-year-old ancestor that night killed three of the Indian braves, and escaped. He devoted the next eighty years of his life to reducing the Indian population, achieving a personal score of confirmed killed-in-individual-encounters of 189 Indians.

Having learned something of Scots history, I can readily understand why the poor Indian didn't have a chance. The Indians were gentle flowers, nurtured in a warm, and sun-kissed land, compared with the bloody-minded, ferocious old bastitches [sic] of the Highlands!

…T'anyhow—you might have fun with a people who had that sort of highly disciplined, and absolutely unswervable intransigence in your Paratime stories. If they'd ever settled their differences at home, agreed on

a True Philosophy, and set out to Enlighten the heathen in the rest of the world...God help the neighbors!

"Down Styphon!" coming back for some minor revisions.

What you've done here is almost exactly parallel to the sort of thing we used to do in 1930-style science fiction, but in a different line. My early stories, for instance, were loaded with 500 words of action, 2,000 words of hypothetical technology, 500 words of action, 1,000 words of science, 500 words of action, 2,000 words of hypothesis...et cetera.

You've gotten somewhat of a similar effect with _military_ technology that I was getting with _physics_ technology.

The general staff scene (P. 16 et seq.) for instance put over the information—but strictly as a Lecture on Military Tactical Problems by H. Beam Piper.

Vide lectures on physics by John W. Campbell, Jr., in Solarite, Amazing Stories, circa 1931.

An alternative approach would be a scene where Kalvan is trying to get a Hostigos artisan to make one of the weapons he wants, with Chartiphon along, and not being too sharp on catching the need for the new idea.

I know it's hard to see that staff meeting is "a dry lecture by the author" when _you_ know how important the data is to the story. Yeah..._you_ do. But does the reader who wants a good old-fashioned swashbuckler? No, he does not. He resents your "stopping the story to spout hypothetical history."

Can something be done about this—and a couple of similar scenes—in this yarn?

On, another item for another story. During WWII, the Allies caused the death by starvation of several million Bengali. They needed airfields, military bases, barracks and roads built, and hired the Bengali men as laborers, paying high wages.

The result was that these Bengali's did not spend their time farming. They wound up with lots of money, and no food for love or money.

A really vicious little tactic to employ deliberately against a subsistence-level economy, isn't it? You get your money back, of course, after you conquer the famine-decimated enemy country. And the roads you've had them build greatly ease your conquest…and bring in the food they're (literally!) dying to buy at inflated prices.

Not all practical and workable tactics are in the history books as such!

Regards
John W. Campbell

On June 14th, 1964, Piper wrote to Charlie and Marcia Brown:

Dear Charlie and Marcia,

Haven't seen a copy of what they call The Other Human Race, *which I suppose is* Fuzzy Sapiens. *Thank you for letting me know. I don't suppose they've bothered to tell Ken White, either. I question if he'll be any more amused about this than I am.*

I'm glad to hear that the paperback Junkyard Planet *(*The Cosmic Computer, *for Christ's sake!) is selling well. I will probably be reaping the harvest in six months or so; they got the rights on it from Putnam's,* and Putnam's will pay me. A paperback Uller Uprising I have been thinking about for some time; someday something will get done on it.

Paratime stories to date:

Police Operation	Astounding, July 1948
Last Enemy	Astounding, August 1960
Temple Trouble	Astounding, April 1951
Time Crime	Astounding, February and March 1955

Campbell has just bought another Paratime story, "Gunpowder God," and since then I have finished another which is still unreported, and am working on a third at present.

I haven't heard any more from the movie than Jim Blish has from his. Do we have an extradition treaty with Jamaica and the Bahamas? If not, that could be just the reason.

Best wishes, and try to get in touch with you-all the next time I get to NY.

Beam

On the 21st of June, Piper wrote, "Worked all morning and afternoon on revision, got 10 pages done, and then found that most of it will have to be scrapped—which means not only loss of time and effort, but of typewriter paper, in short supply as money at present. It was insufferably hot—wonder what it would be like to fight in armor on a day like this." Still, with all his rewriting, he managed to get the "Down Styphon!" rewrite into the mail to Ken White by June 26th, 1964. Included was the following letter to John Campbell:

Dear John:

You must have had a lot of fun in Scotland. I've never been there, and I should, for the ethnological cocktail which is H. Beam Piper contains a very healthy-sized slug of Scotch. But the farthest north I've ever been was Coventry. If I can make it to the '65 World Convention in London, I'll find or make time for a trip to the Highlands.

"Down Styphon! II" is done, and off to Ken White; you should be getting it along with this. I decided to keep the General Staff meeting, it was the best way I could get all the important Hostigi characters together and re-introduced in a bunch and state the situation Kalvan is facing, and that had to be done. I hope, however, that you'll like it. I got rid of most of the indigestible chunks of tactics, such as the proper employment of cavalry, and why cavalry are better off without lances and musketoons, the precise difference, including weight and caliber, between an arquebus and a caliver, and how many of the militia still had crossbows.

I did have to show that Hostigos was fighting against heavy odds, and I did have to bear down on the artillery, because that was Kalvan's ace-in-the-hole. It is surprising how much difference the invention of trunnions made in artillery. Cannon were used in Europe at least as early as 1327, but they weren't mounted with trunnions until about 1490 (+ or − five or ten years), by the French. Cannon bedded into huge timber stocks and hauled on four-wheel carts seem to be the only kind Machiavelli knew about, which accounts for the low opinion of artillery he expressed in The Prince, The Discourses, *and* The Art of War. One of these simple little things, like the stirrup, or the horse-collar, or the socket bayonet, that nobody but a genius would think of, but it was what really put field artillery in business. The guns with which Alfonso d'Este, Duke of Ferarra, pounded the Spaniards out of a good prepared position at Ravenna, 1512, were so mounted.

The idea of terrain alteration because of diversion of a stream I am saving for a late story, when Kalvan is fighting off a general crusade raised against him by Styphon's House. Before he became interested in medieval and XVI and XVII Century warfare, Calvin Morrison was interested in the Civil War, and knew almost as much about Gettysburg as Robert E. Lee. When they had the Centennial battle reenactment, his superiors at the State Police, knowing of this, assigned him to the detail on duty there. So he thinks he knows all about the ground around Gettysburg, and arranges to fight his big battle there.

The only trouble is, that here-and-now, the beavers have gotten into that area, and in the past hundred or so years they've dammed up all the streams and turned all the best fighting ground into marshes. From a historical probability viewpoint, beavers are entirely random.

The Bengali story's a good one; I may use that, not for a Paratime story but for a Future History story, either Terran Federation or Galactic Empire, probably the latter. Instead of being a piece of deliberate villainy, it will be the stupidity of a lot of helping-handers and do-gooders like Count Erskyll in "A Slave is a Slave." Those kind of people are worse than villains; villains only commit crimes, and they commit blunders, which often do much more harm. We're turning a lot of them loose on the world now.

Machiavelli's comment on our Foreign Aid programme, by the way:

"Amongst other indications by which the power of a republic may be recognized is the relationship in which they live with their neighbors; if these are tributary to her by way of securing her friendship and protection, then it is a sure sign that the republic is powerful. But if these neighboring states, though they may be more feeble than herself, draw money from her, then it is a sure indication of great weakness on the part of the republic."

But, of course, Machiavelli was a dirty old so-and-so. He wasn't a Liberal. He was <u>selfish!</u> For one thing, he didn't believe that friends who could be bought were worth buying.

Best wishes,
H. Beam Piper

After mailing off "Down Styphon!" and a letter to his agent, Piper went straight to work on "Kalvan Kingmaker" and by pure serendipity found another $10.00 in his bank account—"which means a lot, now." He was now writing in longhand on legal pads to save typing paper. But there were other problems: "Second floor denizens had another screaming fight, a lot of it on the sidewalk in front of the house."

This is the first time writing on legal pads (which he used to use at the Altoona car shops) is mentioned in the post-1956 diaries. Another sign that his finances were going straight to hell. Any writer who can't afford his basic tools, like typing paper, is in real trouble.

"Worked on first draft all day," Piper wrote on July 15th, "using too many words to say the same thing too many times. Will have to get hold of this story and give it a good shaking." By the 27th, things were starting to jell with the third Kalvan novella, "Kalvan Kingmaker": "All day on planning for the big battle scene, mostly trying to get the timing right. Tricky job, making everything fit."

On July 30th, "Working on cutting down and recasting what has already been done. Have to jettison a lot of nice bits—may be able to get them back in when I rewrite for book-form. Still nothing from Ken White. Wrote him a letter, par avion, to find out why." "Kalvan Kingmaker" was coming down the backstretch. On August 1st, he wrote: "Worked all morning, early P.M., on planning—up to big battle; have to get my troop-strengths, movements and timing, order of battle; worked on this till mid-afternoon, then out for a walk up town, bought another small box of rice, cutting me down to .23 cents, plus a penny I found. Read in evening, to bed 2330."

By August 4th, the "Down Styphon!" money had come in and Piper was hustling to get the new story out so that he would have some income to get him through the end of the year. *Fuzzies and Other People* was dead in the water and the Piper story inventory was almost as bare as his kitchen cabinets the week before. With John Campbell overbooked with novels and novellas, he couldn't count on writing another novel, like *Space Viking*, to tide him over through the winter. His plan was to sell the three Kalvan novelettes to Campbell, and then sell the ensuing novel to Ace Books.

On the 13th, he wrote, "Past the battle, now, and still have oodles of scenes, action, to get in." In his spare time, he was helping friends set up their exhibits at the Lycoming County Historical Society temporary museum. Mike Knerr noted: "His writing appears almost jaunty during these several days of working with friends at the museum, with no moaning at all about scrapping what he'd written. He was even working in the evening. His old friend Ted Ranck had been enlisted to help with the museum work, together with a Mr. And Mrs. Donald Carson, and there are happy notations in the diary about the men dropping by his place, after work, for a couple of drinks. The story, although parts had to be re-done, was coming along at a fair rate of speed and he even found time to clean his own guns."

There was another official looking letter from France on August 21st, while Piper was cleaning the 9mm Mauser pistol. "Suspect that this is *It*." He went back to cleaning the Mauser and working on "Kalvan Kingmaker," which he was now calling "Hos Hostigos."

He was writing at a good clip, 10 to 15 pages a day, showing that when inspired Piper could still type the keys right off a typewriter. He was going well until he was slapped with "another" tax bill: "Really got slapped with a sackful of shit today; seems I owe the city of Williamsport about $150.00 in taxes and tax penalties."

He finished "Hos Hostigos" and fired it off to Ken White on September 4th. Enclosed was this letter to John W. Campbell:

Dear John:

Here's the third of the Kalvan stories. The original idea was that Kalvan should make his father-in-law, Prince Ptosphes, Great King; for reasons set forth in the body of the story, this didn't seem such a good idea, and Kalvan, as you will see, becomes Great King himself. Now, I am pretty much like Ike Asimov trying to figure out where to put the Second Foundation. Kalvan is Great King and Hos-Hostigos is really beginning to pick up Hos-power, but Styphon's House isn't down yet, let alone out, and the Great King of Hos-Harphax (down around Havre-de-Grace,

Md.) isn't going to take this secession from his realm placidly. To carry the story on further, I'm going to have to do a lot of figuring. I still want to fight the battle of Breitenfeld at Gettysburg—Breitenfeld is an excellent battle for this cultural and technological level, and Gustavus Adolphus had about the same impact on the Austrian Empire and the Catholic Church as Kalvan is having on Hos-Harphax and Styphon's House.

The battle of Fyk, in this story, was actually fought, under the circumstances described, at Barnet, about twenty or thirty miles east of London, in 1471, between the Yorkist army under Edward IV and Richard, Duke of Gloucester, and the Lancastrian army under the Earl of Warwick and the Earl of Somerset, and John Vere, Earl of Oxford, did the same thing to the Lancastrians that Balthames did to the Sasksi. Even the incident of crawling forward and lying all night under the midrange trajectory of the guns is from Barnet.

This penicillin suggestion; this is the very last thing Kalvan would want to do. He doesn't want to shift Styphon's House into a new racket, he wants to smash it. As it stands, with a monopoly on gunpowder, they control the princes. But if he gets them working miraculous cures, he'd give them a popular following, which they now don't have.

I know you like victories by slick tricks, but slick tricks run out, sooner or later, and in any case they're good odds-cutters and that's all. The best answer to slick-trickery is always a fast punch in the nose. The Japanese tried that heroin trick in China, before the formal beginning of World War II, when Chiang Kai-Shek was in control. His answer to it was to kill all the heroin peddlers and all the heroin addicts, he could. Nothing like a hundred-odd grains of copper-jacketed lead injected at six or eight hundred fs at the base of the brain to cure anything. Of course, if Chiang had been a nice humanitarian type, it might have worked, but he wasn't.

> So if Kalvan wants to destroy Styphon's House, and destruction is the only thing he can do about it, and wants to maintain his new Great Kingdom, he'll have to do it where it counts, on the battlefield. He can, and will, soften them up by all sorts of slick tricks; he can start them fighting among themselves—see what happened to Prince Gormoth, in this story—but when they're softened up enough, the troops will have to move in and finish it. As long as soldiers don't let statesmen, professional slick-tricksters, squander their victories at the peace conference, that settles it.
>
> Georges Clemenceau made the remark that "War is too serious a business to trust to generals." Well, judging from the one he helped make at Versailles in 1919, peace is too serious a business to trust to statesmen.
>
> Kalvan's big advantage, as will be noted, is that Styphon's hierarchy don't believe in Styphon themselves. Atheists make excellent clergymen in normal times, they never get scared by their own sermons. But offer them a chance to be martyrs and see what happens.
>
> Yours cordially
Beam

With "Hos-Hostigos" finished, Piper returned to his historical novel: "Worked A.M. on background for historical novel, probable title, "Only the Arquebus," battle of Cerignola. Out P.M., did some shopping, got a haircut. Had dinner at Heylmun's, and home about 1930. Got Sabatini's *Life of Cesare Borgia* and, for the fourth time, Prescott's *Ferdinand & Isabella* out of the library. Spent most of the evening on them…"

September 10th, Piper wrote, "Worked for a while on background and planning. Trying to get a story, with love interest, to fit historical facts. Heavy going." Mike Knerr noted: "Beam got everything he could from the book by Sabatini and shifted his attention to Prescott, but added wearily, '…don't seem to have recovered from the PittCon yet.' Small wonder: conventions of the science fiction community seem to be marathons dedicated to see how long a person can stay on their feet and drink without collapsing."

On September 12th, "Worked on background A.M., got a volume of Guizet's French History at library. Very little in it—Guizet was a patriotic Frenchman and the invasions of Italy by Charles VIII and Louis XII were not greatly to the credit of France. Worked all evening putting what I got from Sabatini together with Prescott. From now on it's going to be mostly Prescott. Still don't have an idea about fiction story."

Piper spent most of the next two weeks in fruitless research and "doodling out notes" for "Only the Arquebus" that didn't work into a story. On September 23rd, 1960, "I do have a lot of history, and have the geography of southern Italy in mind, but still no story." As Mike Knerr says, "H. Beam Piper was not the kind of historian/writer who would tamper with the facts, even in a novel. Historical license was not a phrase he used at all. Piper was 'trying to work up an idea for a love-interest for story, or, rather, trying to invest the idea I have with some color of historical plausibility, and having heavy going at it.'"

When he turned in at midnight on October 2nd, he scribbled, "I wish to Christ I could get something done."

During this time, Piper wrote very little in his diary, either about the stories he was working or the ones he was planning. Most of the story information comes from his letters. In a March 22nd, 1963 letter to Jerry Pournelle, he wrote the only existing summary of his proposed historical novel, "Only the Arquebus:"

Dear Jerry,

> *...Having just finished a story in the VII Century A.E. [Fuzzies and Other People—jfc], I have now dug out the historical novel on which I have been working intermittently, when I have not been pressed by necessity to get something quickly saleable done, for the last couple of years. This is early Sixteenth Century C.E. [Christian Era—jfc]—1502-1503, to be exact—and Ferdinand of Spain and Louis XII of France are fighting over the kingdom of Naples.*

This is strictly a zero-sum game; Ferdinand and Louis have made a treaty partitioning the Neapolitan Kingdom between them, and now each is trying to grab the whole thing and shove the other out completely. Ferdinand is a smart crook and Louis is a stupid one. Louis' commander, the Duc de Nemours, thinks war is a large-scale tournament, and its purpose is to enable gallant knights to perform deeds of valor and gain chivalrous renown; Ferdinand's commander, Gonzalo de Cordoba, thinks the purpose of war is the destruction of the enemy's armed force.

In addition, the Spaniards have a new and terrible weapon, so dreadful as to make war unthinkable; it is called the arquebus. They have a lot of them, and the French haven't. Figure it out for yourself from there. The story will come to its final climax on the battlefield of Cerignola, where Nemours' knights and men-at-arms were shot to scrap-iron by Gonzalo's arquebusiers, a victory strikingly parallel to Andrew Jackson's at New Orleans.

You know, it must have been lovely, living in an era when the Clausewitzian 'extension of politics by other means' was accomplished with nothing more lethal or expensive, especially expensive, than black powder. I suspect that one ICBM with a thermonuclear warhead represents enough money to have financed the whole Neapolitan war, from Charles VIII's first invasion in 1494 to Gonzalo's expulsion of the French after the Garigliano campaign in the winter of 1503, on both sides.

Of course, it must be remembered that there wasn't as much money around then as now, and kings were habitually broke and trying to make the payments on their last palace, and military campaigns were often brought to a standstill because the mercenaries were out on strike for their back pay. What's that French saying about the more it changes the more it's the same thing?

Beam

After mailing the "Hos-Hostigos" manuscript and cover letter to Ken, Piper started work on an article on the use of firearms for a writer's magazine. "Spent morning and early afternoon working on the writers' magazine article in pencil—getting it put into shape. Jan Robbins called on phone, told him about the writers' meeting. About 1900, odd little incident—

"At my desk, heard hall door open stealthily. Thought it might be Jan slipping in prankishly; picked up a cutlass, also prankishly, and went down the hall. Instead, it was some perfect stranger, a young punk in dungarees, who was looking around in the hall. Surprised, scared when he saw cutlass, mumbled something about wanting to rent a room, and got out. Might have had some trouble with him, except for cutlass."

Mike Knerr noted: "That was the old H. Beam Piper and he appeared to be back to his true form, fooling around with guns from his collection or attempting to play a prank with a sword. His writing was picking up and he appeared fine...He got 'Arms and the Writer' finished, mailed it out and launched into the novelized version of the three *Analog* stories."

The book title was *Lord Kalvan of Otherwhen* as Piper explains, "which is probably no worse than what Ace would call it, if they published it." This diary entry puts to rest, for once and for all, all fan rumors that some anonymous Ace editor took the three Kalvan novelettes and cobbled them together and formed them into a novel. Plus, the three novelettes are not complete: "Gunpowder God" (18,960 words), "Down Styphon!" (15,574 words) and "Hos-Hostigos" (19,751 words) for a total of 54,216 words. I have a copy of the third novelette, "Hos-Hostigos," and it contains an introductory scene that was later cut from the finished novel which ran slightly over 65,000 words. Thus, Beam added 10,000 words to *Lord Kalvan of Otherwhen* that were not in the two original published novelettes that appeared in *Analog* as well as the unpublished final third novelette.

He began work on the novel on September 13th, and by the 21st was already on page 155! "On the following Sunday," Mike Knerr wrote, "he was 'within plain sight of the end [of *Lord Kalvan of Otherwhen*]. I dropped in on him, after phoning, to do an article on him and his collection for my newspaper. We photographed many of his pieces on the floor and I took a shot of Beam pulling the sword out of his cane. We talked awhile and I left: Piper went back to work, finally winding up his marathon writing stint on September 30th.

"I suspect there was more than a bit of desperation in his speedy novelization of the Kalvan novelettes. He needed to have some incoming money to take care of him through the winter. On October 3rd, he wrote, 'Another do-nothing day; still fagged from getting Kalvan finished; ought to be snapping back, but seem to have little or no snap left in me. Fiddling with detective story I was working on four or five years ago—will probably waste months on it, get nothing out of it.' He was also working on 'The Tactical Seesaw' for a lecture he was giving at Lycoming College."

On October 8th, Piper noted, "Wrote Ken White to prod him up; hope it gets results. Am beginning to distrust him." What Piper didn't know was that Ken had died on October 2nd. He didn't learn about it until the 12th. "Still working on the lecture, am now up to the Thirty Years' War. Received a phone call from Ken White's wife with news of his death ten days ago. The manuscript of *Lord Kalvan of Otherwhen* is in her hands; doesn't know what's happened with "Hos-Hostigos." A hell of a situation! She gave me name and address of another agent, a friend of Ken's, Max Wilkinson. Will have to get in touch with him, see if he will represent me."

The next day, he fired off a letter to John Campbell inquiring about the third Kalvan novelette, "Hos-Hostigos:"

Dear John:

I was informed yesterday of the death of my agent and good friend, Kenneth White, ten days ago. I had not heard from him for some time previous—I understand that he had been ill for several months—and do not even know if he received the manuscripts of the third Kalvan story or sent it on to you. This story is entitled "Hos-Hostigos." I would much appreciate your letting me know whether you received it and if so what you've decided to do about it.

I have made arrangements by telephone with Mr. Max Wilkinson, of Littauer & Wilkinson, 500 Fifth Avenue, to represent me in the future. Agents are replaceable; friends aren't.

Nice cover for "Gunpowder God," but who told the artist that Pennsylvania State cops wear blue? They don't, they wear gray. And the red keystone doesn't belong, that's 28th Division, PNG. Otherwise splendid!

Yours truly
Beam

He next sent off a letter to Wilkinson, his new agent, and went back to working out his upcoming lecture. On October 14th, he got a letter: "Letter from an agent, Jay Garon, offering his services. A nice letter, shows that I am known and considered. Had to send regrets." As Mike Knerr noted in "PIPER": "It's strange that he didn't try to learn more about Mr. Garon, and put all his eggs in one basket—a basket he was taking on faith." It turned out to be a fatal error as Wilkinson quickly sent off the novel *Lord Kalvan of Otherwhen* to Ace Books without checking back with Piper or John W. Campbell.

Knerr had this to say in "PIPER": "On October 15th, 1964, Beam wrote, 'Not feeling well—cold and cough coming on. It was getting worse all day Saturday.' I showed up in the afternoon and knocked on his door.

"'Come on in,' Beam said and led me into the gunroom.

"I asked what I usually asked: "What do you hear from Ken?"

"Beam had just reached the corner of his desk, now in its winter position, facing west. He spun in surprise, his eyes wide. 'Ken's dead,' he said, after a second or two. 'Didn't you know?'

"It was my turn to be surprised. Finally I shook my head. 'Nobody told me, Beam. What'll happen to our manuscripts?'

"'Some chap named Max Wilkinson, a friend of Ken's, is sorting through things. I don't know how long that'll take.'

"'You have his address?'"

"He gave it to me and we talked shop awhile. My decision was that I just wanted my manuscripts back, and I wasn't really interested in having another agent handling them. It had been fun, this writing venture, but I just had too much to do with the newspaper work to fool around with creative writing. I told that to Beam.

"'You're quitting?' he asked.

"When I nodded, he said, 'Well, you're young, Mike. What the hell can a man my age do?'

"I didn't have an answer. We talked a while longer about one thing and another, and finally I left. Beam walked me to the door and I told him so long.

"I never saw him again."

Four days later, Piper wrote, "Home about 1830, and spent all night reading—fell asleep about 1930, woke, quite sleepless, at 2200, and read till 0600—"Murder Frozen Over"—the Jeff Rand story I never could sell. This is carrying it about as far as I ever have."

He gave his lecture on the 19th to a gathering of the Phi Alpha Theta fraternity and returned home to work on story ideas. On October 21st, he wrote, "Letter, very brief, from John Campbell—"Hos-Hostigos" bounced back to Ken White, with letter, so no money coming in. Campbell probably wants rewrite. Nothing yet from Wilkinson—have I an agent, or haven't I? Morale badly down."

John Campbell wrote:

Dear Beam:

Your letter telling me about Kenneth White's death came as a shock. I hadn't heard.

Hos-Hostigos was returned to Kenneth on September 16th with a letter.

Regards
John W. Campbell

For a man who majored in understatement, Piper's last statement is a telling comment. The death of his friend and agent was a terrible blow; he had already run through several agents and didn't have a lot of faith in the breed. He was unable to get in touch with Wilkinson and was feeling badly adrift. On the 26th of October, he wrote, "Worked on story-planning till 1400—think something has finally arrived. Wrote to Wilkinson—is he or isn't he?—and to Campbell—what about 'Hos-Hostigos?'" The next day his morale was sinking even lower. "Cough and cold persist; don't feel too good. Can't seem to get anything done."

Here's what he wrote in his last letter to John W. Campbell:

Dear John:

Your letter of the 19th arrived. As I think I told you in mine of the 13th, I had a telephone conversation with Mr. Max Wilkinson, of Littauer & Wilkinson, inquiring if he would be willing to take over as my agent. To this he agreed, but since then I have heard nothing from him, although some report on the state of my affairs in Ken's hands at the time of his death seems rather overdue. Now I don't know whether I have an agent or not, and until I hear something positive to that effect, I'll have to act on the assumption that I don't.

For one thing, I have not received the letter which you sent accompanying return of "Hos-Hostigos," and except for your brief note, know nothing about it. Apparently Ken was ill for some time before he died, and never got around to forwarding it on to me. I was delaying answer to yours of the 19th in hope that it would come in.

Do you want a revision of the story? If so, I would be deeply grateful if you would write me, giving me a resume of the letter which accompanied it back to Ken, and telling me what needs to be fixed up about it. If you would do so, I will get to work on it immediately.

I am, with best wishes and thanking you in advance.

Yours Cordially
H. Beam Piper

This letter is as close to begging as Piper ever came, all but pleading for Campbell to send him a carbon of Campbell's revision letter. Sadly, Campbell never replied—or if he did, the letter is lost. He doesn't mention it in his diary and this is what Campbell had to say about it all in a November 18th, 1965 letter to John Clark—the same John Clark who wrote the introduction to the Twayne Triplet, which contained his first published novel, *Uller Uprising*:

Dear John:

That H. Beam Piper story business has caused one helluva mess. It goes this way: We bought the first and second Lord Kalvan stories from Piper, through his agent Ken White. "Hos-Hostigos," the third, was submitted by Ken White, and I sent it back for some revision with an eight page letter of explanation.

Three months later I heard from Piper that Ken White had died suddenly, leaving his affairs in such a mess that nobody had done anything for a couple of months. So Piper didn't know what I'd said about "Hos-Hostigos," and never got my letter. And I, by then, didn't remember the yarn exactly enough to be able to redo the letter without seeing the manuscript.

Obviously, John Campbell didn't have any idea of just how desperate Piper's financial situation had gotten. Campbell, not known for his sensitivity, couldn't or didn't bother to read between the lines of his letter—so Piper was left out on the ledge. He was running out of money, his 'supposed' agent wasn't writing or calling and then another disaster on October 29th, 1964: "Now the city income tax people are on me—I'm damned if I know how I'm going to make out. Letter from Wilkinson—he is acting for me, will go over Ken's files after the first, and he has sent *Lord Kalvan of Otherwhen* to Ace."

As Mike Knerr wrote: "The next day he went to the bank and drew everything out but two dollars, did some shopping and returned to the gunroom for another writing session. There's no mention in the diary of what the new story was about or even a working title. He read his lecture to the writers' club on the 2nd of November."

On Wednesday, November 4th, 1964, Piper wrote, "Up 0930. Worked till mid-P.M. on planning. Out 1600 for a little, read in evening; to be 0030. Yesterday's election a bad—but not unexpected defeat; Goldwater carried Arizona and a few of the Deep South states; Johnson everything else, including Maine and Vermont. The only thing that will save this country now is an Act of God, and God doesn't exist."

Mike Knerr wrote, "On Thursday, November 5th, thinly scrawled in weak pencil is the notation that Beam awoke at 9:00 A.M. and half an hour later it had begun to rain.

"It was a Pennsylvania rain, a weeping, drizzling, persistent rain and, in retrospect, I can see him sitting at his desk looking at the beads and rivulets of water running down over the window pane. Frowning, the way he always frowned when he was deep in thought or perplexed by something. The red diary would be on the desk before him and he would have dropped the pencil. His eyes would be squinched [sic] into thin lines and his brows furled above them. He would be weighing the odds again, the way he always did.

"Did he have an agent? Would Ace take *Lord Kalvan of Otherwhen*? Would 'Hos-Hostigos' sell, or 'Fuzzies and Other People?' Could he afford, with the little bit of money he had, to hold out until something finally came through? Could he go through another starvation period like the ones in the past? Was there any use to it all? He was sixty. Betty was gone. Ken was gone. He was tired, old and just a bit sick, and completely in the dark as to what had become of his work. The Nifflheim with it!

"No matter how long he sat there weighing it all. An hour. Two. It all added up to more than he wanted to deal with. He cleared off the desk, wrote a little note and went into the bedroom for his .38 Colt Marshall and sat down again.

"He put up painters' drop-cloths in the gunroom, sat down in his office chair, brought out his pistol, stuck it into his mouth and fired—"

CHAPTER THIRTY-SEVEN

Afterwards

Mike Knerr wrote in "PIPER" about learning of H. Beam Piper's suicide:

"Sunday, November 8th, the one day I had off, and it was spitting rain. All week long, as a reporter for the *Shamokin Citizen*, I had written stories about traffic accidents, human interest junk, drew editorial cartoons and attended the various meetings of the school board, the fire department and the city council. I'd fought my way through the elections and we'd gotten the weekly newspaper put to bed until next week. On Saturday I'd covered a 'milk bowl' football game, writing up the kids as though they were pros; they loved it, but their parents were always giving me a bad time because little 'Johnny' hadn't been mentioned.

"I'd earned a Sunday of tramping through the woods of Line Mountain, getting chortled at by irate squirrels, squeaked at by nearly invisible chipmunks and snorted at by curious does. I wanted to go check buck rubs and slashings; I wanted to see where the deer were moving, and where I'd be sitting on the opening day of buck season.

"The last thing in the world I wanted was goddamn rain!

"When the State Police officer cruiser slid down the mud of the dirt road, and stopped at the house, I had the sinking feeling that I would have to go to work again. A bad accident? A mine cave in? Nuts! Trooper Kraynak got out and ducked through the rain to the porch, his frayed D.I. hat covered with plastic against the water.

"'Mike,'" he said. "'Do you know an H. Beam Piper?'

"'Sure. Why?'

"'The Montoursville barracks called us,' he went on. 'Asked us to notify you because they can't locate any next of kin. He's dead.'"

"I didn't say anything. I just stared at the rain, and at Kraynak. Beam had always said he would do it. He'd killed himself; I knew it. Somehow I knew it just as sure as I knew where the deer trails were in the woods.

"'You all right?' Kraynak asked.

"'How?' I asked, after nodding to his question.

"'Suicide,' Kraynak said gently. 'He shot himself.'

"'Shit,' I whispered.

"'A neighbor got suspicious,' Kraynak went on, 'when they didn't see him around. Called the city police. They went in and found him. The State Police are trying to locate any next of kin he might have had. You know any?'

"I shook my head. 'He mentioned once that he had some cousins scattered around, but I don't know any names. I guess I'll pack the car and go up. Hey, thanks, Kraynak.'

"'See you, Mike.'

"I watched him climb into the patrol car and drive down the road; then I went in and told my wife. We packed the kids in the car and started driving north through the lousy rain. We didn't talk much."

"The State Police managed to locate one of Beam's relations, Charles O. Piper. He was named executor of the estate. He asked me if I would help in assembling whatever literary material was available. This would be turned over to the attorney, William Askey. I agreed, and the following weekend we both went up and got the key from the city police. They had padlocked the door after they'd taken Beam's body out.

"'Poor lonely old fellow,' Charles said softly.

"For a brief time, we simply wandered through the apartment, not knowing exactly where to start. It was a mess. There was scrap paper all over the place; there were files to go through and manuscripts to sort out. I guided Charles in the literary material, and he guided me in what should be classed as junk.

"The desk was bare of anything but a large pool of dried blood where Beam had fallen forward. Behind the desk chair, the ceiling was a dark black hole with blood splatterings around it. I went out into the kitchen and stared out through the door at the pigeons on the roof of the garage in the alley. 'Shit, Beam,' I said helplessly, then went back to help Charles sort things out.

"It took a lot of weekends."

Marvin N. Katz, a reporter for Grit Publishing, wrote in the *Analog Science Fiction* letter column that there was a suicide note, but it did not give any reasons for Piper's fatal decision. In a typically Piperesque comment, it did state: "I don't like to leave messes when I go away, but if I could have cleaned up any of this mess, I wouldn't be going away. H. Beam Piper."

No one will never know just what it was that forced Piper's hand: illness, chronic pain and depression, drunken despondency, loneliness for Betty, the death of his agent and friend, Ken White; or the difficulties of starting all over with a new agent who never answered his letters, when he felt 'written out' and despaired of going through even one more cycle of starvation and salvation, when another check might or might not arrive 'just in time.'

All of Piper's friends, such as Mike Knerr, Don Coleman and Jerry Pournelle bear a heavy weight of guilt for not having recognized his desperation and loneliness—and for not having put out a helping hand....

Mike Knerr wrote, in his August 26th, 1982, letter, "I didn't know about a note, but then I was pretty broken up at the time—in fact, the reason his 'lost' (*Fuzzies and Other People*) manuscript has been lost for so long is because I'm still pretty broken up about it. It didn't have to happen. Hell, I'd have supported him, had I known. Beam and Ray Bradbury taught me to write and that has to count for something."

Despite the best intentions of his friends, had they known of his desperate financial state, it is doubtful that Piper would have accepted their charity. Piper was a proud and independent man—to a fault. Even if he had, he would not have taken their charity for long, and—barring a best seller—he would have gone broke again, and again. *If*, by some miracle, he could have held out to the late seventies when his work was once again in demand, he would never have gone hungry again. But that's a long fourteen years....

Meanwhile, going hat in hand to each of his dear friends—all of whom, sooner or later, would have gotten tired of bailing out their old friend—was not Piper's style. He knew human nature inside out. Go to the well once, and the well keeper feels Christian charity. Go twice and he mumbles with forbearance. A third time and he curses your very existence.

Sure, Piper could have secretly continued to pawn off his gun collection, selling most of them in New York so that the local collectors wouldn't know how desperate he'd become. However, even unbeknownst to Piper, science fiction was heading into stormy seas, as the New Wave broke over the field: bringing relevance, social reform, sexual freedom and speculative fiction to the forefront. Many of the field's Old Guard, like Jack Williamson, Poul Anderson, Randall Garrett and many others were considered relics—dinosaurs, by the Young Turks led by Harlan Ellison, Judith Merril, Norman Spinrad and Michael Moorcock. Classic adventure fiction and space opera, of the sort Piper wrote, was considered passé and old fashioned.

In this piece written shortly before his death, Piper was eerily prescient, in this answer to the question in "The Double Bill Symposium," written in 1964, on how to enlarge the SF audience: "Not enough people read it, and there doesn't seem to be much of anything to do about it. I remember, years ago, Fletcher Pratt was bemoaning this situation and saying that we must enlarge our readership. I said then that it couldn't be done, and I still don't think so....I am almost sixty now. It gives me the most inexpressible pleasure to reflect that by the time this has happened, I shall be dead." He was sixty years old at the time of his death.

Of all the magazines, only John W. Campbell's *Analog* stayed afloat and healthy. While *Analog* was certainly Piper's major market in the last five years of his life, it was not always a safe harbor. The paperback explosion of the 1970s was still not in evidence in 1964 and there were too few houses to support the many old timers who had thrived during the pulp era.

However, Piper —in the last months of his life—*appears* to have made a huge tactical error. He allowed his "new" agent to sell off the paperback rights of *Lord Kalvan of Otherwhen* to Ace Books before the second installment of the 'series' was published in *Analog*.

Campbell blazed at this effrontery. He expressed some of his feelings in a letter to John D. Clark [the same John Clark, who provided the 'scientific' introduction to the Twayne Triplets, which contained Beam's short novel *Uller Uprising*.]:

That H. Beam Piper story business has caused one helluva mess. It goes this way: We bought the first and second Lord Kalvan stories from Piper, through his agent Ken White. Hos-Hostigos, the third, was submitted by Ken White, and I sent it back for some revision with an eight page letter of explanation.

Three months later, I heard from Piper that Ken White had died suddenly, leaving his affairs in such a mess that nobody had been informed and nobody knew what to do, and nobody had done anything for a couple of months. So Piper didn't know what I'd said about Hos-Hostigos, and never got my letter. And I, by then, didn't remember the yarn exactly enough to be able to redo the letter without seeing the manuscript.

So Beam was broke, and apparently suddenly decided to go out sidewise... suicidewise.

And he'd just contacted a new agent, and left his affairs in a mess, including neglecting to explain to the agent that Analog *had bought some of his stories and not published them yet. So the agent, cleaning out his affairs, sold all the stuff* (the novelization of the Kalvan stories—jfc) *to Ace. And the mess was thereby further glorified and transmigrated. Because Ace didn't own the rights to properly copyright, and we couldn't properly copyright because Ace had improperly copyrighted and the legal situation is twice as complicated!*

The Piper Revival of the mid-1970's was, in large part, a reaction to the New Wave; readers searching out 'classics' from the Golden Age of SF, looking for good story telling, not flashy style and little substance. Within five years most of Piper's short stories and novels were re-published, including a few newly 'discovered' books and suddenly there was a new generation of H. Beam Piper fans.

Ventura II, a fanzine published shortly after Pipers death, included several appreciations of Piper, including this touching eulogy from science fiction author Jack Chalker: "The Lights Go Out:"

H. Beam Piper (He never would tell anyone what the "H" stood for) was a talented and imaginative writer who endeared himself to the science fiction world not just by his superb writings, but also by his sparkling wit and personality at various conventions and conferences. He was one of the special group you looked forward to meeting again and again, and who, you know, would be the same cordial gentleman. No one was too big or too small, too famed or too unknown, that he could not talk with Beam as a friend. His pixie-like mannerisms and his twinkling eyes were always at the center of attention. Beam loved people, all kinds of people, and he was never happy unless there was a group nearby discussing history and antique weaponry, and he was often the life of any party.

He looked somewhat like the classic movie villain, with a thin moustache and a deep, piercing voice—but the twinkle in his eye betrayed his image, and this suited his impish sense of humor.

It was only in the past few years that he truly matured as a writer, and found his forte in the form of the novel, giving the SF world such masterpieces as Space Viking *and the novel that truly won him universal acclaim and recognition by all,* Little Fuzzy. *His juvenile novels for Putnam's,* Four-Day Planet *and* Junkyard Planet," *showed him a master of all levels, perhaps the only man who could equal the gifts of Heinlein and Norton in writing juveniles that did not play down, and were often far superior to the bulk of adult fiction. Beam never wrote for adults or for juveniles—he wrote for everyone.*

By 1964 it was very apparent that H. Beam Piper was one of the truly great SF authors, and from the time when he couldn't sell a novel to the magazine or hardback publishers (Little Fuzzy *was universally rejected*) *he had, in a few short years, come up to where he would be ranked on the SF five foot shelf with every great writer in the business. In one sense he truly surpassed his contemporaries—his public knew and loved him personally as well.*

In 1964 PhillyCon attendees were rather puzzled when Beam failed to appear for the festivities. He was so much a part of the East Coast's affairs that his very absence was almost physically noticeable. It was then that Sam Moscowitz told us that he had received word that on November 11, 1964, just a few days before, Beam Piper had said his farewell to this world and gone on.

Beam's thoughts ran deep. He was a very complex man, a very unique and unfathomable man. Behind the villain's façade, beyond even the twinkling eyes and the pixie manner, there were things that showed in no external symptom, and like the ancient ones he studied and loved, he chose his own time and place of farewell, for reasons concealed from us all.

The news passed like a great snake through the Philadelphia audience. Few would or could believe he was gone. There are those of us who really can't believe it even now.

In a year that saw us lose many great men, for different causes-Hannes Bok, Cleve Cartmill, Mark Clifton, Aldous Huxley, T.H. White, C.S. Lewis, Norbert Weiner, and others—this loss was saddening indeed. To those that had the pleasure of knowing Beam himself, the loss is doubly felt.

H. Beam Piper (1904-1964) is gone—but his name will not be forgotten until men cease to imagine far places, new worlds out among the stars....

* * *

H. Beam Piper was above all a storyteller and teller of tales that resonated with history and real life experience. And he wrote words that still ring with truth and wisdom. During the Depression, Piper had worked as a railroad dick, rousting bums and giving nightstick justice to tramps and thieves in the Altoona car yards—some thirty years' worth. Then he married a wealthy socialite and was a gentleman around town in New York at its peak—The Thin Man. He was an outdoorsman, hiker and gun aficionado. In his last years, a recluse working madly to get his fever dreams down on paper. He knew love, he knew loss; he knew triumph, he knew despair. But most of all: he was the "Typewriter Killer"—H. Beam Piper.

The End

BIBLIOGRAPHY

1. Africa, J. Simpson, *The History of Huntingdon and Blair County* (Philadelphia, PA: Louis H. Everts, 1883).

2. *Altoona Mirror*, Obituaries (Altoona, PA: September 10, 1902).

3. Ashley, Mike, *The Complete Index to Astounding/Analog* (Oak Forest, IL: Robert Weinberg Publications, 1981).

4. Barris, Wess, Roster of Juniata Shops Built GG1s: Steamlocomotive.com.

5. Bowers, Bill and Bill Mallardi, "The double: bill Symposium," (Akron, OH; 1969) p. 16.

6. Campbell, John W., Brass Tacks, *Analog Science Fact - Science Fiction* (New York, NY: Condé Nast, January 1966) p. 153.

7. Campbell, John W., letter to Fred Pohl (New York, NY: January 15, 1951).

8. Campbell, John W., letter to H. Beam Piper (New York, NY: June 26, 1952).

9. Campbell, John W., letter to H. Beam Piper (New York, NY: July 21, 1954).

10. Campbell, John W., letter to H. Beam Piper (New York, NY: May 13, 1959).

11. Campbell, John W., letter to Kenneth S. White (New York, NY: January 20, 1960).

12. Campbell, letter to Kenneth S. White (New York, NY: September 12, 1960).

13. Campbell, John W., letter to Kenneth S. White (New York, NY: Nov. 6, 1961).

14. Campbell, John W., letter to H. Beam Piper (New York, NY: June 5, 1962).

15. Campbell, John W., letter to Kenneth S. White (New York, NY: April 15, 1964).

16. Campbell, John W., letter to H. Beam Piper (New York, NY: May 19, 1964).

17. Campbell, John W., letter to H. Beam Piper (New York, NY: October 19, 1964).

18. Campbell, John W., letter to John D. Clark on (New York, NY: November 18, 1965).

19. Campbell, John W., "Tribesman, Barbarian and Citizen," Editorial, *Analog Science Fact - Science Fiction* (New York, NY: Street & Smith, May 1961).

20. Carr, John F., *H. Beam Piper: A Biography*, (Jefferson, NC: McFarland & Company and Inc. 2008).

21. Carr, John F., "Introduction," *Federation* (New York, NY: Ace Books, February 1981).

22. Carr, John F., "The Last Cavalier: H. Beam Piper," *Analog Science Fact - Science Fiction* (New York, NY: Condé Nast, January 1988) pp. 161-174.

23. Carr, John F., "The Terro-Human Future History of H. Beam Piper, *Bulletin of the Science Fiction Writers of America* (Granada Hills, CA, Fall 1979, #71) pp. 42-51.

24. Chalker, Jack L., "The Lights Go Out," *Ventura II* (Norfolk, VA: 1965), pp. 27-28.

25. Chapdelaine, Sr., Perry, *The John W. Campbell Letters, Vol. I* (Franklin, TN: AC Projects: 1985).

26. Coleman, Don, "The Early Letters" unpublished collection of the H. Beam Piper/Ferd Coleman letters in author's possession (Scottsdale, AZ: 1991).

27. Coleman, Don, letter to author (Cincinnati, OH: October 19, 1991),

28. Coleman, Don, letter to author (Cincinnati, OH: November 19, 1991).

29. Coleman, Don, letter to author (Cincinnati, OH: July 20, 2001),

30. Coleman, Don, letter to the author (Cincinnati, OH: October 19, 2003), p 2.

31. Council on International Education Exchange, Inc. Website, information on the Council on Student Travel (http://www.answers.com/topic/council-on-international-educational-exchange-inc: Jan. 18, 2007).

32. John H. Costello, John H., "H. Beam Piper: An Infinity of Worlds: Part One," *Renaissance,* Vol. 4, No. 4, Fall 1972).

33. de Camp, L Sprague, *Time and Chance: an Autobiography* (Hampton Falls, NH: Donald M. Grant, 1996).

34. Flayhart, William H., letter to author (Dover, DE: March 12, 2003), p. 1.

35. Heinlein, Robert A., From James Forrestal Memorial Lecture to the Brigade of Midshipmen at his alma mater, the U.S. Naval Academy at Annapolis, April 5, 1973.

36. Hines, David, e-mail, including biographical information on H. Beam Piper, to author, May, 3, 2001.

37. Holland, Elwanda, "H. Beam Piper in Paperback (1957-1965)," *Books are Everything!*, Vol. 2, No. 2 (Whole Number 8) (Richmond, KY: March 1989).

38. Horton, Rich on the Internet at alt.books.isaac-Asimov.

39. Katz, Marvin N., Brass Tacks, *Analog Science Fact - Science Fiction* (New York, NY: Condé Nast, March 1965) pp. 92-93.

40. Knerr, Michael E., "PIPER", unpublished manuscript in author's possession (Sausalito, CA: 1983).

41. Knerr, Michael E., letter to author (Sausalito, CA: August 26, 1982).

42. Knerr, Michael E., telephone conversation with the author (Sausalito, CA: September 26, 1982).

43. McGuire, Anne, one-hour taped interview for author (Shrewsbury, NJ: June 9, 2001).

44. McGuire, John J., Jr., telephone interview with author (Shrewsbury, NJ: May 10, 2001).

45. McGuire, Terry, telephone interview with author (Oceanport, NJ: June 9, 2001).

46. McGuire, Terry, e-mail to author (Oceanport, NJ: March 26, 2001).

47. McGuire, Terry, e-mail to author (Oceanport, NJ: June 6, 2006).

48. McMorris, Bill, e-mail to author on October 4, 2005.

49. McMorris, Bill, e-mail to author on January 11, 2007.

50. Piper, H. Beam, *A Catalogue of Henry Wharton Shoemaker Weapons at Restless Oaks in McElhattan Pennsylvania* (Altoona, PA: Times Tribune Co.).

51. Piper, H. Beam, diary entries for January 1, 1955 to August 27, 1955 from Rare Books and Manuscripts, The Pennsylvania State University Libraries (Altoona, PA: 1955).

52. Piper, H. Beam, *Federation* (New York, NY: Ace Books, 1981).

53. Piper, H. Beam, *Empire* (New York, NY: Ace Books, 1981).

54. Piper, H. Beam, letter to John W. Campbell (Altoona, PA: June 18, 1951).

55. Piper, H. Beam, letter to Alan Howard (Altoona, PA: Jan. 12, 1953).

56. Piper, H. Beam, letter to John W. Campbell (Altoona, PA: July 17, 1954).

57. Piper, H. Beam, letter to Freida Coleman (Altoona, PA: September 4, 1955).

58. Piper, H. Beam, letter to Lycoming Historical Society (Altoona, PA: 1956: June 12, 1956).

59. Piper, H. Beam, letter to Freida Coleman (Paris, France: May 17, 1957).

60. Piper, H. Beam, letter to Jerry Pournelle (Williamsport, PA: December 19, 1962).

61. Piper, H. Beam, letter to Jerry Pournelle (Williamsport, PA: March 22, 1963).

62. Piper, H. Beam, letter to Charles and Marcia Brown (Williamsport, PA: July 2, 1963).

63. Piper, H. Beam, postcard to Charles and Marcia Brown (Williamsport, PA: December 20, 1963).

64. Piper, H. Beam, letter to Peter Weston with 4 page attachment titled, "The Future History by H. Beam Piper" (Williamsport, PA: February 16, 1964).

65. Piper, H. Beam, letter to Charles and Marcia Brown (Williamsport, PA: June 14, 1964).

66. Piper, H. Beam, letter to John W. Campbell on (Williamsport, PA: September 5, 1964).

67. Piper, H. Beam, letter to John W. Campbell (Williamsport, PA: October 13, 1964).

68. Piper, H. Beam, letter to John W. Campbell (Williamsport, PA: October 26, 1964).

69. Piper, H. Beam, *Little Fuzzy* (New York: NY: Ace Books, 1984).

70. Piper, H. Beam, *Murder in the Gunroom* (New York, NY: Alfred A. Knopf, Inc.: 1953).

71. Pohl, Frederick, The Way the Future Blogs, http://www.thewaythefutureblogs.com/

72. Pohl, Frederick, telephone conversation with author (Red Bank, NJ: June 14, 1979).

73. Pournelle, Jerry E., conversation with author (Studio City, CA: February 12, 1980).

74. Pournelle, Jerry E., conversation with author (Studio City, CA: April 26, 1982).

75. Pournelle, Jerry E., conversation with author (Studio City, CA: November 14, 1983.

76. Pratt, Fletcher, *World of Wonder* (New York City, N.Y.: Twayne Publishers, 1951).

77. Ramsey, Fred, December 15, 2002 e-mail to "The Works of H. Beam Piper" Internet List: PIPER-L@HOME.EASE.LSOFT.COM.

78. Schuchart, Paul, letter to author (Harrisburg, PA: February 18, 1981).

79. Schuchart, Paul, letter to author (Harrisburg, PA: April 19, 1981).

80. Staff, "Typewriter 'Killer'" (Philadelphia, PA: *Pennsy*, Sept. 1953, Vol. 2, No. 8) p. 7.

81. Starlight website, postscript to the biographical entry from *The History of Huntingdon and Blair County*: http://gwillick.tripod.com/bio/DrHBPiper.html.

82. Weston, Peter, "Future History No. 1," H. Beam Piper, *Zenith #4* (May 1964).

83. Wright, Michael, *Here Comes Sputnik* created August 30, 1997 on web site: http://www.batnet.com/mfwright/sputnik.html.

APPENDIX I

Paratime

PARATIME

I love "Paratime." It was the first time I encountered a book that concentrated on a race that moved between alternate Earths as opposed to books that were set only on one. I'm not sure if it's just me, but all of the 'classic' science fiction future worlds imagined in the 1940's and 1950's always have come across as slightly creepy to me. The robots rolling about serving people's whims, the rocket ships, and general decadence that they seemed to have. That the Home Time Line culture is based on theft and slavery makes them hard to like. One sort of wants to see bad things happen to them.

> Jason Kastich
> Member of the Paratime Study Team

H. Beam Piper showed an early interest in precognition and time travel. Piper's first mention of time travel in print appears in the 1947-1948 issue of a small writers' publication, the *Amateur Spectator*, the official organ of the Spectator Club. In a piece titled, "Precognition and a Theory of Time," Piper writes about his ideas on time and General Semantics. Many of Piper's ideas were derived from J. W. Dunne's essay, "An Experiment with Time." A year later this first Paratime Police story, "Police Operation," appeared in the July, 1948, issue of *Astounding Science Fiction*.

The story, "Sideways in Time," by Murray Leinster was first published in the June 1934 issue of *Astounding Stories* and is one of the first alternate worlds stories in modern science fiction. Paratime was H. Beam Piper's own unique take on the time travel genre, postulating the existence of an entire civilization that could travel through alternate time-lines. Instead of going into the future or the past, Piper created a sideways in time traveling race, who used literally millions of selected time-lines, or alternate worlds, as resource supply bases for their Home Time Line. While alternate world time travel is not wholly Piper's invention, he did put his own unique spin on parallel worlds with his Paratime Police. Piper's Paratime stories have influenced most modern time travel and alternate history science fiction works, including Poul Anderson's Time Traders' books, Andre Norton's Time series, Keith Laumer's Imperium and Harry Turtledove's Crosstime series which is dedicated to Piper.

In his Paratime series, H. Beam Piper postulated an almost infinite number of parallel earthly worlds or time-lines, where in each sector, subsector and belt of time-lines events occurred differently. Unknowingly to the inhabitants, some of these outtime time-lines are exploited by the parasitic inhabitants of the Home Time Line who have invented a way to travel from one time-line to another. The Paratimers use that secret technology to steal raw materials, finished goods, rare artworks, cultural artifacts and technological devices which their own exhausted and resource depleted earth can no longer provide. The Home Time Line culture also appears to be in an ideational, scientific and cultural stasis, and, as a result (although they would never admit it), they hijack not only physical objects but cultural ideas and scientific and technological innovations from the outtime worlds they prey upon.

Most First Level inhabitants view the outtime worlds they rob as backward cultures not worthy of consideration. They display no guilt about their depredations; in general they look upon the natives of the outtime worlds as barbarians, regardless of what cultural or scientific heights these cultures have reached. In fact, a few Second Level time-lines have achieved interstellar spaceflight, but they are still considered backward by the Home timeliners. The Home Time Line society has created the Paratime Police to keep the First Level time-line travelers in check and—most importantly—to protect the secret of Paratime travel.

Piper's Paratime series features the Paratime Police who are responsible for policing the almost infinite number of timelines as well as ensuring that the secret of Paratime Transposition is not discovered by the inhabitants of any other time-line. The Paratime stories feature the adventures of the Paratime Police's top troubleshooter Verkan Vall and his wife, Dalla, who has a penchant for attracting trouble.

The Paratime series as written by H. Beam Piper consists of a number of stories: "Police Operation," "Last Enemy;" "Temple Trouble," "Time Crime," and one novel, *Lord Kalvan of Otherwhen*, all of which involve Verkan Vall and the Paratime Police. There is internal evidence that both "He Walked Around the Horses" and "Genesis" fall under the Paratime umbrella.

The idea of parallel worlds is an old one that appears in mythology and folk tales with roots in the accounts of mythical homes of the gods, fairy tales and astral planes. Mark Twain's *A Connecticut Yankee in King Arthur's Court* was one of the first books to bring the theme of alternate worlds to popular attention. The genre was further popularized for American audiences through L. Frank Baum's children's book, *The Wizard of Oz*, where Dorothy travels to an alternate "dream" world. This groundbreaking children's novel was so popular it spawned not only a successful movie, but also an entire series which continued on long after Baum's death in 1919. Edgar Rice Burroughs, A. Merritt and Henry Kuttner were among the first writers to bring this theme into science fiction.

The usual treatment of the parallel worlds theme has been for the author to create a series of alternate worlds as part of a continuum of increasing historical variation from a template world, usually a present time, or future, version of our own earth. This method is primarily directed at speculations of the "What if" variety, such as what if the Confederacy had won the Civil War, or the Nazis had won World War II. The "What If" question has long been popular among professional and amateur historians; there are dozens of websites on the Internet dedicated to Alternate Worlds, many of which offer elaborate alternative histories for readers to enjoy. One of the most prominent is Uchronia, which gives out their Sideways Award for best short form story and novel alternate history work each year.

Most of these "alternates" are based on a historical branching, that is, history taking a different path at some critical juncture of Western Civilization—usually a war or pivotal battle, such as Carthage winning the Punic Wars with Rome, or Napoleon defeating Wellington and so forth. The further in the past these branches occur, the more bizarre and unusual the alternative world appears to the travelers from the template world, i.e. our own world.

British SF author Kenneth Bulmer put a new spin on Paratime by creating alternate world portals or gates which have become standard fare for many alternate world yarns. His Keys to the Dimension series ran to seven novels: *The Key to Irunium*, *The Key To Venudine*, *The Wizards of Senchuria*, *The Ships of Durostorum*, *The Hunters of Jugundai*, *The Chariots of Ra* and *The Diamond Contessa*. Bulmer's first Keys to the Dimension novel didn't appear until 1967 and was heavily influenced by Piper.

Keith Laumer came up with his own sideways time travel slant in the Imperium. This series is a continuum of parallel worlds policed by the Imperium, a government based in an alternate Stockholm. *The Worlds of the Imperium* was published in 1962 and undoubtedly influenced by Piper's Paratime. The Imperium and Paratime technologies describe an angled path across the lines because they move forward at normal time rate while moving sideways. The Imperium is formed in an alternate history where the American Revolution did not occur, and the British Empire and Germany merged into a unified empire in 1900. The protagonist, an American diplomat, Bayard, is kidnapped by the Imperium because in a third parallel Earth he is waging war against his abductors. Further adventures follow after Bayard decides to remain in the service of the Imperium.

The Imperium has a different view of the timelines, seeing them as a tangle rather than an infinite number of straight, parallel lines. Their technology has been developed on several time-lines but in many cases has caused damage and destruction to multiple time-lines, including the massive area called the Blight that was thought to consist of only lines where all life except on the Imperium line had been destroyed or massively mutated, yet two other untouched lines exist, this one we inhabit (or is it?)—Bayard's home line—and one other where Bayard's enemies tried to strand him. There are also at least two other vastly divergent lines where the species that became sapient are not *Homo sapiens* and have developed timeline traveling technology similar to the Imperium, with one having developed a system that's a form fitting suit.

Other Piper influenced examples of sideways time travel include Richard Meredith's Timeliner Trilogy books, Robert Adam's Castaways in Time series, Leo Frankowski's Cross-Time Engineer series, Michael McCollum's A Greater Infinity and Harry Turtledove's Crosstime Traffic series, of which the first title is *Gunpowder Empire*, a nod to Piper's *Lord Kalvan of Otherwhen*.

Paratime has even reached other media, the *Sliders* television show being the most successful media version. The television shows *Fringe, Spellbinder,* and *Parallax,* were TV series that used this device quite successfully.

As most writers do, Piper freely used autobiographical incidents in his work. In *Murder in the Gunroom*, Piper gives us his view of science fiction writing, when he has one of his characters—a science fiction writer—give the following answer as to what he's writing:

"Science fiction. I do a lot of stories for the pulps...Space Trails, and Other Worlds *and* Wonder Stories;' *mags like that. Most of it's standardized formula-stuff; what's known in the trade as space-operas. My best stuff goes to* Astonishing [a barely disguised Astounding—jfc]. *Parenthetically, you mustn't judge any of these magazines by their names. It seems to be a convention to use hyperbolic names for science fiction magazine; a heritage from an earlier and ruder day. What I do for* Astonishing *is really hard work, and I enjoy it. I'm working now on one of them, based on J.W. Dunne's time-theories, if you know what they are."*

J. W. Dunne's essay's, "An Experiment with Time," provided the basis for many of Piper's ideas concerning Paratime, although he did drop most of the pseudo-scientific trappings after his first Paratime Police story,

"Police Operation." After noticing a strange mixture of past and future events in his dreams, J. W. Dunne—an Irish aeronautical engineer—began to systematically study them. He noted that there was a fifty-fifty split in them between the future and the past. This precognitive element of dreams led Dunne to speculate that there must exist a second-level "supertime" which measures the rate at which time passes. This of course implies the existence of other "supertimes," which lead him to the idea of serial time—an infinite series of different "times." Dunne went on to create the "supermind" to explain how we could survive in an infinite number of "times."

In his first Paratime story, "Police Operation," Piper took Dunne's "supermind" and renamed it the extraphysical ego component. The sideways time device the Paratimers developed was based on the Ghaldron-Hesthor Transposition Field, which was a three-way collaboration between Ghaldron (who was working to develop a spacewarp drive), Hesthor (who was working on the theoretical basis for linear time travel) and Rhogom (who was studying precognition). Rhogom's Doctrine—which is based on Dunne's time theories—states "We exist perpetually in all moments within our lifespan; our extraphysical ego component (EPC) passes from the ego existing at one moment to the ego existing at the next. During unconsciousness, the EPC is 'time-free': it may detach, and connect at some other moment, with the ego existing at that time-point. That's how we pre-cog. We take an auto hypno and recover memories brought back from the future moment and buried in the subconscious mind."

Using Dunne's time theories, Piper explains the concept of time-lines in this manner: "All time-lines are totally present, in perpetual co-existence. The EPC passes from one moment, on one time-line, to the next moment on the next time-line, so that the true passage of the EPC from moment to moment is a two-dimensional diagonal.... Now, what we do, in Paratime transposition, is to build up the hyper-temporal field to include the time-line we want to reach, and then shift over to it. Some point in the plenum; same point in primary time—plus primary time elapsed during mechanical and electronic lag in the relays—but a line of secondary time."

In "Police Operation," the first Paratime story, Piper postulates a near infinity of First Level Time-Lines with a Verkan Vall variant in each one; this is glossed over in later stories, probably because of the paradoxes it creates. Most importantly, if there is more than one First Level origin civilization there is no Paratime Secret. Furthermore, it leaves us with an infinity of Verkan Valls (our main protagonist); therefore, why should readers care if any single one of them dies since there's always another replacement Verkan on another nearby First Level time-line? This of course kills reader suspense as well as any identification with the main character, who is in effect—immortal.

Like Asimov with his Foundation series and Heinlein with his future history, Piper found himself with some elements in his Paratime creation that he had to either modify or eliminate. Therefore, Piper jettisons all this talk of the EPC and detached ego after his first Paratime Police yarn and it never appears again in any of the newer Paratime stories.

H. Beam Piper's origin point for Paratime is the Home Time Line (often referred to as First Level), which contains an advanced civilization based on the successful Martian colonization of Earth between 75,000 to 100,000 years ago. Home Time Line is not the most civilized time-line, but the only time-line that has uncovered the secret of Paratime transposition. The Home Time Line Paratimers have a very bad track record, starting with their home world, Mars. After having exhausted Mars of natural resources, the Martians (*homo-sapiens* or Cro-Magnon Man) launched five rickety ships to Earth whose arrival, or not, created the base levels of Paratime probability. Over the ensuing millennia the newcomers depleted the resources of Earth and the rest of the solar system as they had back on Mars.

Paratime as a whole includes parallel universes on the order of 10 to the 100,000 power lines of probability. This is an enormous number of timelines. Piper divided the Paratime alternate worlds into levels, sectors, subsectors, belts and individual time-lines. There are five primary levels of Paratime, all of which are based on the different outcomes of the Martians' attempt to colonize earth (or Terra) over 75,000 to 100,000 years ago. Areas on different levels that show common cultural origins and characteristics are called sectors. Sectors are then somewhat arbitrarily divided into subsectors, which are further broken into belts—areas within subsectors that share common conditions resulting from a recent divarication, or break from the parent subsector. The individual worlds are called a time-line.

As Piper puts it: "Few, on First Level [the primary time-line], realized just how many of these uncountable time-lines had never seen man's imprint. Even after twelve thousand years of parasitism upon other Second, Third, and Fourth level time-lines. First Level Para-topographers had described less than one tenth of one percent of all the 'known' time-lines. In actuality it was an impossible job; few Paratime theorists still believed they would ever completely map this near infinity of diverging time-lines."

* * *

Piper's Paratimers travel inside mesh-covered conveyors, or dome-shaped inter-dimensional time buses, or trucks, which pass through alternate time-lines like frames in a film projector. These paratemporal conveyers are primarily used by the Home Time Line to loot precious metals, artifacts, new inventions, technology, cultural treasures, resources and *objects d' art* from a near infinity of alternate worlds. The Home time-liners are an admitted race of parasites, preying off other time-lines by stealing their goods and resources. It's the Paratime Police's job to make sure things don't get out of hand and the Paratime Secret is kept inviolate.

The transpositional conveyers—which are based on the Home Time Line (First Level)—shift through the levels, sectors, subsectors, belts and time-lines via the Ghaldron-Hesthor field generator. As Piper explains, "the Ghaldron-Hesthor field-generator is like every other mechanism; it can operate only in the area of primary time in which it exists. It can transpose to any other time-line, and carry with it anything inside its field, but it can't go outside its own temporal area of existence, any more than a bullet from that rifle can hit the target a week before it's fired. Anything inside the field is supposed to be unaffected by anything outside. Supposed to be is the way to put it; it doesn't always work. Once in a while, something pretty nasty gets picked up in transit."

Travel between time-lines is measured in parayears, each one consisting of ten thousand time-lines. The transposition from one time-line to another takes half an hour, which is the time required to build up and collapse the transpositional field. It is therefore impossible to make transtemporal jumps of less than ten parayears, or a hundred thousand time-lines. This creates some real difficulties for the Paratime Police in "Time Crime," when the Paratime cops have to chase down the Wizard Traders, a large gang of First Level time slavers, who have bases on several levels and sectors—many on nearby time-lines.

The transposition field is impenetrable except when two Paratime conveyers, going in opposite *directions*, interpenetrate. When this occurs—far more often than the Paratime Commission likes due to the high volume of conveyers traveling between time-lines—the field weakens and material objects and even lifeforms can enter the field. *Lord Kalvan of Otherwhen* is the story of what happens when a Pennsylvania State Police Officer is picked up by a cross-time conveyer and dropped off on a primitive time-line, on Aryan-Transpacific, Styphon's House Subsector.

FIRST LEVEL

After having depleted Mars of resources and faced with a dying world, losing water and oxygen, the Martians are forced to send jury-rigged spaceships to Earth in a desperate attempt at survival. On the First Level the Martian colony was a complete success and it begins with the remnants of Martian society and technology. First Level is four standard deviations left of mean and covers just one half of one percent of all lines of probability. On First Level the new colony was a complete success, so much so that the Martian colonists began to repeat the same mistakes they'd done on Mars, which had rendered that planet devoid of life.

As Verkan Vall puts it: "Our ancestors had pretty-well exhausted the resources of this planet [Earth]. We had a world population of half a billion, and it was all they could do to stay alive. After we began Paratime transportation, our population climbed to ten billion, and there it stayed for the last eight thousand years.... We've tapped the resources of those other worlds on other time-lines, a little here, a little there, and not enough to really hurt anybody. We've left our mark in a few places—the Dakota Badlands, and the Gobi, on the Fourth Level, for instance...."

First Level civilization is the ultimate parasite culture, drawing secretly on the resources and populations of billions of other time-lines. It's no wonder that the Paratime Secret is sacrosanct and guarded so rigidly by the Paratime Police, who have only one inflexible law regarding outtime activities: "The secret of Paratime transposition must be kept inviolate, and any activity tending to endanger it is prohibited."

First Level society sees itself as a rational culture, based on the fundamental laws and rules of science. They have, in Piper's words, "forgotten all the taboos and terminologies of naturalistic religion and sex inhibition." The government is loosely patterned on the British parliamentary system, but without the monarchy. They have an Executive Council which passes laws and is powerful enough to censure the Paratime Police. They also have an hereditary nobility which commands respect, much like the British monarchy, but Piper never makes it clear whether or not they have any governing function.

One of the most powerful institutions on Home Time Line is the Bureau of Psychological Hygiene. The Bureau's job is to ensure social and mental stability among the Home Time Line population. "We define people as criminals when they suffer from psychological aberrations of an antisocial character, usually paranoid—excessive egoism, disregard for the rights of others, inability to recognize the social necessity for mutual cooperation and confidence. On Home Time Line, we have universal psychological testing, for the purpose of detecting and eliminating...crime and/or anti-social behavior."

The Bureau of Psychological Hygiene is the major First Level institution for social control; it's effective, but—as shown in "Time Crime"—far from perfect. Of all the First Level's unsavory institutions the Bureau of Psycho-Hygiene is the worst. The idea behind such a bureau seems rooted in the (racial) hygiene movements of the 1930s and the communist re-education camps. The mental purity of a people is no more possible than racial purity. However, in their arrogance, the Home Timeliners believe that it proves they are more civilized than the various outtimers they scavenge from.

One of their cures for mental instability (which could mean anything from outright psychosis to criminal psychopathology) is psycho-rehabilitation, which is described as "a year of unremitting agony, physical and mental, worse than a Khiftan torture rack"—leaving the patient with a new personality. In some ways, the cure sounds worse than the ill. In "Time Crime" it's obvious that there are a number of citizens living on First Level who are emotionally unstable and outright criminal. And noises are made about investigating the Bureau to find out how "people with potentially criminal characteristics missed being spotted by psychotesting."

By the mid-fifties, when Piper wrote "Time Crime," First Level civilization was beginning to show its warts. Utopias are inherently dull—if the human condition is perfected, there's very little conflict for good stories—and Piper was first and foremost a great storyteller. Furthermore, Piper, as reflected in his letters and fiction, was growing increasingly cynical about the nature of the human beast and the future of democratic institutions. Despite all of the Bureau of Psychological Hygiene's testing and hypno-conditioning, we learn it has been infiltrated and compromised by a criminal conspiracy.

Along with psychological adjustment, most Home Timeliners have perfect recall, and access to memory dumps through hypno-mech via narco-hypnotic tapes. In "Time Crime," we see how it is used to learn outtime cultures and language: "'I'll need a hypno-mech for Kharanda, myself.' While he slept, the Kharand's language, with all its vocabulary and grammar, became part of his subconscious knowledge, needing only the mental pronunciation of a trigger-symbol to bring it into consciousness."

Not surprisingly, Home Time Line is supported by the labor and, in some cases, outright slavery of outtime peoples. On First Level there is a large subject population of indentured servants, who appear to be little more than slaves, with only token rights. "As far as that goes, what's the difference between that [what the outtime slave dealers are doing] and the way we drag those Fourth Level Primitive Sector-Complex people off to Fifth Level Service Sector to work for us?" The paratimers rationale is: "We need a certain amount of human labor, for tasks requiring original thought and decision that are beyond the ability of robots, and most of it is work our Citizens simply wouldn't perform."

There's a great deal of prejudice against these Fourth Level servants and it takes many generations of service and an enlightened master before they can earn First Level Citizenship. The Proles, as they are called, have their own subculture and live in ghettos or in servant quarters in their masters' homes. By the end of "Time Crime," First Level society—far from being a utopia—looks like a funhouse mirror image of our own society.

Home Time Line may be a singularity, but it's not the only First Level society. We also have the Dwarma Sector and the Abzar Sector:

Dwarma Sector

The people of the First Level Dwarma Sector [mentioned in "Time Crime"] after having successfully colonizing Terra had an overpopulation crash. They were reduced by starvation to a tiny handful, had abandoned their cities and renounced their technologies and created for themselves a farm-and-village culture without progress or change or curiosity or struggle or ambition, and a way of life in which every day was like every other day that had been or that would come. The Dwarma Sector is one where the Martian colonizers never developed transtemporal transposition and without the other time-lines to live off of became decivilized and reverted to primitive social forms.

Nor do they have any need for policing: "When somebody does something wrong, his neighbors all come and talk to him about it till he gets ashamed, then they all forgive him and have a feast. They're lovely people, so kind and gentle. But you'll get awfully tired of them in about a month. They have absolutely no respect for anybody's privacy. In fact, it seems slightly indecent to them for anybody to want privacy."

Abzar Sector

The Abzar people [mentioned in "Time Crime"] made the same mistakes as Dwarma Sector. "They had wasted their resources to the last, fighting bitterly over the ultimate crumbs, with fission bombs, and with muskets, and with swords, and with spears and clubs, and finally they had died out, leaving a planet of almost uniform desert dotted with vast empty cities which even twelve thousand years had hardly begun to obliterate."

On Home Time Line the Paratime Police are not only commissioned to protect the Paratime Secret, but to maintain order throughout all surveyed time-lines of Paratime. Paratime Police Chief's Special Investigator Verkan Vall and his on again, off again wife Dalla Hadron are the predominant viewpoint characters in all the Paratime stories. *Lord Kalvan of Otherwhen*, which features a hijacked Pennsylvania State Trooper, Calvin Morrison, is the lone exception. In this novel, Verkan Vall is a secondary character, but now soon to be Paratime police chief when Chief Tortha Karf retires. This is due to the fact that it is Morrison's story.

This is how the Paratime police view their outtime job: "Now, it's just not possible to frame any single code of laws applicable to conditions on all of these. The best we can do is prohibit certain flagrantly immoral types of activity, such as slave-trading, introduction of new types of narcotic drugs, or out-and-out piracy and brigandage. If you're in doubt as to the legality of anything you want to do outtime, go to the Judicial Section of the Paratime Commission and get an opinion on it. That's where you made your whole mistake. You didn't find out just how far it was allowable for you to go."

The Paratime Police Department is huge with over two million agents, one third of them on Home Time Line running the department while the other two-thirds are out in the field. The Paratime Police Chief is Tortha Karf, a competent though somewhat blustery chief reminiscent of Perry White in the *Superman* TV show. However, even with all these agents, the Paratime Police are hard-pressed to maintain order throughout Paratime. Tortha Karf's overview of the Paratime Police states: "We're jugglers, trying to keep our traders and sociological observers and tourists and plain idiots out of trouble; trying to prevent panics and disturbances and dislocations of local economy as a result of our operations; trying to keep out of out-time politics—and, at all times, at all costs and hazards, by all means, guard the secret of Paratime Transposition."

It's the Paratime Police's job to keep this immense ball of yarn from unravelling and, while they're doing their best, there are a lot of places where it's beginning to unravel—and that's where the fun is. This fascinating society of cross-time travelers makes for some great stories and it's no wonder this series was one of John W. Campbell's favorites.

SECOND LEVEL

Second Level is where the Martian colonization attempt on Earth had been almost as successful as it had been on First Level. "Its timelines descend from the probability of one or more shiploads of colonists having come to Terra from Mars about seventy-five to a hundred thousand years ago, and then having been cut off from the home planet and forced to develop a civilization of their own here. The difference was there had been wars and catastrophes that had created dark-age intervals. Still, some Second Level civilizations had developed over-light-speed drives for interstellar ships, which First Level had yet to do. Other than the Ghaldron-Hesthor Transposition-Field, most of its sectors were as civilized as First Level." As on First Level, there is contact and colonies on Mars and Venus.

First Level has learned a great deal from viewing the experiences on

Second Level: "During the Crisis, after the Fourth Interplanetary War, we might have adopted Palnar Sarn's 'Dictatorship of the Chosen' scheme, if we hadn't seen what an exactly similar scheme had done to the Jak-Hakka Civilization, on the Second Level. When Palnar Sarn was told about that, he went into Paratime to see for himself, and when he returned, he renounced his proposal in horror."

Most of the Paratime stories, except for "Last Enemy," focus on either the First Level or the Fourth level, although there are references to really sophisticated time-lines such as Second Level Triplanetary.

Akor-Neb Sector

The Akor-Neb civilization on Earth is almost the equal of First Level. "Like all the Second Level, Akor-Neb civilization is of a fairly high culture-order, even for Second Level. An atomic-power, interplanetary culture; gravity-counteraction, direct conversion of nuclear energy to electrical power, that sort of thing. We buy fine synthetic plastics and fabrics from them."

From "Last Enemy" we learn from Verkan Vall more about the Akor-Neb: "They have a single System-wide government, a single race, and a universal language. They're a dark-brown race, which evolved in its present form about fifty thousand years ago; the present civilization is about ten thousand years old, developed out of the wreckage of several earlier civilizations which decayed or fell through wars, exhaustion of resources, et cetera. They have legends, maybe historical records, of their extraterrestrial origin."

Khiftan Sector

The Khiftan Sector is one of the Second Level societies that didn't recover from its dark age. The Sector is ruled by a theocracy called the Khiftan priesthood. It's used throughout the Paratime stories as a particularly heinous place to be. The priests dress in fringed robes and cloth-of-gold sashes and conical caps. They specialize in instruments of torture: "the whip showed a cylindrical handle, indicated as twelve inches in length and one in diameter, fitted with a thumb-switch. 'That's definitely Second Level Khiftan,' Vall said, handing it back. 'Made of braided copper or silver wire and powered with a little nuclear-conversion battery in the grip. They heat up to about two hundred centigrade; produce really painful burns.' 'Why, that's beastly!' Dalla exclaimed. 'Anything on the Khiftan Sector is.'"

The Khiftan gods are often used as First Level curse words: "He mentioned Fasif, Great God of Khift, in a manner which would have got him an acid-bath if the Khiftan priests had heard him." The Khiftans are slave holders and all in all it's a terrible place to get stranded, but a nice place to exile troublesome First Level enemies.

THIRD LEVEL

Third Level is the probability of an abortive attempt to colonize Earth from Mars about a hundred thousand years ago. In "Time Crime" Verkan describes it thusly: "A few survivors—a shipload or so—were left to shift for themselves while the parent civilization on Mars died out. They lost all vestiges of their original Martian culture, even memory of their extraterrestrial origin. About fifteen hundred to two thousand years ago, a reasonably high electrochemical civilization developed and they began working with nuclear energy and developed reaction-drive spaceships. But they'd concentrated so on the inorganic sciences, and so far neglected the biosciences, that when they launched their first ship for Venus they hadn't yet developed a germ theory of disease."

"What happened when they ran into the green-vomit fever?" Dalla asked.

"About what you could expect. The first—and only—ship to return brought it back to Terra. Of course, nobody knew what it was, and before the epidemic ended, it had almost depopulated this planet.

"Since the survivors knew nothing about germs, they blamed it on the anger of the gods—the old story of recourse to supernaturalism in the absence of a known explanation—and a fanatically anti-scientific cult got control. Of course, space travel was taboo; so was nuclear and even electric power. For some reason, steam power and gunpowder weren't offensive to the gods. They went back to a low-order steam-power, black-powder, culture, and haven't gotten beyond that to this day. The relatively civilized regions are on the east coast of Asia and the west coast of North America; civilized race more or less Caucasian. Political organization just barely above the tribal level—thousands of petty kingdoms and republics and principalities and feudal holdings and robbers' roosts."

Most of Third Level is proscribed for Home Time Line exploitation and infiltration due to too many thermo-nuclear weapons and too many competing national sovereignties, always a disaster-fraught combination. The colonists have lost all traces of Martian civilization and culture, even memory of their mother world, while on Mars civilization withers away. There are whole Sectors on Second and Third Levels that are off-limits to Paratimers due to biological and chemical poisoning.

Esaron Sector

In "Time Crime," the Wizard Traders (a First Level criminal syndicate specializing in outtime slavery and theft) have a base in the Esaron Sector, which Verkan describes. "The principal industries are brigandage, piracy, slave-raiding, cattle-rustling and inter-communal warfare. They have a few ramshackle steam railways, and some steamboats on the rivers. We sell them coal and manufactured goods, mostly in exchange for foodstuffs and tobacco. Consolidated Outtime Foodstuffs has the sector franchise...."

Other than the names of a few other sectors, such as Third Level Luvarian Empire Sector which is pretty advanced, the Third Level Khanga pirates of the Caribbean Islands and the Third-Level Illyalla people, Piper has little to say about the Third Level.

FOURTH LEVEL

Fourth Level is the largest of all the levels and the level where we find our own time-line (or should I say Piper's time-line) on the Europo-American Sector. On Fourth Level a disaster occurred to the original colonists and the result was all civilization and technology were lost. Therefore, the inhabitants believe they are an indigenous race with a long history of savagery. The other levels devolved from low-probability accidents; Fourth Level is the maximum probability. It was divided into many sectors and subsectors in which civilization had first appeared in the Fertile Crescent and Nile River Valley, and on the Indus and Yangtze Rivers. Europo-American Sector is the big one where the Paratimers obtain most of their resources, although it's dangerous, too, with too many thermonuclear weapons and competing nations.

Fourth Level is divided into three basic sector groups:

Nilo-Mesopotamian Basic Sector-Group

As Piper describes in *Lord Kalvan of Otherwhen*: "On most Nilo-Mesopotamian sectors, like the Macedonian Empire Sector, or the Alexandrian-Roman or Alexandrian-Punic or Indo-Turanian or Europo-American, there was an Aryan invasion of Eastern Europe and Asia Minor about four thousand elapsed years ago. On this sector, the ancestors of the Aryans came in about fifteen centuries earlier, as Neolithic savages, about the time that the Sumerian and Egyptian civilizations were first developing, and overran all southeast Europe, Asia Minor and the Nile Valley. They developed to the bronze-age culture of the civilizations they overthrew, and then, more slowly, to an iron-age culture. About two thousand years ago, they were using hardened steel and building large stone cities, just as they do now. At that time, they reached cultural stasis. But as for their religious beliefs, you've described them quite accurately. A god is only worshiped as long as the people think him powerful enough to aid and protect them; when they lose that confidence, he is discarded and the god of some neighboring people is adopted instead." This level is the most fertile ground for First Level exploitation and resource theft, especially in regards to art, cultural innovations and technology. It's also the home of Piper's own time-line.

Indus-Ganges-Irrawaddy Basic Sector-Group

The Indus-Ganges-Irrawaddy Basic Sector-Grouping was derived from the probability of civilization having developed late on the Indian subcontinent, with the rest of the world, including Europe, in Stone Age savagery or early Bronze Age barbarism. Most of the civilizations in this Sector have a pre-mechanical, animal-power, handcraft, edged-weapon culture.

Yangtze Basic Sector Group

Piper never describes this Sector in any of the Paratime stories but it may be another backward sector, another Oriental Hydraulic Despotism where the government maintains social control through the dispensation of water resources. These governments were typical throughout most of the Orient with centralized governments maintaining power through their control of water resources.

In his Paratime series Piper mentions enough combinations of cultures and historical analogs to tantalize any history buff as well as keep him anxious for more stories. With ten to the hundred thousandth possible time-lines, Piper could justify almost any historical possibility: such as Aryan-Transpacific Sector where he turned the Indo-Aryan migrations around, provided them with ships and sent them to the coast of North America where they slaughtered the American Indians and began a new civilization that would not change for several thousand years—until the arrival of an unwitting transtemporal conveyor hitchhiker, Pennsylvania State Trooper, Calvin Morrison.

FIFTH LEVEL

The Fifth Level is the probability of the complete failure of Martian colonization. No human population was established and only indigenous quasi-human life evolved on Earth; nature not man was triumphant. In *Lord Kalvan of Otherwhen,* Piper described it: "And Fifth Level on a few sectors, subhuman brutes, speechless and fireless, were cracking nuts and each other's heads with stones, and on most of it nothing even vaguely humanoid had appeared."

Fifth Level is also home to the Paratime Police Terminal, where a duplicate of Paratime Police Headquarters had been built. Pol-Term, as it's often referred to, is much more secure than First Level Police Headquarters. Only Paratime personnel or authorized persons may visit: as stated in "Time Crime:" "Dalla had never been on Police Terminal Time Line; very few people, outside the Paratime Police, ever had." Police Terminal is also covered with transposition depots at the site of every major city, town and important junction that exists on every major Level and Sector within Paratime, which enables the Paratime Police to transpose to any place where they were needed.

The majority of humans on Fifth Level are Proles who are sent there to work in the Service and Industrial Sector worlds with First Level overseers. They labor there to keep heavy and light industrial installations off Home Time Line. "The Service Sector Proles were not indigenous to the Fifth Level, but were brought from time-lines of near savagery, which they voluntarily left for a better life. The Paratime Transpositional Code limited the colonization of Service Sector time-lines to natives below second-order barbarism. The Serv-Sec Proles were the ones who did most of the administrative and record keeping for Home Time-Line. The proles who were dumped in the Fifth Level, Industrial Sectors, where the machines and robots of First Level were manufactured, were at the bottom rung of the Service Sector. Here were the survivors of Paratime screw-ups, when policy or criminal mistakes had made it necessary to transplant entire tribes and sometimes nations to protect them from their hostile neighbors, or to protect the Paratime secret. No matter—it seemed—how diligently the undermanned and overworked Paratime Police worked, there were always new bodies to fill another industrial time-line on Fifth Level."

In "Time Crime" Javrath Brend states: "We recruit those Fourth Level Primitives out of probability worlds of Stone Age savagery, and transpose them to our own Fifth Level time lines, practically outtime extensions of the Home Time Line. There's absolutely no question of the Paratime Secret being compromised."

"Beside, we need a certain amount of human labor, for tasks requiring original thought and decision that are beyond the ability of robots, and most of it is work our Citizens simply wouldn't perform," Thalvan Dras added.

"Well, from a moral standpoint, wouldn't these Esaron Sector people who buy the slaves justify slavery in the same terms?" a woman whom Vall had identified as a Left Moderate Council Member asked.

"There's still a big difference," Dalla told her. "The ServSec Proles aren't beaten or tortured or chained; we don't break up families or separate friends. When we recruit Fourth Level Primitives, we take whole tribes, and they come willingly...."

The Proles are the other dirty secret of Paratime. The Paratimers depend upon their proles to do the jobs they no longer want to do. On the other hand, Proles are also Home Time Line's greatest fear. Like Rome and the Deep South, one of their biggest bugaboos is a Prole insurrection. Here Ranthar Jard speaking with Verkan Vall says: "Where in blazes did he get them all?" Ranthar Jard demanded. Verkan replies: "They're guard troops, from Service Sector and Industrial Sector. We'll get you the same sort of a force. I only hope we don't have another Prole insurrection while they're away—"

Fifth Level is also where many Home Timeliners have outtime villas and mansions, on uninhabited time-lines. Some choose to relax surrounded by robot servers, or impress visitors by surrounding themselves with big clans or groups of outtimers who were on the wrong side of someone's war or were survivors of disasters. Chief Tortha has his own tribe of servants on his private hideaway, a Fifth Level equivalent of Sicily.

Piper's last novel was a Paratime story, *Lord Kalvan of Otherwhen*, and remains one of his most beloved novels.

H. Beam Piper was quite aware of how important his Paratime series was. In a conversation about time travel with Mike Knerr, Piper said: "'Yes, anyone can write about time travel.'
"But not about parallel time and a police force?" Knerr asked.
"'No. I own the copyright to that.'"

APPENDIX II

PIPER STORY LOG

PIPER STORY LOG

H. Beam Piper's Story Log first appeared in the paperback collector's fanzine "Books Are Everything," Vol. 2, No. 2, dated March 1989. In the introduction to "H. Beam Piper in Paperback," editor Elwanda Holland explains the origin of the Story Log: "A friend was kind enough to lend me Piper's personal notebook, where he recorded his literary gains from his first professional sales to the last sale before his death. The friend wishes to remain anonymous because...the notebook is not for sale at any price. I felt many of you would be interested in seeing them and to my knowledge, they have never been published before."

This first appearance of Piper's Story Log occurs five years after Mike Knerr's "discovery" of the contents of the Piper trunks, the two trunks which contained the surviving contents of H. Beam Piper's apartment on 35 Wordsworth Avenue. I strongly suspect that it was Mike Knerr who loaned a copy of the original Story Log to Editor Elwanda Holland.

[Published]	1946	[Received]
9/25/'46	*Time and Time Again* (mailed, 6/22/'46) Astounding Science Fiction Pub. 3/'47	147.50

	<u>1947</u>	
7/11/'47	*He Walked Around The Horses* (mailed, 6/5/'47) Astounding Science Fiction	200.00
	<u>1948</u>	
1/16/'48	*Police Operation* (mailed, 1/2/'48)	300.00
7/2/'48	Anthology rights on *Time and Time Again* (A Treasury of Science Fiction, Crown Publishers)	<u>37.80</u> 337.80
	<u>1949</u>	
4/8/'49	*The Mercenaries* (mailed, 1/10/'49) Astounding Science Fiction	200.00

	<u>1950</u>	
4/8/'50	*Last Enemy* (mailed, 1/17/'50) Astounding Science Fiction	500.00

3/23/'50	*John Mosby - Rebel Raider*)
	True, per Fred Pohl - 1200.00
	          Commission - <u>120.00</u>
	                        1080.00
		1080.00

5/16/'50	*Operation RSVP* Amazing, per Pohl - 200.00 <u>20.00</u> 180.00	180.00
5/15/'50	*Dearest* Weird Tales, per Pohl - 70.00 <u>7.00</u> 63.00	63.00
8/2/'50	*Immunity* Future Stories, per Pohl - 80.00 <u>8.00</u> 72.00	72.00
10/19/50	*Dearest* Weird Tales, per Pohl - 240.00 <u>24.00</u> 216.00	216.00

	<u>1951</u>	
4/14	*Day of the Moron* (mailed, 6/5/'47) ASF per Pohl, 390.00 <u>39.00</u> 351.00	351.00
6/6	Film Rights on Rebel Raider Per Pohl 2000.00 (Disney Studios) <u>- 200.00</u> 1800.00	1800.00
10/11	*Genesis* (Future, per Pohl) 80.00 <u>- 8.00</u> 72.00	72.00
	<u>1952</u>	
5/21	Radio Rights, *Time and Time Again* 100.00 <u>10.00</u> 90.00	90.00
8/12	Anthology Rights, *Operation RSVP* and *He Walked Around the Horses* 50.00 <u>- 5.00</u> 45.00	<u>45.00</u> 135.00

10/17	Adv. Royalties, *Pistols For Everybody*, Knopf
	      (*Murder in the Gunroom*) 750.00
	                          <u>- 75.00</u>
	                          675.00	

10/31	1/2 share *Null-ABC* , ASF etc 494.22	675.00 <u>494.22</u> 1294.00

	1953	
2/26	On account, *Uller Uprising, Space* 300.00	300.00
	Advance, " " Twayne Pub. 50.00 350.00 -35.00 315.00	315.00
6/10	Remaining due on *Uller Uprising*	405.00
	1954	
2/6	Royalties on *Last Enemy*	13.43
8/3	Royalties on *Last Enemy*	1.51
8/13	*Time Crime* 1260.00 - 10%	1134.00
9/25	French Rights, *Operation RSVP* 50.00 - 10%	45.00
	1955	
7/18	Bonus (.01 per word) on first part of *Time Crime* 210.00	189.00
	1956	
2/9	Anthology Rights, *Police Operation*	45.00
2/25	Anthology Rights, *Time and Time Again*	5.69
10/14	Anthology Rights, *Time and Time Again*	.39
10/15	*Omnilingual* 630 - 10%	567.00
12/20	*Lone Star Planet* half of solo price, shared w/J.J. McG	110.00
12/28	*The Knife Edge*	360.00

	<u>1957</u>	
2/9	Adv, Royalties *Null - ABC*	225.00
2/16	Bonus on *Omnilingual* (ASF)	81.00
3/23	*The Keeper* (Venture)	175.50
8/19	Adv. Royalties *Null - ABC* $250.00 less 10% to White	225.00
9/2	*Graveyard of Dreams* (Galaxy)	189.00
10/25	Anthology (Faber) *He Walked Around the Horses* $41.76 - 10%	37.56
	<u>1958</u>	
2/28	On Ace paperback publication *Lone Star Planet* (250 less 10% to K. White)	225.00
7/8	*Ministry of Disturbance* (Astounding $756.00 less 10%)	680.40
7/14	On Ace paperback, *Lone Star Planet* $250 less 10% K.W.	225.00

	1959	
4/23	*The Other Road* Fantastic Universe	(50.00) 45.00
9/10	*Oomphel in the Sky* (Astounding)	(570) 513.00
9/14	*He Walked Around the Horses* (English, Murray)	20.85
9/14		14.60
12/17	*He Walked Around the Horses* (Italian, Einzudi)	45.00
	The Answer (Fantastic Universe)	
	1960	
8/25	*Four Day Planet* (Putnam's)	900.00
12/17	Bonus on *Oomphel in the Sky*	85.00
12/31	Advance on *Junkyard Planet*	450.00
	1961	
3/14	Second Advance on *Junkyard Planet*	450.00
5/3	Anthology Rights on *Omnilingual*	112.00
5/23	*Naudsonce* (*ASF*)	502.00
10/11	*Little Fuzzy* (first advance)	787.50
10/31	*Little Fuzzy* (second advance)	787.50
12/22	*A Slave is a Slave* (*Analog*)	545.00

	__1962__	
5/15	Bonus on *Naudsonce*	83.30
5/25	Advance on *Space Viking*	800.00
5/31	Balance on *Space Viking*	1714.00
7/28	Bonus on *Slave*	112.50
9/1	Miscellaneous, incl. *The Return* from Pohl	258.37
10/1	Advance on *Fuzzy Sapiens*	787.50
11/16	Additional Royalties *Prologue to Analog* (*Omnilingual*)	45.00
	__1963__	
3/11	Advance from Ace on *Space Viking*	675.00
3/27	*Fuzzy Sapiens*, second installment	787.50
5/15	For Italian rights on *Little Fuzzy*	226.41
6/29	Bonus, *Space Viking*	303.50
8/19	Bal. Due from Ace, *Space Viking*	675.00
11/16	Advance movie rights *Little Fuzzy* (MPC)	900.00
	__1964__	
5/19	*Gunpowder God*	684.00
8/4	*Down Styphon*!	513.00

APPENDIX III

Piper's History of the Future

PIPER'S HISTORY OF THE FUTURE

By H. Beam Piper

(This short but concise piece by H. Beam Piper on his future history was written at the request of a young British fan, Peter Weston. The original letter has been lost, but the four-page piece on Piper's future history has survived and originally appeared in Peter Weston's science fiction fanzine, *Zenith* #4, May, 1964 (Peter Weston, ed.), "Future History No. 1," by H. Beam Piper, pp. 11-14.)

A Note on Atomic Era Dating

The Atomic Era is reckoned as beginning on the 2nd of December 1942, Christian Era, with the first self-sustaining nuclear reactor, put into operation by Enrico Fermi at the University of Chicago. Unlike earlier dating-systems, it begins with a Year Zero, 12/2/42 to 12/1/43 CE. With allowances for December overlaps, 1943 CE is thus equal to Year Zero AE, and 1944 CE to 1 AE, and each century accordingly begins with the "double-zero" year, and ends with the ninety-nine year.

Dates AE and CE are converted by adding or subtracting 1943: thus 1964 CE is 21 AE, and 1066 CE is reckoned as 877 PreAtomic. Atomic Era dating did not become official until 2nd December, 2143, or 200 AE. The Gregorian calendar, with all defects, was adopted, merely setting back Jan. 1st to December 2nd. It took about fifty years for everybody to agree to it, and some fanatical religious sects opposed it to the end of the Terran Federation history.

First Century AE

World War II, 4 P.A.E. to 2 A.E. Nuclear energy, atomic bombs, V-2 rockets. Organization of UN., Korean War, A.E. 7-10. Artificial satellites, space-probes, etc. First landing on Luna, A.E. 27.

Collapse of UN owing to disputes as to national sovereignty over, and militarization of, Luna.

World War III (Thirty Days War). Organization of First Terran Federation 32 A.E.

First landing on Mars. (Cyrano Expedition, Col. Hubert Penrose.) 53A.E. (OMNILINGUAL: *Astounding SF*, February, 1957.)

Further explorations of Mars, Venus, Asteroid Belt and Moons of Jupiter. First Federation begins to crack under strains of colonial claims and counter-claims of member states.

Contragravity, direct conversion of nuclear energy to electric current, and collapsed matter for radiation shielding. Serious financial dislocations.

Second Century

World War IV. (First Interplanetary War.) 106-109A.E.; minor wars for ten years thereafter. Complete devastation of Northern Hemisphere of Terra. Second Federation organized by South Africa and New Zealand, Brazil, the Argentine, etc. Wars of colonial pacification and consolidation; the new Terran Federation imposes System-wide pax.

Keene-Gonzales-Dillingham Theory of Non-Einsteinian Relativity, A.E. 172. Dillingham Hyperdrive developed, A.E. 183; First expedition to Alpha Centauri, 192 A.E.

Third Century, to Eighth Century

Atomic Era dating adopted, A.E. 200.
Period of exploration, colonization, and expansion.
FOUR DAY PLANET—Mid - IV Century (Putnam's; 1963)

ULLER UPRISING—526 A.E. (in, *The Petrified Planet*, Twayne, 1953)

LITTLE FUZZY—654 A.E.   (Avon, 1962)

FUZZY SAPIENS—   (Avon, 1964)

NAUDSONCE—Early VIIIth Century (*ASF* January 1962.)

Ninth Century

By this time, the Federation Government began to get into the hands of left-wing "Liberals," welfare-statists, planned-economy socialists, do-gooders, etc.

OOMPHEL IN THE SKY—812 A.E. (*ASF* Nov 1960.)
Fox Travis on Kwannon as captain on staff of Maj. Gen. Maith. Growing resentment to restrictions and controls, especially on newly-colonized planets. Formation of System States' Alliance to resist encroachments on colonists' rights by Federation Government.

Secession of System States Alliance from Federation, 839 AE. System States War, 842-854. Foxx Travis now General in command of Third Fleet-Army Force.

Complete defeat of Alliance; escape of Alliance Fleet from Abigor; they discover and colonize a planet outside Federation sphere of influence, which they name Excalibur, 855 A.E.

The Federation, already overstrained and top-heavy, begins to crack under strains of the System States War. Economic and political "time of trouble."

JUNKYARD PLANET -- 894 A.E.   (Putnam's, 1963)
...expanded from GRAVEYARD OF DREAMS, (*Galaxy*, Feb 1958)
Breakup of Federation continues at accelerating rate. Disintegration of TF Space Navy due to apathy and even hostility of "Liberal" government; resulting in spreading anarchy.

Tenth to Eighteenth Century

Terran Federation completely vanished by 1100 A.E. A few planets, Odin, Marduk, Baldur, Aton, Isis, etc., retain civilization, including hyper drive. The rest have sunk to low-order civilization in isolation or out-and-out savagery.

The Old Federation: Interplanetary and Interstellar Wars, Civil Wars, revolutions, anarchy. Rise of Neobarbarians.

The Sword-Worlds: Civilization established on Excalibur, colonization of other planets, Joyeuse, Durendal, Haulteclere, Flamberge, Gram, etc.

Development of loose feudalism from earlier and even looser town-meeting democracy. Technological advances, final stagnation.

About 1450 A.E., Sword World ships enter Old Federation space-volume, visit former Federation planets. Raiding expeditions set out, rise of the Space Vikings. By the beginning of the Seventeenth Century, Space Vikings have conquered Old Federation planets and established bases.

SPACE VIKING—Early XVIII Century (*ASF* Nov. 1962 - Feb. 1963)

Lucas Trask organizes League of Civilized Worlds; work continued by the Bentriks, reigning house of Marduk.

By the time of the Nineteenth Century, the League has turned into the Galactic Empire. The Sword Worlds have declined to near-barbarism.

Twentieth Century AE corresponds to the First Century Imperial

Period of Interstellar Wars. House of Bentrik firmly established by end of First Century; center of Empire transferred from Marduk to Odin by Stevan IV.

A SLAVE IS A SLAVE—Mid Third Century Imperial (*ASF* April 1962)

Empire completely consolidated by end of Fourth Century.
Period of cultural and political stasis and self-satisfaction.

MINISTRY OF DISTURBANCE—Twelfth Century Imperial (*ASF* Dec. 1958.)

Emperor Paul XXII and Prince Yorn Trevann undertake to arouse the Empire to new efforts.

Beyond this, with the exception of one story, THE KEEPER, about 30,000 years in the future, when the Fifth Empire was at the height of its power, and Terra was in the middle of another glacial age, I have not gone. THE KEEPER was published in the now defunct *Venture*.

Nothing else, with the possible exception of a novelette called THE EDGE OF THE KNIFE, *Amazing*, May 1957, belongs to the History of the Future. This was a story, time 1973 CE, about a history professor, who got his past and future confused, and had a lot of trouble as a result. It was written and published shortly before Sputnik I invalidated a lot of my near-future stuff, and made me swear off doing anything within a couple of centuries of now.

APPENDIX IV

The Terro-Human Future History

THE TERRO-HUMAN FUTURE HISTORY

By John F. Carr

There remain questions (about Piper's death). His extensive notes have never been found; yet I know that he kept a well-organized set of loose leaf notebooks with entries color-coded; a star map of the Federation and Empire; a history of the System States War; and other materials including some of my own letters which answered historical questions he had posed. Somewhere out there is a gold mine.

It isn't all lost. I have his letters; and some of his notes can be deduced from his writing. Beam firmly believed that history repeated itself; or at least that one can use real history to construct a future history. The casual reader will not easily deduce the historical models Beam employed. He was familiar with forgotten details: as an example, one of the battle scenes in *Lord Kalvan of Otherwhen* is drawn directly from the obscure Battle of Barnet in the Wars of the Roses. He knew the grand sweep of history, but he also knew the small tales; the intrigues and petty jealousies, heroism and cowardice, honor and betrayals.

This, I think, is why his stories have such a ring of truth. They seem real because many were real. Such things as happen in Piper's statecraft have happened time and time again to real politicians.

    Jerry Pournelle
     Federation

The most successful of the science fiction future histories incorporate either a strong socio-economic or political theme, or use a powerful historical philosophy (such as James Blish's Spenglerian approach to the Cities in Flight series and Isaac Asimov's Gibbon-influenced Foundation future history) or turn historical events into plot frameworks. H. Beam Piper welded all of these elements in his crowning creation, the Terro-Human Future History, a unique chronicle of the future spanning more than four millennia.

H. Beam Piper had a lifelong love affair with history. Off and on during the last few years of his life he was working on a major work, "Only the Arquebus," a historical novel about Gonzalo de Córdoba and the Italian wars of the early sixteenth century. Jerry Pournelle still remembers many an evening spent with Piper in his hotel room discussing historical figures and events and how they might apply to the future. Piper had many keen insights into the past and often expressed a longing that he wished he'd been alive in the simpler days of the Christian Era, when Clausewitzian politics and nuclear wars were a faraway nightmare.

Unfortunately, Piper's notebooks and star charts as described by Jerry Pournelle either never existed (according to Mike Knerr) or were destroyed or lost after his death. In a September 9th, 2009 e-mail, John McGuire's daughter Terry confirmed their existence: "I can tell you from personal observation that Beam always had a notebook where he jotted down interesting facts, words and ideas. He always had possible plotlines and outlines of stories in these books. My father picked up the habit from him, but switched to Steno notebooks since my Mother always had these around. He also drew diagrams such as the configuration of whatever universe he was plotting and the location of the planets therein. I have mentioned in the past he outlined each major character and the personality so he could stay 'in character.'"

In a March 22nd, 1963 letter to Jerry Pournelle, Piper gives a plot summary of his historical novel, "Age of the Arquebus:" "Having just finished a story in the VII Century A.E. [*Fuzzy Sapiens* jfc], I have now dug out the historical novel on which I have been working intermittently, when I have not been pressed by necessity to get something quickly saleable done, for the last couple of years. This is early Sixteenth Century C.E. [Christian Era—jfc]—1502-1503, to be exact—and Ferdinand of Spain and Louis XII of France are fighting over the kingdom of Naples."

In several of his works Piper created characters who were historians or studied history as a hobby. In "The Edge of the Knife," a story about a college history professor who can sometimes see into the future, the professor says: "History follows certain patterns. I'm not a Toynbeean, but any historian can see that certain forces generally tend to produce similar effects." In *Space Viking*, Otto Harkaman, a Space Viking ship captain whose hobby is the study of history, says: "I study history. You know, it's odd; practically everything that happened on any of the inhabited planets had happened on Terra before the first spaceship." Vilfredo Pareto, a famous mid-twentieth century sociologist, said just about the same thing: almost every form of government or political-science possibility existed at one time or another among the Italian city-states of the Renaissance.

First, I will discuss Piper's major political themes and how they've molded his future history. I have identified eight major and minor themes, most of them interrelated, which run through Pipe's published works. The three major political themes are as follows: the self-reliant man (or John W. Campbell's "Citizen"), the fragility of civilization and its correlate: the barbarian threat from within and without.

It was the early Robert Heinlein and H. Beam Piper, of all the *Astounding* science fiction writers, who most epitomized Campbell's philosophies. In the fanzine *Renaissance*, John H. Costello wrote a Piper retrospective, "H. Beam Piper: An Infinity of Worlds," in which he states: "Into his stories he [Piper] put a great deal of philosophy—of the Campbellian sort.... Piper was a 19th Century Liberal, a creature with whom neither conservatives nor libertarians can be completely comfortable; and like their creator, he did not believe that anyone had a right to automatic sustenance. Throughout his career, he remained a 19th Century Liberal and a Citizen in the Campbellian sense—quite firmly dedicated to the ideal of Civilization and individual self-reliance."

In many ways H. Beam Piper epitomized the Citizen, as described by Campbell: "The fully developed Citizen actually seems to be every bit as hard-headed, ruthless and dangerous a fighter as any barbarian—he just uses his ruthless determination wisely instead of egocentrically." The essence of the Piper hero is best described by himself in "Oomphel in the Sky," as a person who "actually knows what has to be done and how to do it, without holding a dozen conferences and round-table discussions and giving everybody a fair and equal chance to foul things up for him." This is a fair description of Pappy Jack from *Little Fuzzy*, Conn Maxwell of *Cosmic Computer*, Lucas Trask of *Space Viking*, Calvin Morrison of *Lord Kalvan of Otherwhen*, Campbell's Citizen and for that matter Piper himself.

As with most of Campbell's favored authors, Piper's heroes were cut from the same self-reliant mold: Jack Holloway of the Fuzzy novels, Conn Maxwell of *The Cosmic Computer*, Verkan Vall of the Paratime series, Lucas Trask of *Space Viking* and Calvin Morrison of *Lord Kalvan of Otherwhen*. Their foils are the fools, the venal, the misguided, the lazy, the do-gooders and the mad King John figures, like psychotic Andray Dunnan and his Hitler-like creature, Zaspar Makann of *Space Viking*.

Piper, like John W. Campbell (who was fascinated by the Dean Drive, Dianetics, psi talents and Rhine's research), had a strong interest in psychic phenomena. While this mystic element looms prominently in Piper's Paratime series, with its D.W. Dunne-based rationale and stories such as "Dearest," it is noticeably absent in the stories and novels that comprise The Terro-Human Future History.

While Piper's idolization of the self-reliant man was of great importance in shaping his entire body of work, he was not a firm adherent to the "Great Man Theory of History" popularized in the mid-Nineteenth Century by Thomas Carlyle. Carlyle believed that: "The history of the world is but the biography of great men." These great men and heroes are highly-influential individuals who by their personal charisma, intelligence, strength of will (or Machiavellianism) utilized their personal strengths in such a manner that it had a decisive historical impact. In Carlyle's book *On Heroes, Hero-Worship and the Heroic in History,* he put forth the idea that history was turned on the decisions of Great Men, such as Attila the Hun, Mohammed, Napoleon, Shakespeare and Martin Luther.

Despite the best efforts of Piper's "heroes" in his books, it is quite clear from his works that Piper believed that no human civilization would ever be more than a stanza before the next verse of human civilization: Nor could his heroes change the march of history. Nor that such a stanza would always be progressive. Conn Maxwell of *The Cosmic Computer* is unable to single-handedly prevent the coming long night of barbarism that will follow the fall of the Second Federation. Nor is Lucas Trask of *Space Viking* able to restore the light of civilization to the remnants of the Old Federation with Trask's League of Civilized Worlds.

Instead it is the ongoing dialectical struggle between his themes of the vulnerability of civilization versus the threat of barbarism from within and without that determines the course of history in his Terro-Human Future History. From statements by his friends and his correspondence, it is quite apparent that Piper valued civilization greatly but feared for its demise by the extension of Clausewitzian policies—especially in regards to nuclear weapons. A self-admitted Machiavellian, "one author who influenced me most was Nicco Machiavelli," Beam did believe in *Realpolitik*, that is, a system of politics based on material and practical objectives rather than outmoded morality or ethical objectives.

Lucas Trask, near the end of *Space Viking*, sums up Piper's view of human history quite well: "It may just be that there is something unworkable about government itself. As long as Homo sapiens terra is a wild animal, which he has always been and always will be until he evolves into something different in a million years or so, maybe a workable system of government is a political-science impossibility." This is a political reality which Piper accepts as neither good or bad—just a law like that of the Second Law of Thermodynamics.

Not even the First Galactic Empire, the proud successor to the Terran Federation, is immune from the decay of civilization. In "A Slave is a Slave," Prince Trevannion states: "But we will not again permit the plague of competing sovereignties, the condition under which war is inevitable. The first attempt to set up such a sovereignty in competition with the

Empire will be crushed mercilessly, and no planet inhabited by any sapient race will be permitted to remain outside the Empire." However, even the Empire's strongest sanctions cannot prevent her decline; in "The Edge of the Knife," a story about a history professor plagued with visions from the future, the professor foresees the disintegration of the First Galactic Empire.

And just who are these barbarians busy undermining the foundations of civilization? Piper tell us: "These are homemade barbarians. Workers and peasants who revolted to seize and divide the wealth and then found they'd smashed the means of production and killed off all the technical brains. Survivors on planets hit during the Interstellar Wars…who lost the machinery of civilization. Followers of political leaders on local-dictatorship planets. Companies of mercenaries thrown out of employment and living by pillage. Religious fanatics following self-anointed prophets." Near the end of *Space Viking*, Piper draws an even finer picture: "There is not one of them [our rulers]…who is devoted to civilization or anything outside himself, and that's the mark of a barbarian."

H. Beam Piper's barbarian is very similar to José Ortega y Gasset's conception of mass-man as defined in Ortega's *The Revolt of the Masses*. As described by Ortega, mass-man feels at one with everyone else regardless of station or achievement and reacts to being evaluated with resentment and hostility. Mass-man is natural man, desiring to impose his will upon the rest of the world. When mass-man determines the course of Government, the result is hyperdemocracy and then fascism.

When Piper describes the barbarians in *Space Viking*, his description parallels Ortega's: "The barbarians are rising…. Every society rests on a barbarian base. The people who don't understand civilization, and wouldn't like it if they did. The hitchhikers. The people who create nothing, and who don't appreciate what others have created for them, and who think civilization is something that just exists and that all they need to do is enjoy what they can understand of it—luxuries, a high standard, and easy work for high pay….

"It wasn't the war that put Hitler into power. It was the fact that the ruling class of his nation, the people who kept things running, were discredited. The masses, the homemade barbarians, didn't have anybody to take their responsibilities for them."

In 1930 when Ortega wrote *The Revolt of the Masses*, he believed that most of the European representative governments were approaching a state of mass anarchy, which he termed hyperdemocracy, a state where mass-man dominates government through the flux of public opinion and competing pressure groups. Hyperdemocracy comes about when mass-man has discredited his governmental representatives or they abrogate their own authority.

Piper describes such a situation in *Space Viking* on the planet Marduk, which is ruled by a representative government with a titular monarchy (like that of Great Britain's). "What they have on Marduk is…[a] ruling class that has begun to believe that the masses are just the same as they are, which they manifestly are not. And a ruling class that won't use force to maintain its position. And they have a democracy, and they are letting the enemies of democracy shelter themselves behind democratic safeguards."

Interestingly enough, José Ortega y Gasset believed that it is only "Noble man"—Piper's self-reliant man—who is capable of governing ideally in a representative government, with restraint and purposeful decision. According to Ortega, Noble man is not the aristocrat of birth, but the aristocrat of intellect, one who is self-surpassing, a man who has lifted himself out of the masses and given himself character. As described earlier, this is very similar to the description Piper gives of the self-reliant man in "Oomphel in the Sky."

Ortega also believed that the best possible form of government was that of a liberal democracy, even though it was endangered by the very freedom that it offered to mass-man. Despite mass-man's egoistic demands, Ortega believed that it was possible for Noble man and mass-man to coexist in a continual state of tension within a representative government.

Piper was also an advocate of representative government, as in the Terran Federation; although in his later years, he appeared to be leaning toward an enlightened monarchy—perhaps as a means to overcome the resistance of bureaucrats and welfare advocates to simple solutions and direct action. He was also aware of the tension between self-reliant man and the mass man, as in *Space Viking* when Lucas Trask says to Prince Simon Bentrik: "You have to learn, too, that a ruler cannot afford to be guided by his fears of what people will say about him. Not even what history will say about him. A ruler's only judge is himself."

Jerry Pournelle mentions having discussed Ortega's ideas with Piper, but there is no record of such. However, Piper and Ortega share much of the same pessimistic view of humanity and civilization.

As James Blish stated in his Spenglerian overview of science fiction in "Probapossible Prolegomena to Ideareal History" (*Foundation*: No. 13, May 1978), there are two kinds of historical philosophy, the cyclic and the linear. Most linear historians believe that history follows a predetermined course towards some type of positive state: This group includes the Christian determinists, the utopian socialists (such as Sir Thomas More, H.G. Wells and the Fabian socialists), the positivists (like Saint-Simon and Auguste Comte) who believed the human sciences would one day attain the unity and elegance of natural science, the social Darwinists (like Herbert Spencer) who believed in the evolutionary struggle of societies) and the economic determinists (such as Charles A. Beard and Karl Marx) who believed in the materialist conception of history and the "perfection of man."

The major proponents of the cyclical theory of history were: Oswald Spengler, who held that every culture passes through a life cycle similar to that of the four seasons. Georg Hegel, who divided history into a series of succeeding epochs, each of which expresses a particular phase in the development of the "World Sprit." Vilfredo Pareto, who viewed history as the circulation of elites with few, or no, positive consequences for the "people." Fredrich Nietzsche, who believed history was not only cyclical but repeated itself in fine detail and Arnold J. Toynbee, whose somewhat cyclical view also held that the course of history was determined by psychic forces as well as economic and social forces.

There are other theories of history: geographical determinism and the Great Man in History theory—Emerson once held that all that was important in history could be told in the biographies of the great men. However, neither of these offer a coherent philosophy of history.

Piper himself held a cyclic view of history: the Terro-Human Future History covers the rise and fall of the Terran Federation and four galactic empires. There are a number of interesting similarities between Piper's and Arnold Toynbee's view of history. Piper makes mention of Toynbee on a number of occasions in his diaries; in "The Edge of the Knife" he has his history professor protagonist state: "History follows certain patterns. I'm not a Toynbeean, by any matter of means, but any historian can see that certain forces generally tend to produce similar effects." For help with his short story "A Slave Is a Slave," Mike Knerr wrote in his unpublished biography, "PIPER": "Piper dug out his copy of Toynbee's *A Study of History*, searching for something to write about."

Piper's Terro-Human Future History has much of the breadth of Toynbee's *A Study of History* and his civilizations pass through some of the same phases as Toynbee's: such as the *universal state*, the *time of troubles* and the *interregnum*. Toynbee's "universal state," an entire society incorporated into one universal state, is found in Piper's Terran Federation and the First Galactic Empire, both of which encompass all known human worlds. By the end of *The Cosmic Computer*, the Terran Federation is no longer creative and is in a state of decline. *Space Viking* chronicles the interregnum after the fall of the Terran Federation and before the emergence of the First Galactic Empire.

In *Space Viking* there is an example of Toynbee's "chaotic intrusion of a barbarian heroic age" as the Space Vikings savage the Old Federation. By the time of "A Slave is a Slave" the Space Vikings have taken on an almost mythic quality: "Then they erupted, suddenly and calamitously, into what was left of the Terran Federation as the Space Vikings, carrying pillage and destruction, until the newborn Empire rose to vanquish them."

Where Piper and Toynbee diverge in their conception of history is on the question of psychic forces determining the course of history. Toynbee wrote: "It is clear that if the geneses of civilizations are not the result of biological factors or geographic environment acting separately, they must be the result of some kind of interaction between them.... The first stage, then, of the human protagonist's ordeal is a transition from Yin to Yang through a dynamic act—performed by God's creature under temptation from the Adversary—which enables God Himself to resume His creative activity. But this progress has to be paid for; and it is not God but God's servant, the human sower, who pays the price. Finally, after many vicissitudes, the sufferer triumphant serves as the pioneer. The human protagonist in the divine drama not only serves God by enabling Him to renew His creation but also serves his fellow men by pointing the way for others to follow."

Piper was a self-admitted atheist and—despite his interest in psychic research and Rhine's work—definitely antagonistic towards organized religion, whether it be Christianity ("...I was considerably amused at the account of your war with the local Jesus-brokers, who seem to be a rather swinish lot."—hbp) or Buddhism or some other organized religion. Nor is there any analogy in Piper's work between the fall of the Roman Empire (Hellenic Society) and surviving Church, which becomes Toynbee's womb from which Western Civilization will emerge. Throughout the Terro-Human Future History (unlike Jerry Pournelle's CoDominium/Empire of Man future history) Piper's only use of religion is satirical. In *Space Viking* Piper describes the Gilgamesh religion thusly: "Their society seemed to be a loose theo-socialism, and their religion an absurd potpourri of most of the major monotheisms of the Federation period, plus doctrinal and ritualistic innovations of their own."

José Ortega y Gasset's philosophy of history provides the best paradigm for understanding Piper's Terro-Human Future History. Ortega, unlike Marx and the other economic determinists, believed that the historical epoch was determined not by production but by man's consciousness of the possible. "Not every age has [felt] itself inferior to any past age, nor have all believed themselves superior to any past age. Every historical period displays a different feeling in respect of this strange phenomenon of the vital attitude...."

In his seminal work, *The Revolt of the Masses*, Ortega sets forth three kinds of historical consciousness by which we can judge different historical epochs; the *decadent*, which describes an epoch of decay and shrinking vitality; the *plentitude*, an epoch of history in which the people of that period feel they have attained a full, definitive height or it is thought that the end of a journey has been reached; and the *vitality*, an epoch in which man feels himself "possessed of greater potentiality than ever before and in all previous times being dwarfed by the contrast," a time where everything is possible, including the best and the worst. Throughout Piper's Terro-Human Future History, Ortega's three kinds of consciousness appear and disappear in regular cyclical patterns.

It is in the early years of exploration and interstellar expansion of the Terran Federation that we find an epoch of "vitality." In "The Edge of the Knife" Piper compares the Federation's period of early discovery to that of the Spanish conquest of the Americas. This feeling of expanded and unlimited possibilities extends throughout most of the early Terran Federation stories: *Uller Uprising*, "Omnilingual," and *Four-Day Planet*.

At the twilight of the Terran Federation, after it has been ripped asunder by the System States War and temporarily patched back together, there is an epoch of "decadence." The Federation's expansion has slowed; it is a time of limited expectations, where many war-devastated worlds have begun the long fall into barbarism. When Merlin, the super-computer in *The Cosmic Computer*, is asked to forecast the future, it answers: "The Terran Federation is overextended, had been cracking for a century before the War; the strain of that conflict had started an irreversible breakup. Two centuries for the Federation as such; at most, another century of irregular trade and occasional war between planets. Galaxy-full of human-populated planets as poor as Poictesme at its worst."

The novel, *Space Viking*, takes place several centuries past the peak of Sword-World civilization and is now heading into an epoch of decadence and decline. "The whole level of Sword-World life was sinking…so slowly as to be evident only from the records and monuments of the past." The best and boldest of the Space Vikings have left their homes on the Sword-Worlds for planetary base worlds in the Old Federation from where they can raid and plunder the surrounding Neobarbarian worlds.

By the end of the book, Lucas Trask, ruler of one of the Space Viking base worlds, believes that civilization will most likely be rekindled inside the boundaries of the Old Federation. "Sooner or later, civilization in the Old Federation would drive them [Space Vikings] all home to loot the planets that had sent them out."

In a "Slave is a Slave," which takes place about five centuries after *Space Viking* during the final expansion phase of the First Empire, there is a period of "vitality." This story concerns a small fleet of Imperial spaceships which have been sent to the outer fringes of the Old Federation to bring these worlds Imperial rule. When they discover Aditya—a former Sword-World base that has fallen into a state of what can only be described as feudal-socialism—the Imperials give Aditya's leaders the following warning: "There must be one and only one completely sovereign power. The Terran Federation was once such a power. It failed, and vanished; you know what followed. Darkness and anarchy. We are clawing our way up out of that darkness. We will not fail. We will create a peaceful and united Galaxy."

Another eight centuries pass before the next story, "Ministry of Disturbance," in which the Empire now consists of 3,365 worlds. This epoch finds the First Galactic Empire in a state of "plentitude," a fulfillment of the past. Paul XXII says this about the empire: "The supplementary [economics] chart for the past five centuries told the real story—three perfectly level and perfectly parallel lines." In an attempt to disrupt the inertia in a positive manner, the Emperor decides to create social change: "… [we] agreed upon this long ago, when we were still boys at the University. The Empire stopped growing, and when things stop growing, they start dying, the death of petrification. And when petrification is complete, the cracking and the crumbling starts, and there's no way of stopping it. But if we can get people out onto new planets, the Empire won't die; it'll start growing again."

Despite his good intentions and planning, Paul XXII is not able to save the First Empire. Piper has his history professor in "The Edge of the Knife" give a preview of its collapse: "But, as he walked home, he was struck by the parallel between the buccaneers of the West Indies and the space-pirates in the days of the dissolution of the First Galactic Empire…."

The final story in Piper's Terro-Human Future History is "The

"Keeper." This short story takes place thousands of years after "Ministry of Disturbance" and gives us a good overview of Piper's cyclic and pessimistic view of civilization. "The glaciation hadn't started in the time of the Third Empire. There is no record of this planet [Terra] during the Fourth, but by the beginning of the Fifth Empire, less than a thousand years ago, things here were very much as they are now."

Piper also used historical events as plot models and for inspiration for his future history. In *Uller Uprising*, the first published work in Piper's Terro-Human Future History, he used the Sepoy Mutiny, a revolt in nineteenth century British-held India, when Bengalese soldiers were issued cartridges coated with what they believed to be the fat of cows (sacred to Hindus) and pigs (anathema to Muslims).

This is confirmed by Piper in "The Edge of the Knife," an interesting story that fits sideways into his future history, in which the history professor who sees into the future compares the planetary rebellion in Fourth Century A.E. (the *Uller Uprising*) to the Sepoy Mutiny. "He thought for a time of the Sepoy Mutiny, and then rejected it—he could 'remember' something much like that on one of the planets of the Beta Hydrae System in the Fourth Century of the Atomic Era"

Uller is the second planet of the star Beta Hydrae and the planet Uller is described in some detail in the introduction to *The Petrified Planet* by John D. Clark. This Twayne Science Fiction Triplet is a collection of three short novels by different authors, written around the premises set down by an eminent scientist. *Uller Uprising* was first published in *The Petrified Planet* and Piper incorporated much of Clark's background details into the story. *Uller Uprising* is the first true Terro-Human Future history yarn and set up the template for future works.

Later, in "The Edge of the Knife," Piper's historian protagonist remarks: "there were so few things, in the history of the past, which did not have their counterparts in the future." This idea, of course, is not new with Piper; Vilfredo Pareto once stated that every political science possibility imaginable had, at one time or another, flourished in the Italian city-states during the Renaissance. Most of the works in Piper's Terro-Human Future

History—including the Fuzzy novels, where the Zarathustra Company's treatment of the Fuzzies has a number of parallels to the treatment of the East Indians by the British East India Company—are modeled on real historical events and situations.

Another historical analog used by Piper was the War in the Pacific during World War II. In *Cosmic Computer*, the planet Poictesme, the former headquarters of the Third Terran force during the System States War, has become in the post-war period a deserted backwater. Most of those remaining on Poictesme earn their living by salvaging and recycling old army vehicles and stores—a way of life that continued for some time on many of the Pacific atolls and islands after the war had ended. The survivors have created a belief system based on Merlin, the legendary supercomputer that was reputed to have won the war for the Federation against the System States, which is reminiscent of the Cargo cults much in vogue among the more isolated Pacific Islanders after the parachute drops of W.W. II.

Piper also paid great attention to historical detail, more so than any other previous SF writer since Olaf Stapleton. In *Space Viking*, Piper gives the names of over fifty different planets and goes into historical, sociological and political detail on about twenty of them. This detail ranges from a short clause to pages of exposition concerning Federation history, past wars and historical figures, as well as comments on their political and sociological foibles.

Where are the American-Sino-Soviet superpowers in Piper's Terro-Human Future History? And what has happened to the cultural domination of Europe and North America?

The answer to this question lies in Piper's earliest short stories and novelettes, many predating the creation of his Terro-Human Future History. Throughout his body of work, Piper shows a predilection for certain themes: nuclear war, the cyclical nature of civilization, the threat of barbarians from within society and from without, the citizen patriot, reincarnation, time travel, para-psychological phenomenon, etc. In many of his stories published in the 1940s and '50s the threat of a global nuclear holocaust is clearly on his mind—as it was on the mind of any sane person who lived during that era of nuclear brinkmanship.

Piper's first short story, "Time and Time Again," is where he first mentions a Third World War, one that takes place in 1975 (only one year prior to the date given to the Third World War in his History of the Future letter to Peter Weston). In "Flight From Tomorrow" (re-titled from "Immunity"), which was published in 1950, is the first story using Atomic Era (A.E.) dating and the first one to explore the rise and fall of civilization on earth. There are some glaring inconsistencies with later stories, which makes it impossible to place "Flight From Tomorrow" in the Terro-Human Future History, and the central idea—that man could over time *adapt* to radioactivity—is wrong, although that was not obvious at the time the story was written. It is certainly one of the more interesting stories in the Piper canon, and contains many of the ideas which we find in later Terro-Human Future Histories stories.

"Day of the Moron" could almost be called a part of the Terro-Human Future History; in this early story, Piper is clearly working out some of the background he later uses in his future history. However, there is no internal evidence that would make it a part of his Terro-Human Future History (nor does Piper place it there in his letter to Weston).

The origin story of the Terro-Human Future History began in the short novel, *Uller Uprising*. *Uller Uprising* has an interesting history of its own; it first appeared as one of three short novels in a Twayne Triplet (a series of three novels along a similar theme published in one large book by Twayne) in 1952. A shorter version, by some 20,000 words, was later published in 1953 in *Space Science Fiction*. It's very unusual for a book to be serialized after its initial book publication. All the stories in *The Petrified Planet* were based on a science essay by noted scientist Dr. John D. Clark, chief chemist at the Naval Air Rocket Test Station. The find of several so-called Piperisms, such as the curse "Niflheim," for example, come right out of Clark's essay.

But while the *Uller Uprising* is a treasure trove of information on the Fourth Century, A.E., it doesn't tell us much about the early Terran Federation. Instead we have to go to "The Edge of the Knife" about the professor who *sees* into the future. The professor gets visions from the Third World War through the Third Imperium, storing his data in file folders, much as Piper was reputed to do. However, this story is most valuable for data on the early Federation:

There would be an Eastern (Axis) inspired uprising in Azerbaijan by the middle of next year; before autumn, the Indian Communists would make their fatal attempt to seize East Pakistan. The Thirty Days' War would be the immediate result. By that time, the Lunar base would be completed and ready; the enemy missiles would be supplied. Delivered without warning, it should have succeeded except that every rocket port had its secret duplicate and triplicate. That was Operation Triple Cross; no wonder Major Cutler had been so startled at the words, last evening. The enemy would be utterly overwhelmed under the rain of missiles from across space, but until the moon rockets began to fall, the United States would suffer grievously.

The end result, according to Piper, is World War III—the nightmare, in the fifties and sixties, everyone had dreaded come to life. The new order is the Pan Federation, otherwise known as the First Federation, formed after the Thirty Days War. According to a security officer, who talks to our future visionary: "It's all pretty hush-hush, but this term Terran Federation (is) for a proposed organization to take the place of the U.N. if that organization breaks up..."

In "The Mercenaries," mention is made of the Islamic Kaliphate and a Fourth Komintern, which almost puts this story, which first appears in *Astounding* in 1949, into the Terro-Human Federation canon. Obviously, H. Beam Piper was already synthesizing his "view of the near future" as early as 1946 in "Time and Time Again" with the Hartley Presidency. I suspect, like Asimov and Heinlein, that had Piper lived into the 1980s, he would have found a way to unite all his yarns into one grand "universe."

FIRST FEDERATION

There are clues throughout Piper's early Terro-Human Future History stories about the Federation and its organization. In *Space Viking*, it's stated that the First Terran Federation was said to be based on "Corporate State, First Century Pre-Atomic Era on Terra. Benny the Moose." Benny the Moose was one of Mussolini's nicknames. In Italy Mussolini style-fascism was comprised of large corporations, trade unions and syndicates. Rather than a legislative body, Mussolini formed a National Council of Corporations. Thus, the First Federation might be compared to a mercantile state under the aegis of a president. It's not world government, but is comprised of various national factions. In his "The Future History" Piper states that the first landing on the moon occurred in the year 27 Atomic Era. Shortly after "The collapse of the U.N. owing to disputes as to national sovereignty over, and militarization of, Luna.

The Terran Federation is formed just after World War III (Thirty Days War) in 32 A.E., and so its seat at first is probably in New York in the former United Nations' offices. There was little time to find new facilities, and besides the UN buildings the Federation even appropriate its emblem, a wreathed globe on a light blue field.

The Federation headquarters presumably remains in New York until destroyed in World War IV, making it the Terran Federation capital for almost a century (A.E. 32 to A.E. 127). Since Washington is also destroyed in WWIII (see "Operation Triple Cross"), the US government probably moves elsewhere, but Piper does not provide us with the new location.

"Omnilingual" takes place in 53 A.E. (1996 A.D.) during the early exploration phase of the First Federation. It chronicles the first human expedition to Mars as well as the discovery of an extinct Martian civilization. In his "The Future History" piece, Piper writes: "Further explorations of Mars, Venus, Asteroid Belt and Moons of Jupiter. The First Terran Federation begins to crack under strains of colonial claims and counter-claims of member states."

The First Federation collapses during World War IV, or the First

Interplanetary War which takes place from 106 to 109 A.E. Piper states: "Minor wars for ten years thereafter. Complete devastation of Northern Hemisphere of Terra. Second Federation organized by South Africa and New Zealand, Brazil, Argentina, etc. Wars of colonial pacification and consolidation. The new Terran Federation imposes System-wide pax."

Piper never wrote any stories covering the events on earth after the Thirty Days War, or World War III. This is total war and it devastates the major powers (most in the Northern Hemisphere) and all the big cities and arms depots are destroyed. World War IV (the First Interplanetary War) was probably just as devastating. In *Space Viking*, he writes: "[Even Terra] had anti-technological movements after Venus seceded from the first Federation, before the Second Federation was organized."

The Fourth World War

Piper mentions a Fourth World War in several places. In "When in the Course…" he mentions "the Atomic Wars" which include both World War III and World War IV. Where are the Sino-American-Soviet superpowers and how are they involved in these calamitous events? And what happened to the cultural domination of Europe and North America?

To answer these questions we have to take a close look at Piper's early short stories and novelettes, many of which are not officially part of his Terro-Human Future History. Throughout his body of work, Piper shows a fondness for certain themes: atomic devastation, lost Martian races, the Middle East as the fire-starter for the next World War, the cyclical nature of civilization, the threat of barbarians from within and without, the citizen patriot, etc. In the stories published in the early 1950s (and in some of his letters, too) it is the threat of a global nuclear holocaust that is clearly on his mind—as it was on the mind of any aware person living in the era of nuclear brinksmanship.

Most of our knowledge about the early Federation comes from Piper's story about the history professor with precognition problems, "The Edge of the Knife." The professor's foresight is phenomenal, from the Third

World War to the Third Imperium, and the professor stores his data in folders much as Beam was reputed to do by Jerry Pournelle. This story is most valuable for its information on the early Federation:

He sighed and sat down at Marjorie's typewriter and began transcribing his notes. Assassination of Khalid ib'n Hessein, the pro-Western leader of the newly formed Islamic Caliphate; period of anarchy in the Middle East; interfactorial power-struggles, Turkish intervention. He wondered how long that would last; Khalid's son, Tallal ib'n Khalid, was at school in England when his father was—would be—killed. He would return, and eventually take his father's place, in time to bring the Caliphate into the Terran Federation when the general war came. There were some notes on that already; the war would result from an attempt by Indian Communists to seize East Pakistan. The trouble was that he so seldom "remembered" an exact date.

Another story that contributed important elements to Piper's Terro-Human Future History is "Flight From Tomorrow," reprinted in Ace Books *The Worlds of H. Beam Piper.* Published in 1950, this is the first story where Piper introduces his Atomic Era dating and one in which he explores the rising and ebbing of civilizations. There are some glaring inconsistencies with later stories which makes it impossible to place it within the T-HFH and the central idea—that man can adapt to radiation—is false, although that wasn't so obvious when the story was written. It is certainly one of the more curious tales in the Piper canon, and is a springboard for many of the ideas which crop up in later stories.

The next early story of interest is "Time and Time Again,' Piper's first published story. In this story the Third World War is featured prominently, and occurs in 1975 (only one year before the date given for WWIII in his T-HFH future history). The story "Day of the Moron" almost fits into Piper's Terro-Human Future History; here he was clearly working out some of the background he used in later T-HFH stories. However, there is no internal evidence that allows us to place it legitimately in the Terro-Human Future History.

While "The Answer" (published in 1959 in *Fantastic Universe Science*

Fiction) is not officially part of the Terro-Human Future History it was written during the period where most of Piper's stories took place in his history of the future. However, it is a key story in unraveling Piper's thoughts on a global tragedy, and what happened to the Northern Hemisphere during World War IV. The story concerns two survivors—one Russian, one American—of a catastrophic negamatter explosion from outside the solar system. Unfortunately, in the post-World War III armed camp, it is the trigger for a massive nuclear holocaust. The two survivors are now working for the Argentines to learn the causes. "The memories of all those tests, each ending in an Everest-high mushroom column, rose in his mind. And the end result—the United States and Soviet Union blasted to rubble, a whole hemisphere pushed back to the Dark Ages, a quarter of a billion dead…"

Nuclear holocausts are a familiar theme throughout most of Piper's oeuvre. In "The Answer" Piper writes about what happened to northern hemisphere after it was blasted by multiple nuclear strikes:

"Our friends here in Argentina have been doing very well by themselves since El Coloso del Norte *went down.*

"And there were the Australians, picking themselves up bargains in real estate in the East Indies at gunpoint, and there were the Boers, trekking north again, in tanks instead of ox-wagons. And Brazil, with a not-too-implausible pretender to the Braganza throne, calling itself the Portuguese Empire and looking eastward.…

"You know, there were people inside the Soviet Union—not many, and they kept themselves well hidden—who were dedicated to the overthrow of the Soviet regime. They, or some of them, might have thought that the devastation of both our countries, and the obliteration of civilization in the Northern Hemisphere, would be a cheap price to pay for ending the rule of the Communist Party.

"Could they have built an ICBM with a thermonuclear warhead in secret?" he asked. "There were also fanatical nationalist groups in Europe, on both sides of the Iron Curtain, who might have thought our mutual destruction would be worth the risks involved.

"There was China, and India. If your country and mine wiped each other out, they could go back to the old ways and the old traditions. Or Japan, or the Moslem states. In the end, they all went down along with us, but whatever criminal ever expects to fail?"

The "United States would suffer grievously" from the World War as would Russia, China, the Caliphate and Britain, the last nation to join the Terran Federation. With the Northern Hemisphere poisoned and destroyed, the fear of another global holocaust would force the survivors to work closer together. The American and European refugees would bring with them their education and talents, as well as a desire to recreate their former homelands in the Southern Hemisphere. Unfortunately, Piper doesn't go into this side of the war and we only have a few hints as to what occurred after World War IV.

Second Terran Federation

After World War IV, the Second Terran Federation emerges Phoenix-like out of the ashes of the First Federation. Unfortunately, again, Piper provides few details. He never mentions the new location of the Second Federation capital, but it very might well be Montevideo. The University of Montevideo is mentioned as a great—if not the greatest—center of learning in several places. Conn Maxwell goes there for his computer science education. It would make sense for the Second Terran Federation capital to be situated on the larger and more populous South American continent than in Africa or Australia, despite its connection to Great Britain. The selection of Uruguay as the capital is surprising; it's possible that it was a compromise selection between Argentina and Brazil, either of which might have otherwise dominated the nascent Second Federation. The city of Montevideo is adjacent to the Rio de la Plata, a major river estuary in a temperate climate.

As described in *Four-Day Planet*, the Second Terran Federation has a government with a parliament and an executive, "the President of the Federation," which governs under the Federation Constitution. This is probably some combination of the American and British political systems. Certainly, even after America itself is destroyed in WWIV, it still maintains substantial business, corporate and personal forces within the new world body. The Federation combination of President and Parliament could as reflect some influences from the former British colonies in the Southern Hemisphere, such as Australia, South Africa and the remaining African colonies. Most South America nation states have US-style Presidents, while South Africa, Australia, and New Zealand are former British colonies with parliaments and a prime minister.

There is no mention of any provisions guaranteeing national rights; however, if Piper based the Terran Federation on the government of the Confederate States of America—with which he had a lot of sympathy—it's possible that the resulting constitution allowed certain national rights.

During the Age of Exploration, we see the Federation expanding to new worlds at an explosive rate. Piper compares the later Federation government to that of Georgian England, a representative government with colonies and member states, rather than a strict monarchy. There are also charter companies (much like the British East India Company) that discover and develop new planetary colonies, such as the Chartered Uller Company, and the Chartered Zarathustra Company which argues against Fuzzy sapience in *Little Fuzzy* in order to maintain their control over the colony. In the Federation, there are certain restrictions put on planets with indigenous native races.

Piper, in "Edge of the Knife," compares Federation colonial expansion to: "…when Mars and Venus are colonized, there will be the same historic situations, at least in general shape, as arose when the European powers were colonizing the New World, or for that matter, when the Greek city-states were throwing out colonies across the Aegean." Later he compares the early Federation with the Spanish Conquest, with events like the Uller Uprising and the Loki Enslavement. Many Federation planets have their own colonial governors who can only be overthrown by direct military intervention, and which are governed through and with the consent of a legislature.

The later Terran Federation includes an area of over two hundred billion cubic light years with over five million planets that could sustain life in a natural or artificial environment. Although internal evidence (in *The Cosmic Computer* and *Space Viking*) leads us to suspect that only a few thousand of these worlds were ever inhabited by mankind during the Federation period, we do know that there were new worlds being colonized up until the time of the System States War in the Ninth Century A.E., when the Federation began to turn back in upon itself. The language of the Federation was the universal Lingua Terra, an English-Spanish-Afrikaans-Portuguese mixture of old Terran languages. In the Federation, time is kept according to Galactic Standard, which is based on Terran [Earth] time in seconds, minutes and hours.

Piper was quite advanced—for the time period—in his views of race and integration. By the First Century Atomic Era, Homo sapiens terra has become racially homogeneous; in *Four-Day Planet*, Piper writes: "The amount of intermarriage that's gone on since the First Century, [had made] any resemblance between people's names and their appearances purely coincidental." By the Seventh Century Lingua Terra had become universal: "spoken, in one form or another, by every descendant of the race that had gone out from the Sol System in the Third Century."

Most of Piper's Federation stories, with the exception of "Graveyard of Dreams" and the novel it inspired, *The Cosmic Computer*, involve the Federation's exploration and subjugation of new planets. *The Cosmic Computer* takes place after the disastrous System States War (a thinly disguised version of our own Civil War), when the Federation has clearly entered its Toynbeean "time of troubles." In the follow-up novel, *Space Viking*, which takes place in the "interregnum," Piper writes that the System States War led to a period of instability and the eventual dissolution of the Second Federation. The Space Vikings, whose ancestors fled after the defeat of the System States Alliance, flee far beyond the boundaries of the Federation and create a dozen worlds named after famous swords.

The later Terran Federation itself is well mapped out by *Four-Day Planet*, *Uller Uprising*, *Little Fuzzy*, *Fuzzy Sapiens*, *Cosmic Computer* and half a dozen short stories; however, only one novel, *Space Viking*, and three short stories exist to describe the next four to five thousand years. Furthermore, *Space Viking* takes place several hundred years before the First Galactic Empire, leaving some rather large holes in Piper's tapestry of the future.

Eventually, the Interstellar Wars begin and the Second Federation is thrown into chaos, with only a few older worlds, like Marduk and Odin, retaining any vestiges of civilization and starfaring spacecraft. In *Space Viking*, the descendants of the System States Alliance who fled from the Federation return to prey on the worlds of the Old Federation which have over the centuries descended into barbarism.

Pipe wrote only one short story, "A Slave Is a Slave," where he explores the First Galactic Empire during its expansion period as it rediscovers the lost worlds of the former Federation. "A Slave Is a Slave" further illuminates some of the events after *Space Viking*, but leaves us with more questions about where the Empire began and how it rose to power than it answers. "Ministry of Disturbance" takes place some eight hundred years later when the Empire is at peace and stagnating. This story sheds some light on a few of the previous Emperors, their reigns and the state of the once mighty Sword-Worlds, but again provides us with nothing concerning the genesis of the First Empire.

"The Keeper" is enigmatic at best, taking place in the Fifth Empire and reveals few clues regarding the fates of the previous four Empires and the current epoch. All we learn in this story is that Terra, after several atomic wars, has fallen into barbarism and is experiencing an ice age. Earth has even been "lost" during the interregnums of several galactic empires. Terra is now only an outpost of the Fifth Galactic Empire, with only a nearby naval base for company. There are hints that civilization has spread far and wide throughout the galaxy, but certainly it is a backwater world.

Sadly, Piper's premature death deprived us of the full expanse of his History of the Future as well as some cracking-good yarns. However, throughout the Terro-Human Future History, H. Beam Piper carefully interwove the threads of history and invention, creating the patterns of a unique but unfortunately incomplete cloth. Other future histories might span more centuries or more greatly illuminate the highlights of several decades, but until a rival is created with more historical depth and attention to historical detail, H. Beam Piper's Terro-Human Future History will stand as the Bayeux Tapestry of science-fiction future histories.

APPENDIX V

The Terro-Human Future History Chronology

TERRO-HUMAN FUTURE HISTORY CHRONOLOGY

The Atomic Era is reckoned as beginning on the 2nd December 1942, Christian era, with the first self-sustaining nuclear reactor, put into operation by Enrico Fermi at the University of Chicago. Unlike earlier dating-systems, it begins with a Year Zero, 12/2/1942 to 12/1/1943 CE. With allowances for December overlaps, 1943 CE is thus equal to Year Zero AE, and 1944 CE to 1 AE, and each century accordingly begins with the "double-zero" year, and ends with the ninety-nine year—H. Beam Piper.

(All dates in the Chronology are based on Atomic Era dating—jfc)

0	First self-sustaining nuclear fission reactor in Chicago.
27	First unmanned rocket, the *Kilroy*, lands on the moon.
31	The United Nations collapses.
31	Terran Federation formed.
32	The Thirty Days' War (World War III).
53	First human exploration of Mars; the *Cyrano* Expedition.
55 – 100	Further exploration of Mars, Venus, asteroids and moons of Jupiter.

92	Contragravity is developed.
95 – 105	First Federation begins to crack under strains of colonial claims and counter-claims of member states.
105	Venus secedes from the First Terran Federation.
106	World War IV (First Interplanetary War). Entire Northern Hemisphere devastated by nuclear bombardments.
109	World War IV ends.
110	First Terran Federation is re-centered in the Southern Hemisphere. Australia, New Zealand, South Africa, Brazil, Argentina, Uruguay agree to abolish nation states, creating a completely unified world. This marks the beginning of a new civilization. Lingua Terra begins taking shape.
119	South Africa, Australia, New Zealand, Brazil and Argentina form the Second Terran Federation.
127	Reformed Second Terran Federation establishes a single-world sovereignty when Britain becomes the last nation to join.
172	Keene-Gonzales-Dillingham Theory of Non-Einsteinian Relativity developed.
174	Venus secedes from the First Terran Federation.
183	The First Terran Federation is dissolved and the Second Terran Federation is established. New Federation imposes system-wide pax.

183	Dillingham hyperdrive developed.
192	First expedition to Alpha Centauri.
200	Atomic Era dating adopted.
200 – 800	Period of exploration, colonization and expansion.
350	Marduk colonized.
380	Fenris Company chartered and Fenris settled.
390	Chartered Fenris Company goes bankrupt, most colonists evacuated.
480	Anton Gerrit, leader of the Loki enslavement, captured on Fenris.
500	Federation forces intervene on Fenris with nuclear weapons.
526	Native revolt on Uller against Chartered Uller Company.
629	Zarathustra is discovered and settled.
650	Poictesme is discovered by Genji Gartner and settled.
654	Fuzzy sapience is recognized and Zarathustra reclassified from Class III to Class IV world.
716	Svantovit discovered and Svants encountered.
782	Foxx Travis born. Later he becomes the commander of the Third Fleet-Army Force headquartered on Poictesme.
812	Miles Gilbert and Foxx Travis thwart native revolt on Kwannon. Aditya is discovered.

839	System States Alliance secedes from the Terran Federation.
842 - 854	System States War.
851	Federation forces destroy city of Kindelburg on Ashmodai.
855	Ten thousand refugees from Abigor and the remnants of the System States Alliance Navy flee the Terran Federation and settle Excalibur, the first Sword-World.
871	Conn Maxwell is born.
888	The 'Fawzi Office Gang' sends Conn to school on Terra; the prestigious University of Montevideo.
894	Conn returns from Terra to Poictesme.
895	Merlin is discovered and the Maxwell/Merlin plan to save the Federation is hatched.
895	Sword-Worlds Joyeuse, Durendal and Flamberge colonized from Excalibur.
915	Sword-World Haulteclere colonized from Joyeuse.
935	Sword-World Gram colonized from Haulteclere.
950	Aditya abandoned by the Federation, as it pulls back from the frontiers.
1000	The Interstellar Wars begin, a series of wars and uprisings which lead to the break-up of the Terran Federation.

1100	The final dissolution of the Terran Federation as war breaks out on Terra and the Sol System. The colony worlds turn on the mother world.
1200	The Interstellar Wars come to an end, more through exhaustion than desire. Only a dozen or so worlds still have the capability for interstellar flight.
1242	A fleet from Osiris attacks Poictesme and is repulsed after heavy damage, including the nuclear bombardment of the capital, Storisende.
1268	First Gilgameshers arrive on Vishnu.
1450	First Sword-World ship returns from the Old Federation. Aditya occupied by Morglay.
1533	Wulf Hellmut raids Baldur and a dozen planets in the *World Smasher* and brings home over a billion and a half stellars of plunder back to the Sword-Worlds.
1572	Captain Erlic Sanchez, the Planet-Buster's, raid on Isis is one of the richest Space Viking raids ever made in the Old Federation.
1595	After an unsuccessful raid on Aton by six ships from Haulteclere, Space Vikings no longer raid 'civilized' worlds in the Old Federation.
1600	Aditya is abandoned during a dynastic war on Morglay.
1615	Skathi, a Space Viking base world, is abandoned.
1650	Marduk-Odin 'false war.'

1665	Planetary Nationalist Party takes control of Aton during the crisis after the war with Baldur.
1716	Lucas Trask, seeking revenge for the death of his new wife, leaves Gram aboard the *Nemesis* for Tanith in the Old Federation.
1718	The Battle of Beowulf.
1723	The Battle of Adhumla between Trask's allies and Andray Dunnan's Space Vikings.
1723	Dagon, a Space Viking base world, is raided by Otto Harkaman for attacking Ganpat, a Tanith trade world.
1725	Battle of Marduk between alliance of Lucas Trask's allies and loyalist Mardukan forces against Andray Dunnan's Space Vikings and Zaspar Makann's Mardukan rebels.
1730	King Lucas of Tanith and Prince Simon of Marduk establish the League of Civilized Worlds.
1880	House of Bentrik proclaims Galactic Empire.
1900	Imperial Era (IE) dating system begins: 20th Century corresponds to 1st Century IE.
1980	Emperor Steven IV transfers capital of Galactic Empire from Marduk to Odin.
2035	Sword Worlds added to the Galactic Empire.
2150	Aditya conquered by the Galactic Empire.
2295	Rodrik VI completes consolidation of (first) Galactic Empire.

APPENDIX VI

The "Lost" Fuzzy Novel

THE "LOST" FUZZY NOVEL

John F. Carr

For a little history: *Fuzzies and Other People* over the passing years became known as the legendary "Lost" Piper novel. Shortly after Beam's death, there was considerable controversy among Piper fans whether or not he had written a sequel to *Fuzzy Sapiens* (first published by Avon Books as *The Other Human Race* and later in the 1960s by Ace Books under the title *Fuzzy Sapiens*). It was no secret that Beam had grown contemptuous of his most famous creation after laboring for almost a year over the first sequel. Others scoffed and said it was a myth. The Fuzzies were Piper's most popular creation and it was only natural that fans would want more, even to the extent of believing in a third Fuzzy novel. The only evidence we had that it existed were remembrances from fans and this attribution in a July 2nd, 1963 letter from Piper to Charlie and Marcia Brown: "...For the last three months, I have been working on the historical novel, "Only the Arquebus." I have the story all plotted, and a good start made on the first draft. It is now shelved, however, since I have just had a letter from my agent telling me that Avon wants a sequel to the sequel to *Little Fuzzy*, and I want that finished and accepted as soon as possible, so the arquebus has been hung up temporarily. Inasmuch as this story is going to run to about 100-150,000 words, I never had any expectation of getting it all finished at one uninterrupted writing." This is the only mention of the sequel to *Fuzzy Sapiens* which Piper wouldn't start working on for several months.

There was no other evidence that Piper ever finished this unnamed sequel or even wrote it. For the next decade there were rumors in the science fiction field about the missing book, in fact, several fans claimed they had read the "Lost" Fuzzy novel, although only Odin knows how and where?

Fred Pohl once mentioned that Piper's agent had submitted it to *Galaxy Science Fiction* magazine while he was editor, but when I queried him about it in 1978 he couldn't remember having seen it—"Too many manuscripts over the transom."

He did remember thinking that it did not stand on its own without the prior books which were never serialized in *Galaxy*. Pohl's "questionable recall," plus the words of a few fans who claimed to have read it and Beam's letter to Charlie and Marcia Brown where he mentions that Avon "wants a sequel to the sequel to *Little Fuzzy*," were the only evidence that a third Fuzzy book ever existed.

I learned about the discovery of the "Lost" Fuzzy novel at the Science Fiction Writers of America's Nebula Banquet at the Claremont Resort and Spa in Berkeley on the weekend of April 24th, 1982. At the Ace Publisher's Party, I was approached by then Ace Editor, Beth Meacham, who came up to me in obvious excitement, saying, "John, I just talked with a man who 'claims' to be H. Beam Piper's protégé! His name is Michael Knerr. Have you ever heard of him?"

My response was negative. None of my Piper informants had ever mentioned Knerr's name, nor had it appeared in any of the Piper correspondence I had accumulated.

Ace editor Beth Meacham went on to say that Mike Knerr had first written Ace Books complaining about factual errors about H. Beam Piper in my introductory essay to the Piper short story collection, *Federation*. They had replied to Knerr, promising to forward them to me. He had called Beth back and told her that after writing the letter he had decided to go through the Piper "trunks" in his possession and that he had come across the "Lost" Fuzzy novel.

I was quite excited about this discovery and made Beth promise to call me when, or if, it showed up at the Ace offices. She called about two weeks later, informing me that Knerr had sent Ace a photocopy of what Knerr referred to as the "second or third draft" of the "Lost" Fuzzy novel, entitled, *Fuzzies and Other People*. After reading the manuscript Beth was convinced that it was the "Lost" Piper manuscript and told me that Ace was planning to publish it the next year.

I first heard from Mike Knerr about a month later when his undated letter to me was forwarded by Ace Books.

Dear Mr. Carr:

Susan Allison, being kind enough to forward this letter to you, may end up as kind of a go-between in future conversations.

You don't know me—let me introduce myself. I'm a writer and long-time friend of H. Beam Piper's. I have his diaries, at least the last nine years of his life, and a lot of other things that might have been thrown out when he died. Nothing spectacular, but a few items. Your introduction in Federation *prompted me, not only to write you, but to begin a biography of Beam* [the unpublished "PIPER"—jfc].

Some of your information was wrong, some questionable and the main art very astute and—I thought—brilliant.

I'd like to mention some facts on the matter of Beam's life (I helped clean up the apartment) and ask permission to quote you in the upcoming biography – if I may. I'm sorry for the somewhat confusing address listed above, that being my girlfriend's address, but I live on a 30-foot sloop and am a bit out of touch with the normal world.

At the risk of your anger, let me begin by saying that I unwittingly had a copy of Fuzzies and Other People, *which has since been turned over to Ace—and for which I apologize. I didn't know I had it. Beam was very close and for a long time I couldn't bear to even read his diaries, let alone dig through the material I came to own. Not being especially interested in science fiction, it was through the efforts of Susan Allison and Beth Meacham that the novel was found at all. My dear friend, Mindy, located a copy of* Federation *and that, of course, led to this letter.*

...I didn't know about a (suicide) note, but I was pretty broken up at the time—in fact, the reason his "lost" manuscript has been lost for so long is because I'm still pretty broken up about it. It didn't have to happen. Hell, I'd have supported him, had I known...

At any rate, John, Susan suggested that I write you about using quotes from your work in Federation. *May I? I think it's high time the Piper story has been told, if for no other reason than to stop the crap that shows up in newspapers from time to time...*

Sincerely,
M. E. Knerr

Shortly after receiving this unexpected letter, I called Mike at the telephone number provided in his letter. We had a friendly chat, exchanging information about Beam, and I gave him verbal permission to quote freely from my introduction to *Federation*. We also talked about the "Lost" Fuzzy novel. Mike was convinced it was an early draft, and that the final manuscript was lost forever. However, Ace Books was quite happy to have it. I asked him if they had given him the "finder's fee" for the book. (Jerry Pournelle had convinced Jim Baen to keep the fee under five grand; otherwise, some starving SF writer would "recreate" the damn thing!)

Mike later told me he turned it down: "It's blood money, John! I don't want any part of it. In exchange for the book, I offered to write Beam's biography. They'll pay me for that, but it'll be for honest work. I'm really looking forward to getting the truth out about Beam and his life."

The next letter from Mike was undated but postmarked September 26th, 1982.

Dear Mr. Carr:

Thank you for your kind permission to quote you. It was, by the way, the story that Jerry Pournelle related about Beam's statement about having been born on another time line. Piper was a trifle strange about that sort of thing and <u>loved</u> to bullshit people when he could. I'm afraid he did the same thing to me on several occasions—so I wanted to use it as an example of how he was.

There was about 30-odd pages written on "Only the Arquebus" that I saw some weeks prior to Beam's death, but they did not surface when we cleaned up the apartment. A lot of things were missing at that time—among them "Piper's history of the future" and I think he might have burned them. I don't know for sure.

I must apologize, to you and the SF fraternity, for whatever loss I may have contributed to in sorting out the aftermath of Beam's death. There just wasn't much left, other than what we turned over to William Askey, the attorney. Not being a science-fiction writer, or a fan, I was totally unaware of Beam's new found success. I simply got mad at another of those dumb stories about him that appear in the news from time to time, and that prompted a correspondence between Beth Meacham and myself. Somehow a biography got itself into the mill and I'm working on it.

All of what I salvaged, with the blessings of Charles O. Piper, are in two trunks—one in Williamsport and the other in Lock Haven. The diaries, from 1955 to 1964, are with me. In the future I hope to go back east and check out the trunk in Lock Haven to see if I have anything that would be of value to Ace or yourself. I'll be more than happy to turn it over to you or Beth, if it's of import.

Beam was a close friend of mine, but not close enough to let me in on a lot of things where writing was concerned. He was like that. I never saw, for example, the "notebooks" of Piper's terro-human future history. All he ever showed me was a kind of outline laid out on pieces of cardboard—never any notebooks.

The copy of Fuzzies and Other People, *which I turned over to Ace, is not the final draft according to the diaries; but it is all that's left. How I got a copy still baffles me, yet I am glad that I had it. It would have been destroyed, along with a lot of other things, had I not grabbed it. At the time of Beam's death, all of us who were involved were a bit too upset to cover all the bases. We tried, but perhaps not well enough. We all of us have that cross to bear....*

Sincerely,
M. E. Knerr

I didn't learn anything more about the Lost Fuzzy novel until the spring of 1984 when I received this flier from The Berkley Publishing Group:

NEWS FROM ACE SCIENCE FICTION

QUEST FOR THE LOST FUZZY

In 1963, the respected, but then little-known writer, H. Beam Piper told his friends and fans that he had finished a sequel to his joyously received new novel, Little Fuzzy; *and that he was hard at work on a third Fuzzy book. Only months later, Piper was dead.*

But when Piper's literary estate was gathered, no trace of that third Fuzzy book could be found—no manuscript, no notebooks, no fragments. Yet, as time passed, rumors of the lost Piper novel continued to swirl and surface. Various fans, authors, editors, swore that they had seen, even read, the lost Fuzzy book.

And, as years went by, Piper's canon was finally discovered by a large and ever growing legion of readers—especially the fans who fell in love with the Fuzzies. Something about those little golden-furred critters touched the hearts of hundreds of thousands of readers. We at Ace Science Fiction & Fantasy commissioned two fine authorized adaptations of the series. Still, we were besieged with requests to publish Piper's third Fuzzy novel.

But how could we publish a book we couldn't even prove existed? Then, in March, 1982, an Ace editor received an angry letter from a Mr. Michael Knerr, who was upset over a highly inaccurate article about H. Beam Piper which had appeared in a national news magazine. Mr. Knerr, we learned, had known Piper well, was irritated by the misinformation about the man he had come to look on as friend and father, and wanted to set the record straight. Thus, he set out to publish Piper's biography.

Meanwhile, both Knerr and Charles Piper (H. Beam Piper's cousin), who had assembled Piper's literary estate, insisted that there was no third novel at all. It didn't exist—never had.

Naturally, we were dismayed: the legend had proved false. Then, during the course of his research, Mike Knerr decided to go through Piper's trunk of junk. The contents seemed of little use—just some letters, bills, and a box labeled "Pens and Second Sheets." On impulse, Knerr opened the box....

That week, he called us with the news: "I've got a carbon copy of the third Fuzzy novel I told you didn't exist. I'm going to put it in the mail to you today." Well, he didn't, of course. First, he made a copy, then sent it Federal Express. We weren't taking any chances on losing it a second time!!

In "Fuzzies and Other People," Jack Holloway and Little Fuzzy are off again into the untamed forests of Zarathustra, on separate missions to seek a wild Ghashta capable of committing an act undreamt of in Fuzzy philosophy. This time, Holloway, must prove the Fuzzes are not just intelligent—but all too human.

Ace is proud to present "Fuzzies and Other People"—a long lost novel—to the world.

This was my last contact with Mike Knerr until April 26th, 1987, when I called him for permission to quote some of his comments from our telephone conversations and from his letters for my H. Beam Piper essay, "H. Beam Piper: The Last Cavalier," for *Analog Science Fiction and Fact,* which later appeared in the January 1988 issue. At that time, Mike told me he hadn't found anything else of literary value in the trunks, but that Ace Books had turned down his Piper biography, which he had entitled "PIPER." He was very distraught over what he considered Ace's betrayal of both him and Beam.

"Those bastards at Ace made me a deal, and I spent years writing that biography. And then they turned it down without a qualm.... They totally screwed me!" I remembered the $5,000 dollar reward that Jerry had said that Ace had offered for the "Lost" Fuzzy novel, which Mike (totally out-of-character, as I learned later) had turned down not wanting to "profit from the death of my good friend, Beam!"

I sympathized with him, telling him that "the bloom" was off the Piper revival, since no new Piper related works had appeared since my own sequel to *Lord Kalvan of Otherwhen, Great King's War* was published in 1985.

I told Mike that Ace had started to de-emphasize the kinds of books Piper wrote (men's SF adventure books) around 1986 and that he shouldn't take it personally. The woman editors—often referred to as the Berkley Matriarchy (the contingent of female editors who joined Ace Books when Berkley Books was subsumed by Ace) were in complete control of the publishing house. The irony is in 1985 Ace was the #1 paperback house; today it's not even in the running.

"I'm just going to burn it!" Mike declared with great vehemence. "I'm getting ready to take my sloop on a trip around the world and I don't know when I'll be coming back." [I later learned from his son, Daniel, that this "trip around the world" was a common refrain in the Knerr household and Mike's big dream, but one he never fulfilled before his death.—jfc]

"Don't destroy it!" I pleaded. "What you've written is irreplaceable—part of history, Beam Piper's history. Don't burn it up. Instead, give a copy to Penn State [which has a small Piper collection in the Special Collections] or send me a photocopy. He growled and said, "I gotta go." That was the last time I ever talked with him.

At that time, Mike was living with a girlfriend, Mindy, on a houseboat in Sausalito and rarely—if ever—answered his telephone. I know, because I tried calling him numerous times over the next few months and never reached anyone—not even an answering machine.

So it was to great surprise when I went to my post office box in Granada Hills, California, a few months later, to find a large paper box, the size of a ream of paper. I was even more surprised when I saw the name M. Knerr as the sender.

I quickly opened the box: nestled inside was the complete manuscript titled "PIPER" by Michael Knerr! When my heartbeat slowed down, I leafed through the pages and could barely believe my eyes. Here was the complete final manuscript of Knerr's Piper biography—not a photocopy—and quite possibly the only existing copy! Mike had an earlier draft of the biography on the other side of the pages; like a lot of writers from the last century, he saved paper (he may have even learned this trick from Piper) by reusing the backs of previous drafts and/or discarded stories and novels.

That was the last time I ever heard from Michael Knerr despite numerous attempts to contact him.

The "Lost" Fuzzy novel came out to mixed acclaim. A few people thought *Fuzzies and Other People* was counterfeit Piper, some thought it was an early draft, but in the main Fuzzy fans were pleased. A number of reviewers and readers began referring to this version as an early draft—even Knerr believed that to be true. I always thought it was a submission copy, but there was no proof either way.

That is until 2008 when original manuscript collector, Tom Rogers, e-mailed me about a Heritage rare book and manuscript auction that included a carbon copy of H. Beam Piper's *Fuzzies and Other People*. He was very interested in bidding on it, but wanted my opinion. My advice was: "Go for it! At worst, it was the Mike Knerr carbon that he found in one of the Piper Trunks and thus of great historical value. At best, it was the "Lost" Fuzzy manuscript that Ken White was peddling shortly before his death.

The auction was several weeks away, and Tom promised to e-mail me as soon as the results came in. We were both excited about the possibility that he might *win* the auction; however, our enthusiasm was tempered by the fact that a lot of high-priced Lovecraft, Bradbury and other rare items were listed—which would bring out the "heavy" money. The good news was that the Fuzzy ms. was sandwiched in between a Lovecraft piece and a rare Doc Smith manuscript.

I was very interested in the carbon copy of the "Lost" Fuzzy novel because for once and for all it could settle the question of whether or not the Knerr carbon copy of *Fuzzies and Other People* was from the final manuscript, or an early draft. I already suspected it was from the final manuscript because when I used to use a typewriter I only used carbon paper for final drafts. It didn't make sense that Piper, who was chronically short of funds, would "waste" his money on carbon paper for the numerous (first, first draft, first second draft, etc.) early drafts of his novels and short stories. However, that was only a supposition; only the carbon itself might reveal the answer.

Tom Rogers called me two weeks later, right after the auction. The floor bid was quite high, about the limit of what he could afford, so it wouldn't take much to put him out of the running. However, it turned out Tom was the ONLY bidder for the Piper manuscript—amazing! Especially, when many of the Lovecraft and Arkham House items were selling in the mid-five figure range!

I asked Tom to contact me the minute the ms. arrived as I was very interested in any provenance, condition and whether it was an original carbon or photocopy.

If it was the carbon copy, then it was probably the Knerr "second sheets" that he had discovered in the Piper trunk. I remembered Mike telling me over the phone that he was sending Ace Xerox copies of the *Fuzzies and Other People* carbons, which was verified by Ace Book's flyer announcing the book. Knerr had told me that it was in an 8 1/2 by 11 paper box with the words "Second Sheets" on the top in Piper's hand. When Mike was cleaning out Beam's apartment, he had thought it contained random writings and threw it in the box. He was very familiar with Beam's writing habits, which included first, first draft, first second draft, first final draft, second final draft and so on and so forth.

At the time, I didn't much care what draft it was; I was just blown away that the bloody thing had literally jumped out of a box, so to speak. After all, the important thing was that the Lost Fuzzy novel was found: first, second or third draft, who cared? I could read it—at long last.

Mike also told me that one of the two trunks also contained Beam's miniature brass cannon and a lot of the knickknacks he kept on his desk and shelf. So I knew a lot about the trunks. When I talked on the phone with Daniel Knerr, Mike's son, in 2006 he was surprised at how much I knew about his father—more than he did. It was sad, but Mike left his family in Pennsylvania (for the second time; the first was in 1963) and moved permanently to California in the mid-1970s, when Dan was 11 or 12, and then reinvented himself. Dan knew nothing about his father's relationship with Beam Piper—didn't even know Piper's name. But he did know about those damn trunks! His father hauled them around from apartment to apartment after Beam's death, and he wouldn't let anyone look inside them or discuss what they contained.

They moved a lot as Mike went from job to job, but Dan remembered vividly that in one house they lived in his Dad had kept a "private room" in which he kept his keepsakes and the Piper trunks. He didn't know they were the Piper trunks, but he knew that his father promised a beating to any one of the boys who dared open it. Mike had a very gruff exterior and could be quite intimidating, but there was an aura of mystery about him and the trunks. Of course, that made them irresistible.

Being an intelligent and inquisitive lad, Dan thought a lot about getting into Mike's "private room." And, when he was alone and knew his father was going to be gone for a few hours, he broke into the room and picked the simple lock on the trunks. Inside were all kinds of fascinating items, including Piper's "eensy weensy brass cannon" and some kind of artillery-shell ashtray. Plus, all kinds of manuscript boxes and papers; all of no interest to young Dan.

One of the trunks is missing, but the surviving Piper trunk now resides in California with Mike's last wife, Bunny; she won't relinquish control of it despite Dan's and his brother Chris's requests. Dan is now very curious about the contents and promises to give me a look at anything he uncovers, assuming he can ever get his hands on the elusive last Piper trunk....

Naturally, knowing so much about the history of the Lost Fuzzy manuscript made me very curious as to the provenance of this carbon copy of *Fuzzies and Other People*."

On March 8th, 2008, Tom Rogers e-mailed me the following:

Well, my insanity seems to know no bounds. Despite several arguments to the contrary, almost all financial, I bit the bullet and wound up bidding on the Fuzzies and Other People *manuscript that was auctioned by Heritage Auctions 2 weeks ago. No one else placed a bid. The manuscript arrived in my mail yesterday.*

I was wondering if you could shed any light on what Mike Knerr actually found in the trunk, i.e. was there more than one copy of the manuscript found? The one I purchased has Beam's handwritten corrections throughout, and the editing marks appear to be identical to those on the other manuscripts I have collected. It is a carbon copy typescript, so there had to be at least one other copy produced (the top ribbon copy). All I know is that Knerr found it in an unmarked box at the bottom of the trunk he had, and that it had been overlooked for years because of this. I also know that you were one of the first people to see it after its rediscovery.

I would love to put a little background note into the file to go along with the manuscript, as I have done with the others. If it isn't too much trouble, could you help me with this? Tom Rogers

I immediately phoned Tom and we discussed the "Lost" Fuzzy manuscript, which he claimed was in very good condition for a carbon copy some 55 years old. I asked him to do a quick comparison analysis of the ms. against the published version of *Fuzzies and Other People*. (I remember talking with Beth Meacham, the Ace Editor who negotiated with Mike, and she mentioned that it was complete, but an early draft.) Over the phone, Tom compared the text in five or six places with the published text; in all cases, they read identically. I was certain that somehow he'd obtained Knerr's trunk copy; however, I knew that Penn State had two photocopies of the Knerr Fuzzy manuscript. I wanted to check this new discovery against the Penn State copies, so I told Tom, to photocopy and send me a dozen or so copies of the carbon copies, especially those pages where there were obvious hand corrections by Piper.

Tom's letter reads:

> *Here are a few pages from the Fuzzy ms.*
> Page 65 has the reference to the end of the Terran Federation.
> The copies are not nearly as legible as the original.
> All edit marks/crossouts are in red on the ms.—all underlined words are in black ink (no carbon impressions).
> The drawing on page 15 is in black ink (not carbon impression).
>
> Thanks
> Tom

> *P.S. Note: Page 82 does not exist—The ms. goes from page 81 to 83. At the top of page 83 is written (in red ink in Beam's handwriting), "page 82 is omitted."*
>
> *There is also page 166 and 166A (this gets the pagination back on track).*

I compared the manuscript corrections to several of the Piper manuscripts in my possession: the corrections were obviously in Beam's hand. I next contacted my good friend Dennis Frank, who is a knowledgeable Piper scholar and the Archivist at St. Bonaventure University, which contains the John F. Carr Archives and a number of Piper documents I have donated. I told Dennis that it would be great fun to go to Penn State archives together, and that between the two of us we could authenticate Tom's newly discovered manuscript. Dennis was as thrilled as I was about the possibility of nailing down the manuscript's provenance and agreed to come down to State College as soon as his schedule allowed.

It took a couple of weeks before we settled on a date. Dennis arrived at 10:00 A.M. sharp and we drove over to Penn State. It turned out that our timing couldn't have been better! We arrived at Pattee Library to learn they were scheduled to move the Piper Collection off-site the next day. The Curator, Sandra Stelts, chided us for not contacting them earlier, but I explained we had made our plans at the last minute.

"Well, you're very lucky then!" she snapped.

Dennis and I took seats and played literary detectives: we compared the photocopies of Tom's newly discovered ms. against the photocopied manuscript of *Fuzzies and Other People* in the archive's Piper files. At first, it appeared they were identical. All the strikeouts were the same—as if from a ruler. Immediately, we were able to establish that this carbon was from the same draft that Mike Knerr had provided Ace Books over 30 years before. The next question: was it the same manuscript?

That was more difficult to determine: the first anomaly appeared on page 3. The hand corrections were different: in the Knerr ms. only the s was inserted in sapien (s) on line ten, while there was a ^ with the s on top on the Rogers ms. My blood pressure shot up and Dennis got a big smile; we were onto something.

We found two different penciled-in corrections on page 14. Things were suddenly getting a lot more interesting! Especially with page 15, which contained a hand-inked drawing by Beam of a bullet cartridge two-thirds of the way down the page. (See page 12 of the *Fuzzies and Other People* book.) The hand-drawn case heads are different. The Knerr page shows a much larger primer pocket with a dot in the center, plus there are carbon striations running a third of the way down to the bottom on the Knerr carbons, which do not appear on the Rogers ms. It was hard to keep quiet in a library, but we managed. Our excitement was growing....

Maybe we had the final submission copy in our hands, the very one Ken White had sent to various editors!

The conclusive evidence came on page 166, the new page with a strike of the 5 and the added 6. On the Knerr ms. the entire number 165 was crossed off and 166 was written over it. There were also vastly different strikeout lines in paragraph 3 for both manuscripts! We found more evidence on the following page, enough to convince even the toughest jury.

The bottom line: the newly discovered Rogers' manuscript was one of the "Lost" Fuzzy carbon copies. My guess is that Beam sent Ken White (his agent) two copies for submission. The Knerr trunk carbon being a "safety copy," for use if and when the original typescript ms. was too shopworn to be mailed as a submission copy to the publishing houses.

For this Fuzzy ms. to turn up now was bizarre and unexpected. It was our good fortune that a noted Piper collector and enthusiast discovered and purchased the manuscript. For Dennis and me, it was a fun day of literary detection.

But the story wasn't over! On September 15th, 2008, I got the following e-mail from Tom Rogers:

Dear John,

On the Piper front, there have been some very, very big developments. I am not quite sure where to begin, so I'll just spill it out. I have just come into possession of the Knerr copy of Fuzzies and Other People *as well as Beam's personal copy of Dillin's* [book] The Kentucky Rifle.

The Kentucky Rifle *has numerous notations throughout in Beam's cursive handwriting—and at least one comment by "MEK" (Michael E. Knerr) that calls a Piper notation "Horseshit!" The book is signed by Beam as his own personal copy in 1929, and specifically refers to a page about the Covenhoven rifle mentioned on page 36 of your biography in a letter from Beam to Ferd. Included with the book are a printer-copy of an article from a Williamsport newspaper of recent vintage about Piper, and an original article about Capt. Dillin from about the late 1920's.*

The Fuzzies and Other People *ms. is complete and foliated. It is the same, but not the same, as the other copy I have. The kicker: it's in the original damn box Knerr found it in! The box has three notations on it: (1) "Blues + Pen"; (2) "Partially Finished Books"; and (3) "Thy Hapless Sons," all in Beam's handwriting. Included with all of this is a copy of a page from an auction catalogue from 1983 which shows that a number of Piper manuscripts were auctioned in 1983, including the* Fuzzies and other People *ms. (which is mentioned as being about to be published in 1984 by Ace) as well as "Oomphel in the Sky," "The Other Road (!)," "A Slave is a Slave," "Gunpowder God," "Down Styphon," "Hos-Hostigos" and "Lord Kalvan!"*

Several of the manuscripts appear to have had a notation of "MK II" on them according to the catalogue. Mike Knerr, perhaps? There are notations on the ms. that would seem to indicate that my copy of "Oomphel in the Sky" might have originated from the same auction. I will have to examine all of my mss. more carefully, but I am beginning to smell something.

I can't tell if there were any more mss. auctioned that day, or if The Kentucky Rifle *was part of the same auction, but several ideas occur to me—Mike Knerr took a lot more from the apartment than he ever admitted; that the "Trunk" was probably emptied and its literary contents sold over 25 years ago; and Piper didn't burn his ms. library (or at least not a significant portion of it) on the night of his death!*

I am currently trying to see if I can trace the provenance of both items back further. I'll let you know what I find. There is a lot more, but I think that will suffice for any questions you might have.

Man! What the hell did go on back then? Is everything about Piper an enigma wrapped in a mystery?

Best,
Tom

This e-mail came as quite a shock! It appeared that Mike Knerr actually sold many of his Piper "treasures" back in 1983. From talking with Mike, as well as the content of his letters, this was a development I never foresaw. To my mind, the original "Lost" Fuzzy manuscript was still in one of the famous trunks.

Recently, I've been in contact with Monty M., an old friend of Mike's and one of the members of the Williamsport Creative Writers' Forum in the early 60s when H. Beam Piper was a member. He was never close to Beam, but he had some rather startling things to say about his old friend, Mike Knerr. It seems that Michael was as big a bullshitter as Beam Piper.

Here's what Monty, in a May 19th, 2008 letter, had to say about the Mike Knerr:

...Like many of us, Mike had some character flaws that defined him, but only if you knew him well. Like I said earlier, he was a big time bullshitter.... I never in my entire life saw or heard him yell at someone or ever get into a fistfight. Mike wasn't that kind at least not before the aneurysm. His temperament changed a little then. On the phone, however, he was one of the characters in his books. Threatening and to the point, but I guess you know that. Mike often mixed himself up with his characters, depending on the situation he was in.

Mike did not have a whole lot of loyalty in him. I'm not going to go into that a great deal. On a personal experience he abandoned me in favor of someone else—several times. He was also attracted to women he shouldn't have been. He left his wife and only son to go to California to write those sleaze novels around '61, off of which he couldn't make a living.

There's much more, a lot of it about Knerr's failure to sell his novels and non-fiction Colonial books. It's apparent that Mike was a bit of a gypsy, and liked to live on the fly. I suspect he auctioned off the Piper manuscripts to supplement his meager finances. However, he did it under the table and until Tom "discovered" the Knerr Lost Fuzzy novel. Such a deception wouldn't be possible now in the Internet Age, where most book auctions are online.

On September 17th, 2008, I received the following e-mail from Tom Rogers:

Dear John:

Well, one theory has apparently bitten the dust.
I have received fairly reliable information that The Kentucky Rifle book was part of a recent estate sale in Williamsport. The items supposedly came from an estate in Lock Haven. It all makes sense and seems probable. Also, there is a commercial insert from 1972 laid in about rifles which makes me think the book was held by a firearms enthusiast since at least the late 60's/early 70's. So, this book was probably not in the Trunk(s) and probably not kept by Mike Knerr, probably....
Got some more feelers out there and will keep you informed of my progress.
Tom

My reply was as follows:

Hi Tom,
Hmmm... Very interesting, however, how did Mike Knerr's "bullshit!" entry appear? I can't see him marking up the book while Beam was alive.

I don't know if I ever wrote it, but Mike was born in Williamsport and worked numerous places throughout the area. Also, Mike was a firearms enthusiast himself...

He might have given it to a family member, or close friend.

John F. Carr

From Mike's own comments I knew that one of the Piper trunks had been cached in Lock Haven so it's quite possible he gave or sold Beam's copy of *The Kentucky Rifle* to a flintlock enthusiast or friend.

From all the available evidence it is now clear that the published version of *Fuzzies and Other People* was the definitive version, not a first or second draft. The first photocopiers did not arrive until 1959 and were mostly for commercial use. Before then, writers were forced to use carbons, or face losing their work if the original manuscript was damaged during submission or by coffee spills. Beam was not one to make multiple carbon copies of drafts; for one thing—talking from experience—it's a pain in the ass to keep the pages/carbons from shifting and getting jammed in the platen. For another, Piper couldn't afford the paper costs. Reams of paper in the 1950s and early 1960s were $5.00 or more, far more expensive than they are today—according to the Inflation Calculator, $5.00 in 1958 is now the equivalent of $40.43 in 2015. In the Piper diaries, Beam frets about running low on paper and how expensive it is.

Therefore, the two existing carbon copies of *Fuzzies and Other People* conclusively prove that the published version is the final draft and the one Ken White submitted for publication.

APPENDIX VII

The Continuing Worlds of H. Beam Piper

THE CONTINUING WORLDS OF H. BEAM PIPER

H. Beam Piper published only five Paratime stories, and none after 1955 until "Gunpowder God." Some Piper reviewers have speculated that he 'discarded' the series, but in his diaries he writes about a possible idea for a Paratime story in the late 1950s, although no additional Paratime stories were mentioned in the dairies until the first Kalvan story in 1964. In retrospect, considering the state of Piper's finances and the difficulties he had in selling his work, it was probably a mistake for him not to capitalize on the Paratime Series, which was popular both with *Astounding Science Fiction* editor, John W. Campbell, and his magazine readership. Piper, however, was a rugged individualist and never took the easier road.

Due to H. Beam Piper's suicide and the confusion afterwards regarding who owned the rights to his literary estate, Piper's novels and short stories fell out-of-print, after his final novel, *Lord Kalvan of Otherwhen*, was published in 1965 by Ace Books. It didn't help that Piper's straightforward story writing-style and traditional narrative structure went out of fashion during most of the 1960s and early '70s, when the "New Wave" of Science Fiction reached its peak.

Piper's novels and short stories languished out-of-print for nearly a decade, and the Piper paperback books, *Little Fuzzy*, *Space Viking* and *Lord Kalvan of Otherwhen* were only available at collector's bookstores at "rare" book prices. This would change in the late 1970s as interest in the science fiction backlist and Piper in particular began to build. Jerry Pournelle,

Bill Tuning, Marty Massoglia and Frank Gasperik were among a number of prominent writers and fans who were talking up Piper at science fiction conventions and encouraging publishers to look into purchasing the Piper estate with the purpose of publishing his long out-of-print novels and short stories.

Piper was always very concerned with his literary legacy, even before his first story was published. He was also a very private individual who frequently changed and re-wrote his sparse biography. As a boy, John McGuire, Jr. recounted how he used to watch in fascination as Beam and his father, the late John J. McGuire, would get drunk and burn rejected manuscripts. "They would dance like wild Indians around the barrel-sized ashcan in the backyard, after their stories had made one too many rounds of the New York based science fiction magazines."

In a phone conversation, Mike Knerr told me that when he went to clean up Beam's apartment, the fireplace was full of ashes and partially burned paper. He used to visit Beam a lot before his marriage and they both would discuss works in progress. A number of Piper's manuscripts that he personally was aware of, including his historical novel "Only the Arquebus" and the "Lost" manuscript of *Fuzzies and Other People* (although, he found the "Lost" ms. a year later upon closer examination), never turned up when he sorted through Beam's personal effects.

In the decade following Beam's death, Mike Knerr speculates, in his unpublished manuscript "PIPER," that the trunk of manuscripts that he presented to the "estate" lawyer were probably thrown out. No lawyer, unless a 'close' friend of the deceased, will store "worthless" items for a long period of time. Fred Ramsey, in a March 30th, 2001, e-mail Fred provides a more recent look into what befell the Piper estate:

> As to the Piper estate issues, I tried to get info in Williamsport, but much of the paperwork was damaged in the great flood of 1972. The probate judge was long dead and Piper's fourth cousin's granddaughter was the only family member I could actually find. She never knew Beam. Her grandfather, whom I think was the beneficiary, or one of the beneficiaries of the estate, passed away in the mid-80s. I finally hired a local estate attorney to look over the

known facts and asked him to give me the most logical legal outcome and reasons for that outcome.

The attorney thought that it was basically a fairly simple estate complicated by the lack of close relatives and the shambles in Ken White's life. He thought that it wasn't till Ace began looking for the estate owner to purchase the rights that anyone cared enough to finish the probate.

Piper's ex-wife's only comment, when given the news of Beam's death via the telephone, was "Let the guns bury him!" Betty had no interest in his literary estate. Charles Piper, a cousin, was Beam's closest living relative. He and Beam did keep in sporadic contact as evidenced in the diaries; in fact, he's the only relative mentioned after the death of Harriet Piper. Charles Piper was also the only member of the family who attended Beam's funeral.

However, there's no evidence that Charles or any other member of the family made any attempt to preserve Beam's literary legacy. During the decades following his death, almost all of Piper's unpublished short stories and novels (a large number of which are mentioned in his diaries and letters to his best friend, Ferd Coleman) were lost or destroyed forever.

* * *

In 1977, Jim Baen, Editor-in-Chief of *Galaxy SF Magazine*, left the magazine for the position of vice-president of Ace Books. Jim had worked closely with Jerry Pournelle, who was the science columnist at *Galaxy*, and thanks to Pournelle was familiar with H. Beam Piper's literary legacy. After Jim left *Galaxy*, one of his first acts as the new vice-president was to locate and purchase the literary estate of the late H. Beam Piper. What Jim purchased as Piper's 'literary estate' was a disorganized mess containing a few old science fiction pulp magazines, Ace and Avon paperbacks and a few surviving manuscripts.... Tragically, the majority of Beam's unpublished works were destroyed either in earlier ashcan fires, or in Beam's Williamsport apartment fireplace before his death.

Once Ace Books had purchased the "rights" to the Piper estate in 1978, Jim Baen quickly learned that most of Piper's magazine short stories and novellas were missing from the "estate." When Jim Baen asked Jerry if he knew anyone who had copies of Piper's published works, Jerry informed him that *I* had copies of all of Piper's published works including rarities such as "Dearest" (*Weird Tales*) and "Flight From Tomorrow" (*Future Science Fiction*). Jim called me and I provided him with photocopies of Piper's magazine stories.

In the course of going over the surviving manuscripts from Charles Piper, Jim Baen discovered two unpublished H. Piper works "When in the Course..." and the short novel, *Full Cycle*. Of course, at the time I knew nothing about these unpublished stories. To set the scene: Studio City, Los Angeles, in late March of 1979 Jerry was working in his newly constructed second floor office and Great Hall, which was filled with beautiful bookshelves constructed by a pair of Hollywood set designers to mimic the library in the movie *My Fair Lady*. Jerry's office, computer workroom and Great Hall occupied almost 2000 feet of the upstairs addition.

I sat at a big desk at the bottom of the stairs in Jerry's former office, lined with bookshelves filled to the bursting with SF books and magazines, including a run of *Astounding/Analog Science Fiction* issues from the early 1940's to the present. To this day I can remember Jerry bounding down the wide stairway with a package of manuscripts. "John," he boomed, "You will not believe what just came in from Baen—two unpublished Piper manuscripts! I want you to read them and give me your opinion on whether or not they're publishable."

My pulse raced—I would be one of the first editors since the early 1960's to read unpublished H. Beam Piper stories!

I quickly read the shorter of the two, "When in the Course...," which I promptly identified as taking place in Piper's Hostigos. I was startled to discover this story was also the origin of the Kalvan stories—only without Kalvan! Several of the early Hostigos scenes that take place in "When in the Course..." are almost identical to those which turn up later in "Gunpowder God," the first Kalvan novelette, even down to the character names such as Rylla, Ptosphes, Harmakros and Chartiphon.

It wasn't until a few pages later that I realized this story was set in

Piper's Terro-Human Future History with a different hero, Roger Barron, a member of an interstellar exploration outfit, Stellar Explorations. The plot of "When in the Course..." concerns an interstellar discovery ship that's been searching for a habitable planet and its crew is about at the end of their string of luck. They arrive only to find another sentient humanoid race. To be able to colonize the planet, they have to come to some accommodation with the natives and pick the outlying small princedom of Hostigos as their contact point. "When in the Course..." covers a lot more ground time-wise than the three Kalvan novellas, and it is not without serious flaws. But interesting as Hell, for all that!

On the other hand, the other manuscript of *Full Cycle* was a disappointing parable of the Cold War with two alien races standing in for Americans and Russians. It was definitely a work of the early 1950's (there is convincing evidence that this novel was written as a fourth Twayne Triplet, but never published when that press folded); and flawed at that. My recommendation to Ace Books was that it not be published. I was very disappointed when Ace Books released it anyway under Jim's successor.

"When in the Course..." is an intriguing piece of work for Piper and Kalvan fans. The opening war council scene in Hostigos was almost lifted verbatim from "When in the Course..." and put into "Gunpowder God." The primary conflict of both stories is the small princedom of Hostigos versus the Goliath of Styphon's House which controls the production of gunpowder, or "fireseed" as they call it. Only on Freya the weather is better and on this "smaller continent" there are only three Kingdoms (not five), Hos-Harphax, Hos-Rathon and Hos-Bletha.

The biggest difference in regards to the plot between the two stories is that in "When in the Course..." the protagonist, Roger Barron, brings the full might of a Federation space ship against the pike and shot armies of Styphon. This quickly finishes off any conflict between Hostigos and Styphon's House, although there is some *business* about the ship being low on ammunition just to keep the story moving. Piper realized the story was lagging about midway through "When in the Course..." and attempts to create dramatic tension out of the question of whether Federation non-interference rules make helping the Freyans illegal under Federation law.

In contrast to *Lord Kalvan of Otherwhen*, Styphon's House in "When in the Course…" turns out to be a paper tiger and the fireseed secret, once disseminated throughout the continent, results in a complete rejection of this heinous religious theocracy. Despite the pat ending, there are some excellent characters and dramatic scenes; "When in the Course…" is a flawed but, still, above average (for the time) science-fiction story; although, it is clearly a lesser Piper work.

"When in the Course…" proved unsaleable for several good reasons. The Freyan natives turn out to be not only humanoid, but also interfertile with humans. (This is what the title refers to: "when, in the course of human events, a couple of humans of different sexes get married—") Parallel evolution was not an unusual concept in the 1930s and 1940s, but highly suspect by late 1950s and early 1960s. Piper often used the Martian origin of humanity idea in both the Paratime stories and the Terro-Human Federation series, but there's no mention of the Ancient Martians in "When in the Course…" However, the Terrans and Freyans might well be of Martian stock, which would explain their inter-species fertility, or even the product of alien seed ships, another popular convention for explaining parallel evolution. Near the end of the story, Piper does offer an explanation of convergent evolution, but it's hardly convincing—even to his own characters!

I was able to include it among the stories in *Federation*—the first collection of H. Beam Piper stories I edited for Ace Books. Despite the story's flaws, it was quite a coup to be able to publish a "new" Piper short story, made even more so by the fact that it is the *origin* story of the Kalvan stories.

The major plot problem is that the story conflict is minimized; the villain (Styphon's House) remains mostly faceless and is quickly neutralized, leaving the plot to wrap up both too neatly and too quickly. The idea behind Styphon's House, the sinister theocracy of both "When in the Course…" and *Lord Kalvan of Otherwhen*, is a very good one: only the highpriests of Styphon's House know the formula for gunpowder, which they call the Fireseed Mystery. The Temple's fireseed monopoly puts them in the empire-building business; if you want to defeat your enemies, do as we say or we'll give your enemies fireseed and cut you off. "If you don't like that, put it in your pipe and smoke it!"

The Styphon's House cast of characters would have been right at home in Renaissance Italy for all the high church politics and dirty dealings—Machiavelli would have recognized this lot!

In "PIPER," Mike Knerr mentions an incident which he believes may have been the genesis of Styphon's House: "When he (Piper) taught me about black powder, I started reading about it and told him that I'd found that when it was moistened into cakes (in the old days) they used urine. According to the book, the urine of a wine drinker was good, but that of a priest was considered best. 'Yes,' Beam retorted, laughing, 'and I'll bet they made a tidy profit from it!'"

Piper often re-used the better elements of his unsold stories and in this case he took out the Hostigos of "When in the Course…" transplanting it into the Paratime series as a small princedom in the Great Kingdom of Hos-Harphax on Forth Level, Europo-American, Aryan-Transpacific.

As Campbell noted, the major problems with "When in the Course" are its meandering plotline, numerous subplots that for the most part go nowhere and a flat resolution that solves the problem in far too simple a manner, robbing the reader of satisfaction. Yet, there are some good characters: Rylla, Ptosphes and Harmakros make their first appearance and the gunpowder theocracy of Styphon's House is introduced. It's actually fortuitous that *Fantastic Universe*, *Amazing Stories* or some other 1960s' salvage market didn't pick up the story, preventing Beam from reinventing it as "Gunpowder God"—the first of the Lord Kalvan novelettes he wrote.

It was Jim Baen who came up with the titles for the first three Piper collections: *Federation*, *Paratime* and *Empire*. Originally, he tried to negotiate with Jerry Pournelle (whose career, at the time, was hot as a pistol due to the bestseller status of *The Mote in God's Eye*, *Lucifer's Hammer* and *Oath of Fealty*) to edit the Piper collections, update the technology, as well as remove the smoking references, etc. (like Baen did with the Chris Anvil books some twenty years later) and write story introductions. The deal floundered when Jerry demanded a royalty percentage; the higher-ups at Ace balked and as a result the deal died.

Before Jim was able to put the Piper collections together, he left Ace Books in 1980 to become Vice-President and Editor of Tor Books under Tom Doherty. Jim, who was known for writing up contacts on the back of luncheon receipts, left a mess of disorganized and missing paperwork behind him when he left Ace Books. Unfortunately for Ace, the Piper photocopies of the Piper stories that I had sent to Jim also disappeared.

When Ace Editor, Beth Meacham contacted Jerry about replacing the missing stories, he told her that I was the one who had provided the Piper stories for Jim. Beth called me and asked for the copies. She offered to pay me for the photocopies, but I told her I would give them to her, but only if I was able to put the collections together. After a year and a half of reading and researching Piper's works, I believed Beam's work had to be treated with respect and that Ace (in the typical slipshod Ace manner) would screw the collections up, having some junior editor assembling them by Ouija Board or 52-pickup.

I sent her a copy of the essay, "The Terro-Human Future History," that I had just written for *The Bulletin of the Science Writers of America* Special Issue on "Science-Fiction Future Histories." We later came to terms and I sent her photocopies of the missing stories; unfortunately, I wasn't given editorial credit, but I believed then (and still do) that the most important thing was putting the books out correctly by someone familiar with Piper's future history and overall writings. The Ace editorial team retained Jim's original titles, but wanted the introductions yesterday. I quickly put together the stories and wrote up the *Federation* book and story introductions. Ace was so pleased with the results that they put *Federation* out as a trade paperback with a smashing cover by Michael Whelan. Whelan was the artist who had already done the covers for the new Ace Piper novels; they were quite arresting and made quite a stir in science-fiction circles, especially the Fuzzy covers. The book sold very well and made Ace a lot of money.

Almost immediately Ace Books wanted the introductions to *Paratime* and *Empire*. I did those over the next six months and Ace put them out quickly to take advantage of the Piper revival. After I finished them, as payback, Beth Meacham called me and asked me if I wanted to do a sequel to the Fuzzy novels. I told her I was more interested in a *Lord Kalvan of Otherwhen* sequel, but that William Tuning was a big Piper fan (they had even met at a few east-coast conventions) and would do a good job.

Later, Ace contacted Bill and he wrote the Fuzzy sequel, *Fuzzy Bones* and it was released in 1981. It was quite good (he had a lot of help from Robert A. Heinlein who did a major edit on the first draft) and it was by far the best thing Bill ever wrote. Unfortunately, Bill died in 1982 before completing the sequel, *Captain Fuzzy*. Of course, none of us knew at the time that the "Lost" Fuzzy novel would ever turn up.

* * *

"Lord Kalvan of Otherwhen" had long been one of my favorite novels and, as a Renaissance warfare buff, I enjoyed the realistic battles and Piper's military expertise. It's also one of the best adventure stories ever written, with great action scenes, suspense, romance and a hero for all ages. It only has one problem; the story is incomplete. There's no resolution. While re-reading it for the fourth or fifth time, I came up with an idea for a sequel based on a Styphon's House counter-reformation. I shared my ideas with Jerry Pournelle and he liked them. However, Jerry was in the middle of a new novel with Larry Niven and suggested I get together with Roland Green.

They had just finished their collaborative novel: *Janissaries: Clan and Crown*, a novel heavily influenced by Piper and *Lord Kalvan of Otherwhen*. By a strange coincidence, or synchronicity (your call), Roland, another military science-fiction writer, had also just talked with Jerry about co-authoring a *Lord Kalvan of Otherwhen* sequel. Jerry brought the two of us together and wisely got out of the way.

Next, we contacted Ace Books, who were still reveling in the success of Bill Tuning's *Fuzzy Bones*; they gave us an enthusiastic thumbs-up on the Kalvan sequel with a decent advance. Ace was pleased with Roland's contributions to the second Janissaries book and Ace had made a lot of money with the four Piper short story collections I had edited for them. Roland and I had never met in person, but we found an immediate rapport over the phone on matters Kalvan and Hostigos. Roland flew out to Los Angeles in early 1984 and stayed in our Chatsworth home for about two weeks, while we hammered out the plot and worked out the background for *Great Kings' War*. The plot outline of the book turned out to be more ambitious than we originally thought, so we divided it into three parts, covering the three years following *Lord Kalvan of Otherwhen*.

We saw lots of possibilities for the sequel, but all would come to naught if Styphon's House proved to be the paper tiger it was in "When In The Course..." Our first job was to stiffen the spine of Styphon's House, which was reeling from Kalvan's initial military success in Hos-Harphax. We put some iron in the Inner Circle by bringing the Machiavellian Archpriest Anaxthenes and the Savonarola of Styphon's House, Archpriest Roxthar, as well as creating the Order of Zarthani Knights (The Teutonic Knights of Aryan-Transpacific) as a counter-balance to Hos-Hostigos' growing military and political power.

To see how well we worked together as a team, Roland and I wrote the ending of our three part novel first. Writing the ending first is an old writer's trick, because it allows the author, as he writes the book, to tie up the plot line very tightly. Often times, endings are the most difficult part of the story to pull off, thus, knowing the tough part is already finished can be very liberating.

Our initial idea was to open *Great Kings' War* about a year after *Lord Kalvan of Otherwhen*. After Roland left to return home to Chicago, for the next month we brainstormed ideas over the phone concerning the period of time between *Lord Kalvan of Otherwhen* and the opening of our proposed sequel. The back story we came up with was so interesting that we decided to open the novel with it. As a result, *Great Kings' War* starts only a few months after *Lord Kalvan of Otherwhen*.

We began writing the book by alternating between different chapters. Later, I started writing the first draft on all the new Styphon's House characters and the mercenary, Captain Phidestros. The writing went very well, maybe too well! About four months into the novel and some four hundred pages later, it dawned on us that we were less than a third of the way through our original plot outline! After a few telephone conversations, we concluded that we'd better bring the book to a swift conclusion, or we were going to have a book the size of *Lord of the Rings*, as well as a very ticked-off publisher. In the mid-1980's a paperback over four hundred pages had to be printed on a special and more costly press and this was not done lightly, certainly not because the authors decided the book should be double the length of the contracted novel!

Since we were having a lot of fun writing *Great Kings' War* together and had already planned to do five or six follow-up novels, we ended the book just where the first third of our outline came to an end, and then: Voila!, Part One ended up becoming *Great Kings' War*, book two of the Kalvan Saga.

The book was written in high spirits with lots of long-distance calls between Chicago and Southern California. For both of us, collaborating on the sequel to one of our all-time favorite novels, was a whale of a good time and one we hoped to repeat soon. After reading the galley proofs science fiction luminary, Andre Norton, asked us when we were going to write the sequel. The initial success of the paperback (it reached #1 on the *Locus* Paperback Bestseller List) boded well for future books. The first edition sales were very good for a paperback original.

Roland's career, meanwhile, went white hot and was suddenly doing a series for Tor Books and two series for Ace Books, Peace Company and Star Cruiser Shenandoah. Since the agent representing us was Roland's agent, she was much more concerned about pushing Roland's solo efforts than our collaboration. She saw this as make it or break it time for Roland's career as an SF writer. She was right, but in retrospect she may not have given him the best career advice...since both of the other series eventually tanked.

Meanwhile, I was chomping at the bit to get back to work on the next Kalvan book, which we had tentatively titled *Gunpowder God*. So while Roland's agent kept putting obstacles, i.e. higher priority Roland Green books in the way, I went ahead and began writing the sequel myself in 1986.

At that time, Jerry Pournelle and I were editing a number of successful anthology series, including *Imperial Stars*, *The Endless Frontier*, *There*

Will Be War and *War World*, an original shared-world anthology that takes place in Jerry Pournelle's CoDominium/Empire of Man future history.

I was also Treasurer and Vice President of the Science Fiction Writers of America so it was a busy time for me as well. It was also an exuberant time for things related to Kalvan and Aryan-Transpacific, Styphon's House Subsector. I was corresponding with a number of Kalvan and Piper fans who had written to me after the publication of the book. This group featured Jim Landau and the then fledgling SF writers Harry Turtledove and S.M. Stirling, both big Kalvan fans. Ideas, theories and research on Sixteenth Century military warfare, Aryan-Transpacific geographical boundaries, Aryan migrations, Home Time-Line politics, Styphon's House revival and all sorts of things flew back and forth across the continent via snail mail. In the midst of this flurry of activity and research, I worked on the sequel until I finally brought it to a conclusion in 1988.

I found myself with a complete first draft of *Gunpowder God* that ran over 700 pages and a collaborator who didn't have the time to read what I'd written, much less do a final draft. That's where the *Great Kings' War* sequel stayed until finally, at my insistence, Roland's agent approached Ace Books in 1988 about a contract for the sequel. Ace sat on it for a few months, until pressured, whereupon Ace's chief editor said they were no longer interested in doing the book!

I still believe that had we presented the outline and first three chapters to Ace Books a few months after *Great Kings' War* was published, Ace would have jumped on *Gunpowder God* and it would have sold well enough to establish the Kalvan Saga for good. But this was not to be. Ace books had been bought up by Putnam's and their editorial direction had changed; they were no longer interested in science fiction adventure novels with heroic characters and strong male protagonists.

I suspect it's no surprise that Ace Books, at that time the number one paperback publisher of science fiction (according to *Locus Magazine*), is now near the bottom of the list.

Our agent did do us one big favor; after Ace rejected *Gunpowder God*, she asked Ace Books for the revision of rights to *Great Kings' War*, since Ace was clearly no longer interested in the Kalvan series. Without protest—at the time Roland's agent was Mr. Heinlein's agent and had mojo clout—Ace reverted the rights to us; the rights to an "orphan series" (since they still owned *Lord Kalvan of Otherwhen*). Because of this, no other publisher has wanted to touch the series unless we could guarantee that Ace would "allow" them to re-print the original Kalvan novel, which wasn't likely to happen unless they paid Ace Books some Big Bucks.

After *Fuzzies and Other People* (the Lost Fuzzy novel) was published, Ace quietly let most of Piper's backlist fall out-of-print, including *Space Viking*, *The Cosmic Computer* and *Lord Kalvan of Otherwhen*. The Fuzzy books were still available, in an omnibus edition, but the rest of Piper's canon was relegated to the dustbin.

Meanwhile I was able to publish a portion of *Gunpowder God* in *There Will Be War: Volume VIII, Armageddon* under the title, "Siege at Tarr-Hostigos." A while later, author Bob Adams, a big Kalvan fan, asked me to excerpt another portion of the unpublished Kalvan novel for the alternate-worlds science-fiction anthology *Alternatives* he was editing. I expanded the role of Ranjar Sargos and Great Master Soton and the story was published in *Alternatives* under the title "Kalvan Kingmaker."

Over the years I thought about having a small press put out a limited edition version of the book, but nothing ever came of it. I continued to get letters from Kalvan fans and kept up my correspondence with Jim Landau about future Kalvan books. Every time I visited A&M Book Cellars, Marty Massoglia would ask me when *Gunpowder God* was coming out? I even talked with several editors I knew about re-releasing *Great Kings' War* and the sequel, but they weren't interested in buying and promoting an orphaned series. Without clear title to *Lord Kalvan of Otherwhen* no major publishing house or specialty press was going to touch the Kalvan series.

When I went on the web to see if there were any Piper sites, the first place I visited was David Johnson's website, www.Zarthani.com, a tribute site to H. Beam Piper and his great stories. We started to exchange e-mails and David convinced me to join the Piper List, which put me in touch with some wonderful Piper fans and readers.

For over a decade Marty Massoglia had tried to talk me into reprinting *Great Kings' War*, and then, if it was successful, publish the sequels. When old paperback copies of *Great Kings' War* in good condition were selling for $40.00 and more in the late 1990s, Marty was convinced that he could sell a hardcover version for twice that amount. I wasn't interested, at that point, in reprinting *Great Kings' War* since it was still available—even though it was outrageously overpriced for an out-of-print paperback.

The series stayed dormant until early 1999, when I decided that I was either going to publish the books myself, or let the series die. If I was going to do them, I was going to do them right. Rather than re-publish *Great Kings' War* as my first release, I decided to return to the already written sequel and go forward, not backward and try to put *Gunpowder God* into print. Once I began the rewrite, which included scanning the manuscript and converting it into readable text, I noticed the story was already beginning to grow, as I added new scenes and even chapters. I soon realized that if I didn't do something quick, the book would soon rival *Dune* in length.

So, I went back to the original outline and discovered that my sequel included both the second and third parts of the plot outline as originally conceived. Voila!, problem solved. I cut the book in half and decided it needed a new title. Since the manuscript of "Gunpowder God," included the novella, "Kalvan Kingmaker," I decided *Kalvan Kingmaker* would be the title, (which was a nod to Beam since the original title of the Kalvan novelette "Down Styphon!" had been "Kalvan Kingmaker"). With the title problem solved, I broke the book into two halves, and *Kalvan Kingmaker* practically wrote itself. I had a hell of a good time writing this book! Not only was it fun to write, but the expansion allowed me to more fully develop the First Level plot, expand the battle scenes, and provide more about detail on life in Aryan-Transpacific. The final manuscript came in at around 584 pages. Pequod Press published a limited edition of 1,000 copies of *Kalvan Kingmaker* in 2001. A corrected 2nd edition with new maps was published by Pequod in January of 2010 after the 1st edition sold out.

Over the next two years I rewrote and fleshed out the second half of the unpublished sequel, and it was published in 2004 under the title

Siege of Tarr-Hostigos. My plan was to keep publishing a new volume every three or four years—so that I wouldn't get burned out—until I finished the entire Kalvan Saga. I took a step back in 2006 to do a major rewrite of *Great Kings' War*, adding almost 60,000 new words and fixing some long-standing continuity issues. Also I wanted to add some new maps and had Alan Gutierrez, who did the original cover and has since created the cover art for all the sequels, do several including a color map of Hostigos Town. The 2nd edition of *Great Kings' War* was published in 2006 by Pequod Press.

Fireseed Wars was the next volume, appearing in 2009. This book begins right after the final scene in *Siege of Tarr-Hostigos* and takes us another year in the life of Great King Kalvan, who now has an entirely new set of problems and obstacles... *Gunpowder God*, the next book in the series, was published by Pequod Press in 2011. A sidebar novel to *Siege of Tarr-Hostigos*, titled *The Hos-Blethan Affair* was published in 2014. I'm already at work on the final volume, *Down Styphon!*, of the Kalvan versus Styphon's House story arc; it will be published in 2016.

* * *

In the late 2000s a most interesting thing happened to the Piper canon; Ace Books did not renew the copyrights on any of the pre-1963 books. Suddenly, most of Piper's work, except for the Kalvan series, was in the Public Domain! This meant anyone who was so inclined could write their own sequels to Piper's classic works, including *Four-Day Planet*, *The Cosmic Computer*, *Little Fuzzy* and *Space Viking*.

Wolfgang Diehr, a fellow Piper fan and correspondent, started writing his own Fuzzy sequel, *Fuzzy Ergo Sum*, in 2008 and asked me to evaluate it. I read it, liked it but gave him a critique and told him to cut it by two-thirds (there was a 60 page prologue that was well-written, but did not move the story forward) and start over. Surprisingly, he did—but not until howling like a bear that just got its nose caught in a door! A year later he sent me the first dozen chapters; I read them and liked them—enough that I told him that when he finished it I would publish it under the Pequod imprint.

Wolf worked slowly and methodically on the book for the next year. Then in 2010, we learned that John Scalzi was doing a reimagining of *Little Fuzzy*. I told Wolfgang the time had come to fish or cut bait. If his book came out after Scalzi's it would look as if he were riding on his coattails rather than writing his own sequel to *Little Fuzzy*. He got to work and turned in a completed draft of *Fuzzy Ergo Sum* in November of 2010. I thought he had captured the feel and voice of the original novel and published *Fuzzy Ergo Sum* in early 2011. The story was big enough that it demanded a sequel and he went right to work on *Caveat Fuzzy*, which Pequod published a year later in 2012. He is currently hard at work on a new Fuzzy novel, "The Fuzzy Conundrum," in collaboration with me.

Wolfgang put me in touch with another Piper aficionado, Michael Robertson, after telling me Mike had written a very interesting *Space Viking* sequel and that I ought to read it. I told Wolfgang that I already had two *Space Viking* sequels in mind; the first one, a follow-up to the original novel featuring Lucas Trask; the second one, "Space Viking's Return," which I had completed almost thirty years ago for Jerry Pournelle. Since it was never rewritten and *Space Viking* was now in the public domain, I thought the time had come to put that novel out.

Then Wolf pointed out that Mike's novel took place a century after *Space Viking* and was a completely different animal; "and, really, you ought to take a look at it." I got in contact with Mike and he sent me the original work which was entitled "Sarpanitum." I liked it a lot; he had managed to get the scope of the original novel down, which was no small thing. However, there were some problems; I told him I liked it enough to do a rewrite and publish it as a collaboration. He agreed and I got to work; I doubled the length of the original ms. and, when I sent it out to my first readers, they felt it was too long. I reread it and agreed. Adventure novels, SF or otherwise, work better at between 80,000 and 100,000 words. Fortunately, there was a nice break at the end of Part II and Pequod Press published the first half as *The Last Space Viking* in 2012. A year later and with another major rewrite, the companion volume, *Space Viking's Throne*, came out in 2013.

My next Space Viking work will be "Space Viking's Revenge," which I'm currently working on. When that's published, I will release "Space Viking's Return," the story of Arthur Trask, Lucas Trask's son and his adventures.

There are plans for more surprises in the future. Other writers have published *Space Viking* sequels. However, I have stayed away from them since I don't want to compromise my own vision of how Lucas Trask and the League of Civilized Worlds move into the future.

APPENDIX VIII

H. Beam Piper
BIBLIOGRAPHY

H. BEAM PIPER BIBLIOGRAPHY

H. Beam Piper Bibliography, by David Johnson

(piperfan@zarathani.net)

A bibliography of original Piper works (novels, short fiction, non-fiction, and other work) and reprints or reissues by the year of first publication as provided by David Johnson.

1927

A Catalogue of Early Pennsylvania and other Firearms and Edged Weapons at "Restless Oaks," McElhattan, Pa., Henry W. Shoemaker and H. Beam Piper, Altoona, PA: Times Tribune Co., 1927 (non-fiction).

1947

"Time and Time Again," H. Beam Piper, *Astounding Science Fiction*, Vol. XXXIX, No. 2, April 1947, pp. 27-43, short story (~7000 words) with interior illustration by Vincent Napoli, reprinted in (or adapted as):

- *A Treasury of Science Fiction*, Groff Conklin, ed., New York: Crown, 1948.
- *Dimension X*, Episode #39, NBC Radio, aired July 12, 1951, 30 minutes, script adapted by Ernest Kinoy, directed by Fred Way, with cast including David Anderson (young Allan) and Joseph Curtin (Allan's dad).
- *Überwindung von Raum und Zeit*, as "Zeit und weider Zeit," Otto Schrag, translator, Gotthard Gunther, ed., Frankfurt: Rauch, 1952 (German translation).
- *X Minus One*, Episode #33, NBC Radio, aired January 11, 1956, 30 minutes, script adapted by Ernest Kinoy, directed by Daniel Sutter, with cast including Jack Grimes (young Allan), Peter Fernandez, Joe DeSantas, Joseph Bell, Clark Gordon, Herm Dinken, Dick Hamilton, and James Ducas.
- *Häpna!*, Vol. 7, No. 1, January 1960, as "Tid efter annan," unknown translator, pp. 59-77 (Swedish translation).

- *The Worlds of H. Beam Piper*, John F. Carr, ed., New York: Ace, 1983, pp. 9-28, with retouched cover illustration of scene from the 1968 film *The Green Slime*.
- *Isaac Asimov Presents the Great SF Stories: 9 (1947)*, Isaac Asimov and Martin H. Greenberg, eds., New York: DAW, 1983.
- *Die Vierziger Jahre II*, as "Zeitsprung," Otto Schrag, translator, Hans Joachim Alpers and Werner Fuchs, eds., Stuttgart: Hohenheim, 1983 (German translation).
- *The Golden Years of Science Fiction: Fifth Series*, Isaac Asimov and Martin H. Greenberg, eds., New York: Bonanza/Crown, 1985.
- *Crossroads of Destiny: Science Fiction Stories*, P.D. Cacek, ed. (uncredited), Rockville, MD: Wildside Press, 2006.
- *Time and Time Again and Other SF*, Alan Rodgers, ed., Northridge, CA: Ægypan Press, 2007.
- *Short Science Fiction Collection 003*, Cori Samuel, book coordinator, Web: LibriVox, February 2008, audiobook read by R. J. Davis.

1948

"He Walked Around the Horses," H. Beam Piper, *Astounding Science Fiction*, Vol. XLI, No. 2, April 1948, pp. 53-70, novelette (~8000 words) with interior illustration by Edd Cartier, reprinted in:

- *World of Wonder*, Fletcher Pratt, ed., New York: Twayne, 1951.
- *Best SF 3*, Edmund Crispin, ed., London: Faber and Faber, 1958.
- *Aspects of Science Fiction*, G. D. Doherty, ed., London: John Murray, 1959.
- *Le Meraviglie del possibile - Antologia della fantascienza*, as "Passò intorno ai cavalli," Bruno Fonzi, translator, Sergio Solmi and Carlo Fruttero, eds., Turin: Einaudi, 1959 (Italian translation).
- *Häpna!*, Vol. 7, No. 5, May 1962, as "Mannen från ingenstans," unknown translator, pp. 7-26 (Swedish translation).
- *Science Fiction Through the Ages 2*, I. O. Evans, ed., London: Panther, 1966.
- *Narraciones de Ciencia Ficción*, as "Fue a echar una ojeada a los caballos," unknown translator, Óscar Hurtado, ed., Madrid: Castellote Editor (Básica #15), 1969 (Spanish translation).
- *A Science Fiction Argosy*, Damon Knight, ed., New York: Simon and Schuster, 1972.
- *Space Mail*, Isaac Asimov, Martin H. Greenberg and Joseph D. Olander, eds., Greenwich, CN: Fawcett, 1980.

- *Isaac Asimov's Science Fiction Treasury*, Isaac Asimov, Martin H. Greenberg and Joseph D. Olander, eds., New York: Bonanza/Crown, 1981.
- *Paratime*, John F. Carr, ed., New York: Ace, 1981, pp. 14-37, with cover illustration by Michael Whelan.
- *The Golden Age of Science Fiction*, Kingsley Amis, ed., London: Hutchinson, 1981.
- *Orbites*, No. 3, September 1982, as "À i'instant où il contourna les chevaux,» Brigitte Cirla, translator) (French translation).
- *Isaac Asimov Presents the Great SF Stories: 10 (1948)*, Isaac Asimov and Martin H. Greenberg, eds., New York: DAW, 1983.
- *Histoire de la 4ème dimension*, as "L'Homme qui apparut," Alain Rague, translator, Demètre Ioakimidis, Gérard Klein, and Jacques Goimard, eds., Paris: Livre de Poche/Librairie Générale Française, 1983 (French translation).
- *Sternenpost 3*, as "Er ging um die Pferde herum," Eva Malsch, translator, Isaac Asimov, Martin H. Greenberg, and Joseph H. Olander, eds., Rastatt: Möewig, 1984 (German translation).
- *Parazeit*, as "Der Mann, der um die Pferde herumging," Lore Straßl, translator, Günter M. Schelwokat, ed., Rastatt: Möewig (Utopia Classics #66), 1984 (German translation).
- *Le grandi storie della fantascienza 10*, as "Camminò intorno ai cavalli," Giampaolo Cossato and Sandro Sandrelli, translator, Isaac Asimov and Martin H. Greenberg, eds., Milan: SIAD, 1984 (Italian translation).
- *The Golden Years of Science Fiction: Fifth Series*, Isaac Asimov and Martin H. Greenberg, eds., New York: Bonanza/Crown, 1985.
- *Alternate Histories*, Charles G. Waugh and Martin H. Greenberg, eds., New York: Garland, 1986.
- *Schöne verkehrte Welt: Phantastische Geschichten zur Geschichte*, as "Der Mann, der um die Pferde herumging," Lore Straßl, translator, René Oth, ed., Neuwied am Rhein: Luchterhand, 1988 (German translation).
- *The Amis Story Anthology: A Personal Choice of Short Stories*, Kingsley Amis, ed., London: Hutchinson, 1992.
- *The Complete Paratime*, John F. Carr, ed. (uncredited), New York: Ace, 2001, with cover art by Dave Dorman.
- *Crossroads of Destiny: Science Fiction Stories*, P.D. Cacek, ed. (uncredited), Rockville, MD: Wildside Press, 2006.
- *I segreti del Paratempo*, as "Girò intorno ai cavalli," Roberto Marini, translator, Giuseppe Lippi,, ed., Milan: Mondadori (Urania No. 1514), 2006, with cover illustration by Victor Togliani (Italian translation).

- *Time and Time Again and Other SF*, Alan Rodgers, ed., Northridge, CA: Ægypan Press, 2007.
- *Short Science Fiction Collection 026*, Gregg Margarite, book coordinator, Web: LibriVox, September 2009, audiobook read by "tabithat."
- *Paratime!: The Collected Paratime Stories*, uncredited editor, Rockville, MD: Wildside Press, 2010.
- *The Complete Paratime*, John F. Carr, ed. (uncredited), Palo Alto, CA: Benetech, 2011 (submitted by Allison Hilliker), Braille Refreshable Format (BRF) and Digital Accessible Information System (DAISY) talking book for the visually-impaired.

"Police Operation," H. Beam Piper, *Astounding Science Fiction*, Vol. XLI, No. 5, July 1948, pp. 8-35, novelette (~12K words) with interior illustration by Edd Cartier, reprinted in or reissued as:

- *Space Police*, Andre Norton, ed., Cleveland and New York: World, 1956.
- *The Best of Astounding*, Anthony R. Lewis, ed., New York: Baronet/Analog, 1978, with interior illustration by Edd Cartier.
- *Science Fiction Stories 66*, as "Der venusische Wuerger," Dolf Straßer, translator, Walter Spiegl, ed., Frankfurt: Ullstein, 1977 (German translation).
- *Paratime*, John F. Carr, ed., New York: Ace, 1981, pp. 39-75, with cover illustration (scene from "Police Operation") by Michael Whelan.
- *Parazeit*, as "Polizeiaktion," Lore Straßl, translator, Günter M. Schelwokat, ed., Rastatt: Möewig (Utopia Classics #66), 1984 (German translation).
- *Analog: The Best of Science Fiction*, editor uncredited, New York: Galahad, 1985.
- *The Complete Paratime*, John F. Carr, ed. (uncredited), New York: Ace, 2001, with cover art by Dave Dorman.
- *Naudsonce and Other SF*, Alan Rodgers, ed., Northridge, CA: Ægypan Press, 2006, with cover illustration by Leo Morey (interior illustration from "Naudsonce" from January 1962 edition of *Analog*).
- *I segreti del Paratempo*, as "Operazione di polizia," Roberto Marini, translator, Giuseppe Lippi, ed., Milan: Mondadori (Urania No. 1514), 2006, with cover illustration by Victor Togliani (Italian translation).
- *Five Sci-Fi Short Stories by H. Beam Piper*, Mark Nelson, book coordinator, Web: LibriVox, January 2007, audiobook read by Mark Nelson.
- *Police Operation*, H. Beam Piper, Web: LibriVox, October 2008, audiobook read by Alex Buie and "kelcymx."

- *Paratime!: The Collected Paratime Stories*, uncredited editor, Rockville, MD: Wildside Press, 2010.
- *The Complete Paratime*, John F. Carr, ed. (uncredited), Palo Alto, CA: Benetech, 2011 (submitted by Allison Hilliker), Braille Refreshable Format (BRF) and Digital Accessible Information System (DAISY) talking book for the visually-impaired.

"Precognition and a Theory of Time" (part 1), H. Beam Piper, *Amateur Spectator*, Vol. 1, No. 4 (Mailing Number 4), September 1948 ("pro-zine" published by The Spectator Club), pp. 15-25 (non-fiction).

"Precognition and a Theory of Time" (part 2), H. Beam Piper, *Amateur Spectator*, Vol. 1, No. 5 (Mailing Number 5), November 1948 ("pro-zine" published by The Spectator Club), pp. 27-36 (non-fiction).

1950

"The Mercenaries," H. Beam Piper, *Astounding Science Fiction*, Vol. XLV, No. 1, March 1950, pp. 57-77, novelette (~8500 words) with interior illustration by "Brush," reprinted in:

- *Science Fiction Stories 59, Drel Ergahlungen von H. Beam Piper*, as "Im Dienst der Sache," Wim Koll, translator, Walter Spiegl, ed., Frankfurt: Ullstein (Ullstein Buch Nr. 3225), 1976 (German translation).
- *The Worlds of H. Beam Piper*, John F. Carr, ed., New York: Ace, 1983, pp. 29-56, with retouched cover illustration of scene from the 1968 film *The Green Slime*.
- *Crossroads of Destiny: Science Fiction Stories*, P.D. Cacek, ed. (uncredited), Rockville, MD: Wildside Press, 2006.
- *Time and Time Again and Other SF*, Alan Rodgers, ed., Northridge, CA: Ægypan Press, 2007.

"Last Enemy," H. Beam Piper, *Astounding Science Fiction*, Vol. XLV, No. 6, August 1950, pp. 5-60, novella (~24K words) with cover and interior illustration by "Miller," reprinted in or reissued as:

- *The Astounding Science Fiction Anthology*, John W. Campbell, Jr., ed., New York: Simon and Schuster, 1952.
- *The Second Astounding Science Fiction Anthology*, John W. Campbell, Jr., ed., London: Four Square Books, 1965.
- *Fiction spécial: Astounding 1947-1951*, No. 9, April 1966, as "Le Dernier ennemi," Pierre Billon, translator (French translation).

- *Science Fiction Stories 59, Drel Ergahlungen von H. Beam Piper*, as "Der letzte Feind," Wim Koll, translator, Walter Spiegl, ed., Frankfurt: Ullstein (Ullstein Buch Nr. 3225), 1976 (German translation).
- *Paratime*, John F. Carr, ed., New York: Ace, 1981, pp. 77-147, with cover illustration by Michael Whelan.
- *Parazeit*, as "Der letzte Feind," Lore Straßl, translator, Günter M. Schelwokat, ed., Rastatt: Möewig (Utopia Classics #66), 1984 (German translation).
- *Robert Adams' Book of Alternate Worlds*, Robert Adams, Pamela Crippen Adams, and Martin H. Greenberg, eds., New York: New American Library/Signet, 1987.
- *The Complete Paratime*, John F. Carr, ed. (uncredited), New York: Ace, 2001, with cover art by Dave Dorman.
- *Graveyard of Dreams: Science Fiction Stories*, P.D. Cacek, ed. (uncredited), Rockville, MD: Wildside Press, 2006.
- *I segreti del Paratempo*, as "L'ultimo nemico," Roberto Marini, translator, Giuseppe Lippi, ed., Milan: Mondadori (Urania No. 1514), 2006, with cover illustration by Victor Togliani (Italian translation).
- *Last Enemy*, H. Beam Piper, Northridge, CA: Ægypan Press, 2007.
- *Thousand Suns: Transmissions from Piper*, John Appel, Vaclav G. Ujcik, and Greg Videll, eds., Web: Rogue Games, 2009.
- *Last Enemy*, H. Beam Piper, Web: LibriVox, May 2009, audiobook read by Mark Nelson.
- *Paratime!: The Collected Paratime Stories*, uncredited editor, Rockville, MD: Wildside Press, 2010.
- *The Complete Paratime*, John F. Carr, ed. (uncredited), Palo Alto, CA: Benetech, 2011 (submitted by Allison Hilliker), Braille Refreshable Format (BRF) and Digital Accessible Information System (DAISY) talking book for the visually-impaired.

"Flight from Tomorrow," H. Beam Piper, *Future* combined with *Science Fiction Stories*, Vol. 1, No. 3, September/October 1950. pp. 36-49, novelette (~8100 words) with interior illustration by Lawrence Sterne Stevens, reprinted in:

- *The Worlds of H. Beam Piper*, John F. Carr, ed., New York: Ace, 1983, pp. 36-49, with retouched cover illustration of scene from the 1968 film *The Green Slime*.
- *Flight from Tomorrow: Science Fiction Stories*, P.D. Cacek, ed. (uncredited), Rockville, MD: Wildside Press, 2006.

- *Flight from Tomorrow and Other SF*, Alan Rodgers, ed., Northridge, CA: Ægypan Press, 2006.
- *Five Sci-Fi Short Stories by H. Beam Piper*, Mark Nelson, book coordinator, Web: LibriVox, January 2007, audiobook read by Mark Nelson.
- *Short Science Fiction Collection 006*, Cori Samuel, book coordinator, Web: LibriVox, July 2008, audiobook read by Jerome Lawsen.

"Rebel Raider," H. Beam Piper, *True: The Men's Magazine*, Vol. 28, No. 163, December 1950, pp. 128-140, with interior illustration by Mario Cooper (fictionalized historical account), reprinted in (or adapted as):

- *Willie and the Yank*, Harold Swanton, screenwriter (Michael O'Herlihy, director), Walt Disney Productions, 1967, screenplay adaptation broadcast in two-parts on *Walt Disney's Wonderful World of Color*, National Broadcasting Company (NBC), January 8 and 16, 1967.
- *Mosby's Marauders*, Harold Swanton, screenwriter (Michael O'Herlihy, director), Walt Disney Productions, 1967, theatrical release of *Willie and the Yank*.
- *Willie and the Yank*, Harold Swanton and Stuart Ludlum, New York: Scholastic Book Services, 1967, trade paperback (novelization of screenplay).
- *Crossroads of Destiny and Others*, Alan Rodgers, ed., Northridge, CA: Ægypan Press, 2007.

1951

"Operation R.S.V.P.," H. Beam Piper, *Amazing Stories*, Vol. 25, No. 1, January 1951, pp. 52-58, short story (~2900 words) with interior illustration by Robert Jones, reprinted in:

- *World of Wonder*, Fletcher Pratt, ed., New York: Twayne, 1951
- *Amazing Stories: 40th Anniversary Issue*, Vol. 40, No. 5, April 1966.
- *The Worlds of H. Beam Piper*, John F. Carr, ed., New York: Ace, 1983, pp. 135-146, with retouched cover illustration of scene from the 1968 film *The Green Slime*.
- *Amazing Science Fiction Stories: The Wild Years 1946-1955*, Martin H. Greenberg, ed., Lake Geneva, WI: TSR, 1987.
- *Flight from Tomorrow: Science Fiction Stories*, P.D. Cacek, ed. (uncredited), Rockville, MD: Wildside Press, 2006.
- *Graveyard of Dreams: Science Fiction Stories*, P.D. Cacek, ed. (uncredited), Rockville, MD: Wildside Press, 2006.

- *Flight from Tomorrow and Other SF*, Alan Rodgers, ed., Northridge, CA: Ægypan Press, 2006.
- *Short Science Fiction Collection 014*, Cori Samuel, book coordinator, Web: LibriVox, April 2009, audiobook read by William Haseltine.

"Dearest," H. Beam Piper, *Weird Tales*, Vol. 43, No. 3, March 1951 (November 1951 in Britain), pp. 68-78, short story (~6400 words) with interior illustration by Vincent Napoli, reprinted in:

- *The Worlds of H. Beam Piper*, John F. Carr, ed., New York: Ace, 1983, pp. 57-75, with retouched cover illustration of scene from the 1968 film *The Green Slime*.
- *Crossroads of Destiny: Science Fiction Stories*, P.D. Cacek, ed. (uncredited), Rockville, MD: Wildside Press, 2006.
- *Crossroads of Destiny and Others*, Alan Rodgers, ed., Northridge, CA: Ægypan Press, 2007.
- *Short Science Fiction Collection 027*, Gregg Margarite, book coordinator, Web: LibriVox, September 2009, audiobook read by "Ric F."

"Temple Trouble," H. Beam Piper, *Astounding Science Fiction*, Vol. XLVII, No. 2, April 1951, pp. 6-34, novelette (~12K words) with cover and interior illustrations by Hubert Rogers, reprinted in or reissued as:

- *Science Fiction Stories 5*, as "Machtkampf der Gotzen," Bodo Baumann, translator, Walter Spiegl, ed., Frankfurt: Ullstein (Buch Nr. 2804), 1970, pp. 7-41 (German translation).
- *Paratime*, John F. Carr, ed., New York: Ace, 1981, pp. 261-295, with cover illustration by Michael Whelan.
- *Das Zeitverbrechen - Zeitpolizisten im Einsatz*, as "Tempelschwierigkeiten," Lore Straßl, translator, editor uncredited, Rastatt: Möewig (Utopia Classics #68), 1984 (German translation).
- *The Complete Paratime*, John F. Carr, ed. (uncredited), New York: Ace, 2001, with cover art by Dave Dorman.
- *I segreti del Paratempo*, as "Traffici nel tempio," Roberto Marini, translator, Giuseppe Lippi, ed., Milan: Mondadori (Urania No. 1514), 2006, with cover illustration by Victor Togliani (Italian translation).
- *Five Sci-Fi Short Stories by H. Beam Piper*, Mark Nelson, book coordinator, Web: LibriVox, January 2007, audiobook read by Mark Nelson.
- *Time and Time Again and Other SF*, Alan Rodgers, ed., Northridge, CA: Ægypan Press, 2007.

- *Temple Trouble*, H. Beam Piper, Web: LibriVox, August 2008, audiobook read by Phil Chenevert.
- *Paratime!: The Collected Paratime Stories*, uncredited editor, Rockville, MD: Wildside Press, 2010.
- *The Complete Paratime*, John F. Carr, ed. (uncredited), Palo Alto, CA: Benetech, 2011 (submitted by Allison Hilliker), Braille Refreshable Format (BRF) and Digital Accessible Information System (DAISY) talking book for the visually-impaired.

"Day of the Moron," H. Beam Piper, *Astounding Science Fiction*, Vol. XLVIII, No. 1, September 1951, pp. 7-34, novelette (~11K words) with cover and interior illustration by Hubert Rogers, reprinted in:
- *The Worlds of H. Beam Piper*, John F. Carr, ed., New York: Ace, 1983, pp. 199-231, with retouched cover illustration of scene from the 1968 film *The Green Slime*.
- *Naudsonce and Other SF*, Alan Rodgers, ed., Northridge, CA: Ægypan Press, 2006, with cover illustration by Leo Morey (interior illustration from «Naudsonce» from January 1962 edition of *Analog*).

"Genesis," H. Beam Piper, *Future* combined with *Science Fiction Stories*, Vol. 2, No. 3, September 1951, pp. 8-21, 37, novelette (~8400 words) with interior illustration by Virgil Finlay, reprinted in:
- *Shadow of Tomorrow*, Frederik Pohl, ed., New York: Doubleday, 1953.
- *American Science Fiction Magazine*, No. 35, March 1955 (Australian edition).
- *S-F Magazine*, No. 64, January 1965, as "Genesis," Hisashi Asakura, translator, with cover illustration by Tooru Kanamori (Japanese translation).
- *SF3*, as "Genesis," Masami Fukushima, translator, editor uncredited, Tokyo: ShueiSha, 1969, with cover illustration by Tooru Kanamori (Japanese translation).
- *If I Forget Thee Oh Earth*, as "Genesis," Hisashi Asakura, translator, Masami Fukushima, ed., Tokyo: Haga Shoten (Haga SF Series), 1972 (Japanese translation).
- *(untranslated title)*, as "Genesis," Hisashi Asakura, translator, Masami Fukushima, ed., Tokyo: KodanSha (BX12), 1975 (Japanese translation).
- *Science Fiction Stories 59, Drel Ergahlungen von H. Beam Piper*, as "(unknown title)," Wim Koll, translator, Walter Spiegl, ed., Frankfurt: Ullstein (Ullstein Buch Nr. 3225), 1976 (German translation).

- *The Worlds of H. Beam Piper*, John F. Carr, ed., New York: Ace, 1983, pp. 147-170, with retouched cover illustration of scene from the 1968 film *The Green Slime*.
- *Isaac Asimov's Wonderful Worlds of Science Fiction # 6: Neanderthals*, Isaac Asimov, Martin H. Greenberg and Charles G. Waugh, eds., New York: New American Library/Signet, 1987.
- *Flight from Tomorrow: Science Fiction Stories*, P.D. Cacek, ed. (uncredited), Rockville, MD: Wildside Press, 2006.
- *Graveyard of Dreams: Science Fiction Stories*, P.D. Cacek, ed. (uncredited), Rockville, MD: Wildside Press, 2006.
- *Flight from Tomorrow and Other SF*, Alan Rodgers, ed., Northridge, CA: Ægypan Press, 2006.
- *Paratime!: The Collected Paratime Stories*, uncredited editor, Rockville, MD: Wildside Press, 2010.

1952

Uller Uprising, H. Beam Piper, *The Petrified Planet*, Fletcher Pratt, ed. (uncredited), New York: Twayne, 1952, pp. 74-196, novel (~50K words), reprinted in or reissued as:

- "Ullr Uprising, " *Space Science Fiction*, Vol. 1, No. 4, February 1953, pp. 4-75, serial (part 1 of two parts) with interior illustration by Paul Orban (serialization of 1952 novel).
- "Ullr Uprising, " *Space Science Fiction*, Vol. 1, No. 5, March 1953, pp. 120-156, serial (part 2 of two parts) with illustration by Paul Orban (serialization of 1952 novel).
- *Uller Uprising*, New York: Ace, 1983, with cover illustration by Gino D'Achille, including original introduction ("The Silicone World" and "The Flourine Planet") by Dr. John D. Clark, reprinted from *The Petrified Planet*, pp. xi-xx.
- *Der Uller-Aufstand*, H. Beam Piper, Dolf Straßer, translator, Frankfurt: Ullstein (#3306), 1977, with cover illustration by Paul Lehr (German translation).
- *Uller Uprising*, H. Beam Piper, Northridge, CA: Ægypan, 2007, hardcover without dust jacket.
- *Uller Uprising*, H. Beam Piper, Northridge, CA: Ægypan, 2007, trade paperback with cover illustration by "Ebel" (unrelated scene from February 1953 edition of *Space Science Fiction*).
- *Uller Uprising*, H. Beam Piper, Rockville, MD: Wildside, 2007, with dust jacket illustration by "Fyletto."

- *Uller Uprising*, H. Beam Piper, Rockville, MD: Wildside, 2007, paperback with cover illustration by "Fyletto."
- *Uller Uprising*, H. Beam Piper, Web: LibriVox, December 2008, audiobook read by Ralph Snelson, Morgan Saletta, Acacia Wood, Sean O'Hara, and Anthony Wilson.

1953

"Null-ABC," H. Beam Piper and John J. McGuire, *Astounding Science Fiction*, Vol. L, No. 6, February 1953, pp. 12-54, serialized (part 1 of two parts) novella (~35K words) with interior illustration by H. R. Van Dongen, and

"Null-ABC," H. Beam Piper and John J. McGuire, *Astounding Science Fiction*, Vol. LI, No. 1, March 1953, pp. 112-153, serialized (part 2 of two parts) novella (~35K words) with interior illustration by Gordon Pawelka, reprinted in or reissued as:

- *Crisis in 2140*, H. Beam Piper and John J. McGuire, New York: Ace (D-227), 1957, with cover illustration by Ed Emshwiller ("double novel" combined reprint of 1953 serialization, with *Gunner Cade*, Cyril Judd, alias for C.M. Kornbluth and Judith Merril).
- *Null-ABC*, H. Beam Piper (and John J. McGuire, uncredited; Heinz Nagel, translator, Frankfurt: Ullstein (#2888), 1972, with cover illustration by John Schoenherr (German translation).
- *Krisenhahr 2140*, H. Beam Piper and John J. McGuire, unknown translator, Hamburg: Semrau, 1972, with retouched cover illustration by Ed Emshwiller (German translation).
- *Null-ABC*, H. Beam Piper and John J. McGuire, Rockville, MD: Wildside Press, 2006.
- *Null-ABC*, H. Beam Piper and John J. McGuire, Ægypan Press, 2006.
- *Null-ABC*, H. Beam Piper, Web: LibriVox, October 2011, audiobook read by Corinna Schultz.

Murder in the Gunroom, H. Beam Piper, New York: Knopf, 1953, novel (~67K words) with dust jacket illustration by Georgianna Schiffmacher, and reissued as:

- *Murder in the Gunroom*, H. Beam Piper, Baltimore: Old Earth Books, 1993 (facsimile).
- *Murder in the Gunroom*, H. Beam Piper, Northridge, CA: Ægypan Press, 2006.
- *Murder in the Gunroom*, H. Beam Piper, Web: LibriVox, February 2009, audiobook read by Anthony Wilson.

1954

"The Return," H. Beam Piper and John J. McGuire, *Astounding Science Fiction*, Vol. LII, No. 5, January 1954, pp. 70-95, novelette (~11K words) with interior illustration by Kelly Freas, and reprinted in or reissued as:

- *The Science-Fictional Sherlock Holmes*, Robert C. Peterson, ed., Denver: The Council of Four, 1960, pp. 105-137 (expanded version of 1954 novelette).
- *Empire*, John F. Carr, ed., New York: Ace, 1981, pp. 183-214, with cover illustration by Michael Whelan.
- *Crossroads of Destiny: Science Fiction Stories*, P.D. Cacek, ed. (uncredited), Rockville, MD: Wildside Press, 2006.
- *Time and Time Again and Other SF*, Alan Rodgers, ed., Northridge, CA: Ægypan Press, 2007.
- *Crossroads of Destiny and Others*, Alan Rodgers, ed., Northridge, CA: Ægypan Press, 2007.
- *The Return*, H. Beam Piper, Web: LibriVox, November 2007, audiobook read by Reynard T. Fox.

1955

"Time Crime," H. Beam Piper, *Astounding Science Fiction*, Vol. LIV, No. 6, February 1955, pp. 8-49, serialized (part 1 of two parts) novella (~37K words) with cover and interior illustration by Kelly Freas, and

"Time Crime," H. Beam Piper, *Astounding Science Fiction*, Vol. LV, No. 1, March 1955, pp. 85-131, serialized (part 2 of two parts) novella (~37K words) with interior illustration by Kelly Freas, reprinted in or reissued as:

- *Science Fiction Stories 6*, as "Sklaven der Zeit," Bodo Baumann, translator, Walter Spiegl, ed., Frankfurt: Ullstein, 1971 (German translation).
- *Paratime*, John F. Carr, ed., New York: Ace, 1981, pp. 149-259, with cover illustration by Michael Whelan (combined reprint of 1955 serialization).
- *Das Zeitverbrechen - Zeitpolizisten im Einsatz*, as "Das Zeitverbrechen," Lore Straßl, translator, editor uncredited, Rastatt: Möewig (Utopia Classics #68), 1984 (German translation).
- *The Complete Paratime*, John F. Carr, ed. (uncredited), New York: Ace, 2001, with cover art by Dave Dorman.
- "*Time Crime*," H. Beam Piper, Northridge, CA: Ægypan Press, 2006.
- *I segreti del Paratempo*, as "Crimini nel tempo," Roberto Marini, translator, Giuseppe Lippi, ed., Milan: Mondadori (Urania No. 1514), 2006, with cover illustration by Victor Togliani (Italian translation).

- *"Time Crime,"* H. Beam Piper, Rockville, MD: Wildside Press, 2009.
- *Paratime!: The Collected Paratime Stories*, uncredited editor, Rockville, MD: Wildside Press, 2010.
- *The Complete Paratime*, John F. Carr, ed. (uncredited), Palo Alto, CA: Benetech, 2011 (submitted by Allison Hilliker), Braille Refreshable Format (BRF) and Digital Accessible Information System (DAISY) talking book for the visually-impaired.
- *Time Crime*, H. Beam Piper and John F. Carr, Boalsburg, PA: Pequod Press, 2010, with dust jacket illustration by Alan Gutierrez (expanded version of 1955 novella).
- *"Time Crime,"* H. Beam Piper, Web: LibriVox, May 2013, audiobook read by Mark Nelson.

1957

"Omnilingual," H. Beam Piper, *Astounding Science Fiction*, Vol. LVIII, No. 6, February 1957, pp. 8-46, novelette (~16K words) with cover and interior illustration by Kelly Freas, reprinted in or reissued as:
- *Prologue to Analog*, John W. Campbell, Jr., ed., Garden City, NY: Doubleday, 1962.
- *Analog Anthology*, John W. Campbell, Jr., ed., London: Dobson, 1965.
- *Great Science Fiction Stories About Mars*, T. E. Dikty, ed., New york: Frederick Fell, 1966.
- *Apeman, Spaceman*, Leon E. Stover and Harry Harrison, eds., Garden City, NY: Doubleday, 1968.
- *S-F Magazine*, No. 115, December 1968, as "Omnilingual," Hisashi Asakura, translator, with interior illustration by Tooru Kanamori (Japanese translation).
- *Mars, We Love You*, Jane Hipolito and Willis E. McNelly, eds., Garden City, NY: Doubleday, 1971.
- *The Days After Tomorrow*, Hans Stefan Santesson, ed., New York: Little and Brown, 1971.
- *Where Do We Go from Here?*, Isaac Asimov, ed., Garden City, NY: Doubleday, 1971.
- *Antologia scolastica n. 3*, as "Omnilingue," Beata Della Frattina, translator, editor uncredited, Milan: Mondadori (Urania No. 593), 1972, with cover illustration by Karel Thole (Italian translation).
- *Fiction*, No. 235, July 1973, as "Langage universel," Bruno Martin, translator (French translation).

- *Tomorrow, and Tomorrow, and Tomorrow . . .*, Bonnie L. Heintz, Frank Herbert, Donald A. Joos, and Jane Agorn McGee, eds., New York: Holt, Rinehart and Winston, 1974.
- *Science Fiction Novellas*, Harry Harrison and Willis E. McNelly, eds., New York: Charles Scribner's Sons, 1975.
- *Federation*, John F. Carr, ed., New York: Ace, 1981, pp. 2-55, with cover illustration by Michael Whelan.
- *From Mind to Mind*, Stanley Schmidt, ed., Philadelphia: Davis, 1984.
- *Isaac Asimov Presents the Great SF Stories: 19 (1957)*, Isaac Asimov and Martin H. Greenberg, eds., New York: DAW Books, 1989
- *Le grandi storie della fantascienza 19 (1957)*, as "Omnilinguista," Giampaolo Cossato and Sandro Sandrelli, translators, Isaac Asimov and Martin H. Greenberg, eds., Milan: Armenia, 1989, with cover illustration by Dino Marsan (Italian translation).
- *The World Turned Upside Down*, David Drake, Jim Baen, and Eric Flint, eds., Riverdale, NY: Baen, 2005.
- *Ministry of Disturbance and Other SF*, Alan Rodgers, ed., Northridge, CA: Ægypan Press, 2007.
- *Omnilingual*, H. Beam Piper, Web: LibriVox, March 2007, audiobook read by Mark Nelson.
- *Omnilingual*, H. Beam Piper, Web: LibriVox, October 2014, audiobook read by Phil Chenevert.

"Lone Star Planet," H. Beam Piper and John J. McGuire, *Fantastic Universe Science Fiction*, Vol. 7, No. 3, March 1957, pp. 4-66, novella (~30K words) with cover illustration by Virgil Finlay, reprinted in or reissued as:

- *A Planet for Texans*, H. Beam Piper and John J. McGuire, New York: Ace (D-299), 1958, with uncredited cover illustration ("double novel" combined reprint of 1957 novella, with *Star Born*, Andre Norton).
- *Four-Day Planet and Lone Star Planet*, editor uncredited, New York: Ace, 1979, pp. 219-340, with cover illustration (scene from *Four-Day Planet*) by Michael Whelan.
- *Planet der Texaner*, H. Beam Piper (and John J. McGuire, uncredited), Horst Hoffmann, translator, Rastatt: Möewig (Terra Astra #485), 1980, with uncredited cover illustration (German translation).
- *A Planet for Texans*, H. Beam Piper (and John J. McGuire, uncredited), Rockville, MD: Wildside Press, 2006, with uncredited dust jack illustration.

- *Lone Star Planet*, H. Beam Piper (and John J. McGuire, uncredited), Northridge, CA: Ægypan Press, 2007.
- *Lone Star Planet*, H. Beam Piper (and John J. McGuire, uncredited), Web: LibriVox, October 2009, audiobook read by Mark Nelson.

"The Edge of the Knife," H. Beam Piper, *Amazing Stories*, Vol. 31, No. 5, May 1957, pp. 6-50, novelette (~16K words) with uncredited interior illustration, reprinted in or reissued as:
- *Empire*, John F. Carr, ed., New York: Ace, 1981, pp. 13-59, with cover illustration by Michael Whelan.
- *Flight from Tomorrow and Other SF*, Alan Rodgers, ed., Northridge, CA: Ægypan Press, 2006.
- *The Edge of the Knife*, H. Beam Piper, Web: LibriVox, February 2009, audiobook read by "jfmarchini."

"The Keeper," H. Beam Piper, *Venture Science Fiction*, Vol. 1, No. 4, July 1957, pp. 80-100, novelette (~9500 words) with interior illustration by Cindy Smith, reprinted in:
- *Fiction*, as "Le Diadème," René Lathière, translator, No. 76, March 1960 (French translation).
- *Empire*, John F. Carr, ed., New York: Ace, 1981, pp. 217-242, with cover illustration by Michael Whelan.
- *Ministry of Disturbance and Other SF*, Alan Rodgers, ed., Northridge, CA: Ægypan Press, 2007.

1958

"Graveyard of Dreams," H. Beam Piper, *Galaxy Science Fiction*, Vol. 15, No. 4, February 1958, pp. 122-144, novelette (~7900 words) with interior illustration by Leo and Diane Dillon, reprinted in or reissued as:
- *Galaxie*, as "Le Cimetière des rêves," translator uncredited, No. 54, May 1958, with interior illustration by Leo and Diane Dillon (French translation).
- *Federation*, John F. Carr, ed., New York: Ace, 1981, pp. 173-199, with cover illustration by Michael Whelan.
- *Flight from Tomorrow: Science Fiction Stories*, P.D. Cacek, ed. (uncredited), Rockville, MD: Wildside Press, 2006.
- *Graveyard of Dreams: Science Fiction Stories*, P.D. Cacek, ed. (uncredited), Rockville, MD: Wildside Press, 2006.

- *Flight from Tomorrow and Other SF*, Alan Rodgers, ed., Northridge, CA: Ægypan Press, 2006.

- *Five Sci-Fi Short Stories by H. Beam Piper*, Mark Nelson, book coordinator, Web: LibriVox, January 2007, audiobook read by Mark Nelson.

"Ministry of Disturbance," H. Beam Piper, *Astounding Science Fiction*, Vol. LXII, No. 4, December 1958, pp. 8-46, novelette (~16K words) with interior illustration by H. R. Van Dongen, reprinted in:

- *Seven Trips Through Time and Space*, Groff Conklin, ed., Greenwich, CN: Fawcett, 1968.

- *7 Viajes a Través del Tiempo y del Espacio*, as "Ministerio de Disturbios," Rafael Zavala, translator, Groff Conklin, ed., Mexico City: Editorial Novaro (Nova Dell, #177), 1972 (Spanish translation).

- *Science Fiction Stories 46*, as "Ministerium für Unruhe," translator unknown, Walter Spiegl, ed., Frankfurt: Ullstein, 1975 (German translation).

- *Empire*, John F. Carr, ed., New York: Ace, 1981, pp. 131-179, with cover illustration by Michael Whelan.

- *Isaac Asimov's Wonderful Worlds of Science Fiction #1: Intergalactic Empires*, Isaac Asimov, Martin H. Greenberg and Charles G. Waugh, eds., New York: Signet/New American Library, 1983.

- *Regni stellari*, as "Il ministero del disordine," Iva Guglielmi and Gianni Pilo, translators, Isaac Asimov, Martin H. Greenberg, and Charles G. Waugh, eds., Rome: Fanucci (I Magici Mondi di Asimov No. 2), 1987, with cover illustration by Peter Jones (Italian translation).

- *Nova SF No. 13*, as "Ministero del disordine," Stefano Carducci, translator, editor uncredited, Bologna: Perseo Libri, 1988, with cover illustration by "Allison" (Italian translation).

- *Ministry of Disturbance and Other SF*, Alan Rodgers, ed., Northridge, CA: Ægypan Press, 2007.

- *Thousand Suns: Transmissions from Piper*, John Appel, Vaclav G. Ujcik, and Greg Videll, eds., Web: Rogue Games, 2009.

1959

"Hunter Patrol," H. Beam Piper and John J. McGuire, *Amazing Science Fiction Stories*, Vol. 33, No. 5, May 1959, pp. 20-45, novelette (~11K words), reprinted in or reissued as:

- *Thrilling Science Fiction*, No. 31, June 1973, pp. 80-104, 115.

- *The Worlds of H. Beam Piper*, John F. Carr, ed., New York: Ace, 1983, pp. 77-109, with retouched cover illustration of scene from the 1968 film *The Green Slime*.
- *Crossroads of Destiny: Science Fiction Stories*, P.D. Cacek, ed. (uncredited), Rockville, MD: Wildside Press, 2006.
- *Crossroads of Destiny and Others*, Alan Rodgers, ed., Northridge, CA: Ægypan Press, 2007.
- *Hunter Patrol*, H. Beam Piper, Web: LibriVox, July 2012, audiobook read by Phil Chenevert.

"Crossroads of Destiny," H. Beam Piper, *Fantastic Universe Science Fiction*, Vol. 11, No. 4, July 1959, pp. 4-13, short story (~4400 words), reprinted in:
- *The Worlds of H. Beam Piper*, John F. Carr, ed., New York: Ace, 1983, pp. 185-197, with retouched cover illustration of scene from the 1968 film *The Green Slime*.
- *Crossroads of Destiny: Science Fiction Stories*, P.D. Cacek, ed. (uncredited), Rockville, MD: Wildside Press, 2006.
- *Crossroads of Destiny and Others*, Alan Rodgers, ed., Northridge, CA: Ægypan Press, 2007.
- *Short Science Fiction Collection 005*, Cori Samuel, book coordinator, Web: LibriVox, April 2008, audiobook read by Alex C. Telander.
- *Short Science Fiction Collection 044*, Gregg Margarite, book coordinator, Web: LibriVox, November 2011, audiobook read by "litarvan."

"The Answer," H. Beam Piper, *Fantastic Universe Science Fiction*, Vol. 12, No. 2, December 1959, pp. 4-12, short story (~4400 words) with uncredited interior illustration, reprinted in:
- *The Worlds of H. Beam Piper*, John F. Carr, ed., New York: Ace, 1983, pp. 171-183, with retouched cover illustration of scene from the 1968 film *The Green Slime*.
- *Flight from Tomorrow: Science Fiction Stories*, P.D. Cacek, ed. (uncredited), Rockville, MD: Wildside Press, 2006.
- *Graveyard of Dreams: Science Fiction Stories*, P.D. Cacek, ed. (uncredited), Rockville, MD: Wildside Press, 2006.
- *Flight from Tomorrow and Other SF*, Alan Rodgers, ed., Northridge, CA: Ægypan Press, 2006.
- *Five Sci-Fi Short Stories by H. Beam Piper*, Mark Nelson, book coordinator, Web: LibriVox, January 2007, audiobook read by Mark Nelson.

- *Short Science Fiction Collection 002*, Cori Samuel, book coordinator, Web: LibriVox, November 2007, audiobook read by "Nicodemus."

1960

"Oomphel in the Sky," H. Beam Piper, *Analog Science Fact—Science Fiction*, Vol. LXVI, No. 3, November 1960, pp. 120-158, novella (~17,500 words) with interior illustration by "Bernklau," reprinted in or reissued as:

- *Federation*, John F. Carr, ed., New York: Ace, 1981, pp. 114-171, with cover illustration by Michael Whelan.
- *Ministry of Disturbance and Other SF*, Alan Rodgers, ed., Northridge, CA: Ægypan Press, 2007.
- *Oomphel in the Sky*, H. Beam Piper, Web: LibriVox, March 2007, audiobook read by Mark Nelson.

1961

Four-Day Planet, H. Beam Piper, New York: G.P. Putnam's Sons, 1961, novel (~57K words) with dust jacket illustration by Charles Geer, and reprinted in or reissued as:

- *Four-Day Planet and Lone Star Planet*, editor uncredited, New York: Ace, 1979, pp. 1-216, with cover illustration (scene from *Four-Day Planet*) by Michael Whelan.
- *Die Vier-Tage-Welt*, H. Beam Piper, translator unknown, Rastatt: Möewig Terra Astra , 1981, with cover illustration by Eddie Jones (German translation).
- *Four-Day Planet*, H. Beam Piper, Rockville, MD: Wildside Press, 2006, paperback with cover illustration by Spectral/Fotolia.
- *Four-Day Planet*, H. Beam Piper, Northridge, CA: Ægypan Press, 2006, hardcover without dust jacket.
- *Four-Day Planet*, H. Beam Piper, Northridge, CA: Ægypan Press, 2007, trade paperback with cover illustration by Leo Morey (unrelated interior illustration from «Naudsonce» from January 1962 edition of *Analog*).
- *Four-Day Planet*, H. Beam Piper, Rockville, MD: Wildside Press, 2006, with dust jacket illustration by Spectral/Fotolia.
- *Four-Day Planet*, H. Beam Piper, Web: LibriVox, December 2010, audiobook read by Mark Nelson.

1962

"Naudsonce," H. Beam Piper, *Analog Science Fact—Science Fiction*, Vol. LXVIII, No. 5, January 1962, pp. 6-44, novelette (~17K words) with interior illustration by Leo Morey, reprinted in or reissued as:

- *Richiamo all'ordine e altri racconti*, as "Pernonac," Beata Della Frattina, translator, editor uncredited, Milan: Mondadori (Urania No. 376), 1965, with cover illustration by Karel Thole (Italian translation).
- *Außerirdische mal drei*, as "Naudas," Eduard Lukschandl, translator, editor uncredited, Rastatt: Erich Pabel (Nr. 565), 1968, pp. 3-34, with cover illustration by Rudolf Sieber-Lonati (German translation).
- *Federation*, John F. Carr, ed., New York: Ace, 1981, pp. 57-112, with cover illustration by Michael Whelan.
- *Naudsonce and Other SF*, Alan Rodgers, ed., Northridge, CA: Ægypan Press, 2006, with cover illustration by Leo Morey (interior illustration from "Naudsonce" from January 1962 edition of *Analog*).
- *Thousand Suns: Transmissions from Piper*, John Appel, Vaclav G. Ujcik, and Greg Videll, eds., Web: Rogue Games, 2009.
- *Naudsonce*, H. Beam Piper, Web: LibriVox, November 2012, audiobook read by Phil Chenevert.

"A Slave is a Slave," H. Beam Piper, *Analog Science Fact—Science Fiction*, Vol. LXLX (sic), No. 2, April 1962, pp. 62-82, 113-142, novella (~21K words) with interior illustration by John Schoenherr, reprinted in:

- *Empire*, John F. Carr, ed., New York: Ace, 1981, pp. 63-127, with cover illustration by Michael Whelan.
- *Ministry of Disturbance and Other SF*, Alan Rodgers, ed., Northridge, CA: Ægypan Press, 2007.
- *A Slave is a Slave*, H. Beam Piper, Web: LibriVox, July 2012, audiobook read by Phil Chenevert.

Little Fuzzy, H. Beam Piper, New York: Avon (F-118), 1962, novel (~59K words) with cover illustration by Victor Kalins, reprinted in or reissued as:

- *Il piccolo popolo*, H. Beam Piper, Bianca Russo, translator, Milan: Mondadori (Urania #298), 1962, with cover illustration by Karel Thole (Italian translation).
- *Der kleine Fuzzy*, H. Beam Piper, Heinz Zwack, translator, Rastatt: Möewig Terra Sonderband, 1964, with cover illustration by Karl Stephan (German translation).

- *Il piccolo popolo*, H. Beam Piper, Bianca Russo, translator, Milan: Mondadori (Oscar Ragazzi #19), 1973, with cover illustration by Paul Scharff (Italian translation).
- *Little Fuzzy*, H. Beam Piper, New York: Ace, 1976, with cover illustration by Michael Whelan.
- *Was ist los auf Planet Zeno?*, H. Beam Piper, Heinz Nagel, translator, Zürich: Albert Müller (Rüschlikon), 1976, with cover illustration by Beni LaRoche (German translation).
- *Encuentro en Zarathustra*, H. Beam Piper, J. L. Yarza, translator, Barcelona: Bruguera (Libro Amigo #472), 1976 (Spanish translation).
- *The Fuzzy Papers*, editor uncredited, Garden City, NY: Doubleday (SFBC), 1977. with dust jacket illustration by Michael Whelan.
- *Little Fuzzy*, H. Beam Piper, London: Futura Orbit, 1977, with uncredited cover illustration.
- *Les hommes de poche*, H. Beam Piper, Jacqueline Huet, translator, Paris: Librairie des Champs-Elysées (Le Masque SF #64), 1977, with cover illustration by J. J. Vincent (French translation).
- *The Fuzzy Papers*, editor uncredited, London: Futura, 1979, with uncredited cover illustration.
- *Der kleine Fuzzy*, H. Beam Piper, Heinz Peter Lehnert, translator, Rastatt: Erich Pabel (Terra #319), 1979, with cover illustration by Michael Whelan (German translation).
- *Fuzzy/Ruimteiking*, translator uncredited, editor uncredited, Bussum, Netherlands: Centripress, 1979, with cover illustration by Michael Whelan (Dutch translation).
- *The Fuzzy Papers*, editor uncredited, New York: Ace, 1980, pp. 1-197, with cover illustration by Michael Whelan and interior illustration by Victoria Poyser.
- *The Adventures of Little Fuzzy*, H. Beam Piper with Benson Parker, New York: Platt and Munk, 1983, with cover illustration by Michael Whelan (children's adaptation).
- *Little Fuzzy*, H. Beam Piper, Mariko Sakawa, translator, Rastatt: Tokyo: Sogen Mystery (685-01), 1984, with cover illustration by Hitoshi Yoneda (Japanese translation).
- *The Complete Fuzzy*, editor uncredited, New York: Ace, 1998, with cover illustration by Michael Whelan.
- *Little Fuzzy*, H. Beam Piper, Northridge, CA: Ægypan Press, 2006, hardcover without dust jacket.

- *Little Fuzzy*, H. Beam Piper, Northridge, CA: Ægypan Press, 2006. trade paperback with uncredited cover illustration.
- *Little Fuzzy*, H. Beam Piper, Wildside Press, 2006, trade paperback with cover illustration by Michael Whelan (from 1976 Ace edition).
- *Little Fuzzy*, H. Beam Piper, Wildside Press, 2006, paperback with cover illustration by Michael Whelan (from 1976 Ace edition).
- *Little Fuzzy*, H. Beam Piper, Web: Maria Lectrix, August 2006, audiobook read by Maureen O'Brien.
- *Little Fuzzy*, H. Beam Piper, Web: LibriVox, November 2009, audiobook read by "tabithat."

Space Viking, H. Beam Piper, Analog Science Fact—Science Fiction, Vol. LXX, No. 3, November 1962, pp. 6-52, serialized (part 1 of four parts) novel (~69K words) with cover and interior illustration by John Schoenherr, and

Space Viking, H. Beam Piper, Analog Science Fact—Science Fiction, Vol. LXX, No. 4, December 1962, pp. 104-146, serialized (part 2 of four parts) novel (~69K words) with interior illustration by John Schoenherr, and

1963

Space Viking, H. Beam Piper, Analog Science Fact—Science Fiction, Vol. LXX, No. 5, January 1963, pp. 111-55, serialized (part 3 of four parts) novel (~69K words) with interior illustration by John Schoenherr, and

Space Viking, H. Beam Piper, Analog Science Fact—Science Fiction, Vol. LXX, No. 6, February 1963, pp. 120-162, serialized (part 4 of four parts) novel (~69K words) with interior illustration by John Schoenherr, reprinted in or reissued as:

- *Space Viking*, H. Beam Piper, New York: Ace (F-225), 1963, with uncredited cover illustration (combined reprint of 1962-63 serialization).
- *Vikingo espacial*, H. Beam Piper, F. Sesén, translator, Barcelona: Vertice (Galaxia No. 48), 1966, with cover illustration by "Scholler" (Spanish translation).
- *I vichinghi dello spazio*, H. Beam Piper, Mauro Cesari, translator, Piacenza: Casa Editrice La Tribuna (Galassia No. 92), 1968, with cover illustration by Paola Pallottino (Italian translation).
- *Lord Kalvan d'altroquando I vichinghi dello spazio*, as *I vichinghi dello spazio*, Mauro Cesari, translator, editor uncredited, Piacenza: Casa Editrice La Tribuna (Bigalassia No. 6), 1971, with uncredited cover illustration (Italian translation).
- *Space Viking*, H. Beam Piper, New York: Garland, 1975, limited edition without dust jacket.

- *Die Weltenplünderer*, H. Beam Piper, Dolf Straßer, translator, Frankfurt: Ullstein (#3223), 1976, with cover illustration by Chet Morrow (German translation).
- *Space Viking*, H. Beam Piper, New York: Ace, 1977, with cover illustration by Michael Whelan.
- *Space Viking*, H. Beam Piper, London: Sphere, 1978, with cover illustration by Melvyn Grant.
- *Space Viking*, H. Beam Piper, Jun Kazami, translator, Tokyo: Tokuma (Space Adventure Series), 1978, with cover illustration by Sadao Naito (Japanese translation).
- *Fuzzy/Ruimteiking*, translator uncredited, editor uncredited, Bussum, Netherlands: Centripress, 1979, with cover illustration by Michael Whelan (Dutch translation).
- *Space Viking*, H. Beam Piper, Jean-Pierre Pugi, translator, Paris: Temps Futurs (Space-fiction #3), 1982, with cover illustration by Philippe Adamov and François Allot (French translation).
- *Space Viking*, H. Beam Piper, Northridge, CA: Ægypan Press, 2007, hardcover without dust jacket.
- *Space Viking*, H. Beam Piper, Northridge, CA: Ægypan Press, 2007, paperback with cover illustration by John Schoenherr (from November 1962 *Analog* serialization).
- *Space Viking*, H. Beam Piper, Rockville, MD: Wildside Press, 2007, with dust jacket illustration by "Ericus."
- *Space Viking*, H. Beam Piper, Rockville, MD: Wildside Press, 2007, paperback with cover illustration by "Ericus."
- *Space Viking*, H. Beam Piper, Palo Alto, CA: Benetech, 2008 (submitted by Roger Drewicke), Braille Refreshable Format (BRF) and Digital Accessible Information System (DAISY) talking book for the visually-impaired.
- *Space Viking*, H. Beam Piper, Web: LibriVox, September 2008, audiobook read by Mark Nelson.
- *Space Viking*, H. Beam Piper, Boalsburg, PA: Pequod, 2011, with dust jacket illustration by Alan Gutierrez.

Junkyard Planet, H. Beam Piper, New York: G.P. Putnam's Sons, 1963, novel (~64K words) with dust jacket illustration by Herb Mott (expanded edition of 1958 novelette "Graveyard of Dreams"), reissued as:

- *The Cosmic Computer*, H. Beam Piper, New York: Ace (F-274), 1964, with cover illustration by Ed Valigursky (uncredited) and interior illustration by Jack Gaughan (uncredited) (reissue of expanded *Junkyard Planet*).

- *The Cosmic Computer*, H. Beam Piper, New York: Ace, 1963, with cover illustration by Michael Whelan.
- *Der Verschollene Computer*, H. Beam Piper, Dolf Straßer, translator, Frankfurt: Ullstein (#3167), 1975, with cover illustration by Chet Morrow.
- *Der kosmische Computer*, H. Beam Piper, Juergen Saupe, translator, Rastatt: Erich Pabel (Terra #335), 1981, with uncredited cover illustration (German translation).
- *The Cosmic Computer,* H. Beam Piper, Web: LibriVox, January 2007, audiobook read by Mark Nelson.
- *The Cosmic Computer*, H. Beam Piper, Northridge, CA: Ægypan Press, 2007, hardcover without dust jacket.
- *The Cosmic Computer*, H. Beam Piper, Northridge, CA: Ægypan Press, 2007, trade paperback with cover illustration Ed Valigursky (from 1964 Ace edition).
- *Junkyard Planet*, H. Beam Piper, Rockville, MD: Wildside, 2007, paperback with cover illustration by Julio Rodriguez.
- *Junkyard Planet*, H. Beam Piper, Rockville, MD: Wildside, 2007, with dust jacket illustration by Julio Rodriguez.
- *The Cosmic Computer*, H. Beam Piper, Boalsburg, PA: Pequod, 2013, with dust jacket illustration by Alan Gutierrez.

1964

The Other Human Race, H. Beam Piper, New York: Avon (G1220), 1964, with uncredited cover illustration (sequel to 1962 novel *Little Fuzzy*), reprinted in or reissued as:
- *Fuzzy Sapiens*, H. Beam Piper, New York: Ace, 1976, with cover illustration by Michael Whelan.
- *Wollie Sapiens*, H. Beam Piper, translator unknown, Rotterdam: Netherlands: Scala, 1976, with cover illustration by Michael Whelan.
- *The Fuzzy Papers*, editor uncredited, Garden City, NY: Doubleday (SFBC), 1977. with dust jacket illustration by Michael Whelan.
- *Fuzzy Sapiens*, H. Beam Piper, London: Futura Orbit, 1977.
- *Tinounours sapiens*, H. Beam Piper, Jacqueline Huet, translator, Paris: Librairie des Champs-Elysées (Le Masque SF #76), 1978, with cover illustration by Atelier P. Vercken.
- *The Fuzzy Papers*, editor uncredited, London: Futura, 1979, with uncredited cover illustration.

- *Torna il piccolo popolo*, H. Beam Piper, Enzo Ruscica, translator, Piacenza: Casa Editrice La Tribuna (Galassia No. 236), 1979, with cover illustration by Franco Storchi (Italian translation).
- *Fuzzy sapiens*, H. Beam Piper, Heinz Peter Lehnert, translator, Erich Pabel (Terra #319), 1979, with cover illustration by Michael Whelan (German translation).
- *The Fuzzy Papers*, editor uncredited, New York: Ace, 1980, pp. 198-406, with cover illustration by Michael Whelan and interior illustration by Victoria Poyser.
- *The Complete Fuzzy*, editor uncredited, New York: Ace, 1998, with cover illustration by Michael Whelan.

"Future History No. 1" (aka "The Future History"), H. Beam Piper, *Zenith*, No. 4, May 1964, Peter Weston, ed. (fanzine), pp. 11-14 (non-fiction article about the Terro-human Future History).

"Gunpowder God," H. Beam Piper, *Analog Science Fiction—Science Fact*, Vol. LXXIV, No. 3, November 1964, pp. 17-36, novella (~25K words) with cover and interior illustration by John Schoenherr, reprinted in:

- *Planetoidenfänger*, as "Der Schießpulver-Gott," Elke Kamper, translator, Wolfgang Jeschke, ed., Munich: Lichtenberg, 1971 (German translation).
- *Created by Poul Anderson: Time Wars*, Martin H. Greenberg and Charles G. Waugh, eds., New York: Tor, 1986, pp. 27-74.
- *The Good Old Stuff*, Gardner Dozois, ed., New York: Griffin/St. Martin's Press, 1998.
- *Astronavi & mondi lontani*, as "(unknown title)," translator uncredited, Gardner Dozois, ed., Milan: Mondadori (Urania #1405), 2001, with cover illustration by Franco Brambilla (Italian translation).

1965

"Down Styphon!," H. Beam Piper, *Analog Science Fiction—Science Fact*, Vol. LXXVI, No. 3, November 1965, pp. 10-46, novella (~18K words) with cover and interior illustration by Kelly Freas (sequel to 1964 novella "Gunpowder God"), reprinted in:

- *Robert Adams' Book of Soldiers*, Robert Adams, Pamela Crippen Adams, and Martin H. Greenberg, eds., New York: Signet/New American Library, 1988, pp. 132-171

Lord Kalvan of Otherwhen, H. Beam Piper, New York: Ace (F-342), 1965, with cover and interior illustration by Jack Gaughan (uncredited), (expanded combination of 1964 novella "Gunpowder God" and 1965 novella "Down Styphon!"), reprinted in or reissued as:

- *Der Mann, der die Zeit betrogs*, H. Beam Piper, Helmut Bittner, translator, Hamburg: Winther, 1967 (German translation).
- *Lord Kalvan di Altroquando*, H. Beam Piper, Cesare Gavioli, translator, Piacenza: Casa Editrice La Tribuna (Galassia No. 87), 1968, with cover illustration by Paola Pallottino (Italian translation).
- *Lord Kalvan d'altroquando I vichinghi dello spazio*, as *Lord Kalvan di Altroquando*, Mauro Cesari, translator, editor uncredited, Piacenza: Casa Editrice La Tribuna (Bigalassia No. 6), 1971, with uncredited cover illustration (Italian translation).
- *Kalvan d'outre-temps*, H. Beam Piper, Michel Deutsch, translator, Paris: Opta, 1972 (Galaxie bis 24), with cover illustration by Claude Lacroix (French translation).
- *Lord Kalvan of Otherwhen*, H. Beam Piper, New York: Garland, 1975, limited edition without dust jacket.
- *Lord Kalvan of Otherwhen*, H. Beam Piper, New York: Ace, 1977, with Michael Whelan cover illustration.
- *Gunpowder God*, H. Beam Piper, London: Sphere, 1978, with uncredited cover illustration.
- *Lord Kalvan d'Altroquando*, H. Beam Piper, Roberta Rambelli, translator, Bologna: Libra (Classici della Fantascienza No. 38), 1979, with cover illustration by "Allison" (Italian translation).
- *Lord Kalvan of Otherwhen*, H. Beam Piper, Ryukio Sekiguchi, translator, Tokyo: Hayakawa (SF344), 1979, with cover and interior illustration by Jun'ichi Murayama (Japanese translation).
- *Der Mann, der die Zeit betrogs*, H. Beam Piper, translator unknown, Rastatt: Erich Pabel (Utopia Classics #29), 1981 (German translation).
- *The Complete Paratime*, John F. Carr, ed. (uncredited), New York: Ace, 2001, with cover art by Dave Dorman.
- *Astronavi & mondi lontani*, as *Il dio della polvere da sparo*, Vittorio Curtoni, translator, Gardner Dozois, ed., Milan: Mondadori (Urania #1405), 2001, with cover illustration by Franco Brambilla (Italian translation).
- *Lord Kalvan of Otherwhen*, H. Beam Piper, Palo Alto, CA: Benetech, 2004, Braille Refreshable Format (BRF) and Digital Accessible Information System (DAISY) talking book for the visually-impaired.

- *Lord Kalvan d'Altroquando*, H. Beam Piper, Roberta Rambelli, translator, Milan: Mondadori (Urania Collezione No. 040), 2006, with cover illustration by Franco Brambilla (Italian translation).
- *The Complete Paratime*, John F. Carr, ed. (uncredited), Palo Alto, CA: Benetech, 2011 (submitted by Allison Hilliker), Braille Refreshable Format (BRF) and Digital Accessible Information System (DAISY) talking book for the visually-impaired.

"Untitled," H. Beam Piper, *Ventura II*, May 1965, Phillip A. Harrell, ed. (fanzine), p. 97 (freehand sketch).

1981

"When in the Course—," H. Beam Piper, in *Federation*, John F. Carr, ed., New York: Ace, 1981, pp. 201-284, with cover illustration by Michael Whelan, novella (25K words), previously unpublished , variant version of 1964 novella "Gunpowder God."

1982

First Cycle, H. Beam Piper with Michael Kurland, New York: Ace, 1982, with uncredited cover illustration (possibly by Wayne Barlowe).)

1984

Fuzzies and Other People, H. Beam Piper, New York: Ace, 1984, with cover illustration by Michael Whelan (sequel to 1964 novel *The Other Human Race/Fuzzy Sapiens*), reprinted in:
- *The Complete Fuzzy*, editor uncredited, New York: Ace, 1998, with cover illustration by Michael Whelan.

www.ingramcontent.com/pod-product-compliance
Lightning Source LLC
Chambersburg PA
CBHW032057090426
42743CB00007B/152